NEVADA

Nevada
TOWNS & TALES

Volume II — South

edited by Stanley W. Paher
cover etching by Roy E. Purcell

Nevada Publications
Box 15444
Las Vegas, Nevada
89114

Acknowledgments

There is in every book an attempt to chronicle everyone who assisted in the project and to thank those who contributed research materials. Often an apology is included for those who may have been omitted or overlooked in acknowledging their help and services. In this book effort, hundreds of people graciously volunteered in some way, whether it was hospitality for a weary editor in his travels or a lead to an unpublished story or priceless photos.

To our authors we extend special thanks for their time and materials in compiling and presenting a story for inclusion in this volume. Many others besides authors offered special help and encouragement from time to time. People such as: Don Payne of the Las Vegas News Bureau, Allan Krieg of the Union Pacific Railroad, Marlene Olsen of the Reno Chamber of Commerce, Jack McCloskey of Hawthorne, Florence Robinson of Tonopah, and Phil Earl at the Nevada Historical Society.

Nevada artist Roy Purcell graciously provided the color etching on the cover ''Comin' In.'' The sketch on the half-title page also is by Purcell.

The county sections are introduced with maps artistically drawn and illustrated by Kelly Fleming.

Picture Credits

Picture credits are as follows (an ''a'' after the page number denotes the top of the page, ''b'' and ''c'' are pictures in descending order):

John Beville, 342; the Binion family, 362-364; Ann Brauer, 345-346; Marjorie Brown, 350b; Tom Brown, 304 a, c, dc 309; Don Bufkin map, 317; Mrs. Jack Burns, 258a; Roberta Childers, 246; Mary-Ellen Clark, 239.

The Delmue family, 311; Binnie Douglas, 347; the Elam family, 382; Elbert Edwards, 337; Murl Emery, 348-349; Leonard Fayle, 330; Marshall Fey, 354-355 all; Gerald Fisher, 298; Theron Fox, 268b, 270, 386-387 all.

Fraser photo, 253; Estelle Funke, 255b, 257b, 392; Charles Gallagher, 296a; ''Scoop'' Garside, 338, 409; Charles George, 423; Captain R. A. Gibson, 324; G. I. Gooden, 341; Nan Grant, 289; Leo Grutt, 260; Ed Halstead, 382a.

Harvey Hardy, 327; *Harper's Weekly,* 261t, 292, 304b; Harrah's Casino, 416; John Harrington, 333(2); H. H. Heisler, 271, 272; Fred Holliday, 237, 238a; F. D. Howard, 236; Huntington Library, 244c; Dorothy Jennings, 254, 255a.

Phil Jensen, 423b; Hank Johnston, 273; Florence Lee Jones, 344; Grace Kendrick, 421; Kennecott Corporation, 295, 296b; Las Vegas News Bureau, 322, 323, 343, 352-353, 357, 358, 381, 408; Las Vegas *Review-Journal,* 302.

Phyllis Leavitt, 340(2); Margaret P. McCarran, 278; Frank Maggio photo, 316; Jeanne Mercer, 248a; William Metscher, 258a; Sebastian Miculich, 414-415; Frank Mitrani photos, 269(2), 371; David F. Myrick, 371.

Nevada Historical Society, 238b, 261b, 262b, 279a, 407(2). Olive Norton, 293; B. J. Owen, 265; Orlo Parker, 243(2), 245, 248b, 394; Alberta Perkins, 320; Pomona Public Library, 263t, 279b; Art Radar, 412.

Effie Read, 306b; Ressie Read, 294; Mrs. Larry Reiley, 249; Reno Chamber of Commerce News Bureau, 368, 385, 389b, 410; Marion Rosevear, 276(2), 350a; Mort Saiger, 365-366; Byrd Wall Sawyer, 290; Jim Seagrave, 360, 374-380; Hugh Shamberger, 247(2); Summa Corporation, 405; Ben Sweet, 406.

Mark Twain's *Roughing It,* 292c, 426-427. Union Pacific Railroad, 413; United Airlines, 418; U.S. Atomic Energy Commission, 257, 397-403; University of California, Bancroft Library, 240; University of Nevada, Las Vegas Special Collections, 329b.

Harold Weight, 389a; Wells Cargo, 417; Wells Fargo Bank, 394a; Ruth Wilkerson, 312-313; Walter Wilson, 268a; Bill Wright, 420, 425. Pictures not credited above are from the collection of the publisher.

Table of Contents

ESMERALDA COUNTY 234-249
Desert Justice as told to Sessions S. Wheeler   235
Goldfield's Brownstone Mansions by F. D. Howard   236
The Earp Brothers in Goldfield by Fred Holliday   237
J. J. Noone by Mary-Ellen Clark   239
Growing Up With Goldfield by Lela Halsell Hempton   241
Boom Town Goldfield by F. D. Howard   244
The Flood Side of Town by Roberta Childers   246
Goldfield's Blind Miner by Hugh A. Shamberger
   and L. K. "Ken" Wilson   247
The Fire From My Window by Jennie Mercer   248
Joy by Mrs. Larry Reiley   249

MINERAL COUNTY 250-265
Aurora's Deadly Growing Pains by Bob Stewart   251
Knapp's Landing by Helen McInnis   253
Shockley at Candelaria by Nanelia S. Doughty   255
Man About Town by Lorena Edwards Meadows   256
Stingaree Gulch by Harold O. Weight   259
Desert Transport by Richard C. Datin   261
Modern Desert Rat by Jean Reid   262
Hawthorne Legend by B. J. Owen   264
The Great Safari by B. J. Owen   265

NYE COUNTY 266-283
Spanish Springs Station by Walter C. Wilson   267
Belmont's Other Court House by Theron Fox   269
The Bullfrog District by Grace Dini   271
Scotty in Rhyolite by Hank Johnson   273
Curious Newsboy by Vincent McGinn   274
Growing Up in Tonopah by Marion Dobrowsky Rosevear   275
Young Lawyer in Tonopah by Jerome E. Edwards   278
Supply Point for Scotty by Hank Johnson   280
Bootlegger's Bylaws by Helen McInnis   281
Gold Nuggets for an Apple Pie by Ruth Fenstermaker Tipton 282
The Transient's Repentance by Captain R. A. Gibson   283

WHITE PINE COUNTY 284-299
Frontier Indian Life by Howard Egan   285
"Fast Mail" by Betty Orr   287
The Story of Kinnemich by Laura Gallagher Werner   288
Two Buxom Gals by Nan Millard Grant   289
Midwives of Nevada by Byrd Wall Sawyer   290

Doctor at Hamilton by Elsa & Jerry Culbert   291
First Train by Olive Stanton Norton   293
Dr. A. P. Lagoon by Stella Heit   294
First Church by Mrs. Thelma Ireland   294
The Charmed Circle by Ressie Walls Read   295
Memories of McGill 1917 to 1922 by Georgia Shaver   296
On the South Side in '23 by Effie O. Read   298
Speak Easy But Prudently — Bootleg Days in White Pine
    County by Effie O. Read   299

LINCOLN COUNTY 300-313
Valley of Lakes by Joe C. Cathcart   301
Delamar Sunsets by Corrine Walker   302
Tales of Old Delamar by Wayne Lytle   303
Tikapoo by Wayne Lytle   305
Watered Milk by Wayne Lytle   306
So They Dug Frank's Grave by Walter Averett   307
Burial of Sport Watkins by Effie O. Read   307
Our Family at Fay by Myrtle Damrow Bliss   308
A School Boy's View of Prince by Arthur H. Dietz   309
School Daze by Ruth Bradley Wilkinson   312

CLARK COUNTY 314-349
First in Vegas Valley by Frank Maggio   315
The Lost County of Pah-Ute by Donald Bufkin   318
The Last Indian Raid by Alberta Perkins   320
Brigham Young in Nevada by Elbert Edwards   321
Fight for Survival by Kenley Reese   322
Gunwoman by Captain R. A. Gibson   324
Duel at Copper City by Walter Averett   326
Las Vegas Christmas by Harvey Hardy   327
The Great Booster by Janice Haupt   328
Jean and Goodsprings by Leonard R. Fayle   330
Temperance Town by Charles "Pop" Squires   332
Ghost Orchard by John Harrington   333
El Dorado Doctor by Arda M. Haenszel   334
Two Story Man by Larry Strate   335
The Last Paiute Chief by R. A. Gibson   336
Burro King by Joyce Jones   337
The Legend of Lorenzi Park   338
Depression Pioneers of Boulder City by Phyllis M. Leavitt   339
Colonel Bob by John Beville   342
Magic Theatre by James M. Greene   343
Norman D. Nevills by Florence Lee Jones   343
A Resting Place by Ann Brauer   345
Nellis Air Force Base by Binnie Douglas   347
Colorado River Boatman   348

GAMBLING 350-367
History of Chance by Frank H. Johnson   351
The Fabulous Slots by Marshall Fey   354

Father of Modern Nevada Gambling by Don Stubbs 356
Dealer's Choice by Phyllis Darling 357
The First Strip Hotel by Jim Daley 358
Bugsy Siegel by John F. Cahlan 360
Spirit of a Gambling Town by Sam Bowler 361
Family Operation 362
Guardian of the Games 365

ENTERTAINMENT 368-381
The Origins of Casino Entertainment in Nevada
   by Paul A. Leonard 369
Elvis-Wayne-Liza; That Superstar City by Bill Willard 370
Entertain Them...But by Mildred M. Wilson 380

POTPOURRI 382-393
Nevada — I Love The Name by Norman Kaye 383
Ins and Outs of Rustlers by Don Bowman 384
Nevada by M. Burrell Bybee, Sr. 384
Walker Lake Fish by Estelle Moore 385
Poetical Location 385
Ghost Town Landmarks, Desert Storms and Vandals
   by Theron Fox 386
Poor Little Pupfish by Jim Yoakum 387
Restless Houses by Harold O. Weight 388
The Tree That Made Nevada's Silver by Ronald M. Lanner 390
Little Brown Nut by Mary K. Miller 391
Prospector's Heaven by Laura Bell 392

BUSINESS AND INDUSTRY 394-419
Nevada Banking History by Jordan J. Crouch 395
A Wise Indian 396
The Nevada Test Site by David Jackson 397
Las Vegas' Wing Fong 404
Howard R. Hughes Industrialist 404
Industrial City by Ben Sweet 406
Bankers Named George by Dennis Pletzke 407
Two Griffiths by Florence Lee Jones 408
Warehousing and Nevada's Freeport Law by Sonja Mosse 410
Nevada Railroads by Art Rader 412
Nevada's Bus-man by Douglas McDonald 414
First Flight 416
Specialized Hauling 417
Historic Landing 418
Joseph Kelley 419

COLLECTABLES 420-425
Nevada Collectables 420
Old Bottles by Grace Kendrick 421
Obsolete Stock Certificates by Clint Thomas Maish 422
Postage Stamps by Charles W. George 423
Gaming Chips by Phil Jensen 423

Books and Pamphlets by Stanley W. Paher   424
Merchant Trade Tokens by William V. Wright   425

LITERARY 426-436
Mark Twain's Nevada by Jeanne Elizabeth Wier   426
Nevada Poetry by Joseph T. Goodman and Bret Harte   428
Walter Van Tilburg Clark's Jason White
    edited by Robert Morse Clark   429
Old Button by Robert Laxalt   433

Introduction

The collection of Nevada stories and anecdotes included herein, originally published as *The Nevada Bicentennial Book* in 1976, has proven to be one of the most successful and well-received works ever published about this state.

Part of the success of the original edition stemmed from the enormous diversity of subject matter represented in these stories. While most of them are placed into chapters according to their county of origin, these vignettes cover a broad cross-section of the past twelve decades throughout all of Nevada.

Traditional western themes are present in stories about gunfights, robberies, stage lines, cowboys, railroads, mining, and ghost towns. Many lesser-known subjects are also touched upon here in such topics as midwifery, hobos, Tommy Knockers, suffrage, and pupfish. Still more tales highlight some little-known aspects of previous years in telling of bootlegging in Nye County, prostitution in Reno and Rawhide, the robbing of the Carson City Mint, and the last Indian battle in Nevada.

Glimpses into the lives of some famous, or infamous, people are also present here in stories concerning Howard Hughes in Las Vegas, Wyatt Earp in Goldfield, Brigham Young in southern Nevada, the hanging of Mr. and Mrs. Potts in Elko, the first woman sheriff in Austin, Josie Pearl in the Black Rock Desert, and the Paiute Princess Sarah Winnemucca.

Entire chapters on important aspects of Nevada's history are included under the headings of gambling, mining, transportation, politics, entertainment, banking, and agriculture. Also present are segments on Chinese, Indians, Italians, Basques, and blacks in the state's past.

Collectors of the artifacts and ephemera of Nevada's history will find stories on such fields as coins, books, bottles, stock certificates, postage stamps, gaming chips, and trade tokens. And, for the lovers of Nevada literature, there are original poems and previously unpublished writings by two of the state's great authors, Walter Van Tilburg Clark and Robert Laxalt.

The great variety of material contained here in some 264 stories was made possible by searching out the 200 people who authored them. Most were long-time Nevada residents who were well-versed in their particular interests or experiences but some were located as far away as South Carolina, Pennsylvania, and New York. Credit for the amassing and editing of this huge volume of material must be given to the staff of the original *Bicentennial book,* but most particularly to Stanley Paher. In his capacity as chief editor, Paher personally contacted most of the authors, searched out photographs for illustrations, supervised the editing of all the submissions, and generally acted as the driving force in bringing this enormous project to a successful conclusion.

Upon its publication in 1976 the original volume was an immediate success in both its soft-bound and hard cover editions. Today, over five years later, the demand for this collection of stories is still running high, although the original work is now out of print.

Again it is Paher who has arranged with the copyright holders to make this treasure trove of Nevada material available to the public in a two-volume set. Permission has been granted to reprint a large majority of the original material in these two volumes, thus severing all connections these stories had with either the State of Nevada or the North American Revolution Bicentennial Commission.

Never before has such a collection of anecdotes, legends, and stories pertaining to Nevada been brought together and it is fitting that it be kept in print as long as possible.

Douglas McDonald
Reno, Nevada

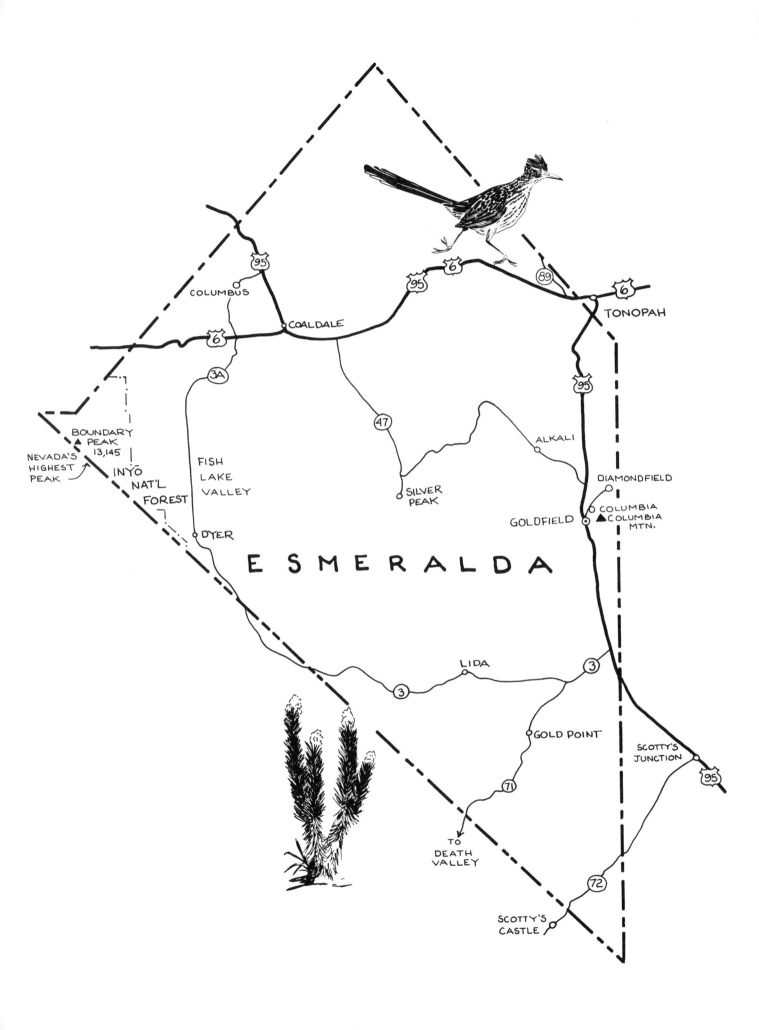

COLUMBUS

95

COALDALE

6

95

6

89

6

TONOPAH

3A

95

47

ALKALI

BOUNDARY
PEAK
13,145

NEVADA'S
HIGHEST
PEAK

INYO
NAT'L
FOREST

FISH
LAKE
VALLEY

SILVER
PEAK

DIAMONDFIELD

COLUMBIA
COLUMBIA
MTN.

GOLDFIELD

DYER

E S M E R A L D A

LIDA

3

3

GOLD POINT

SCOTTY'S
JUNCTION

95

71

72

TO
DEATH
VALLEY

SCOTTY'S
CASTLE

Esmeralda County

Desert Justice

As told to

Sessions S. Wheeler

During the fall of 1888, itinerant construction workers traveled on foot from Frisco, Utah, through Snake Valley, Nevada, en route to the hydraulic operations at the placer mining camp of Osceola. Sixty miles of the eighty-mile trip were desert, and some of the tired men stopped at our Snake Valley ranch to spent the night. One of them was named Tom Notes.

Notes was a large, handsome man of about forty-five who hoped someday to be a rancher. Because of this interest, my father offered him a job; and during the following months Notes developed into an efficient ranch hand.

To a five-year-old boy, he soon became a hero. He bought me candy, told me stories, and called me his partner. He singled me out from my five brothers and, to me, there was no better man in all Nevada.

During the winter of 1888, Tom somehow obtained information that a certain 160 acres of land, lying near the center of a large ranch holding, was open to homesteading. In those days legal descriptions and fencing of large ranches were faulty, and land within their boundaries was sometimes unclaimed. The Utah-Nevada state line bisected Snake Valley and Tom proved his finding in the Millard County, Utah, courthouse. He then homesteaded the quarter section of rich land.

He was starting to build his log cabin and barn when the owners of the surrounding ranch made their first offer to purchase the property. His refusal to sell brought threats, which increased in their seriousness during the following months.

It was in the summer of 1889 that Tom Notes was murdered. He was found lying between his new house and barn; he had been shot in the back.

Authorities were far away, transportation was slow, and it was three days before a sheriff's posse arrived. There were no clues, but on the strength of their threats, the owners of the surrounding ranch were arrested and brought to trial in Millard County. Because of insufficient evidence they were acquitted, and eventually the case was forgotten—forgotten by everyone except me, a six-year-old kid who swore that someday he would find the murderer of his partner.

To give my brothers and me proper schooling, my father moved to Utah. Years later, I returned to northern Nevada to work as a cowpuncher.

It was in April, 1903, that I got the mining fever and headed for Tonopah. In August of that year, I left Tonopah on a prospecting trip to the unorganized mining district called "Grandpa," later to be named Goldfield, and during the following spring located claims there on land which eventually became a part of the city.

During the winter of 1904, there were three saloons, one grocery store, and two feedlots in the town. Johnnie Jones, Bert Higgins, and Bob Martin owned the Gold Wedge saloon which consisted of a tent about twenty feet long and fourteen feet wide, framed and floored with pine. There was little money in circulation in the camp, but we could get whiskey on credit at the Gold Wedge bar, and there was heat from a big stove in the center of the tent where we played cards—providing there was enough wood to keep the stove hot.

Wood was supplied to the town by a grizzled old Frenchman called Jerry. A booze-fighter, he earned his whiskey money hauling piñon and juniper logs to the camp on a battered freight wagon pulled by two ancient crowbait horses. The wood supply was uncertain, depending on whether Jerry had recovered from the alcohol that money or credit always bought.

However, of more concern to us than the uncertainty of our wood supply was Jerry's neglect of his horses. A horse or a mule was a valuable asset to a desert mining camp—something on which a man's life might depend. Although we were a rough bunch, we took care of our animals and they were fed before a man looked to his own meal. And so when two half starved horses stood unharnessed night after night, the population of Goldfield became concerned.

Reprimands and warnings were given the old drunk, but they had no effect. Finally a group of us decided to hold a kangaroo court, a mock trial to attempt to scare old Jerry into taking better care of his horses.

Plans were made around the stove on a cold winter night. I was chosen to act as sheriff, an ex-lawyer was selected as district attorney, and a hard-rock miner, who knew something about legal procedures, was appointed judge. A jury was formed from the rest of the men, and we planned the trial carefully.

On the night of February eighteenth, during a heavy snowstorm, I located Jerry in another bar and arrested him. Court was called to order in the saloon, where the prisoner, confused and unsteady with alcohol, was pushed into a chair. Above him a hangman's noose hung from a crossbeam.

Witnesses were called who testified as to the drunkard's treatment of his horses. There was no defense attorney, and Jerry did not deny the accusations. The district attorney made a dramatic summary; the judge notified the prisoner that if the jury returned a verdict of guilty, he would be hung by the neck until dead; and the jury was charged. Minutes later the six men returned; their verdict was guilty.

The judge turned to the prisoner and said, "You have been found guilty of cruelty to animals in the desert. You will, therefore, be hung immediately. If you have anything on your conscience that you want to confess before you die, now is the time."

I was standing in the back of the room watching the old Frenchman's face. Under the light of the kerosene lamps, I could see the sweat on the sides of his thin, wrinkled cheeks. The trial seemed to be having the desired effect but, for a moment, I felt sorry for him. Suddenly tears began running down his face and his voice in broken English came across the room.

Then, hardly believing what I heard, I listened to a confession of a murder committed sixteen years before —the killing of my friend, Tom Notes.

Time weakens desire for revenge; and, as the broken old man finished his confession and sat hunched and frightened in his chair, I kept my silence. Such matters as murder were not uncommon in those days, and when Jerry promised to take better care of his horses, he was released.

He kept that promise for the next seven months— until he was found dead from too much whiskey and exposure. I guess he paid for his crime. I like to remember his trial as desert justice.

Goldfield's Brownstone Mansions
by F. D. Howard

Some of the original homes of Goldfield were colloquially referred to as "brownstone mansions." The need for their construction was determined in the winter of 1902 following the discovery of gold the preceding summer. One winter at an altitude of almost six thousand feet, near the summit of the Saw Tooth Range, was enough to convince the hardiest of miners that a tent or packing-box shanty was not a satisfactory shelter for such a clime.

In the summer of 1903 the digging done in Goldfield was not entirely for gold. The thought of another winter in improvised shanties was not a warming thought. Holes for homes were dug along the banks of Coyote Wash. Brown stones from the canyons of the Malapai Mesa were hauled in to close the fronts of these hurriedly dug caves making them suitable for occupancy against the cold of winter and the heat of summer. They proved to be quite adequate dwellings.

Most of these homes were destroyed in the flood of 1913. Some parts of them were still evident as late as the early 1940s. Since that time, with the combined efforts of wind, rain, and the artifact hunter it is almost impossible to determine where these interesting creations of dual architecture once stood.

With the passing of these dug-out homes and other items from the past has gone a never to be forgotten era of excitement, challenge, and glory. Excitement was found in the challenge itself, glory was obtained by subduing the challenge. The glory of Goldfield was gold! Those who discovered it worked hard, and those who dug it worked hard and were paid a fair day's wage. They were paid in gold or in notes backed by gold. Today man sometimes wonders what excitement is found in subduing the challenge if the glory one obtains rings with a dull thud.

These were the original dugout houses of Goldfield, built in 1903 when materials were scarce.

The Earp Brothers in Goldfield

by Fred Holliday

It was in October, 1881, that the Earp brothers, Wyatt, Virgil and Morgan, along with their compatriot, "Doc" Holliday, rose from the obscurity of serving as non-descript lawmen at Tombstone, Arizona, to make headlines in every major newspaper in the United States, when reports of their thirty-second gunfight at the O.K. Corral reached the outside world.

Indicted for murder, Wyatt stood trial at Tombstone and was cleared of all charges. Virgil was ambushed on December 28, 1881, and had most of his left elbow shot away, while Morgan was murdered less than a year later, each by assailants unknown.

During the next two decades Wyatt roamed across the Northwest, while Virgil remained in California with his family.

Wyatt returned from Alaska in 1898, to pursue mining interests in California and Nevada. He drifted into Tonopah in 1902, where he worked for young Tasker Oddie for a few weeks, running claim-jumpers off the Tonopah Mining Company's property. Then he started his Northern saloon, only to sell out a few months later to concentrate on developing claims in the newly-opened Goldfield area.

Wyatt had kept in touch with Virgil since their Tombstone days and now wrote him to move to Goldfield—where money flowed like wine.

But his wife didn't want her husband to start chasing rainbows again. By now his left arm had atrophied and he experienced difficulty walking as a result of a mine accident. However, the challenge of starting anew seemed to rejuvenate Virgil and when he promised to buy her another home in Nevada, she agreed.

They arrived at Goldfield in the spring of 1904. Initially hired as special officer by the National Club, Virgil was soon sworn in as a deputy sheriff. His quiet and unassuming manner, coupled with the reputation of being a pushover for anyone with a hard-luck story, soon won him a host of friends.

In February 1905, promoter Tex Rickard opened the Northern, Goldfield's most celebrated saloon and gambling house, in a building adjoining the National Club. Wyatt, who had met and become friends with Tex in Nome, Alaska, was hired to be one of his pit bosses, overseeing the club's gaming tables.

Rickard's Northern boasted a 50-foot long bar, dispensing six barrels of whiskey daily. It became great fun for habitues to greet the great gunfighter Wyatt Earp at Rickard's saloon and then drift next door to have a drink with his brother Virgil.

Wyatt Earp

However, only a short time later, Virgil came down with a bad cold which developed into pneumonia. On the critical list for several days, he finally recovered and resumed work at the National.

Then, on July 8, 1905, Goldfield suffered its first major fire when a stove exploded in the Bon Ton Millinery shop. The flames soon spread to adjoining structures as volunteer firemen and hundreds of town residents rushed to the scene. Virgil, as deputy sheriff, was undoubtedly on the fireline.

Goldfield's fire hydrants had been turned on at the start of the conflagration, materially diminishing the water supply. By the time wiser heads turned them off, little water remained to fight the flames. In at least one instance, beer was used as an extinguisher—according to the July 9, 1905, issue of the Tonopah *Daily Sun:*

"The buildings of the Enterprise Mercantile Company were saved by the free and unlimited use of beer. Barrel after barrel was used and had a most desirous effect. Had it not been for the liquid the entire stock of goods of the company would have been ruined. The Enterprise Mercantile building is a stone structure and had the effect of checking the flames to a great extent, while the beer acted as an extinguisher. . . ."

Goldfield was saved when the wind shifted to the southeast, but not before two blocks of business houses burned to the ground.

Virgil Earp

Incredibly, only eight days later, the adjacent mining town of Columbia caught fire and its residents, assisted by Goldfield's firemen and law officers, fought the flames for more than two hours before it was brought under control.

Three months later, Virgil suffered a relapse and again contracted pneumonia. This time he was so ill the doctor cut him off his favorite cigars. On October 20, 1905, he seemed to rally and Allie later recalled what happened:

" . . . he said to me, 'Get me a cigar.' Believing he was feeling better I did so.

" 'Now,' he said, 'put Hickie's (Allie's grand-niece) last letter under my pillow, light my cigar, and stay here and hold my hand.' "

Virgil died before he finished the cigar. He was only 62.

Wyatt left Nevada shortly after Virgil's death and spent many years mining in the Whipple Mountains, on the California side of the Colorado River. He died of uremic poisoning on January 13, 1929, at the age of 80, while living in a small motor court at Los Angeles.

Thus the Earps passed into eternity, but not before leaving their indelible mark upon the history of the western frontier.

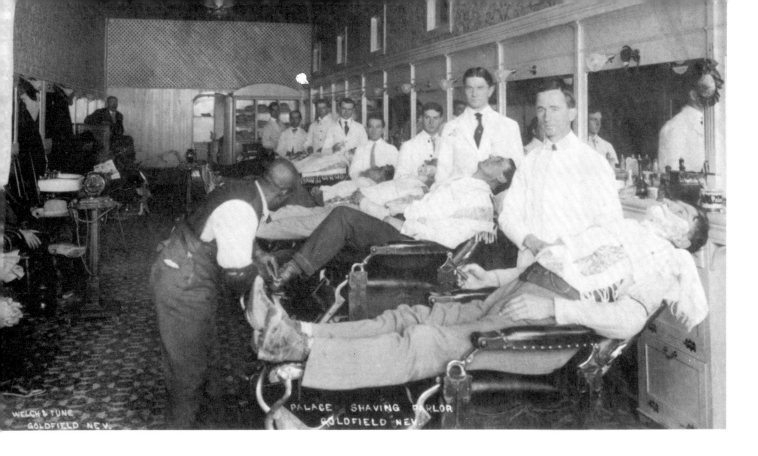

PALACE SHAVING PARLOR
GOLDFIELD NEV.

WELCH & TUNE
GOLDFIELD NEV.

J. J. Noone

by Mary-Ellen Clark

Youthful J. J. Noone held the first chair of this busy Goldfield barber shop, in 1906. On the opposite page is the very heart of Goldfield's saloon district which included the famous Tex Rickard's Northern. The holiday crowd enjoys a drilling contest which tested the strength and stamina of husky miners. The champion driller of the event was the man who could punch a hole deeper into a solid granite boulder in less time than his opponents, using a single jack and drill bit.

In Nevada's mining camps resourceful men often had to work in several different jobs. J. J. Noone was one of these men who earned his living as a barber, mortician, mill worker, taxi operator, justice of the peace, deputy sheriff and postmaster in several western Nevada towns.

Noone arrived in Goldfield in the summer of 1904 on one of the first trains into the camp. Within two years he was partner in a thriving 14-chair barber shop, the Palace Shaving Parlor, which rivaled any establishment in San Francisco at the time. It was a prosperous business. On one occasion, Noone had to order an entire carload of barbersoap to keep up with the demand. However, the strike of mine workers in Goldfield and the national financial panic in 1907 eventually forced him to give up the shop.

He began working in the Consolidated Mill at Goldfield and as a steward at the local Elks club to support his young family. By 1915 he launched a new career by obtaining a mortician's license from the state. Noone moved to Luning in 1916 where he was soon dealing with the effects of a dreaded influenza epidemic. He also operated a barber shop and a taxi service to bring miners to the saloons and gambling halls of Luning.

Jack Noone's trade as a barber served him well. After leaving Luning, he opened up shop in Tonopah in 1919. He moved back to Goldfield in 1922, to open still another shop, and bought the mortuary business of Thomas F. Dunn. Maintaining these two businesses provided an adequate living. However, his shop was one of the many businesses burned to the ground on Main Street in the great 1923 Goldfield fire. Like many others of his generation, this setback did not mean failure. He soon set up business in the Goldfield Hotel and later the Elks' building.

Although people in mining towns struggled through many hardships, they were not without sources of diversion. For example, the fight in 1906 between Joe Gans and Battling Nelson for the world lightweight championship drew thousands of people to Goldfield and gained national publicity. Noone was one of the leaders who helped promote the event and collect the $30,000 purse, the largest ever put up for a boxing match at the time. He also coached local boxing and baseball teams which kept up a healthy rivalry with nearby towns, especially Tonopah. When there was excitement lacking around town, the men drove their cars out to dry lake beds to race them, while the wives stood cringing on the sidelines.

The passing years saw a steady decline in Goldfield's population and importance as a mining center. Also, the gloom of the Depression had settled over the country. During these years Noone maintained his mortuary business and ran for public office. At different times he was appointed to serve as justice of the peace, deputy sheriff, and postmaster. These jobs had their exciting moments, too. One night, during his term as postmaster, his safe was blown open in a robbery. While serving as deputy sheriff in Esmeralda County he was severely beaten by two assailants who left him for dead by the roadside, then stole his car. They were later apprehended in California.

It was not long after this incident that Noone expanded his mortuary business to Hawthorne, frequently shuttling back and forth between there and Goldfield. Simultaneously operating two towns 130 miles apart gives an indication of the vitality of this man who was then in his seventies. Continuing this dual operation for thirteen years, Jack Noone partially retired when he sold the Hawthorne business in 1955. But it wasn't until 1963 that he conducted his last funeral service in Goldfield, at age 89.

Until his death, at 96, he lived in Hawthorne with his daughter and family, regaling interviewers with colorful stories and first-hand accounts of life in Nevada's boom towns.

Growing up with Goldfield

by Lela Halsell Hempton

In 1904, the fastest way to travel through Nevada was by railroad. When Papa got the mining fever, we headed west to Reno to board the Virginia & Truckee and ultimately the Carson & Colorado Railroad to Sodaville, its southern terminus. From there we caught the new narrow gauge into booming Tonopah.

I remember well the ride on the narrow gauge. When the engine needed water, it would stop and the passengers would take short walks into the desert. The sun burned brightly against a white-as-snow alkali flat.

When we arrived in Tonopah, I was cheated out of riding in a regular stage coach outfitted by six galloping horses because Uncle John hired a rig, a spring wagon pulled by only two horses. We started the slow ride across 26 miles of desert to our new home in Goldfield, where it was hot and dry, so very different from green, humid Missouri.

The first sight of the Goldfield district was the little suburb of Columbia. As we passed a new hotel, a pretty woman called out to us, "Merchant's Hotel—best hotel in town." Later I learned she was Mrs. Casey who had been the inspiration for Rex Beach's Cherry Malotte in his Alaskan story, "The Spoilers."

Uncle John had rented a room for us at Barlow's Rooming House and we ate our meals with Aunt Sina and Uncle Dan. Aunt Sina was a young bride and Mama was supposed to teach her to cook. Mama's culinary efforts were a failure, for she knew nothing of cooking in a high altitude.

Goldfield and Tonopah were tent cities. Papa bought a big 12 × 24 tent, with a long ridge pole to hold it up and board siding. The floor was just desert soil covered with burlap sacks, but when sprinkled with water the floor was hard and smooth. Our only "boughten" furniture were bed springs and a cook stove. Boxes served as chairs with tables and cupboards made of precious lumber.

We loved the desert. Mama enjoyed her new freedom; no garden to tend, no canning, and no cooking for threshers on hot summer days. She dabbled in mining stock at an exchange in Goldfield.

Papa did assessment work and took leases on claims belonging to others. Each day he was sure he would strike it rich. What fun it was to watch him pound his samples of ore with the mortar and pestle and then pan the powdered rock in a small pan! Precious water washed away the waste and the heavier gold remained in the pan. If there were no "colors," he was sure he would strike it the next day. Sometimes he worked in the big mines earning the coveted $4 for an eight hour shift. However, his pay was not the key to riches because we had to buy all our food. Mama called it "living out of a paper sack."

My first hobby was collecting tin cans tossed outside the tents. I was completely fascinated by the syrup cans made in the shape of log cabins, ranging from half pints to two gallon containers. I built model cities with my collection, cutting doors and windows in the cans with a trusty can opener, a necessity in a desert mining camp.

Water was scarce and was piped to the center of Columbia from a mountain spring. At the water company, we bought a five gallon bucket of water for five cents, but if the water wagon delivered it, the cost doubled. Children could go to the water works and get a little lard bucket of water free. At school, it was a treat to be sent with a friend for a bucket of water. The water bucket was passed up and down the aisles with everyone drinking from a common dipper. One was supposed to empty the dipper, it being bad manners to put any water left back into the bucket.

The Nevada nightingale, or burro, was ever present; so the trick was to catch a burro and ride. The stubborn burros often balked, but what is that to a child with a whole day to play? When I was twelve a movie theatre was opened in Goldfield. Piano music accompanied the silent pictures. A magic lantern threw the pictures on the screen while local talent sang the songs. On Saturday night, after a bath in the family wash tub, my hair was put up in rags for the long curls I was to wear to Sunday school. Sunday was a special day with nice clothes to wear and that quiet "day of rest" feeling.

We did not have a phonograph, but we could listen to the ones owned by more affluent neighbors. Tents are not sound proof, and the shrill voice of the announcer at the beginning of each record told the name of the artist and the selection, followed by the name of the recording company, such as "by Columbia Records," which was announced very dramatically. Usually opera at its loudest followed.

Besides dabbling in stocks, Mama was in the real estate business. When a neighbor moved, Mama bought their tent house, which she later either rented or sold. Sometimes she kept boarders, single men who liked home cooking. Once, I remember our table was full, but the next day only our family was seated. There was a gold strike at Manhattan, and the men were off to discover a fortune.

Miners were never discouraged. They looked forward to when their luck might change. Restless when working for wages, they would announce, "deep enough," and quit their jobs in search of new adventures. Their positions were easily filled by men rustling for work as the shifts changed. The men worked seven days a week and changed shifts every two weeks. Mama was always afraid that some of her Missouri

Shown here is the very heart of Goldfield's saloon district which included the famous Tex Rickard's Northern. The holiday crowd enjoys a drilling contest which tested the strength and stamina of husky miners. The champion driller of the event was the man who could punch a hole deeper into a solid granite boulder in less time than his opponents, using a single jack and drill bit. Below is the main street of Goldfield, Columbia Avenue, in November, exactly a year after initial discoveries.

relatives would learn that Papa worked on Sunday—something unheard of before we went west.

Late in 1904 we left Goldfield, but we returned the next summer. By then, stage coaches and twenty-mule freight wagons could not keep up with the transportation demand. In 1905 the Tonopah & Goldfield Railroad was finished; by 1907 two other railroads, the Tonopah & Tidewater and the Las Vegas & Tonopah were completed. One of these trains ran in front of our house, and the tracks of another railroad crossed near our tent. What a clickity-clack was made when a train went over the crossing!

An event on Labor Day, 1906, overshadowed the usual events. The big Gans-Nelson fight was a publicity stunt by Tex Rickard to advertise Goldfield and the mines. Mama, Papa and I were in downtown Goldfield for the Labor Day celebration. The streets were crowded until it was time for the fight, then Papa and all other men went to the arena, leaving a town of women and children. For the first time the saloons were closed.

Joe Gans, world lightweight champion, had been challenged by "Battling" Nelson. Gans won the fight on a foul in the forty-second round. Mama and I could hear the shouting and we could hardly wait for Papa to get home and tell us all about it.

Besides prize fights and drilling contests, there were labor problems. With the big mines hiring so many men, by 1906 there were unions established, the "Wobblies" and the WFM.

By 1907, George Wingfield was the richest operator in the area, and he ordered change rooms built at the Consolidated Mining Company. Then high-grading

was the established thing to do. Most miners felt the very rich ore was a gift of nature and that they were entitled to take what they could. Many methods were used in efforts to bring home the most ore. Papa said he could tell if a lunch pail was filled with high-grade for the miner swings an empty pail, but the heavy pail hangs straight down.

Other labor difficulties resulted in a strike. George Wingfield requested aid from Governor Sparks and in December troops arrived in Goldfield. Then the only trouble was caused by the soldiers because every young girl in the camp fell in love with a soldier. One trooper

visited our Sunday school class. We got his name and address and what a deluge of valentines he must have received, mine among them. The mine operators won the strike and by 1908 the unions were eliminated.

A few years later we moved to Elko County. But I now cherished the true wealth of Nevada lore and history which my family had encompassed while living in a mining camp during the gold rush era.

During the 1905–07 boom numerous animal-driven teams jammed the main streets, creating a confusion of sounds. The sidewalks were thronged with speculators, gamblers, con men, and greenhorns.

Boom Town Goldfield

by F. D. Howard

Ah! Goldfield,
Born of dust and sweat and tears
Bedraggled by many snows
And darkly clouded yesteryears.
Today unveiled of mist
Lay sparkling in your mysteries.

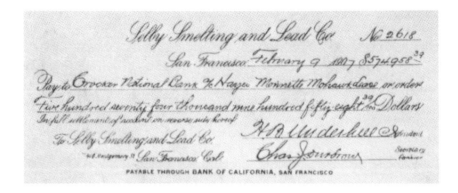

Not from gold alone came your ennobled past.
Ragamuffin of today hold tight
The tattered rainment of yesterday.
Urchin of forgotten streets
Exude the glories of your past.
Lend solace to the wandered
From ghostly ruins still remaining,
Change them little if at all.

Be adorned to fit your need,
Yet do not greatly heed
The siren's song of progress.
We love you as you are
Yet must sometimes think,
Oh, to be a child again
And see the wondrous things to come.

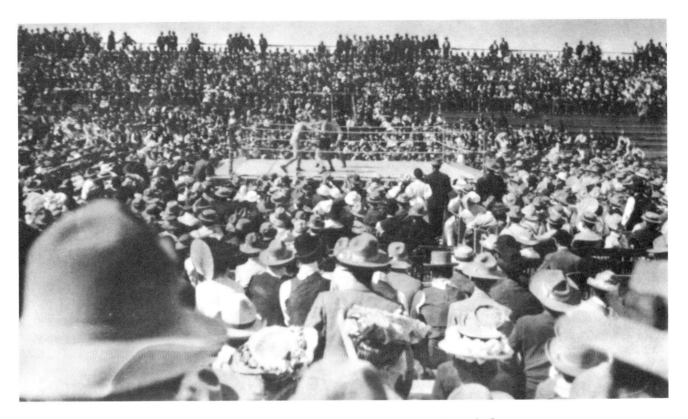

The check (opposite page) was given in settlement for 47 tons of high-grade from the famous Mohawk mine. Sacks of Mohawk gold are shown in the bank vault, awaiting shipment. The Gans-Nelson 42 round world's lightweight championship fight brought the largest gate ever taken by a prize fight until that time. More importantly, the match put Goldfield on the map of public consciousness. Goldfield also was festive during parades (below).

The Flood Side of Town

by Roberta Childers

It was Saturday, September 13, 1913 and this day seemed strangely foreboding. I stood with my face turned up and the rain started falling, getting myself wet and licking the water off my lips, savoring rain in the dry land. The drops were bigger than I had ever seen and hard-hitting, like buckshot. I ran to the house, completely soaked.

Inside we could hear it pouring down, like hammers pounding our shingle roof. The roof leaked, and the ceiling wallpaper bulged with the weight and began to drip. We scurried around placing teacups, pots and bowls.

As suddenly as it began, the storm was gone. Mama said we must walk down the hill to see if the Reynolds family was all right. They lived across the street from our old house, with their back door facing the big gulch which began near the old summit.

A large stream was still running in the gulch but the first high surge had only reached the Reynolds' chicken house. The water had torn away all the ground in front of the coop, and it teetered crazily on the two front posts, ready to collapse into the stream. The door was flapping and two chickens clung to the roost, while the rest clucked excitedly in the front yard.

The Reynolds were out in the street; as were other families further down. Reynolds' was the first house below the old brickyard, although once there had been solid houses beyond. Had there been homes in this section, they would have been washed away.

Suddenly a tub came down the stream, a big boy standing in it with a long pole to steer and slow his swirling rush. He waved and was soon out of sight. The ladies shook their heads. We envied him.

The highest wall of water was in the Brewery gulch on the west side of town, where mama's friend and fellow Methodist church member, Mrs. di Garmo lost her life.

One old man said he had had two sample sacks of gold in his cabin that floated off. On our side of town, a man had buried stolen high-grade and gone away. He returned years later. He did not find the cabin, let alone the high-grade.

When we came home, mama called a taxi and went to see dad who was already aware how bad a storm it had been.

"I heard the boys in the ward hollering 'There goes another one' (they could see both gulches from their high vantage point) and I heard the nuns praying and I knew it was bad, but I didn't worry. I knew you were up on high ground." Score one for the Hayes house, even if it did leak.

The bulk of the cloudburst had hit on the Malapai above the two gulches. Between them, the town sat high and safe. Some of the sporting girls' cabins close to the brewery above the South Main redlight were washed away. The 'famous four' saloons—the Palace, Northern, Hermitage and Mohawk—on the corners of Crook and Main were high enough to escape.

The gulch water dropped down, then took the Moose Hall, roaring on and smashing cabins along the way. The two gulches met far down toward the Consolidated Mill on Columbia Mountain.

Much property was swept away, but because the town already was on the skids, it was not replaced. It took the disastrous fire of 1923 to demolish the big buildings on high ground. Many were still occupied, some were used less frequently. The fire devastated most of them.

In the early 1940's, two Fallonites who heard about the flood stories, were experimenting with a metalscope in mining and took their doodlebug south. They followed the gulch from the old brewery ruins to the mill, several blocks wide and miles long, for several weeks.

There were lots of signals and digging turned up barrel hoops and old pieces of stove. They found the door to a mine car and were sure they had found the safe. Further digging brought disappointment. They failed to find any gold sacks, high-grade or the safe. They did find, just above an old iron wagon wheel buried two feet down, a small silk-lined leather garter or stocking purse in good condition, the type often worn by "one of the girls." It held a 1910, $5 gold piece.

Goldfield's Blind Miner

by Hugh A. Shamberger and
L. K. "Ken" Wilson

Heinie Miller was blinded by an explosion at the Goldfield Consolidated mine in 1927. Olaf Olson, who had known Heinie for many years, related that he was working in a nearby shaft when he heard him cry for help. He had drilled into a hole loaded with dynamite, causing the explosion.

Before the accident, Heinie had staked a claim east of town near Columbia Mountain in the Diamondfield District. Since the explosion cost him his eyesight, his friends ran a continuous wire three miles from his home in Goldfield to the mining property so that he could work his claim.

One of these friends, Joe Fuetsch, owned a lunch counter and bar near Heinie's cabin. Heinie would have breakfast at Fuetsch's restaurant, then begin the walk to his claim by picking up the wire guide and following it to his diggings.

For eight years Heinie left each morning at about six and walked to his property. It took about an hour, "give or take ten minutes," as he put it, "depending if I'm in a hurry or tired. Usually it's an hour and a quarter going home after my shift in the mine. That's a long climb up the shaft at three-thirty in the afternoon."

Heinie, by himself, had sunk a hundred-foot shaft and then tunneled horizontally about forty feet at its bottom. This level showed an ore vein about thirty inches in width and assayed $20 per ton. Earlier, the blind miner had prospected an outcrop of siliceous material and found some rich ore. Then he began sinking his shaft in softer altered country rock on a projection of the outcropping vein, striving for depth to get under that rich find.

By the mid-1930's, Heinie had stopped using his three-mile wire. He walked the trail by instinct and worked his mine without any assistance. He did the drilling, loading, blasting, mucking, hoisting to the surface, and even tramming to his dump site, all on his own.

Heinie's unique conquest of his blindness won him plaudits in the press and a vignette in Ripley's "Believe It or Not." On national radio networks he appeared as a guest on "We The People" and "Death Valley Days," as well as other programs of Philip H. Lord, of Seth Parker fame. As a result of the radio appearances, Heinie gained needed financial support for his mining activities.

In each of his public appearances, much emphasis was placed on Heinie's ability to know the kind of rock he was working by tasting it. By so doing, he could actually distinguish minerals in any piece of rock he was examining. As an experienced miner, and as efficient as a geologist with two good eyes, Heinie recognized the minerals found in dacite, the country or host rock of Goldfield ores, and would taste for an abundance of alunite. For example, he would know the fresh taste of waste dacite and could determine its difference from that of strong mineralization, vein material, or high-grade ore.

Sometime later Heinie purchased the Yellow Rose Patterson claim and worked it alone, as he did the other claims. At one time, according to Olson, he had three or four tons of ore on the dump that assayed $35 to $40 a ton. Some "slicker" came along and talked Heinie into giving him a lease and option. The fast-talker loaded up the ore and that was the last Heinie ever heard of him. He worked the mine for several years, but never found any more good ore.

In the late 1930's Heinie married a widow in Goldfield. A few years later they moved to southern California, where Heinie died in 1950 at the age of 62.

Few mining men in Nevada tried as hard as did Heinie Miller to develop a paying mine.

Following the wire (above).
Tasting the gold ore (below).

The devastating effects of the 1913 cloudburst (on a previous page) and the 1923 fire are apparent The Goldfield Hotel is at the far right. Disasters came to Goldfield in 3's: in 1933 snowstorms buried Goldfield in several feet of snow.

The Fire from My Window

by Jennie Mercer

On July 6, 1923, Goldfield was still a mining town of 5000 people. My husband, Bill, was the Sheriff of Esmeralda County and I was a housewife. About 7 o'clock that morning, while we were sitting down to have breakfast, I looked out of my kitchen window and saw some smoke rising above Parker's Garage, opposite the famous Goldfield Hotel.

We both immediately rose from the table to get a better look.

"Oh, that's a big fire!" Bill exclaimed. He rushed to the door, sped away in his car and did not return until late that night. All day the wind was blowing a gale and the fire spread down Main Street, taking all the buildings with it. Tonopah fire fighters and their truck came to help put out the blaze. Even the fire truck from Ely eventually arrived and worked far into the night.

From our front yard, my mother-in-law and I watched the fire on that terrible day. Toward evening my husband sent many hungry people over to us and we were very busy taking care of them. After 13 hours the flames were brought under control.

The next day we saw what the fire had done. In all, 27 blocks of businesses and houses were destroyed. Fortunately, the Goldfield Hotel was not harmed but many people were homeless and their belongings were gone. The Red Cross soon arrived to house and care for the unfortunates. It was many months before Goldfield was back to normal, but, since the fire, housing and business were never the same.

Joy

by Mrs. Larry Reiley

It was while my daughters and I were helping American Legionnaires look for veterans' graves in the Goldfield cemetery, we saw the unusual headstone, a sandstone slab with the name "Joy" crudely chiseled on the face.

The finding held special significance: when living in Oregon, I had read a book entitled *Autobiography of an Ordinary Woman* by Anne Ellis. One chapter was related to the hardships she and her family, consisting of her husband, a son Earl, and two daughters, Nita and Joy, endured while living in Goldfield.

It was in the year when the I.W.W.s had converged in Goldfield and instigated a miners' strike which lasted many months. The Ellis family had moved from Colorado to Goldfield in 1906. As the strike continued, other work for miners was very difficult to find. Food and fuel were exorbitantly high, credit nonobtainable, and with their meager savings gone, Anne was fortunate to find employment in the home of a stock broker.

During this period an epidemic of black diphtheria swept through the camp. Not realizing her young daughter had become a victim of the disease, Anne sat by Joy's bedside engrossed in reading *The Count of Monte Cristo*. When Joy asked her mother for a drink of water, Anne told her to wait for a minute. When Anne's eyes looked up from the page in her book, she was horrified to see Joy's breathing had stopped. Her baby daughter's life was gone.

Combined with the mother's grief was the remorse that she had ignored Joy's last request. This threw Anne into a deep shock lasting through the private burial. But necessity forced Anne back to the household chores, for the wages so sorely needed by her family. One morning when reporting for work, Anne noticed stones designated for use as steps in the nearly completed Sundog Elementary School. All day long, her grief-stricken mind kept comparing the similarity of sizes of the stones to monuments. That night, after dark, she secretly borrowed the wagon belonging to her employer's boy and managed to lift the heavy stone into the wagon, then pulled it to her home on High-graders' Hill. She used a spike to inscribe the letters "Joy" on one side of the stone and started the long walk to the cemetery. Emerging from the hollow near the Tonopah & Tidewater Railway station, she was stopped by a roving cabdriver, who warned her that people were being shot for stealing wood or coal along the tracks. Upon learning of the contents of the wagon, he charitably drove her to the cemetery and helped her place the stone on Joy's grave.

Having been brought up on an Indiana farm, the life of a miner's wife seemed to me to be comparatively easy, and then having lived years in Goldfield where I had seen such generous responses to alleviate the hardship of needful inhabitants, I was quite skeptical of the story and vowed if we ever returned to Goldfield, I would look for the grave.

And there it was!

My daughter was so impressed she wrote the story which was published in the *Playmate* magazine. Later she received a letter from Nita's daughter, telling of her grandmother's recent death. One of her last expressed wishes was that someone would look after Joy's grave. So my daughter and her schoolmates started the custom of gathering wildflowers to decorate her grave each Memorial Day.

As time went by, the elements took their toll. One Memorial Day, we were saddened to see the widening crack had finally split the stone, almost obliterating the name.

Then we moved from Goldfield and on a revisit to the cemetery we noticed a new stone had been placed at the grave with the benevolence of the Nevada Highway Department employees. It is a molded cement slab, with the outline of a child's toy wagon, and the single word "Joy" marked on it.

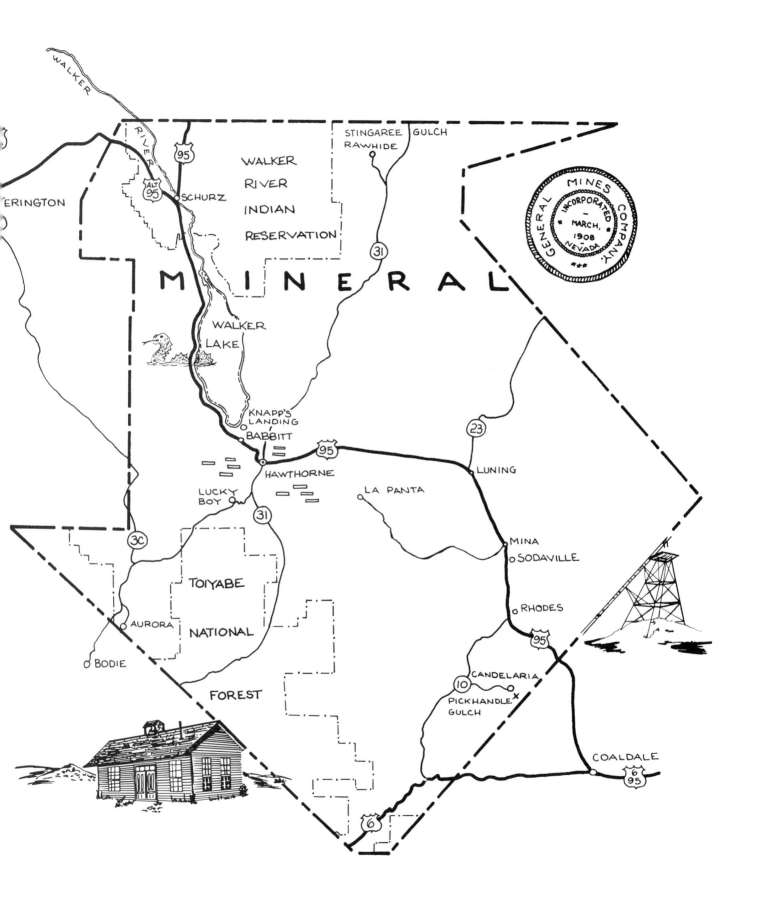

Mineral County

Aurora's Deadly Growing Pains

by Bob Stewart

On February 8, 1864, more than 200 ore stamps stopped hammering and pulverising ore in the seventeen quartz mills around Aurora. The silence permeating the valley remained unbroken for more than a day, until four bodies swung in a gallows constructed by the Aurora Citizens Safety Committee.

The committee had formed on the day W. R. Johnson was murdered, February 2nd, and within a short time 350 names had been enrolled and the organization completed.

Aurora's problem, which began a year before Johnson's murder, stemmed from a dispute between the Pond and the Real del Monte mining companies. Both claimed the same ore ledge, from opposite ends. While arguments were brought before the court, both companies hired gunmen to enforce their right to continue mining and to watch for claim jumpers.

Litigation dragged out for months and the gunmen settled in Aurora. During the ordeal of rule-by-gun, a mine tough named Jimmy Sears stole a horse. W. R. Johnson dispatched one of his employees to catch Sears and bring back the horse. In the line of duty, the employee shot and killed Sears.

All of the gunmen considered themselves "employees" and understood the shooting in those terms. They held the shooting against Johnson, who ordered his workman to action, not against the man who pulled the trigger. Even so, they took no immediate steps toward revenge.

Nine months later, in January 1864, the court suit was resolved. The gunslingers, now well established in Aurora, continued their residency. But resentment among the townspeople grew quickly. Law enforcement officers had been urged by wealthy mine owners to ignore the group of gunmen during the dispute and now it was too late for lawmen to gain the upper hand.

At dawn on February 1, 1864, the high-riding toughs avenged their friend Sears' death by shooting Johnson and attempting to burn his body in the streets of Aurora. This incident brought the townsfolk to action and Aurora lawmen immediately began tracking the outlaws.

Sheriff D. G. Francis and deputy H. J. Teel each led one posse out of town. By February 11, Sheriff Francis telegraphed Gov. James W. Nye that his posse made three arrests, and there were "no apprehensions of a mob—the citizens are acting with me."

The Sheriff then led his posse back out of town in search of the other desperadoes. In Aurora a dozen men were held in a stone structure used as the jail. A coroner's jury was empaneled to consider the murder and it began hearing witnesses.

On February 9, Deputy Teel returned to town to find the Citizens Committee had assumed control. Just before noon, he wired the Governor: "Sheriff Francis is out of town doing his best to find the murderers. Coroner's Jury has indicted four; one for accessory. I have just returned with the last murderer after a very laborious trip. Last evening at five o'clock Deputy Sheriff Demming was taking the supper to the prisoners, the citizens rushed in on him and Marshal [Dan] Pine put them under guard and the jail is now out of the Sheriff's hands. When I brought my prisoner in this morning, he was taken from me and I was ordered under arrest at my residence. The prisoners will be hung in less than an hour . . . everything is in the hands of the citizens."

Sam Youngs, an Aurora civic leader who had watched the San Francisco Vigilance Committee of 1856 hang two men, had sent his old friend Gov. Nye a more explicit telegram a few minutes earlier: "Everything peaceable and orderly. No opposition to officers. Four men will be hung at twelve o'clock."

At half past one, four men clearly involved in the murder—John Daley, William Buckley, John (Three-Finger Jack) McDowell and James Masterson—stretched ropes on the gallows. That night Youngs wrote in his journal: "A trying day for Aurora. Gov. Nye telegraphed me there must be no violence, but the people are the masters."

In Carson City, a rugged two-day stagecoach trip from Aurora, Governor Nye sought to protect the authority of the law. He ordered a detachment of soldiers from Ft. Churchill to Aurora. Accompanied by Warren Wasson, U.S. Marshal for Nevada Territory, and Jacob Van Bokkeleyn, territorial Provost Marshal,

Who owned the green jewel Esmeralda? Holt's 1863 map shows the rich Esmeralda mines of Aurora to be in California; that state and Nevada vied for political control until a survey late in 1863 placed Aurora in Nevada. The town declined after 1881 but a revival before World War I reopened its buildings (below).

Nye himself rode to Aurora.

They arrived more than 48 hours after the hanging.

Gov. Nye, a New York politician of the early Tammany Hall days, was chagrined to face a situation that political machinery could not handle. But Nye's alarmed view of the committee action was eased after an explanation from Van Bokkeleyn, who had served as "chief of police" for the San Francisco Committee of Vigilance of 1851, and had, in that job, conducted lynchings.

Although the Citizens Safety Committee of Aurora did not disband after the hangings, the town was orderly. A month after Johnson's murder, the committee ordered a member of an outlaw gang to leave town. He refused the committee order, but did leave quietly when Sheriff Francis suggested he find a new home.

When Sheriff Francis and Deputy Teel met with the committee three days later, it was ordered to disband.

Gov. Nye, fearing that adverse publicity might affect Nevada's bid for statehood, neglected to mention the incident in his report to Secretary of State William Seward. He did say: "Obstacles that would seem insurmountable in many places, here seem only to quicken the zeal and the energies of our people to apply themselves to their removal, with a will absolutely irresistible. . . ."

S. Vance, a gunman wounded in the aftermath of the Johnson killing, had been locked in the county jail as an accessory to the murder. At the end of March, he gained freedom when two other prisoners used spoons to dig away the mortar and effect an escape from the building.

But Vance, his action demonstrating effectively the return of rule by law to Aurora, went straight to the sheriff's office and surrendered.

Knapp's Landing

by Helen McInnis

Knapp's Landing was once a small freight terminal on the south shore of Walker Lake from 1875 to 1881.

Its founder, Sewell Crosby Knapp, was born in Bradley, Maine and grew up piloting ships with his father on the Penobscot River and Bay. He came to California in the early 1850's and located on the Mother Lode. About 1874, he and his three eldest sons, Sewell Alvin, Edwin and Eugene settled in the northern end of the Mason Valley. Sewell Alvin and a man named R. G. Laws became partners in a mercantile store at Wabuska, while Sewell, Sr., Edwin and Eugene operated a freight line between the Central Pacific railroad station at Wadsworth and the mining camps in the Candelaria region southeast of Walker Lake.

Getting around Walker Lake was a struggle. The sheer sides of the Wassuk mountains created a barrier several miles long on the western shore, and miles of sand dunes on the eastern shore made travel almost impossible. So, the freight wagons had to veer far to the east of the lake, adding additional miles to an already long and arduous journey.

Knapp, with his naval background, soon realized that the fastest and easiest way to move freight southward from Wadsworth and Mason Valley to Candelaria would be by boat. With Edwin and Eugene, he established Knapp's freighting and transportation service across the waters of Walker Lake.

Freight and passengers came to a loading jetty near Wasson's Camp on the Walker River, near present day Schurz. There the boat was loaded, ferried down a few miles to the river's mouth, and piloted across the full 26 miles of Walker Lake to a cove near the mouth of Wild Cat Canyon (the present Cat Creek). This creek flowed down the canyon amid stands of cottonwood and willow trees. It was a good place to locate and the Knapps constructed their landing dock and associated structures at that site.

The road from Candelaria to Aurora and Bodie crossed the valley south of Knapp's Landing and many boatloads of freight, especially fresh produce and hay from the fertile Mason Valley, were picked up at the landing by merchants of Candelaria. Many residents of that region who needed to travel north, favored the shorter trip over the water rather than the long haul on land. Knapp's Landing became a busy place and along with an adjacent ranch, owned by Sam Nickel at the

foot of Big Squaw Canyon, were the first white settlements on the south end of Walker Lake.

In 1881 the Carson & Colorado Railroad was built along the eastern shore of Walker Lake and the town of Hawthorne was established that April. Many people came to reside in the new railroad division point, but more especially, hundreds of prospectors and mine boomers discovered metal-bearing ore in the surrounding mountains. The Cory Creek, Alum Creek, Cottonwood Canyon, and La Panta Districts opened up for settlement. The area boomed and Sewell Alvin Knapp came down from Wabuska to open the first store near the depot of the new town. Knapp and Laws General Merchandise prospered along with hotels, seven saloons, barber shops, harness shops, a hay and grain yard, a blacksmith shop, and three Chinese washhouses. In the spring of 1883 Hawthorne became the seat of Esmeralda county, taking it away from the once prosperous Aurora.

The railroad instantly abolished the need for Knapp's freight service across the lake, and around 1885 the eldest Knapp moved to Stockton, California where he died three years later.

Sewell Alvin sold his interest in the general store to J. E. Adams and J. H. Miller and became involved in the La Panta mines. He and his two brothers built and operated a quartz mill at the south end of Hawthorne, almost directly across from the present Mineral County Library. For several years it processed ore from the La Panta mines. But by 1902 all of the Knapps had left the area.

The accumulation of tailings from the mill still makes a well defined elevation, and the house that Sewell Alvin built for his wife and children stands in use at Fifth and "C" Streets by the Southern Baptist Church. There is nothing at the site of Knapps Landing to show that a busy freight terminal had existed there.

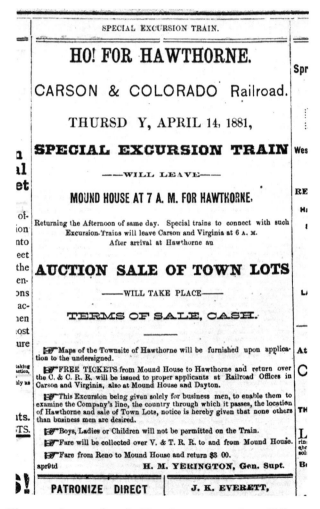

The very heart of early Hawthorne was along E Street, near the Carson & Colorado tracks. The town was founded as a result of an auction which brought speculators from as far away as Reno and Virginia City.

Shockley at Candelaria

by Nanelia S. Doughty

William Hillman Shockley, son of a New Bedford whaling captain, and a mining engineer from M.I.T., came in December 1880 to Candelaria.

Shockley arrived at a fortuitous time. He had emerged from school into a nationwide panic, with the accompanying shortage of jobs. After being exploited in two or three unpaid jobs, he was glad to secure through family friends this post as clerk-assayer-surveyor for the Mt. Diablo Mining and Milling Company.

The Mt. Diablo shaft was located on a branch of the great Northern Belle lode—like all the others in Pickhandle Gulch, adjacent to Candelaria. The mine was just coming into production under Mr. Jones, superintendent of both it and the Northern Belle.

Eighteen months after Shockley's arrival, Superintendent Jones was fatally injured in an accident; and the Company appointed Shockley superintendent of the Mt. Diablo operation.

Candelaria lies in a wide alluvial valley sloping toward the northeast, banked by lava hills to the south. Pickhandle Gulch cuts a steep slot into those grim blue-black hills, rising steeply to the Y, where it was flanked by wood shacks and stone cabins, three boarding houses, four saloons, and one grocery. Winding upward, the road crested at the future reservoir site, then tobogganed south to Columbus and its mill. The steep descent gave the Chinese drivers of the ore wagons a chance for a wild, thrill-packed ride.

Early in 1882 two events alleviated the isolation of Candelaria. The Carson and Colorado Railroad completed a spur line into town, eliminating the 150-mile stagecoach ride which Shockley had endured from Mound House, near Carson City.

Within a week or two the White Mountain Water Company pipe line from Trail Canyon—some nineteen miles—was finished, and began filling the reservoir at the Gulch summit. Pickhandle Gulch got first chance at the gravity-flow line—and the superintendent's house up in the Mt. Diablo cul-de-sac had first call with running water in his house—in 1882.

This was a tremendous change in a community which had been so deprived of water that the telegraph installer had had to descend to the 1,700-ft. level of one of the mines to find a spot wet enough for his ground wire.

A major professional advance was developing, as well. To relieve itself of milling charges, the Mt. Diablo company constructed its own ten-stamp mill at Soda Springs (now Sodaville), in 1886–1887. Here Shockley participated in experiments with a new method of ore extraction being developed by his associates back east. This was the cyanide process, first commercially ap-

Superintendent Shockley is on the far right.

plied to gold ore in 1887–1888. An immediate and obvious application was to rework tailings, retrieving values unrecoverable with earlier methods.

Shockley's steady governance, and the company's regular declaration of dividends, earned him a public endorsement—that the Mt. Diablo Mine and Mill were "very well run." Only the falling price of silver, and a long strike by the miners in 1891–1892, brought a shut down of operations.

Pickhandle Gulch

In the meantime, Shockley had earned renown in another field. The grim lava cliffs of the Gulch which he found repellent and depressing, on arrival, burst into a blaze of flowers and plants after a rather wet winter. Skeptic Shockley had written his mother, a serious botanizer, that "nothing grows here." He was converted. Fascinated by the prodigal display and by the short life-cycle of these desert-adapted plants, he spent his spare time collecting specimens. In February 1882 he sent a packet of plants to Professor Serena Watson at Cambridge. Watson and Gray found several new species among them, and one new genus—a most unusual discovery. In all, Shockley collected first specimens of some fifteen plants which bear his name; and botanists identify him instantly. He presented his herbarium to the University of California at Berkeley.

Shockley's thirst for learning produced one wildly unpredictable effect on his career. He had always studied since coming to Candelaria, as an antidote for isolation and loneliness—mathematics and herpetology, Latin, and modern languages. The discovery that his Chinese cook was no mere "coolie," but a literate man, generated a desire to read and write Chinese. So, for years, the superintendent and Chinese from Candelaria's Chinatown worked on the intonation and writing skills of that tongue.

When he went to London in 1893, Shockley called on various investors' syndicates, seeking employment as a consulting engineer. When they discovered he knew Chinese, he was dispatched at once, in company with a Member of Parliament negotiating loans, to investigate mining opportunities in China. Now the Old Empress, with her prejudice against outsiders, still ruled China. There the "foreign devils" roused hatred —which eventually culminated in the Boxer Rebellion.

But Shockley discovered that the dialect learned in Candelaria enabled him to communicate with the Empress' strong man, Li Hung Chang, more readily than could the British Embassy's interpreter! Li himself was an up-country peasant risen by ability and favor to be the "Bismarck of China." Shockley stayed in the country two and a half years, finally leaving with a price on his head.

His reputation for judgment and honesty brought him consulting assignments on every continent but Antarctica, in the next decade. He never went back to Candelaria; but Nevada drew him after 1900. His old friends B. G. and "Borax" Smith, David Howell Jackson, E. B. Cushman and Ben Edwards all had joined in the boom days of Tonopah and Goldfield. And the Bullfrog strike of 1904 had again electrified the mining fraternity.

Much-travelled Shockley joined them—and at last settled into domestic life, at Tonopah, the great silver camp founded by Jim Butler.

Man About Town
by Lorena Edwards Meadows

In 1885 Ben Edwards went to Candelaria to work in the mines. Candelaria had been discovered in 1864 by Mexican prospectors who named the mine after a Catholic Mass day. The town spread out on a flat below Pickhandle Gulch where the mines were located.

Beginning in 1880 the area began to prosper, and in 1882 a good water supply and a spur of the Carson & Colorado Railroad came to the camp. In its heyday, Candelaria could boast of two hotels, stores, offices for lawyers and three doctors, and countless saloons. Dances, lodge meetings, roller skating and many public gatherings took place at Candelaria Hall, a large room above Billy Thomas saloon.

In 1890 Edwards was employed at Zabriskie & Shockley's bank. Here he learned that the banking business consisted mainly of safeguarding customers' money and dealing in foreign exchange over the telegraph wire. Ben became an influential man, serving as the postmaster, telegraph operator, Wells Fargo agent, notary public and on occasion as mortician and deputy sheriff.

Soon after he brought his bride to Candelaria in 1893, he was alarmed when the financial panic in the country caused mines to close down. As people deserted the camp, Ben also had to decide whether he should stay on or leave. His faith in Nevada's silver ore never faltered and his decision not to move helped keep the town alive.

Dry and uninviting Candelaria was a wooden town subject to fires and extreme temperatures. The wind kicked up dust and sand, making life nearly unbearable. But the dream of silver persisted.

This shaft hoisting works was at the very foot of Pickhandle Gulch, over-looking the town of Candelaria.

Candelaria was a station on the Carson & Colorado Railroad and Ben brought in merchandise and commodities which were freighted to the small, outlying communities of Fish Lake Valley, Silver Peak, Lida, Pigeon Springs and Marietta.

Candelaria was near Columbus and Teel's marshes, where great quantities of borax had been discovered and produced, bringing a large fortune to F. M. (Borax) Smith. Although the supply had diminished, and the Pacific Coast Borax Company had closed its headquarters there, Ben knew there was enough for shipments to a refinery in Alameda, California. He employed hundreds of Chinese "coolies," directed by a "boss Chinaman," and they produced and sacked the crude borax which was then hauled in 14-mule freight wagons to the railway station.

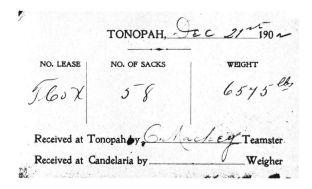

NO. LEASE	NO. OF SACKS	WEIGHT
760 X	58	6575 lbs.

TONOPAH, Dec 21 190 2

Received at Tonopah by C. Mackey Teamster.
Received at Candelaria by _____ Weigher

By 1885 or so, Candelaria's white painted cemetery held more residents than the town itself. Above is a common teamster's receipt for ore.

The following seven years proved difficult for the remaining citizens of Candelaria—now a dry, wind swept, desolate place, bitterly cold in winter and unbearably hot and dry in summer. For two years the water supply was shut off when the pipes froze in the mountains. Water had to be brought in barrels, an expensive means, or obtained from the locomotive tanks.

The mines produced practically nothing during these years, but in 1900 Jim Butler, with his straying burro, discovered rich deposits of silver in Nye County and established the mining district of Tonopah.

Ben Edwards soon traveled the sixty miles to the new camp. He inspected the ore and invested in successful mining claims.

Immediately his Candelaria store received more orders than he could handle. The eager prospectors rushing to Tonopah needed all types of commodities which had to be ordered and reordered. Edwards built a warehouse, guarded by an armed watchman, at the rail station to house the piles of merchandise until teamsters with their large wagons would carry the goods across the desert.

He opened a branch store in Tonopah and put in a telephone line between Tonopah and Candelaria. In 1904 railroad service was extended to Tonopah, by-passing Candelaria. Ben sold his merchandise and fixtures, then transported his family of six and two houses to Bishop, California.

Candelaria was deserted in a short time. Once or twice the area's mining was revived with no lasting success. By World War II it was truly a ghost town.

ARRIVAL OF TEX RICKARDS
DRILL MINING WATER

Stingaree Gulch

by Harold O. Weight

Experts claimed that Rawhide's Stingaree Gulch was the only real rival San Francisco's Barbary Coast ever had. Leo Grutt couldn't judge that—he didn't know the Barbary Coast.

"But I knew Stingaree Gulch," he said. "I saw it grow—and it was something! There must have been five or six hundred girls on the line up there—all nations, all colors!"

Stingaree Gulch occupied the narrow, curving valley separating Grutt and Balloon hills, separated from respectable Rawhide by a low rocky ridge extending down from Grutt Hill. The entire Gulch was upon validly located mining claims; parts of the Gray Eagle, Mascot, Balloon, Sunbeam, Wild West and others. Consequently, none of the inhabitants could obtain legal title to the land, and madams, dance hall owners, saloon keepers and crib girls paid no rent to the claim holders. They were simply squatters. Squatting was accepted in boom towns, as long as mineral rights of claim holders remained unchallenged.

A man called Friday pioneered Stingaree Gulch late in 1907. Gene Grutt discovered his little saloon-dance hall almost completed, and told Friday he was trespassing.

"I'm just squatting," Friday explained.

Gene considered. "Well, understand you have no claim at all to the land."

"Sure," said Friday. "Let's have a drink on it."

"While I was having that drink," Gene told me, "a back door opened and a girl came in. The first girl in Stingaree Gulch—and she used to wait on me in the hotel dining room up in Davenport, Washington!"

After Friday opened the Gulch, the hookers, their macs and madams poured in. The wagon road between Grutt and Balloon hills became Johnson Street, Stingaree's one winding, narrow thoroughfare which was soon lined with buildings for half a mile on both sides, from Jack Hall's Liquor Company to Shorty's hop joint.

Parlor houses, cribs, saloons, dance halls. Hug & Johnson's Big Casino, the Little Casino, the Deuce Spot, Babe Raymond's, Bessie Bell's, Ragtime Kelly's, the Zanzibar, Squeeze Inn. Smaller operations were scattered to the boundaries of the soon legally segregated district. Mixed throughout were the tunnels, surface structures and dumps of numerous mine workings.

The gulch mouth, adjacent to Rawhide, was the only natural entrance to Stingaree Gulch. Here Esmeralda County strategically placed Rawhide's new stone jail. As Stingaree grew and extended, this portal was considered an inconvenience by many patrons of downtown Rawhide and they disliked the close proximity of the jail.

Tex Rickard was loudly applauded when he hired the Tonopah Kid to blast a narrow passage through the rocky ridge some distance north of the jail. The new entrance led past Rickard's Northern Saloon and a few cynics questioned Tex's altruism. The heavy traffic into Stingaree Gulch passed through the front and back doors of the Northern Saloon, with other businesses lacking customers.

The girls in the Gulch came from the red light districts so common in western mining days. Blonde Ada, Sloppy Dora, Gold Tooth Bess and her sister Gold Tooth Molly, Red Bess, Lil Bennett, the Midget Fraction, Little Birdie, Big Kate, Stud Horse Lil, Gypsy LaMarr ("Oh, she was a pretty little girl!"), the Red Top Fraction ("From Goldfield—about four and a half feet tall, weighed about 100 pounds."), The Boiler Maker ("From the Barbary Coast, a great big hard boiled girl, the name fitted her well.").

All kinds of girls from all kinds of places, were in Stingaree Gulch for all kinds of reasons. For some it was the only way to survive in a world that had defeated them. Some, through love or fear, were virtual slaves of their pimps and were addicts to alcohol, cocaine or opium. For many girls existence was a hopeless degra-

Lingering snow of early 1908 in Rawhide is evident on Grutt Hill. Many of the tent dwellings would soon be replaced by wooden shanties.

dation while others were there by choice and would not have accepted any other way of life.

The girls left the line by equally varied ways; violence, disease, the poor conditions under which they lived. Suicide was pitifully common. Lucky or hard-headed ones made their money as planned, retired, enjoyed a peaceful and respectable old age. Others continued until too battleworn to compete, then became madams supervising younger and fresher girls. But surprisingly, many married their customers.

"A girl in the Gulch married and quit the dance hall and everything," said the Tonopah Kid. "Opened a stand in another camp and sold cigars, cigarettes and chewing gum, and nothing else. All us guys who knew her told everybody to buy there. She just done more damn business. And everybody respected her and she never throwed herself open to anybody in any way after that."

The "life of shame" was not all that shameful in Rawhide or any other boom mining camp. They were "sporting women" and often judged as individuals rather than members of the class prostitute.

Why, then, the insistence they be segregated? Partly human nature, partly the knowledge that the very nature of their profession subjected them to the worst elements; usually they came with parasites already attached.

Rawhide limited its district by ordinance, and when two women set up a workshop on the ridge, some 200 citizens moved the half-completed building back into the Gulch. Said the Rawhide *Times:* "There is a determined stand taken by the better element that all questionable establishments shall be embraced in the limits of the Gulch to the west of Nevada Street."

For "west," read "east." Rawhiders must have been upset when the reporter mixed his compass directions. But use of "embraced" was an inspiration. Plenty of that "better element" in Rawhide embraced not only the establishments, but the girls in the Gulch. They just wanted them kept in their place.

In 1877 Harper's Weekly *delighted its readers with this drawing of a camel train in Nevada. The beasts were employed in southwestern deserts as early as 1855 and after the Civil War they were used to pack freight over the Sierra to western Nevada. The cumbersome traction engine at Tonopah (below) was also found at Columbus, in Death Valley and in Eldorado Canyon. All of them were a failure.*

Desert Transport

by Richard C. Datin

Camels and traction engines had much in common. They were unusual, their existence was short-lived, and both failed to live up to their expectations. The primary purpose of this equipment was to transport merchandise across the desert, but repeated attempts were costly failures.

In 1851 the idea to use camels as beasts of burden on the arid plains of the West was promoted by U.S. Secretary of War Jefferson Davis, who believed these animals might be best suited for transporting military supplies to the distant army forts. The camels arrived at Indianola, Texas, in February 1857, but after several

treks across the southwest deserts, the camels' eccentricities surfaced. With the experiments less than successful, the camels were herded together and only used briefly thereafter.

Not to be outdone by the military, fifteen Bactrian camels (the double humped variety) arrived at San Francisco in July 1860. They were shipped from the far east by importer Otto Esche for use in the mining regions of Nevada. The animals then were auctioned off to establish a regular camel train between Placerville and the Comstock. However, this failed to materialize and the beasts were subsequently employed hauling salt to the Carson River mills from the southern marshes. When a more abundant deposit of salt was located near Sand Springs, Churchill County, within seventy-five miles of Virginia City, the use of camels was superseded by wagon teams. For a few years afterwards the animals transported mercantile goods from Virginia City to Austin; a 180 mile trip lasting about 13 days and they hauled from 5,500 to 7,000 pounds of freight at a time.

Eventually these "ships of the desert" were turned adrift but state legislators declared the humpbacks a nuisance. A bill was introduced in the state legislature, "An act to prohibit camels and dromedaries from running at large on or about the public highways of Nevada." This was approved in 1875 and ultimately was repealed in 1899.

The traction engines, a boiler mounted on three or four wheels, eventually replaced the camels. In early 1880 the Nevada Steam Transportation Company introduced a steam wagon for hauling supplies along the Wadsworth-Columbus wagon road. It made about twenty miles a day—empty and on one occasion a team from Columbus had to take wood and water to it.

During the Tonopah boom, near the end of 1901, more than 400 horses and mules transported supplies to Tonopah and returning with sacks of high grade ore to the nearest railroad. These animals worked in teams of twelve to twenty but hauled only fifteen tons of ore per load.

The much heralded 32,000 pound traction engine, with wagons designed to haul freight between Sodaville and Tonopah, arrived at the Carson and Colorado Railway's Sodaville depot in February 1902. Company officials felt this engine would be a great success on its exclusively constructed road between Sodaville and the new bonanza camp, and that its adaptability to the desert would spark revivals of the dormant mining camps. However, after several trial trips the steam tractor had surrendered its job to the mules. The owners had concluded that expense for building this wagon road would not warrant the outlay because the railroad would soon be extended to Tonopah.

The advent of this modern iron horse closed another chapter in Nevada's history and simultaneously introduced an era of efficient and profitable transportation enterprises.

In 1902 Sodaville was the nearest railroad station for the newly discovered Tonopah district. People bound for there rode the Carson & Colorado to Sodaville and then caught a four- or six-horse stage for Tonopah.

Modern Desert Rat

by Jean Reid

Photographic maps and magnetic fields have replaced chance prospecting; hydraulic and pneumatic drills have replaced single and double jacks; but the miner who uses the tools has changed little. His techniques have become more sophisticated, of course, but the vigilant spirit and rugged independence of the "old-timers" is still alive and kicking. However, as with the rest of the Old West, it has been civilized and is showing itself in more socially acceptable ways. A present-day miner would rarely take law into his own hands and shoot a claim jumper in the back, yet the miner feels he could do very well without government regulations such as the EPA controls. Today's miner would still rather work for himself or for something that will be his than for somebody else, but instead of buying a burro, loading up, and going out prospecting, he makes a business out of mining, working from a home base, and going out for days, not months, at a time.

Ike Williams, of Mina, is one such miner. In the business since 1923, Ike obviously has full knowledge of all the new methods of prospecting and mining. In prospecting, he looks at a geological structure for granite and igneous rock contact zones to follow or faults to check out. He also gets photographic maps from the United States Geological Survey or the Bureau of Mines and reads them to help him know where to begin looking. As he says, it makes it "a little faster than 40 or 50 years ago." Even with these methods, though, he admits with a chuckle to drawing blanks about 99 times out of 100, and notes that some mines are found by accident. He relates the tale of some men who were building a road to a mine in Fish Lake Valley and struck a richer mine while building the road.

Although his mining ways are modern, Ike's attitudes resemble the spirit of the old miner. His regard for government controls is about as high as his predecessors' regard for the law. It seems to him the government is trying to stop industry with all the EPA controls its been imposing. He cites, for example, the Kennecott copper mine in Ely closing because of an EPA crackdown on open-pit mining. This crackdown also hampers iron mining because it's uneconomical to go underground. He also refers to a bill in Congress that would force prospectors to get a permit to prospect, and, if they find something, to put it up for auction. This, he adds, would put the independent prospectors out of business because they couldn't afford to bid against the companies. "In the East they don't have an idea (of the problems). In the west, it almost supports us," he explains, adding, "Some of that stuff I get pretty bitter about."

In the 1920's the Sinnott Garage advertised itself as being in the center of town. Mina then had several hundred people.

Ike also possesses the spirit of independence of the old miner. At 74 he has just finished building a road to his mine with the help of "a boy," his 45-year-old partner. Between his mining, on which he says he loses money, the machine shop he runs in the winter, and his social security pension, Ike supports himself in what he considers a comfortable manner. He also adheres to the philosophy that working for oneself is better than working for someone else, and has been in business for himself since 1950. He now has 12 claims, some under lease, some having never been worked, and the one he is working with his partner. Unlike the old miner, however, Ike doesn't go prospecting or working his mine for months at a time. For awhile, he lived in a trailer in Marietta while building the road to his mine, but, as he says, "I got tired of that and it got cold." He had since been commuting to his mine, about 50 miles southwest of Mina, before he stopped work for the winter.

Because of his independence, Ike has the dedication of the old prospector in spending a life looking for that one big strike. Although his career in mining was of necessity (his car broke down in Candelaria on the way to Ely and he needed some money for a new set of tires), mining has become a way of life for him. Mining has gotten into his blood. He's tried other jobs since that first one in Candelaria, but he's "always leaned back toward the mines." Even now he continues to mine, although he had decided to retire five years ago. Ike doesn't need the money it brings in, but he says, "If I didn't keep busy with something like that I wouldn't last long."

Ike can't explain why he likes to mine. His wife Cele explains, "It's hard to say after so many years why you like or dislike something. You just take it as it comes." However, one of the obvious factors that keeps Ike in mining is working underground. He says, "I have to be careful about working underground; it becomes a mania. I get to where I don't want to work anywhere else. . . . It's nice. On cold days in winter it's warmer in the mine; in the summer, it's cool." He sees no more hazard working underground than in any other job. In mining, he explains, one just has to be careful and not take chances.

If his spirit and dedication liken him to the old-time miner, Ike's lack of greed distinguishes him. In the mine he's working now, he extracts just enough to keep him going. He and his wife live in two small one-room houses and a three-room trailer all pushed together to form a home on the outskirts of Mina. They dress simply and their house is furnished in early American odds and ends. As Ike says, "I don't see where anybody'd want to build anything elaborate." About striking it rich, Cele philosophises, "I can't let it excite me; I can't let it bother me. There are so many failures." She tells of two women who divorced their husbands because they didn't get the money from the mines they expected, but she says she can't afford to let it bother her in every day life. She worries now, instead, about Ike's health. Since he's 74, she worries about his working on the bulldozer and coming home at seven or eight in the evening.

Mining is still, as Ike would say, "an interesting but hard life," in spite of technology. The sophistication the machines have brought has tended to make mining more of a science, and the miner more of a scientist, yet the robust spirit of the old-timers lives on.

263

Hawthorne Legend

by B. J. Owen

Mamie Frances Mingle, a legend—and certainly a mysterious figure—around Hawthorne, spent twenty-odd years on a homestead near the south end of Walker Lake, just north of the present U.S. Naval Ammunition Depot concrete batch plant.

A native of Michigan, she initially came to Goldfield shortly after the first strike there, about 1904, to open a boarding house. When nearby Diamondfield was founded a year later, she moved her operation there and then ultimately to Aurora.

The Lucky Boy mine was discovered in 1908, five miles south of Hawthorne and Mamie became the manager of the company boarding house and an important influence in the mine's early development.

The wiry, rugged Mamie, usually outfitted in high boots and short skirts, would refuse to hire any man at her boarding house unless he could prove his strength equal to her own. The test she used for interviews was to carry a side of beef from the storeroom to the butchering block and not every man could complete this feat.

Weighing ninety pounds at the time and only 4 feet 10 inches tall, she acted as bouncer when boarding house miners got out of hand.

When Lucky Boy activity faded, Mamie refurbished her homestead near Walker Lake, raising hundreds of chickens and selling poultry and eggs. Her favorite diversion was spending hours each Saturday fixing a chicken dinner for the children of Hawthorne, who were regaled by stories of the mining camps and homespun advice.

In 1928, the government bought up homesteads and property for the huge Naval Ammunition Depot. Mamie refused to sell her tiny parcel with its windmill water right, ready to fight the United States government if necessary. When it came to a showdown, government authorities backed off and became Mamie's friends and benefactors. Throughout her remaining years, Mamie lived in the shadow of the world's largest ammunition depot.

As huge storage buildings and bunkers went up all around her during the World War II conflict, Mamie's comfort and health were guarded by daily Marine patrols and officials were gravely concerned when she fell down the well shaft on her property. She had rescued herself by bracing her arms and legs against the sides of the shaft, then inching her way to the top, where she was found exhausted, with a badly injured arm.

In 1946, fire consumed her small home, but through the combined effort of the Navy and Mineral County Fire Department all of the many outbuildings were saved. Navy officials remodeled one of these in a matter of days and Mamie was soon doing business as usual from a larger, improved home.

She continued to raise her chickens and received daily visitors, including the Marine Patrol who continued to look in on her as a matter of moral obligation, if not a direct military order. They found her early in the morning on March 11, 1948; she had been dead for a few hours and death was declared to be from natural causes.

Mamie Mingle had known good and bad times in the heyday of the Nevada mining camps, had personified the indomitable spirit of the early pioneer women, and died peacefully at 88 in her home amid one of the largest industrial complexes in Nevada.

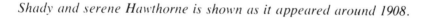

Shady and serene Hawthorne is shown as it appeared around 1908.

The Hawthorne Elks Safari marches proudly up E Street during the Armed Forces Day celebration in 1956.

The Great Safari

by B. J. Owen

The Hawthorne Armed Forces Day parade always has been the biggest celebration in town and was an especially big event in 1954 when the local Elks formed a drill team to compete in it.

Colorful uniforms of surplus Navy white trousers with a royal purple cummerbund were topped off with a white pith helmet encircled by purple trim. The pith explorers helmets suggested the name they finally adopted—the "Elks Safari."

Marching in their first Hawthorne Armed Forces Day parade in 1954, the Safari was an instant success, winning a blue ribbon for their performance, and everyone awed at the precision with which they performed.

The Safari had discovered two problems in their first outing. With no marching music, they had to rely on voice commands alone.

In the next two years they again won the blue ribbon at Hawthorne, and a Scotch drum and bagpipe entry provided rhythmic background for the Safari's march steps.

Flushed with their continuing success, but eager to win more extensive laurels, the Safari went into all out training, refining original steps and adding intricate manuevers to their reportoire. The team could be seen almost every night, swinging up and down "A" Street as they prepared for the Bishop Homecoming parade.

At Bishop they were again placed behind the Scotch Bagpipe entry and they performed flawlessly, bringing the huge marching team trophy home to Hawthorne.

The Safari trained harder than ever for the big one—the Nevada Admission Day parade at Carson City in October 1956.

They arrived early on this cold day, their drill team featuring a large Pink Elephant float.

Clad only in their thin white uniforms, the Safari was half frozen before the parade began and members made frequent trips to the portable bar inside the Pink Elephant.

They were in trouble from the start. The parade Marshal had entered them between a popular dance band from Reno *and* their Scotch Bagpipe friends. They were dismayed when the dance band played "When The Saints Go Marching In," while the Scotch entry broke into a highland fling. The Safari could not select a beat from either band and the din made it almost impossible to hear the vital commands of their leader.

It all fell apart in front of the reviewing stand. The Safari's most dazzling step was an intricate maneuver called "fan blue," a series of "wheels," about-faces, hesitations and obliques that spread them all over the street. The next command, "fan red," was intended to reverse the procedure, reuniting the group into a tight unit.

The order came, "fan blue!" and thirty Safari members broke into the first phase of the manuever, then hesitated, waiting for the order to reunite.

Only this time—whether due to the confusing beats of the competing bands, the numbing moan of the north wind, or too many nips from the Pink Elephant—planned chaos became utter confusion when the commander called "fan red!"

Some heard the order and performed correctly, running immediately into others who were still in their former positions. Then, neither group knowing which manuever was right, the Safari floundered and faltered before the horrified eyes of their admirers.

Some members tried to regroup the best way they could; some stood helplessly, watching the others stumble around; and one walked off the street into the nearest bar—as if that was what he was *supposed* to do all along.

The "Elks Safari" disbanded after that, never to be reorganized. But in its day, it was the best act in Hawthorne.

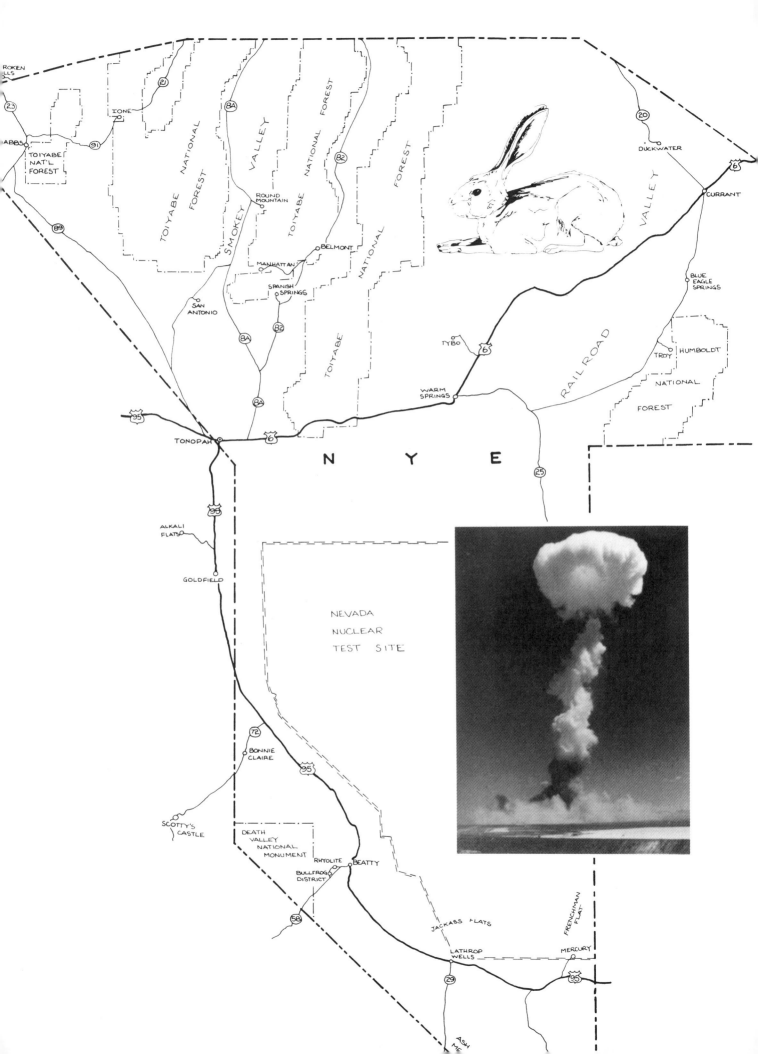

ROKEN
LLS
23
ABBS
91
TOIYABE
NAT'L
FOREST
89
21
IONE
8A
TOIYABE   NATIONAL   FOREST
SMOKEY   VALLEY
82
TOIYABE   NATIONAL   FOREST
ROUND
MOUNTAIN
BELMONT
MANHATTAN
SPANISH
SPRINGS
82
SAN
ANTONIO
8A
TOIYABE   NATIONAL   FOREST
8A
95
6
TONOPAH
6
N   Y   E
25
ALKALI
FLATS
95
GOLDFIELD
NEVADA
NUCLEAR
TEST   SITE
72
BONNIE
CLAIRE
95
SCOTTY'S
CASTLE
DEATH
VALLEY
NATIONAL
MONUMENT
RHYOLITE
BEATTY
BULLFROG
DISTRICT
58
20
DUCKWATER
6
CURRANT
BLUE
EAGLE
SPRINGS
TYBO
6
TROY
HUMBOLDT
NATIONAL
FOREST
WARM
SPRINGS
RAILROAD
VALLEY
JACKASS   FLATS
LATHROP
WELLS
29
FRENCHMAN
FLAT
MERCURY
95
ASH
ME

Spanish Springs Station

by Walter C. Wilson

Soon after John Humphrey's wayward boot kicked rich ore from a gopher hole and Manhattan was discovered on April Fool's Day, 1905, Spanish Springs was established as a station for freighters and other travellers between Tonopah and Manhattan. The Springs was thirty-five miles north of Tonopah and ten miles southeast of Manhattan. Freighters stopped at a station every fifteen miles. Rye Patch was the first, and the Springs the second station on the Tonopah-Manhattan road.

The Springs had been used for many years by nomadic Shoshone Indians. Cowboys and prospectors paused there for water in the late 1860's. A Spaniard, San Pedro, and his group of Mexican prospectors wintered there in 1870. After that the place was called Spanish Springs.

In 1907 Mom and Dad moved to Spanish Springs.

Daddy felt he could make some money operating the station, raising horses, cutting and selling cord wood and doing ten thousand odd jobs.

Mama was chief cook and bottle washer. She cooked meals for the teamsters and other wayfarers, raised chickens, pigs, a vegetable garden and administered to the growing needs of a growing family.

We kids helped with the chores of the station. According to age and talents, we carried water from well to house, chopped wood and carried it from the wood pile to our cook stove and our "central heating system," the pot-bellied stove. We swept and scrubbed floors and cleaned corrals, chicken and pig pens. Mama and Daddy sometimes argued about how much work and how much play was necessary before we'd get dull, but life for us at Spanish Springs was never boring. Mama said that we were good kids. Daddy didn't always agree!

Spanish Springs station gave us a living and a way of frontier life. But, the coming of the freighters was always exciting to us.

"The teamsters are coming, the teamsters are coming!" we shouted when the freighters were but a dust cloud coming up Ralston Valley.

Daddy said: "They're still two hours away." Then he'd put his watch back in his pocket and say: "I'll whale the daylights out of you kids if you don't keep away from those horses and wagons when they get here."

We knew that Daddy wouldn't put up with any monkey business, so when freighters pulled in we sat on the porch and watched.

The huge, heavily-loaded wagons creaked and groaned as they arrived at the station. Their big wheels ground into the sandy road, picking up sand and dropping it out behind, leaving a cloud of dust which was augmented by sand kicked up by the horses' hoofs. The big, shaggy horses looked down at us with wild, roving, distrustful eyes. Sneezing and snorting and tossing their large heads and manes, they creaked their harness and jangled the tug-chains. Usually they were puffing and covered with a white, frothy lather from sweating. They were tired!

"Whoa thar!" Tom Lovelock shouted from his perch on top of the left or "near" wheel-horse. Then he yanked the brake-line which set the wooden brake-blocks against the steel bands of the huge rear wheels. The horses stopped, the wagons stopped, most of the noises ceased. Only the horses remained noisy, breathing heavily and waiting impatiently to be unhitched. "Howdy Cal," Tom said, "how's the missus?" Then, he jumped down, holding the jerk-line which controlled the horses.

Daddy helped him unhitch and unharness the twelve horses and lead them to the water trough and then back to the feed cart where they were haltered to eat their hay and rations of barley during the night. "To give them strength for the long, hard, uphill pull to Manhattan tomorrow," Tom said.

"You're sure good to your horses, Tom," Daddy said.

"Only four of them are mine," said Tom. "Eight belong to Wittenberg Warehouse and Transfer of Tonopah which owns the outfit. Horses, like people, need good food, water and rest to keep going."

Mama came out on the porch and hollered: "Supper's ready." Supper for the teamsters was usually

steak, fried taters and onions, stewed tomatoes and canned corn, with plenty of Mama's baking powder biscuits and coffee.

"Matie, you're the best cook in the world," Tom said; "Here's some candy for the kids."

Mama smiled and said: "You need good food too, Tom. Thank you for the candy."

Then, while Tom and Daddy ate, they talked about the good old days and how things now are going to hell.

"Things are changing too fast," Tom said. "When I ran a freighter outfit from Sodaville to Tonopah and had Summit Station, I thought I'd make a fortune. The railroad came to Tonopah and busted me. All I have left are my four horses. The trucks will put more freighters

out of business soon. I'm going to have to learn to drive a truck."

Daddy said: "I'll think on that too, Tom. Without the freighters Spanish Springs won't have much business. I'd better sell the station while I can."

"We should be moving into Tonopah so the kids can start school in the fall," Mama reminded Daddy who didn't like the reminder.

But, Daddy sold the station and we moved to Tonopah in 1914.

The trucks did replace the freighters in a few years and Spanish Springs became a ghost station long before the mining booms at Manhattan and Tonopah faded. Today there isn't much left of Spanish Springs.

Shown here is the entrance to the dungeon cells in the basement of the old courthouse at Belmont. The spot from where this picture was taken was about where two men were lynched in 1874.

In 1874 when Belmont acquired the county seat, county offices were scattered throughout town, including in the building at left, before the two-story courthouse was finished.

Belmont's Other Court House

by Theron Fox

Visitors to the quaint desert community of Belmont are drawn to the ruins of the old two-story court house. Little do many of them realize, however, that Belmont has still another court house with a unique story of old Nevada.

Built soon after the county seat was removed from Ione, this first courthouse was across the street from the now picturesque ruins of the Cosmopolitan Hotel. Today only the front brick wall remains as a mark of its initial importance to Nye County. The back and two side walls were constructed of local rock. Taking advantage of the natural sloping of the ground, a large full size basement covered the entire space under the main floor, actually extending out under the front sidewalk.

During the spring of 1874 two men, Charlie McIntyre and Jack Walker, drifted into town. There are two versions of what happened after that, one official and another what might be called a legendary account. In some respects the latter seems more plausible. An effort will be made here to give both of them as well as can be reconstructed. First, here is the official version.

Soon after their arrival McIntyre and Walker had an altercation with a local citizen, H. H. Sutherland. During the gunplay that followed, Sutherland was shot and wounded, and the two men were jailed awaiting grand jury action.

Before the grand jury could do its duty, the two men were able to escape from the dungeon type jail cells underneath the front sidewalk, but two days later were found hiding in a nearby abandoned mine shaft. They were jailed again, but during the night the sheriff and his deputy were confronted by a determined vigilante group. The officers were both tied up before the mob adjourned to the basement jail area for the grisly lynching of McIntyre and Walker.

According to the sheriff's report there were no marks of violence on either man except for a bruise on Walker's head, apparently not mentioning the marks caused by the hanging. The sheriff added that no shots were heard and no bullet wounds were found on either body.

This was more or less the official version. Now for the account that is readily told locally even today—a hundred years later.

McIntyre and Walker were said to be union organizers for the Molly McGuires and came to Belmont from the coal fields of Pennsylvania where they had previously engaged in organizing work.

The fight with Sutherland was the result of an argument over their organizing attempts. Upon being jailed they feared violence at the hands of the mine operators. Friendly miners came to the rescue and engineered the escape to the nearby mine shaft. That they had some local support is evidenced by the food and good care they had during the stay in the mine.

After securely tying the sheriff and his deputy on the first floor, the vigilantes went to the basement for the scheduled execution. A rope was passed through a hole in the ceiling, but it is obvious that the short drop was not effective and the attempt at hanging was a fiasco. To end the misery and strangling of the men, a few well-placed shots mercifully completed the slow execution.

One of the victims was a mere boy of about sixteen, and the older man pleaded for his life without avail. The next day both bodies were taken to a spot near the cemetery on the road to San Antone and buried in a common grave.

Which story you receive in the area still depends on to whom you talk. A few years ago a move was started to rebury the bodies in the Belmont cemetery, but some local sentiment was still so severe that the project was abandoned.

Lee Brotherton points to the area on the low ceiling where the rope for the executions went through the floor. Evidently it was not an efficient hanging.

There were autos galore in Rhyolite which was first a wooden town, as above. But concrete blocks soon rose amid these structures. Collapse came after 1909 and now the street has only golden memories. Photographer was A. E. Holt, who also sold real estate and mines.

The Bullfrog District

As told to Ann Rusnak

by Grace Dini

We lived in Rhyolite, the metropolis of the Bull-frog District, from 1907 until 1911. The big silver boom had quieted down and Rhyolite was just a dusty, placid town of hard-working miners.

On the main street were several blocks of businesses. The bank was an impressive concrete building with apartments upstairs. Porter Brothers had a general store in another concrete building. We bought dress materials and groceries there, and also got groceries from Cook's grocery store. There was one ice cream parlor and many saloons. There was a telephone-telegraph office, a bookstore, hotels, and boarding houses. The red light district was one block off main street. A two-story concrete schoolhouse was built within a year of our arrival. Houses were small but many people had planted trees and quite a few had lawns struggling in the dry desert sand.

The small house my stepfather had rented for us had porches front and back, a cellar, and an outhouse. We were pretty crowded when everybody was home. Mama and Jack Holly slept on a roll-down bed in the front room. Eddie had a cot in the kitchen. Freda and I shared a cot in the clothes closet. I wouldn't have minded the smallness—and in summertime, the heat—but having clothes hanging right above us in there did make it an oppressive place to be.

I stayed out of school our first year in Rhyolite,

helping Mama with the washing and taking care of the younger kids. I specialized in ironing. Mama said I was awfully fast at it. My ironing board was a plank covered with cotton batting, balanced between a table and a chair. I used six irons at a time, pressing with one while the other five heated on the stove.

I did house cleaning for neighbors at two bits an hour. For a while I worked regularly at Mrs. Weiburg's boarding house, helping her with cooking and washing up after meals. I didn't like the job, for a couple of reasons. She never used leftovers, so each evening she threw out enough food to have fed my family. It went into a garbage pit in the back yard that attracted cats. Some of them had their kittens in the yard or the cellar, handy to this wonderful source of food. And Mrs. Weiburg made me drown them by putting them in a ten-gallon can of water.

Jack Holly died while working at the Tonopah and Tidewater railroad yard, lifting heavy machinery off freight cars. The exertion was too much for him.

We were so bad off at that time we had to belittle ourselves and borrow money from a neighbor lady to buy me a pair of shoes so I'd be presentable for the funeral.

Thereafter Mama had to work harder than ever. She got a job as janitor at the bank. A little later she took over running the Miners' Hospital. She did well enough then to let the bank keep her janitor's wages in a savings account. That little nest egg never hatched—the bank closed up and she lost all that she had saved.

I quit school to work too. We always did washing and ironing. I did housecleaning and I guess that's how

271

I got my job at the telephone company, working for Mrs. Munger. Her husband managed the AT&T office and she was the switchboard operator. She recommended hiring me when the job got too heavy for her alone.

I was paid $45 a month when I began, at age 15. I worked four or five hours each afternoon—sometimes alone, sometimes with Mrs. Munger. The phone office was in a one-story concrete building. In back was the telegraph office, a storeroom, and a place for the telephone system's power supply—the telephones were powered by huge electric batteries. On a hot day —and we had plenty of 'em—we'd open the doors front and back, and let the wind sweep thru.

My mother's hospital workday routine was long and tiring. Mornings, she collected and delivered laundry. In the afternoon she heated water for washing. In between times she was nursing the patients, making beds, and shopping. Mama made dinner while I worked at the phone company. We bought vegetables from Los Angeles—lettuce, tomatos, radishes, potatos. We had a standing order for a once-a-week shipment. Meat, bread, and dry or canned things we bought in town. Sometimes we made our own bread.

My days were busy too. In the morning I did housework around the hospital. In the late morning I began making lunch for the patients. They usually got a hot meal—meat, potatos, a vegetable and dessert. For dessert I made cakes or Jello or served fruit. I worked in the telephone office till six or seven o'clock. When I came home I ate dinner and then ironed for several hours.

One July Fourth was clouded. My girlfriend Marie Wexelburger and I took the train at 6 a.m. to a picnic at Springdale. Getting up before dawn to dress Freda and Ed in the dark had given me a sick headache. Marie realized on the train that the shoes she had put on in the dark didn't match. So she hid out all day and I hid with her. There was a dance after the picnic lunches were eaten.

Abandoned Rhyolite train depot.

I learned to dance while I was babysitting. I had gone to a schoolhouse dance as nursemaid for the babies and children too young to leave home. One of the bookstore woman's sons talked me into a few minutes away from the nursery, and showed me how to do a little two-step dance.

My only other social activity was church. I taught Sunday school, sang in the choir, and played piano at services. I never felt quite at ease with the preacher because he seemed awfully anxious to get me alone somewhere.

The most common animals were burros. Miners left them at the outskirts of town when they came in for the day, and these burros got pretty lively in mating season. A bunch of them, 18 or 20, would come roaring through town—tromping on porches, leaping low fences, knocking pedestrians aside.

Maude was a burro who stood out from the rest because of her unusually sociable ways. She'd poke her head through the swinging doors of a saloon and wait until some animal-lover bought her a beer. Trouble was, she made the rounds and the saloons were full of animal-lovers. When she got drunk she would lie down in the street and sleep it off.

I had a few bad times at the hospital. One winter we had a portable coal-oil heater in one fellow's room. I heard him yelling and found the whole machine in flames. Somehow I grabbed it and ran outside without getting burned.

There were several general calamities too. Once there was a big cloudburst over Rhyolite and the rain swept everything loose before it. On one of the more prosperous streets, water came in through the back doors and out the front, leaving mud on the carpets and ruining the wallpaper. It filled our cellar. We had canned goods stored there and when the water went down the labels had come off the cans. We had to guess the contents and had some quite interesting mealtime combinations that way.

Mama's laundry business got her another husband, Richard Fisher. He dealt faro at the Sixty-Six Club and was a sharp dresser. I admired the clothes Mama washed for him—pastel-colored silk knit underwear, silk shirts. In 1910 he married Mama and joined us at the hospital. Maybe Mama didn't approve of his job as a gambler; anyway, he quit the club and signed on at the Shoshone mine, processing ore.

Our four years in Rhyolite came to an end when Mr. Fisher decided to move to Tonopah. I was happy with my job as chief telephone operator at $75 a month, so I stayed, boarding with a family I knew. Letters from Mama said that the high altitude in Tonopah made her sick. After six weeks I quit my job to join Mama in Tonopah.

I'd been in Tonopah about another six weeks when we moved to a ranch in Mason Valley. Mama wanted to get back to farming.

Scotty in Rhyolite

by Hank Johnston

In the summer of 1905, Walter E. Scott, an itinerant ex-rodeo rider turned pseudo-prospector, burst into the headlines of America by chartering a special Santa Fe train to break the speed record between Los Angeles and Chicago. Newspapers from coast to coast played up the singular escapade in banner type, thus boosting "Death Valley Scotty," as he soon became known, into national prominence.

Scott's sudden rise to fame occurred coincidentally with the Nevada mining rush of 1904–07. In reality, he had nothing whatever to do with the dramatic ore strikes at Goldfield, Tonopah, and Rhyolite, but the golden madness attending America's last great bonanza provided an ideal setting for his claims of a "fabulously rich mine" hidden somewhere in nearby Death Valley.

Scotty's con game was simple and effective. By appearing to spend money recklessly during his occasional, well-publicized visits to civilization, he enticed grubstakes from gold-hungry investors, which he then used on additional sprees. His earliest notoriety resulted from a series of spendthrift adventures in Los Angeles, the nearest large city, but he also became a familiar figure in the boom camp of Rhyolite.

"Walter Scott is in town again," the *Rhyolite Herald* reported in a typical story in 1907, "holding court at the Southern Hotel. He seemed to have money in every pocket as he toured the usual watering holes last night in company with a gathering of the curious. He says he may soon charter another special train to break his own speed record if his funds hold out."

When grubstakes were lean, Scotty usually arrived in town on his mule "Slim." At other times he sported a large open touring car of the latest design. In either instance, he inevitably attracted considerable attention from local residents who hoped to gain some knowledge of his mysterious diggings. After spending a few days dazzling the populace, Scott would soon be off to other conquests, leaving Rhyolite as uninformed about the source of his supposed wealth as before.

In January 1908, Scotty became involved in an altercation with Al Myers, locator of the famous Mohawk mine at Goldfield, during a drinking bout at Rhyolite's Silver Dollar Saloon. After angry words were exchanged, Myers suddenly knocked Scott to the floor with a well-placed punch, and then kicked his prostrate opponent in the ribs. A few months later, Scotty got more than adequate revenge by leaving Myers stranded in the depths of Death Valley during the peak of the summer heat.

On another occasion, Scotty posed for a widely circulated photograph purportedly showing him "fighting prejudice" by having a picnic lunch on Rhyolite's main street with a Chinese companion. (Chinese were barred from saloons by local ordinance). Actually, Scott owed the Chinese man $1,000 that was long past due, and he was merely using the opportunity to placate his creditor.

Rhyolite's short-lived prosperity ended permanently and abruptly when its mines played out in 1909: Death Valley Scotty, however, moved on to far greater adventures in succeeding years. Eventually, with the backing of a whimsical Chicago millionaire, he became one of the most storied characters in all the history of the Old West.

Curious Newsboy

by Vincent McGinn

The news traveled fast, and soon a bunch of us newsboys gathered around the entrance to the Mizpah Hotel. Suddenly the door swung open, and down the steps bounced a stout, stubby little man dressed in sloppy Western clothes. He didn't look like much, but we all knew that Death Valley Scotty was in town! He stood on the curb for a moment, surveying our expectant faces. Then he reached into a voluminous pocket, and with a bellow of laughter, flung a handful of silver quarters into the street.

During the ensuing scramble he sauntered across Main Street and entered the Tonopah Club, his headquarters while in town. Soon all the high-rollers headed for the club, because they all knew that's where the action would be with Scotty around.

I never witnessed these particular games, but I did work in a cigar store after school hours, and they played some pretty high powered poker in the back room. I remember one session that started about three one

The Tonopah Club rose above the business section. Leasers (below) are next to their windlass.

afternoon and continued non-stop for three days and nights, with thousands of dollars changing hands. Stacks of ten and twenty dollar gold pieces and silver dollars glittered on the green baize of the poker table.

As the game progressed, the whiskey bottles went the rounds, and the play became wilder. They would toss out ten and twenty dollars "without looking," and often they'd have a couple of hundred dollars in the pot even before the draw. One smart aleck sat in the afternoon of the third day, thinking he'd take this bunch of drunks, and he'd lost seven hundred dollars before his chair warmed up.

When I arrived in Tonopah in 1906, aged three months, the town had gone through the initial boomtown phase and had assumed the appearance of a substantial and permanent town, with stone buildings and sturdy frame houses. A two story dance hall, the Big Casino, stood on lower Main Street.

When I was about ten, I worked at Klinger's department store after school. I'd carry merchandise down to the red-light district and wait outside the crib while the girl tried on the dress, corset, or other apparel. I got to know some of the girls pretty well, and considered them a fine, friendly lot. They were generous with tips and, contrary to the dire warnings of my strict Catholic parents, never tried to molest me.

Although the uptown ladies who considered themselves pillars of society despised their less fortunate sisters, I could never see anything very "evil" about these friendly girls. In fact, whenever they passed the hat to help some destitute miner's family, the girls' contributions exceeded those of the "respectable" ladies of the town. In the eighteen years I lived in

Tonopah, I never heard of a man accosting any girl. My mother was never afraid to go out alone at night.

Later, I peddled the *Daily Bonanza* on the streets, then went to work for the morning paper, the *Times*, carrying a paper route. With my bag of papers slung over my shoulder, I'd leave the office, cross dark Main Street to the lighted haven of the Montana Cafe, and consume my daily coffee and sinkers. As part of a nightly ritual, Bill the white-haired waiter would glance at the clock presently, and say, "He's a little late tonight."

"Yes," I'd answer, "Probably had a big night."

"Oh oh! Here he comes," Bill would say. "I'd better tell the cook to put on the steak," and he'd hustle out to the kitchen.

I'd busy myself with a doughnut, while a vision of sartorial splendor strolled in and proceeded to one of the curtained booths along the wall; the same booth every night.

When he was comfortably seated, I'd walk over to the booth and say in a quiet, respectful tone, "Good morning, Mr. Drysdale. Here's your paper, sir."

"Why thank you, my boy," he'd reply, as if I'd bestowed a priceless object. Then he'd flip a silver quarter into the air.

"Thanks, Mr. Drysdale," I'd reply, as I caught the coin and returned to my seat at the counter.

Walter Drysdale was undoubtedly the most elegant saloon keeper in town. He ran the Bank Saloon just around the corner on Brougher Avenue, and every morning, after closing the bar, he'd come into the Montana for supper.

Bill brought in the main dish, a huge porterhouse steak, which covered a platter fully a foot in diameter, along with all the steaming side dishes to go with such a sumptuous meal. As a kid, I know I never tasted such a mouth-watering steak, and have often wondered since if it would have tasted as good as the Kansas City beef I've eaten since. I'll bet it would have—maybe better.

My next stop was down the line in the red-light district, where everything would be going full blast. You could hear the music from the Northern and the Big Casino a block away. The lines of cribs back of the dance halls were brilliantly lighted, with the girls seated in the windows displaying their charms to the eager customers. Several of the girls subscribed to the paper, and they'd always tip me an extra dime or a quarter.

On quiet nights, I'd stop and chat with some of the girls, listening to their troubles. They seemed to like me and would tell some stories they'd never dream of telling the other girls. Even later, after I'd quit the newspaper, I'd come down the line once in a while, just to talk to them, because some of them were old friends. Naturally, my interest eventually became something more than mere friendly chatter, but I'm not going into *that* story, because it's *my* business, isn't it?

Growing Up in Tonopah

by Marion Dobrowsky Rosevear

For a young girl to grow up amid the excitement of a mining camp is a very proud heritage. In those days, around World War I, children created their own entertainment and diversion, and these are memorable experiences.

Packing a light lunch and hiking up the slopes of Mt. Brougher or Mt. Oddie to pick wild flowers was a frequent summer pastime. Three large hillside tanks, two red and one green, were water reservoirs for the town. These were favorite goals for young hikers. Once in a while we built a bonfire to bake potatoes in the hot coals. Of course, they were charred on the outside and raw inside but they tasted delicious after our hike and long wait for them to bake.

Many evenings were spent listening to our old Edison phonograph with the large selection of cylinder type records. Since we had musically inclined parents and a piano in our home, we began taking music lessons from Miss Ethel Murphy, the Catholic Church organist. Then later we studied most diligently with Mrs. Cecil Williams, a very strict and thorough teacher who demanded many hours of practice.

The glorious 4th of July was a gala occasion, with the stores on Main Street elaborately decorated with red, white and blue bunting, banners and flags. Homes, and cars too, displayed the patriotic fervor. Many inhabitants from mining camps several miles away came to Tonopah for the celebration. The festivities began with a parade of colorful floats, Indians, prospectors, burros and horses (with or without riders), marching groups and bands. This was followed by the children's "fevered" contests of hoop or tire rolling, foot races, sack and three-legged races with prizes for the winners—then free ice cream cones for all! Occasionally a carnival would come to town. Kids were

Holidays in Tonopah were special occasions: festivities included parades and rock drilling contests (below). The popular Butler theater is in the background left, while to the right is the east end of Tonopah. Above the town and at the foot of Mt. Oddie is where the principal mines were located (opposite page).

allowed to buy fire crackers, "red devils," cap guns for the boys and cap canes for the girls—anything for noise and excitement. For the adults, rock drilling contests, boxing matches and horse races down Main Street held great interest. At night, dancing was enjoyed at the auditorium on Brougher Avenue. However there were some who preferred gambling and drinking in the bars and clubs, as was expected on a holiday.

About 1920, the Victor Mining Company built Tonopah's first public park with trees, picnic tables, benches, and an indoor wooden swimming pool. This was located on their property northwest of town. Many enjoyable summer outings were provided for those who would take their lunches and spend the day. Most of us learned to swim by hanging on to the secured ropes

around the sides of the pool with one hand and using swimming strokes with the other while kicking our feet.

Alkali Hot Springs, situated to the west of the road between Tonopah and Goldfield, was owned and operated by the Joe Guisti family. This desert spa consisted of a large building housing the dining room, kitchen, bar and dance floor. A separate building enclosed the indoor wooden swimming pool with a built up shallow area in one corner for the children. Outside in front of the dining room were a few tall tamarisk bushes (the only shady area) under which sat a large picnic table and benches where visitors could either bring their own lunches or order from the dining room and eat outside if they wished. At the rear of the resort area was the Guisti home. A Sunday outing and swim at Alkali was a real treat, as was the traditional glass of grape juice over ice from the bar. This was Mr. Guisti's specialty for the young folks. The Friday or Saturday night dances were attended by many from Tonopah.

A frequent visit with friends in Goldfield was usually in anticipation of having dinner at the fabulous Goldfield Hotel. The hotel lobby was beautifully furnished with cushioned leather seats surrounding the large supporting pillars and the huge leather chairs were symetrically arranged around the lobby. The dining room was exquisitely attractive with oil paintings on the walls and crystal chandeliers hanging from the ceilings lighting the white damask covered tables. The waiters, dressed in their white coats and shirts with black ties, presented a very formal but friendly atmosphere. The food was superb and served very properly. The mezzanine floor above the lobby contained rest rooms and a nicely furnished lounge area which opened on to the balcony over the hotel entrance.

A trip to Goldfield was never complete without a visit to "Pete's Candy Store." Nowhere could you find a better selection of candy! "Pete," a jolly fellow, loved children and always saw that they received an extra treat other than their small purchase.

276

Outings were favorite week-end pastimes for the families in Tonopah. Picnic spots were not plentiful as trees were difficult to grow in the alkali soil, and grass was impossible, especially with the limited water supply. However, an occasional well or spring in the desert would produce sufficient water to become a small ranch or a roadside station. These "few and far between" spots usually had a few trees to provide a shady area and cool breeze. The owners or occupants were very hospitable and welcomed their picnicking visitors.

Fishing streams were non-existent close by, but occasionally a trip could be made to Smoky Valley, with its Toiyabe Mountains to the west. It was well supplied with ranches, camping sites and fishing streams. An overnight camp-out was a "must" as it was a *long* drive over rutted dirt roads for the slow-speed vehicles of the day.

At school, classes were strictly disciplined with students being well instructed by devoted and competent teachers. Two "old timers," Anna E. Bradley and Helene Slavin had even taught some of our younger aunts and uncles. A failing student was indeed rare in those days. "After school" sessions or penalties were common in a few instances. While the teacher corrected tests or papers, the student studied or wrote "I will not . . ." one hundred times.

Winters were long and cold but looking forward to the snow was a delight. The fluffy white flakes soon became firmly packed by auto and wagon traffic up the slopes of Brougher and Bryan Avenues. It was then that the myriads of warmly dressed and gaily laughing youngsters pulled their sleds or carried their "Yankee Bumpers" up the long slope, exuberant in anticipation of their rides down the hill. (A "Yankee Bumper" was a barrel stave for the runner with a short upright 2" × 4" supporting a seat on top.) After sleighriding, many cold feet were warmed and "toasted" at home by opening the hot oven of the old wood and coal kitchen range, and sitting with feet propped on the oven door.

Victor Lambertucci, an Italian immigrant, was owner of a farm which became known as the "Sewer Farm" and was located west of town on the road to Millers. His irrigation system was provided by drained sewage from the town. He raised hogs, pigs, and fresh vegetables, with great success. The vegetables, in season, he peddled house to house in Tonopah. He maintained a filtered pond reservoir, which when frozen over in winter provided a skating rink for those who had or could borrow ice skates to enjoy this winter sport.

In the 1920's, Tonopah was a fashion-minded town. People were always stylishly dressed, portraying a metropolitan atmosphere. This was evident by the many ladies' dress shops and men's clothing stores which flourished with the times.

The large social event of the year was the Elks Charity Ball, where men wore tuxedos or "swallow tails" and the ladies displayed the most elegant and latest creations purchased locally or direct from San Francisco, the fashion center of the West.

Growing up in glorious and friendly Tonopah left indelible imprints on our future lives and beloved and cherished memories.

Young Lawyer in Tonopah

by Jerome E. Edwards

Pat McCarran first established his reputation as an attorney with the Barieau case in 1906; an important case that resulted in his being elected District Attorney of Nye County.

According to the Tonopah newspapers, Tom Logan, the popular sheriff of Nye County, was shot and murdered in cold blood by professional gambler Walter Barieau, in the mining town of Manhattan, some forty miles northeast of Tonopah. The shooting occurred at the Jewel saloon, a popular Manhattan "resort" in the red light district. As reported by the Tonopah press, Barieau and another gambler had been quarreling and creating a disturbance, and the bartender of the Jewel called in Sheriff Logan who just happened to be "passing at the time" for the purpose of calming things down. The sheriff, at least according to the first news reports, entered the Jewel and politely requested the men to go home. As Logan began to leave, the drunken Barieau fired five shots at him, killing him. In the view of the Tonopah *Bonanza* there was absolutely no doubt as to Barieau's guilt and this opinion was reflected throughout Tonopah. Barieau was described by the *Bonanza* as a "cowardly murderer, an absinthe fiend and general all-round bad man." It was generally believed, the *Bonanza* asserted, "that the inhuman wretch who committed the foul deed should be given a speedy trial and a chance to dangle at the end of a rope at Carson as soon as possible." It was also pointed out, and this certainly added to the popular excitement, that Sheriff Logan left behind a widow and eight children.

When Barieau was brought into Tonopah to be arraigned, a great crowd was present in the courtroom to see the notorious person who had committed the murder. The judge asked Barieau if he had an attorney and Barieau replied no, because he was broke and asked the court to appoint a defense attorney for him. The judge looked over the room, filled with the most experienced, locally eminent lawyers of Tonopah. By chance he appointed the 29-year-old McCarran who had been in law practice less than a year and who had never tried an important case.

McCarran was stunned and, because of his inexperience, filled with self-doubt. In his own words, "I had heard that there might be occasions in one's life when his knees would go out from under him but I never believed it to be true until that moment, and then for the first time I realized what it was to be possessed of fear,

embarrassment and consternation." Caught off-guard, McCarran remembered some advice that he was given when he was studying the law, "When you get in a tight place, ask for time." He did and it was granted. "I had nothing else to do so I put my whole time into the case from then until the trial."

McCarran's defense directly countered the newspaper version. He placed Barieau on the witness stand, and the defendant told the courtroom how he had innocently gone to the Jewel saloon where he had imbibed only a single drink of wine. This made him sick and he was forced to go to a lounge in the Jewel to lie down. According to his story, Mae Biggs, the proprietess of the Jewel, ordered him to leave, and eventually she started screaming when he failed to move fast enough. The next thing Barieau knew, at least according to his testimony, was that he received a blow which knocked him down, and this happened a second time. Trying to back out of the resort he was again struck on the head with a heavy instrument, whereupon he noticed, for the first time, his assailant had a gun, so he drew his pistol and fired. Barieau swore that he was not acquainted with Sheriff Logan, had never previously met him, and did not recognize him.

McCarran backed up this testimony by a closing, emotional preoration. He was at his most spellbinding. He pictured Mae Biggs as an "enchantress" who had made Logan into "a slave to her every will and wish." The fact that Logan left behind a family of nine was stated in a way unsympathetic to the sheriff. McCarran "touchingly" referred to Logan's family, thundering that "while the sheriff, under the influence of the Biggs woman, was showering presents upon her, the family of the man in Smoky Valley had but few of the necessities of life."

The Tonopah papers which had been so eager to hang Barieau, now were convinced by McCarran's rhetoric. According to the Tonopah *Sun*, "no finer argument, from the standpoint of eloquence and logic, has ever been delivered in the courthouse. During the course of the argument, Attorney McCarran demonstrated that as a dealer in sarcasm and invective he is without a peer at the local bar." The *Bonanza* enthused, "McCarran . . . always eloquent, excelled himself on this occasion and spoke with a feeling that brought tears to the eyes of many in the courtroom."

In a sensational finish to the trial, Barieau was acquitted after a jury deliberation of 17 hours. McCarran had successfully swayed the jury, the press, and the community. His reputation as an attorney was made. The success in this case also directly led to his political advancement. Because of his defense of Barieau, he was nominated by the Democrats as their candidate for District Attorney of Nye County. As the Republicans did not nominate an opponent, McCarran won the November, 1906 election by default.

Devoted to the Interests of Nye County and its Mine...

TONOPAH BONANZA

NO.

TONOPAH NEVADA, SATURDAY, APRIL 7, 1906

POPULAR SHERIFF KILLED!

Thomas Logan is Murdered in Cold Blood by Gambler in Manhattan this Morning

MANHATTAN, April 7, 1906—9 a. m.

To the BONANZA:

Sheriff Thomas Logan was shot at 6 o'clock this morning and passed away a few minutes ago. The shooting was done by Walter C. Barieu, a low Creole gambler.

Barieu and another gambler had been quarreling and creating a disturbance in the Jewell saloon and the bartender called Sheriff Logan, who was passing at the time, to separate the men and prevent trouble. He entered the place and requested the men to go to their respective homes. As he started to leave the place Barieu fired five shots at him point blank, four of them taking effect, and he sank to the floor mortally wounded.

A crowd quickly gathered and while many willing hands cared for the unfortunate sheriff, others seized the cowardly murderer and with Deputy Scott Hickey took him to an improvised jail, there being no detention house at present in Manhattan.

The Sheriff suffered great agony for two hours, before passing to the unknown world. His remains will be taken to Tonopah as soon as possible.

The above dispatch was received this morning and was immediately posted in front of the BONANZA office. A crowd quickly gathered and there was universal regret at the untimely taking off of the popular sheriff.

News of the shooting also reached the Sheriff's office and Deputies George Logan, W. S. Bryden and J. W. Landquist, were soon stirred to action. They engaged a four horse team, and dispatched the messenger to notify the...

QUESTION OF BIG

...Judge Breen this morning... being granted the defendants. The suit involved title to the original locations in the Manhattan district.

Sim claimed that he was entitled to an interest in the claims located through...

...erty Springs, to the Tonop... mining company. In addition t... cash they receive a big block of in the corporation. There a... strong ledges on the property, show splendid values. The ne...

Senator Pat McCarran (1876-1954) learned the political ropes in central Nevada's mining camps. He distinguished himself and his beloved Nevada as its Senator from 1933 until his death at Hawthorne. He was Chairman of the powerful Senate Judiciary Committee and a high ranking member of the Senate Appropriations Committee.

Long line team at Bonnie Claire, c. 1907.

Supply Point for Scotty

by Hank Johnston

About six miles southwest of U.S. 95, just off the Grapevine Canyon Road that descends from Scotty's Junction into the northern edge of Death Valley, a faint, weed-grown crisscross of railroad grades marks the site of Bonnie Claire.

Bonnie Claire, which loosely means "bright, beautiful, robust," never did live up to its euphonious name. Originally known as "Thorp's Wells," it was actually a squalid settlement that managed only a brief period of modest prosperity during the Nevada mining boom of the early 1900's.

Bonnie Claire was established in October 1906, as a milling center for several mines at nearby Gold Mountain when the Bullfrog-Goldfield built its line

through the area to Rhyolite from Goldfield. A tent city soon grew up around the mill, and town lots were laid out in anticipation of a permanent community. A few months later, the Las Vegas & Tonopah Railroad virtually duplicated the BG route, thus creating the unlikely situation of two railroads paralleling each other through an isolated region that could scarcely support even one.

In those rose-colored bonanza days, however, railroad fever seemed to be infectious. The Ubehebe Copper Mines and Smelter Co. began surveying a proposed 48-mile railroad between Bonnie Claire and a copper development near Ubehebe Crater in Death Valley. The Bonnie Claire Bullfrog Mining Co. announced plans for a six-mile spur to connect its mill with the Gold Mountain mines. Another report stated that the Bonnie Claire Townsite Co. was sinking a community well on Main Street to supply the expected influx of new residents.

The Panic of 1907 ended all such optimistic projects. With money in short supply, investors withdrew their support, causing a general suspension of mining operations. By 1914, the collapse of Rhyolite and the decline of the Goldfield mines had forced railroad abandonments. The Tonopah & Tidewater took over tri-weekly service to Goldfield via Bonnie Claire until January 7, 1928.

In the meantime, Bonnie Claire limped along with few permanent facilities and only a handful of residents. Sporadic attempts to reactivate the mills were uniformly unsuccessful. Bonnie Claire, however, would make one last unexpected and significant contribution.

In 1925 a Chicago insurance millionaire named Albert Mussey Johnson began construction of an ornate, Mediterranean-style vacation home some twenty miles down Grapevine Canyon in northern Death Valley. The project generated considerable notice because of Johnson's so-called "partnership" with Death Valley Scotty, a paunchy pseudo-prospector who captured headlines for years with tales of a rich gold mine hidden in Death Valley.

280

In reality, Walter Scott had nothing to do with the design or financing of the strange, $2 million desert mansion (Johnson secretly backed Scotty's antics "for laughs," as he himself put it), but the publicity Scott provided, along with the sheer unlikeliness of its austere location, soon made "Scotty's Castle" one of the most famous private residences in the West.

A complex of nine elaborate structures was undertaken, embracing about 33,000 square feet of floor space in all. The buildings included two main living wings, a cookhouse, powerhouse, stable, guest house with two lavish apartments, gas station, 56-foot clock tower with full Westminster Chimes, and a spacious garage-workshop. Fourteen fireplaces, fourteen bathrooms—many with elaborate Spanish tiling, four kitchens, a sumptuous music room with theater-sized pipe organ, and a Pelton wheel hydroelectric generating system provided all the comforts of urban living. Water piped from springs a mile up Grapevine Canyon was sufficient to sustain a population of a thousand persons.

From 1925 until January 7, 1928, nearly all items involved in the difficult construction job arrived at Bonnie Claire station over the Tonopah & Tidewater Railroad. From Bonnie Claire, an assortment of four-wheel-drive motor trucks and mule-drawn wagons shuttled the final twenty miles to the building site over a rough desert road. Freight cars brought in load after load of material: stacks of assorted lumber, bags of mortar and plaster, crates of tile, bundles of steel and pipe, cartons of fittings and valves, keg upon keg of nails, boxes of bolts, bundles of reinforcing rods, reels of fence and electrical wire, and cases of ornate lighting fixtures. Workers, hired through agencies in Los Angeles, received a railroad ticket to Bonnie Claire as a condition of their employment. Foodstuffs to feed the crew of nearly 100 men also arrived via the T & T. It was Bonnie Claire's greatest activity since the failure of its original mills twenty years earlier.

Scotty's Castle was never finished. When Johnson lost the bulk of his fortune following the stock market crash of 1929, work was halted with the 185-foot swimming pool still only a gaping hole, and assorted lesser amenities not yet fully realized. Nonetheless, the project was already well enough along to insure its eventual position as the Mojave Desert's most intriguing man-made wonder. Today, the unusual edifice is owned and maintained by the National Park Service, which operates guided tours on a regular basis for the several hundred thousand annual visitors.

A few miles up the Grapevine Canyon Road, the little town of Bonnie Claire has long since taken its place among the ghosts of Nevada's historic past. "Bright, beautiful, and robust" it never was, but its brief existence is surely worth remembering.

Bootlegger's Bylaws
by Helen McInnis

During the years when the making and selling of alcoholic liquors was illegal, bootlegging became a big business in Nevada. Many people resented prohibition and took it upon themselves to remedy the situation.

All that was needed to turn innocent, everyday ingredients into a spirited nectar was someone with the knowledge, good water, fuel for a nice steady fire and a secluded location. Ancient ledgers held various recipes for medicinal nostrums which could, after a few alterations, produce a liquid that packed a pretty fair wallop.

The demand for contraband alcohol was vast, and stills were in operation all over the state. Nevada law officers were, for the most part, tolerant when they stumbled upon the location of a still, and usually turned their heads the other way. The only law the moonshiners had to really worry about was the government men or "revenuers."

Stills had to be watched continuously for there was always the danger of an explosion if things weren't kept just right, and the bigger operations with several boilers going at once had to keep men on shift at all times to fill their orders. Occasionally the still tender would test his product too often and become soused. It wasn't uncommon for a still to blow sky high while the tender slept off the effects of too much testing.

Integrity in his dealings was a bootlegger's most valuable asset. The two cardinal rules were to never handle cut or watered whiskey, nor turn information over to the law. A man accused of breaking either one of those rules stood a good chance of getting killed. At Ash Meadows, down in the southern tip of Nye County, a man named Bill broke them both and he paid the ultimate price for his perfidy.

Bill made whiskey for the biggest outfit in the area.

He was a good bootlegger and his whiskey was top quality and consistent, but like so many others he became addicted to his product and began testing it too freely.

As a result of his persistent imbibing his still's given quota was quite often short. To make up for the deficiency he began adding water to the whiskey, not once but several times, thus causing the still's owner to suffer a bad reputation. The time came when he was fired from his job, blacklisted with the other bootleggers, and humiliated in front of his friends. Bill sought revenge and committed the unforgivable sin. He told the revenue men exactly when and where they could confiscate a full truck load of whiskey.

George White, an old-time Ash Meadow resident out checking his trap lines, found Bill's body. He had evidently been walking away from Ash Meadows, heading for the security of Las Vegas, when two men on horseback overtook him and chased him into a mesquite thicket. He had been hung by his arms in the midst of the sharp thorned trees, stabbed several times and shot. None of those cruel inflictions were meant to cause immediate death—his murderers didn't plan for him to die easy, and he didn't. There were pathetic signs of a long and useless struggle among the sharp barbs of the mesquite branches.

A coroner's jury of local men, including the two who had killed him, held an inquest and reported that Bill, in his downcast mood, had committed suicide. That, and a telegram sent to the Sheriff in Tonopah advising him of the death and the jury's decision, took care of the investigation. He was buried, at the place where he died, without a casket, just a thin blanket wrapped around his mutilated body. A prayer was said over his grave—the Ash Meadows women insisted on that.

It was common knowledge who had killed him and why, but no one said a word. Bill was a bootlegger and knew the rules of the game. When he broke them, his death, as harsh as it was, was justifiable.

Gold Nuggets for an Apple Pie

by Ruth Fenstermaker Tipton

The small isolated community of Gabbs in 1952 was experiencing a post-war revival. Only three years before, the defense plant had been purchased from the War Assets Administration by Basic Refractories, the parent company that had pioneered the Gabbs and Henderson war-time magnesium industry. The plant and townsite had experienced some vandalism by salvagers, but Basic had reorganized the mining operation, and the 1950's saw a prosperous beginning for civilian magnesite mining in Nevada.

Gabbs has always had a flavor of the old-time Nevada mining camps. From its birth in 1941, when the miners lived in tents, it provided a novel living experience to the new workers who came into town from all parts of the country. The Fenstermaker family, who came there from Arkansas, was no exception. When they first opened the door of the company house at 205 Ave B, it was evident that a desert sandstorm had recently blasted the town. The mahogany baby-grand piano, sitting in the middle of the floor where the movers had left it, was covered with a shroud of dust. Glasses and plates stacked on the table contained

ample servings of Gabbs Valley sand, and the grit on the floors crunched with every step. If it hadn't been so late at night, the newcomers might have retreated eastward.

The next day revealed more of the primitive living conditions at Gabbs. There were no milk bottles on the doorstep and no daily paper in the evening. The town, surrounded by colorful "no-places" like Gardenia Gulch, Dead Horse Wells, Rawhide, and Broken Hills, was 60 to 80 miles from shopping, banking, and medical facilities. The streets were not paved, and the 50-some company houses which formed a terraced townsite of South Gabbs had only scant lawns with a few elm or poplar trees for shade. Water was pumped from hot wells in the valley to giant wooden cooling towers and storage tanks which supplied both North and South Gabbs.

The Toiyabe School was located in South Gabbs. Both the high school and elementary school were housed in the same building, and as many as three different grades held classes in one room. There was a recreation hall used for Sunday school, basketball games, and pot-luck dinners. A volunteer fire department, a two-room library, and two hotel apartment buildings had been built for the townsite.

In North Gabbs, also known as Smithville after the two Smith brothers who owned most of the business there, was the Toiyabe Supply Company, a general store with a 35-foot soda fountain. The Gabbs Valley Inn was in North Gabbs, as well as a bar called "The Bucket," a restaurant, a Standard gas station, the post office, a swimming pool, a dry cleaners, the sheriff's office, and the town's only telephone. The houses in the Basic townsite had company phones, but calls, other than local, came and went from the phone booth outside the bar. The sheriff would come down to South Gabbs to inform recipients of long distance calls.

Good drinking water was a necessity not found at Gabbs. The town water was heavily chlorinated and high in flouride. Many of the locals carried water jugs with them on their regular supply trips to Fallon or would take their jugs to get cold water at Green Springs or Rusty Run. One enterprising prospector got the idea of starting a water delivery business to Gabbs and he made twice weekly deliveries selling five gallon glass bottles of spring water at $1.00 apiece. Housewives needing water would place a diamond-shaped red sign, that said "water," in the window on water day.

Early in their life at Gabbs, the Fenstermaker family got prospecting fever. Perhaps it was the tungsten boom that was stirring both amateurs and veterans to buy a black light and prowl the hills at night. More likely it was the weekly visit of the waterman who told of gold nuggets, silver ledges, and placer that could "be panned from every wash in Nevada."

Lee Fenstermaker bought a jeep and with his two

daughters began exploring the hills around Gabbs. His wife, Gladys, although enchanted with the stories of gold nuggets in the sand, had heard too many rattlesnake stories and preferred to spend her afternoons with the Gabbs Bridge Club. She admired the samples of "fool's gold" that came home in the sample bags and visited with the waterman on his delivery days telling him about her family of prospectors and their finds.

The waterman told how he, too, had come to Nevada as a youngster from the midwest. Nearly 50 years previously he had come west with his father and grandfather during the boom days of Rawhide and Tonopah and walked the dusty trail from Fallon to Mina prospecting for gold. He insisted there was still gold to be found in that country and promised to bring evidence of it on his next visit.

A few days later the waterman again came through the back door with the five-gallon jug slung up on his shoulder. He placed it in a metal rocker frame from which the water could be poured into smaller containers for refrigeration. He then reached into his pocket and pulled out a tiny vial which he handed to his eager audience. The bottle, about an inch long and as big around as a woman's little finger, was filled with gold dust and several good-sized nuggets. This gold he claimed he had placered from Finger-rock Wash, a picturesque gully halfway between Gabbs and Luning.

After much admiration, someone finally asked if he would consider selling the gold sample. No, he didn't really want to sell the vial; quite a bit of work had gone into obtaining its contents.

Suddenly, the waterman gave the little bottle of gold to the Fenstermakers. Protesting that they couldn't accept such a wonderful gift without payment, they finally found out that what the lonely prospector would like more than anything else—a nice, hot, home-made apple pie.

On the next water day, and often after that, an apple pie, fresh from the oven, was waiting for the waterman to take back to his cabin for supper. The Fenstermaker family made many friends and had many prospecting experiences looking for tungsten in the Paradise Mountains. Although their prospector friend moved on, and they became acquainted with a succession of watermen who delivered spring water to Gabbs, they always had a special fondness for the prospector who gave them their first sample of Nevada gold. The little bottle of nuggets that was traded for an apple pie is still a happy reminder of life in a 20th century mining camp.

The Transient's Repentance
by Captain R. A. Gibson

In 1905, Tommy Williams, a Welshman and mule skinner, was driving a ten-mule string from Las Vegas to Beatty—I accompanied him as the swamper on this trip. A big fellow, fairly well dressed, asked Tommy if he could accompany us to Beatty in the Bullfrog District, which was then on the boom. Tommy said, "Sure, throw your bedroll aboard and crawl aboard yourself." This fellow was very good company and the tales of his travels all over the world and his many experiences kept us entertained.

Crossing the wash at Ash Meadows, just after a very slight rain, the team got a little off the road. Down went the lead wagon to the axles, meaning we had to discharge, snake it out to hardpan, haul the cargo with the trailer and reload. Tommy knew how to cuss better than any sheepherder and, on this occasion, looked up into the sky and said, "Lord, you sent this dam' rain to get me into trouble, dang your hide—now help me get out, dang you to the devil!"

Seemingly out of the heavens came a hollow voice saying, "You call yourself a skinner? Let the kid (me) drive—he'll mind that the teams stay on the road. . . . Who told you how to skin mules anyway?"

Tommy, astride the wheel mule, glared at me and the passenger who, when Tommy turned away, winked at me and without any visible movement of his lips, said, "Now get the cargo out of the wagon, dig out, and don't ever dare to cuss me again."

Tom was visibly shaken, and while I accompanied him on several trips to the Providence mountains and Death Valley, I never heard him take the Lord's name in vain again—nor did he ever mention the affair. I guess he never knew he had an "Edgar Bergen" for a passenger.

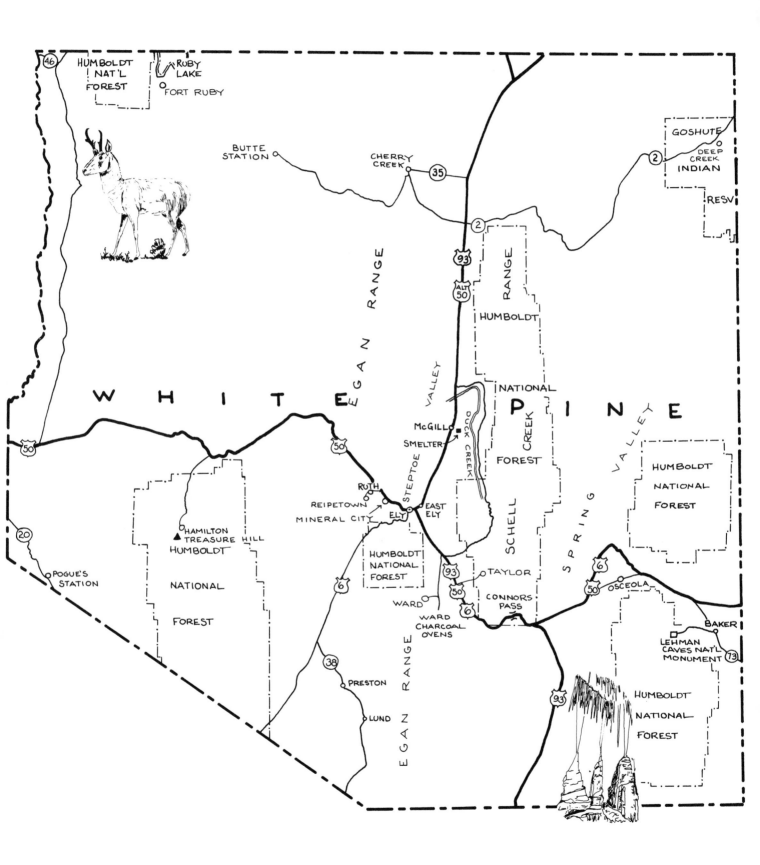

HUMBOLDT NAT'L FOREST
46
RUBY LAKE
FORT RUBY

BUTTE STATION

CHERRY CREEK
35

GOSHUTE
2
DEEP CREEK
INDIAN
RESV

2
93
ALT 50

HUMBOLDT

RANGE

EGAN RANGE

Valley

NATIONAL

CREEK

DUCK CREEK

FOREST

SCHELL

SPRING

VALLEY

W H I T E   P I N E

McGILL
SMELTER

50
50

RUTH
REIPETOWN
MINERAL CITY
ELY
STEPTOE
EAST ELY

HUMBOLDT NATIONAL FOREST

HAMILTON
TREASURE HILL

HUMBOLDT

NATIONAL

FOREST

20

POGUE'S STATION

6

93
50

TAYLOR

CONNORS PASS

6

50
OSCEOLA

HUMBOLDT NATIONAL FOREST

6

WARD

WARD CHARCOAL OVENS

BAKER

LEHMAN CAVES NAT'L MONUMENT
73

38

PRESTON

LUND

EGAN RANGE

93

HUMBOLDT

NATIONAL

FOREST

White Pine County

Frontier Indian Life

by Howard Egan

While building the new Butte station I took a jaunt to the north along the range of mountains, in hopes of locating a log big enough and long enough to make a ridge pole for the rock house. After going ten or twelve miles and not finding one, I returned by another route when I came to a family camp of Indians.

After joining the circle that was sitting around a small fire, we had our peace smoke and I told them what I was hunting. When I was ready to start back, I decided to have some fun. Getting on my pony, I made a large loop with my rawhide lasso and threw it over four or five of them, which caused much laughter. And the old man said, "That would be a good way to catch a Squaw."

I said, "Yes, I will try it on your girl." So I tried. She was very good at dodging, but at the third throw I caught her tight, which seemed to plague her considerably, for she said I could not catch her again so easily.

When about to start home, I swung the rope in the usual way, and looking at the girl, said "Run!" She was off in an instant, but instead of running around the camp she dodged among the trees. After some chasing I was about to throw the loop when she ran around a large tree. My pony being a good lasso animal gave a quick jump aside to head her off and ran under a low limb of a tree which caught under the rim of my saddle, breaking the cinch, and I was on the ground.

There was no use trying to catch my horse, and I offered five cups of flour to anyone who would carry my saddle to the station. "Alright," said the old man, and, pointing to the saddle, said, "You take it" (to the girl). She got the things together and started off. Going about fifty yards she stopped until I got through talking to the old man and got started, when she turned and went ahead.

That was as close to her as I could get; the faster I would go the faster she would. When I reached the station she was standing beside the door, saddle still on her back. I asked her if she was tired and wanted to stay all night.

"No, flour."

"Soon dark; aren't you afraid to go now?" I said.

"No afraid to go; afraid to stay here." So I gave her the flour and a chunk of cold bread; she then started down the hill on the run for their camp.

About a year after, she came to the station with a band of Indians and camped near. She was married. When I went to their camp I said, "I see that a man did catch you."

"Yes, but he did not have a horse and saddle," and she seemed to think the joke was on me.

While on a three days' horseback trip in the wilderness, I had for a companion the Indian called "Egan Jack." We were on a prospecting or exploring trip to the northwest of Deep Creek, or Ibapah as the Indians called it. At one place, as we came out of a canyon onto the bench land, we saw a number of Indians that were quite busy, some digging trenches and some gathering arms full of the tall wheat grass that grew on the flat in the bottom of the canyon. I asked Jack what they were doing.

He said, "Catching crickets for bread."

"Well, we will go and see how they do it."

We went, and saw that they had dug quite a number of trenches about a foot wide and a foot deep and about thirty or forty feet long, and around like a new moon with the horns uphill.

These trenches ran in a north and south direction, the land sloping to the west. The Indians, men, women and children, divided into two parties, one going to the north end and the other to the south end, all carrying a bunch of grass in each hand. They went single file toward the foothills, and making the distance between the parties wider than the length of the trenches. When they had gone what they thought far enough, as judged by the scarcity of grass left by the black insects, the party closed in and, walking back and forth swinging their grass bunches they gradually worked down toward the trenches.

We followed them on horseback and I noticed that there were but very few crickets left behind. As they went down, the line of crickets grew thicker and thicker till the ground ahead of the drivers was as black as coal with the excited, tumbling mass of crickets.

When all had been driven in the Indians set fire to

SHOSHONE INDIAN VILLAGE.

the cooking and eating utensils was as greasy as grease could make them.

The next morning the cook was the first to find out that the whole lot of cooking and eating utensils had taken wings or had been stolen by the Indians. He called the boys and at the same time was looking for tracks of the thief. He soon found a tin plate, then a spoon, or cup.

One of the boys had gone about one hundred yards from the camp when he yelled out that he had found one of the thieves. We all ran to where he was and this is what we saw: A coyote with his head in our largest coffee pot and the bail over his head back of his ears. He was bumping against the brush at every step. He could make no progress.

Chief White Horse would make my visits interesting to me and once he had planned an antelope catch. By daylight all were ready for the start and a number of the young men had left early in the evening before to go to the extreme south end of the ground to be covered. They were to spread apart across the valley, travel in open order back to the north, being careful that not one of the antelope jumped would run, except in a northerly direction.

This valley has a good many hills or knolls along the base of the mountains and a few of them scattered more to the center of the level ground in the middle of the valley. An antelope, when started up, will always run directly for one of these, that lay opposite from where he gets his scare from, and they run hill to hill. They see no one ahead of them but the party behind being constantly increased, and if they undertake to pass around the drivers a buck or squaw sends them off to the center again.

Thus it goes till they come to the line between the outer ends of the arms, which, there, are about four miles apart, but gradually closing in as they get nearer the pen. The arms or leads are started at the extreme ends by simply prying or pulling up a large sagebrush and standing it roots up on the top of another brush, thus making a tall, black object visible for miles.

White Horse and I rode the only two horses in the drive and we went to about half the distance to the ends of the arms and were soon back as fast as possible on the outside to take advantage of the bends and turns and to try and keep abreast of the drivers, who were all on a fast run, yelling like a pack of coyotes. The drive came to an end with a rush and everyone working desperately closing up the entrance, a few small children appearing on the wall at different points around the pen. By the time we had tied our horses and climbed to the top of the wall the entrance had been closed.

The killing was done with arrow and seldom missed piercing the heart. The catch was about twenty-five, mostly all bucks or does, there being only five or

the grass they had in their hands and scattered it along on top of that they had over the trenches, causing a big blaze and smoke which soon left the crickets powerless to crawl out. The squaws were busy gathering up the game into large conical shaped baskets. When they headed back to camp, there were bushels of crickets left in the trenches, which they would gather later in the day.

After the crickets are dried the squaws grind them, feathers and all, on a mill making a fine flour that will keep a long time, if kept dry. Jack says the crickets make the bread good, the same as sugar used by the white woman in her cakes.

On our way to Carson City with a train of four wagons pulled by three yoke of oxen each and teams of six mules we hauled wagons loaded with produce to sell on the way and bring back a threshing machine and other farm machinery, and dry goods to supply our little store at Deep Creek. Our first camp was at Antelope Springs, where we arrived just before dark.

After supper was over, the plates and utensils were all pushed back around the fire and the frying pans, coffee pots and skillets were left close to the fire, where they had been used. Not a thing was washed or taken care of and you can safely bet that every single piece of

GOSHOOT INDIANS HANGING AROUND STATIONS.

"Fast Mail"

by Betty Orr

Elias Dart carried the "fast mail" in White Pine County at the age of 16. Slight of build, daring, bright and courageous, he was the prototype of the West's best riders.

Just as 15 years earlier the Pony Express moved the mail from St. Joseph to Sacramento, the "jackass mail" or "fast mail" was being carried over remote areas of Nevada in the 1870's and 1880's, particularly between far-flung mining camps.

The rider covered 50 miles of wild country in five hours—faster than most Concord stages could travel. After his five hour shift was over, the rider's work was done for the day; he could then catch a little rest at the pony station and think about the adventures of his next ride.

The letters were carried in two leather packs at the side of the saddle. The cost was ten to 25 cents for a writer to have a letter delivered by "fast mail," depending on how far the letter had to be carried, but it was a quick and efficient service.

Elias started his career at Ward, riding to Hamilton or Taylor; from Eureka through the White River Valley; or from Ward to Osceola—wherever his employers sent him.

In his later years Dart loved to tell of his harrowing adventures as a "fast mail" rider and a stage driver. He recalled that Captain De la Mar made his silver bars so large and heavy that robbers could not carry them; a safe on the stage was loaded with the bars. At Taylor, the mine payroll was brought in from San Francisco rolled inside fresh, ice-packed fish to protect it from highwaymen. It was also at Taylor one Christmas that Elias and one of his stage passengers nearly brought down the wrath of the entire camp.

Dart had been directed to drive over to Ward, across Steptoe Valley, to get the current Santa Claus and bring him into camp for the Christmas festivities. Great preparations had been made and hundreds of dollars had been solicited from the miners to buy gifts for the children. The big bash was to be held in the Taylor Opera House on Christmas evening. There would be singing, a program, a tree, and Santa for the children, followed by refreshments and an all-night dance for the adults. In all, it was a typical mining camp Christmas which the Taylor ladies had planned.

But something went amiss.

Because of the unusually cold weather, no doubt, Dart and his passenger imbibed a bit too freely from the jug of spirits the young driver had cached under his seat. First the coach went off the icy road. After being duly rescued and put back in shape, the two men

six yearlings in the bunch. There were five or six bucks killed that day and one of which had tried to jump the fence, but got entangled in the fence and was killed by having his throat cut with a knife. The reason they were not all killed in one day was to give the squaws time to cut up in thin strips the flesh and dry it on a rack built over a small fire, thus curing it so it would keep.

The brains are seldom eaten, but carefully preserved to tan the hide with, by spreading them all over the flesh side of the skin, after the hair has been removed, rolling them up and leaving them this way for a few days, when the skins may be washed clean and wrung as dry as possible, then stretched and pulled and rubbed till dry, when they are soft, white and pliable. Then they are ready for trade or use.

In traveling through Goshute Valley (later called Flower Lake Valley), we were getting very thirsty, having been traveling five or six hours from the last water hole and it being a dry, hot and sultry day I and the horses needed water. The nearest I knew of was about twelve miles distance and that not in the direction of our travel; and our one canteen being empty, I thought we would have to change our course to get water.

I asked Jack, "How far to water this way," pointing the way I wanted to go.

He said, "I do not know, maybe no water."

"Well, are you thirsty?"

"Yes."

"Well, then, think fast and locate water or Indian no better than white man."

I soon left this area and returned to Utah and left other travelers passing through the area to help pioneer the west.

decided to pay a visit to the Monitor mine. Temptation was too much. Finally, after a night of drinking the men arrived in Taylor, just in time for the big "doin's." As they were hustled behind the stage at the opera house, no one noticed that the two revelers were having a nip now and then.

At length, after the caroling and main program, the curtains were opened to reveal two shimmering silver Christmas trees. The children cheered and laughed in delight, anticipating the many gifts which Santa would distribute. They called for Santa Claus. They called again; and yet again.

But, alas, when he made his much awaited appearance, thanks to the help of Dart, Santa was a wreck—no white whiskers, no jolly red suit, no Santa—just a rowdy chap wrapped up in a bunch of sheets with a frightening ghoulish mask.

But most of the time Elias was a dependable and efficient rider or driver. In later years he worked as a teamster on the famous McGill ranch. He never married but concerned himself with his horses, the desert roads and how many miles per day he could make. He loved his life and blushingly admitted it had been "too exciting" to think about matrimony.

At last, when he was close to 70, he settled down in Spring Valley at the Cleveland ranch where he handled odd jobs and entertained the hands with tales of his adventurous life as a rider for the "fast mail."

The Story of Kinnemich

by Laura Gallagher Werner

One day in my early childhood, while my mother and the younger children of the family were alone in our ranch house on Duck Creek, we were startled to see a wizened old face, cupped in brown hands, pressed against the window pane. In some trepidation we went outside to investigate and found an old, old Indian, dressed, not in overalls and shirt as we were accustomed to seeing the Indian men, but in fringed buckskin shirt, leggings and moccasins. He seemed not to understand when we talked to him, but accepted the food which my mother gave him and went away.

We thought it quite an exciting event and were full of talk about our strange visitor when the men of the family came home. Someone said, "Oh, that must have been old Kinnemich, he doesn't often come to this side of the valley." That was the only time that I remember seeing Kinnemich, but this is his story:

In 1863 the Goshute War raged in what is now White Pine County, Nevada.

Numerous depredations had been committed by Indians against the overland stages, their drivers, passengers and stations. Finally, after the destruction of Eight Mile Station, an appeal was sent to Camp Douglas in Utah. A company of Cavalry volunteers, led by Captain S. P. Smith, was sent to Fort Ruby near the southern boundary of what is now Elko County.

Henry Butterfield, who had been appointed as Indian Agent at Fort Ruby, sent out two friendly Shoshone Indians as spies to find out who had committed the outrages, and where the guilty parties could be found. When these two Indians made their report, Captain Smith set out from Fort Ruby with his company of cavalry and, moving with great secrecy and under the guidance of the two Shoshones, arrived at Duck Creek at a point where it enters Steptoe Valley. They made their stand, under cover of darkness, at a point where later stood the Caldwell house, and which later became the home of the W. C. Gallagher family.

There Captain Smith divided his forces with one party going three miles down Duck Creek and crossing over to the south side. The Indians were camped on a hillside in the shelter of a butte, south of the creek, and this party circled the butte, thus approaching the camp from the rear. The party on the north side approached the front of the camp and waited till daybreak when, at a given signal, the slaughter of the sleeping Indians began.

A watch was set for those believed to be out of camp, and when warning of their approach was given, a number of the cavalrymen dashed up the rise to the east and, as they came over the summit, killed three Indians who had been on a night hunting expedition. According to stories from old timers, 23 Indians were killed.

With the destruction of the guilty Goshutes, Captain Smith and his men moved on up Duck Creek, crossed the divide which separates it from Steptoe Creek, then over the Schell Creek range to Spring Valley where a second battle was fought. The Goshutes then asked for peace and the war was ended.

One had escaped by hiding behind rocks and creeping through brush, and reached Duck Creek. There he was sheltered by willows and went in water for several miles, finally reaching the hills on the opposite side of Steptoe Valley.

In later years the other Indians would have nothing to do with him, believing him bewitched because the white man's bullets had failed to kill him. They gave him the name of Kinnemich which means "Never Die."

Kinnemich lived entirely by himself in the hills to which he had escaped, seldom venturing out to any of the ranches. He lived on a diet of gophers and rodents, pine nuts, berries and roots. He never learned to speak English and became a legendary figure, for all the Indians and many of the younger whites believed that he never would die.

He was occasionally seen by prospectors and hunters, and in his later years, citizens of Ely went to his camp leaving him supplies. On one of these visits, about 1909, they found that his name had lost its meaning, for there lay old Kinnemich—dead.

Two Buxom Gals

by Nan Millard Grant

Shelter was a luxury and those not accustomed to the untimely seasons of northern Nevada quickly learned that winter came even in late summer. Then any shield from exposure was a haven.

Our mules, Mollie and Bessie, were not used to easy living. They knew hauling, but usually on open roads, certainly not on roads that were little better than trails. They came on the long uphill climb from southern California. The menfolk had made a distance gauge for the wagon which rang a bell for each mile. Joshua and juniper trees that had given meager shade from scorching sun were also sieve-like wind breaks. On the trail for thirty days, averaging about twenty miles daily, travelers and mules were weary. Water rationing, the state's most precious resource, affected all, Mollie and Bessie especially. They could go on short-feed rations if necessary, but they had to have water. Cognizant of both necessity and emergency, the water keg was indispensable. To moisten a traveler's parched throat, oranges had been stashed away in the wagon.

This journey had been planned for 1901 by the Millard family following their son's graduation from the Colorado School of Mines. The family was eager to locate some promising mining property and after investigating numerous questionable sites along the route, they simply kept on going.

In spite of miles and miles of distance, strangers sometimes crossed paths on the desert. A stray Indian cowpoke drew up alongside the wagon one day. His chivalrous greeting was warm and friendly. After numerous inquiries by all parties, with some informal chitchat, Granddad gave the sweating buckaroo an orange. With thanks he and his cayuse took off like a thunder-bolt. Mollie and Bessie resumed their accustomed pace, as they swished their tails good-bye to the Indian pony.

Finally Mollie and Bessie pulled into Ely, then a small mining camp, and the Millards worked the rich tailings of the nearby Chainman Mine. Later they built the Millard Engineering office building on High Street. The two old buxom gals, Mollie and Bessie, continued daily service with the engineering company in Ely for many years, but progress brought cars, trucks and jeeps which eventually replaced the faithful mules. Mollie and Bessie finally reveled in well-deserved shelter and meadow comfort, shade trees, and bounty on Frank Calloway's ranch where "livin' was easy."

Mules were an important property for desert dwellers. This wagon was used for short transportation with limited hauls.

Midwife
Mary
Oxborrow
in 1927

Midwives of Nevada

by Byrd Wall Sawyer

Midwives pioneering the western frontier were called upon in illness, death and birth to bring comfort and physical help. Usually the midwife was skilled in using medicinal herbs and also applied some of her own secret remedies; her life's work was dedicated to the comfort and health of the community.

The Paiutes, Washoes and Shoshones appointed older women of their tribes to serve as midwives at birthings. Rosie, withered to a sort of agelessness, officiated in Churchill County as late as 1930 and Maggie White Feather was another well-known Indian midwife. Though Indian births generally were not troublesome, Rosie and Maggie immediately sent for the white man's doctor when delivery became complicated.

In 1897 the Deseret Hospital in Salt Lake City initiated a course in midwifery, graduating an outstanding nurse in Mary Leicht Oxborrow. When her husband was relocated to Lund by the Mormon church, Mary brought with her considerable knowledge about medicine and good nursing skills. She was raising a large family, but when needed by neighbors to administer her medical know-how, her own family would have to manage without her until the neighbor could again assume the responsibilities of everyday living. In her 82 years Mary dedicated herself with energy and grace, contributing her compassion and talent to the White Pine community.

Margaret Windows completed her training in midwifery and returned to the White River Valley and throughout her career delivered more than a thousand babies. In forty years Mrs. Windows never lost a mother through childbirth and she delivered 14 sets of twins. After her husband's death Margaret moved to Ely for the position of head-nurse in Dr. Buckle's hospital.

Widely known for her successful ministrations, "Grandma" Henroid of Deep Creek traveled the Utah-Nevada line to attend birthings. Her two daughters came to delivery at the same time, one living in Utah and the other in Nevada, so Grandma spent a long night rushing from one to the other.

During the boom at Ward in White Pine County, Mrs. Clark settled there as a homeopathic doctor. Her successful herbal medicines and home remedies were in great demand and she was often favored over a licensed doctor.

Newark Valley boasted of the brawniest "midwife," Julis Minoletti. He served his community in the 1870's and reputedly never lost a patient. In his prime he had worked as a cowman and was so strong that he could carry a calf draped over his shoulders without effort. Supposedly he had never taken a bath and fortunately his filth and grime never infected mother or child during delivery. When old and decrepit, he was sent to the hospital against his violent protest and the nurses insisted that he be bathed before getting into the sterile bed. Some said that it was the bath that brought on his death a few days later.

Eliza Jane Pulsifer Terry traveled the Clover Valley and Panaca country when she was needed. If her patients could pay, she charged $10 for delivery and care of infant and mother, and she remained there until the woman could take over the responsibilities of home and family once more. In later years Eliza worked as a nurse for a Pioche doctor, investing her earnings in a home in Panaca.

In Virgin Valley, Mary Bunker was trained by a visiting nurse employed by the Mormon relief society, and diligently served her people. But Mary did not restrict her care to just the Mormon population and was severely chastised for this practice, especially when she came to the aid of gypsies camped outside Bunkerville. Unwelcome in town, the desperate father could find no one to help his wife in her delivery until Mary sympathetically listened to his story. Her family was outraged that she should associate with the dirty, thieving gypsies, but she ignored their objections and trudged the mile to the gypsy camp for ten days. She delivered a healthy child and ceased her daily visits only after the mother was fully recovered. While Mrs. Bunker went about her volunteer visits her daughter took charge of the household, but when Mary's husband left for Mexico she never saw him again. Mary Bunker continued caring for the sick and trained younger women for nursing and the midwifery profession until her death in 1906.

Mary Virginia Lytle of Overton lost her first three daughters and was acutely aware of the drastic need for doctors and midwives to care for pregnant women. Mary decided to attend the training school in Salt Lake City and returned to southern Nevada in 1909 as a full fledged midwife. For 31 years she cared for her patients and never lost one of the 198 children she safely delivered.

Battle Mountain employed the services of two generous midwives, Mrs. Dusang and Annie Laurie McCormack. Mrs. Dusang was a seamstress by trade but, whenever sickness or birthing demanded her medical experience, she dropped her sewing and rushed to offer her aid whether in town or at a distant ranch. Annie Laurie's skill as a midwife and nurse kept her very busy and her compassionate service continued, especially in obstetrical nursing, until her health failed. Mrs. McCormack improvised with efficiency and good humor to keep her patients healthy. If there were no hot water bottles available, then newspapers or magazines were heated in the oven and the newborn was cradled within the warm pages. If there was no olive oil the baby would be cleaned with lard. Annie would contrive a crib from towels and she could have the new mother in a clean fresh bed instantly.

In Washoe County Ellen Frances Ross and Mary Kinney, both of Glendale, were on constant call as midwives, nurses and to attend to the deceased in funeral homes. Before a corpse was laid out for viewing, Mary and Ellen would cleanse and clothe the body before the undertaker arrived from Reno with a coffin. The ladies then stayed with the grieving household until family life returned to normal.

Many of these capable and selfless women were taken for granted and they often braved the heat of the desert or the deep snow drifts and biting blizzards to aid the stricken and bring healthy babies into the world. Midwives generally donated their services and while others became popular some of these volunteer ladies were not even known by their given names.

Mrs. Jake Cameron of Spring Valley, Aunt Lena Leavitt of Virgin Valley, Mary Dakin of Elko County and Matilda Mortenson Swallow of Osceola are but a few midwives of the numerous mining camps and frontier villages who have gone unsung but certainly appreciated by the families they served.

For a long time medicine and nursing had hardly any regulation in Nevada. In the codified laws little is said of midwifery and the few provisions established were never enforced. As early as January 1875, legislation had been introduced forbidding anyone to practice medicine without training or registration.

After May 1, 1905 all persons practicing obstetrics were required to pay a fee of $25 and a Nevada statute of March 1911 created a State Board of Health.

The new legal requirements then forced local health officers to gather vital statistics by the 10th of each month. Births were to be registered immediately and all midwives were required to register with the local health officer. A check of all counties reveals no such registrations of midwives. In 1923 nurses had to pass examinations before being registered and with such strict regulations only a few midwives worked on and there would be no new recruits for the demanding profession of midwifery.

Doctor At Hamilton
by Elsa & Jerry Culbert

Doctor H. S. Herrick moved to western Utah Territory in 1860 when he was 41 years old. During his years at Hamilton, 1872–1880, he kept a daily diary of a mining camp that already had declined after its big boom of 1869–1870. He wrote about his patients, presidential nominees and other politics, wars, mining stocks, price of food, and the general dull times and boredom in the camp.

Every day he commented extenuously on the weather:

"Arose about 5, found the winds howling fiercely: all day they have been increasing in their murmurs. . . . Night has again approached. The stars are one by one coming out from the deep blue sky. . . . The whole heavens are decked in bright and glittering constellations; still the winds are howling. My only patient died at 10 o'clock this evening, a poor sufferer. The Irish are having a 'wake' as it is called among them. Retire at 2 o'clock.

"January 2, 1876

This is the first Sunday of 1876. I arose about daylight and found it a clear, cold winter morning. The wind commenced howling at about 9 o'clock blowing from the southwest. Tonight at 10 o'clock it has not ceased its fury. Have spent the whole day at home in reading, writing letters and cooking grub. The snow is now about 2 feet in depth and a fair prospect of an increase. No important news to record. The town is alarmingly dull although distressingly healthy, at least so considered by the sons of the great Escaulapius. The Sabbath is spent, by those who have any pretense to morals in reading and writing, at home—while loafers and bummers spend their hours at the saloons in

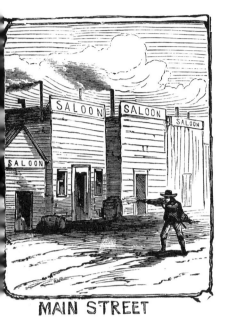

MAIN STREET

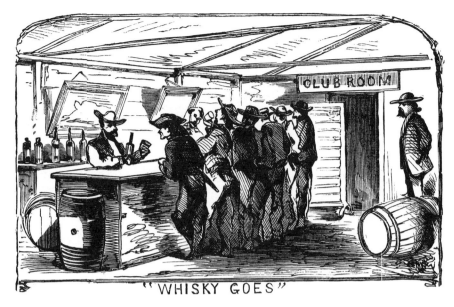

"WHISKY GOES"

Harper's Weekly April 24, 1869 was illustrated with several cartoons of Hamilton. "There are no churches. Every other house on the street is a saloon, and is thronged with drinkers and gamblers. The gambling room is in back of the saloon. Here faro is played, the stakes ranging from $1 to $1,000."

drinking. Hamilton has two churches but no service except Sunday School. The place is too poor to support a divine of any kind. H. Carpenter was married in Eureka on December 30th, which is the first marriage for a long time of any citizen belonging to Hamilton. Carpenter has now two living wives, one here, the other in Salt Lake. Hamilton is not much of a place for marrying but a good place for breeding.

Some of our American women are too proud to have children yet they will not throw aside chances to get married. I must move along for the night and retire to the arms of Morpheus hoping to have a good sleep and rest.

"July 4, 1876

"I arose just at the break of day to the roaring of cannon and popping of fire crackers, announcing that the great and glorious 4th had burst forth in all her ancient greatness. After preparing and eating a hearty breakfast I then made my morning visits, found all improving. At 10 o'clock this town assembled in the center of the street listening to the old Declaration of Independence by W. Forest; poems by W. Pardy; orations by G. Watrep, president of the day; and music by the Hamilton choir. In the afternoon Mrs. Allen held an exhibition of her school at the court; it passed off finely. It was every way a pleasant day in all respects, some drunk but no fighting or much quarreling. Thus ended this glorious fourth in 1876. It is now 10 o'clock let me retire."

In 1880 he recalled the great June 1873 fire:

"Saturday June 26, 1880. I was up at an early hour, found it a clear, beautiful summer morning. All was calm and serene, not a zephyr was stirring in all the region around. I took a short walk around town, found all on the improvement. The news is not important either at home or abroad. Politics is all the good present, stocks have improved some today. Sunday 27th found it a warm clear summer morning. After my usual work I then sit down to read and write and spend the Sabbath to the most proper advantage. Seven years ago today, the 27th of June, Hamilton was lain in ashes by fire. It was a terrible fire demolishing everything in its way. This has been a warm day but nothing like that day. Cohn, the incendiary, spent his time of 7 years in prison, he was released 11 months ago for good behavior. Retire at 10 P.M."

Aultman St., Ely before the railroad

First Train

by Olive Stanton Norton

On September 29, 1906 the railroad came to Ely out of necessity. By then the world needed the ores that the pioneers had mined there. Dave Bartley and Edwin Gray, young engineer-prospectors, bought many claims in the Ruth area from D. C. McDonald and after a few years' work sold them to Mark Requa, who planned further development via his Consolidated Copper Corporation. Gold, silver, and other precious ores had been dug from the ground, sacked, and shipped by mule-back or wagons, but the huge copper ore bodies demanded rail transportation. So the Nevada Northern Railway was built.

Track was laid some 140 miles down Steptoe Valley connecting with the Southern Pacific at Cobre. With neither bridge nor fill needed the railroad reached Ely within a year.

The celebration lasted three days. A select group drove by automobile to Cherry Creek, some forty miles north, to meet the first incoming train. When Cherry Creek had competed with Hamilton some years before in vying for the county seat, it lost by one hundred votes. Now it was being missed by but one mile by the railroad!

Red, white and blue decorations and American flags were abundant, and the entire front of the courthouse was covered with sagebrush wreaths. Excursion fare was $10.50 round trip from Salt Lake City; Pullman was $2.50 each way. Visiting trains were switched to a siding and the Pullman and dining cars were used throughout the weekend.

Huge crowds cheered wildly as the trains from Salt Lake City, Ogden, and San Francisco arrived. Many adults had never before seen a train, and all crowded close to inspect the puffing engine. When the engineer gleefully blew the whistle and called, "Look out, folks; I'm going to turn her around," it was claimed that people scattered in all directions. Indians, leery of such forbidding "creatures," stayed far up on the hillside, venturing down only to feast on the barbecue and the hot coffee of which they were so fond.

Mr. Requa drove the last spike, made at Ruth of nearly pure copper, to complete the railroad. His speech paid tribute to those who had helped with the project and he told of the evolution of copper development to date, saying, "It would be pure folly to think the methods of handling ores have been perfected. . . ." Other speakers included Senator Newlands, Governor Sparks, Thomas Rockhill, and many others.

During the next couple of days baseball games and other entertainment continued, including the famous "badger fight" and a double-jack drilling contest.

Within a year one would have scarcely recognized the mining camp. The coming of the railroad made Ely prosper. In 1907 Ely boasted a population of 3,000 as compared with 500 two years before. The city was being incorporated; a $35,000 school house and an $80,000 courthouse were being built, a few thousand men were employed in mines and smelters nearby; two strong banks carried $1,000,000 on deposit.

There were two daily and three weekly newspapers, and a well-equipped telephone system connecting Ely with mines and plants. The Northern Hotel completed, Tex Rickard and his partners spared no expense to make it the finest in the West. Ely was on the threshold of becoming a great camp. As an early newspaper journalist said, "It was indeed a 'hummer.' "

Dr. A. P. Lagoon

by Stella Heit

Dr. A. P. Lagoon came to Ely in about 1900. With his peg leg, the result of a Spanish-American War accident, he hunted, fished, climbed hills, swore, and could drink anyone under the table. He claimed that he could do more with his peg leg than most men could do with two normal ones. Dr. Lagoon performed operations on kitchen or library tables.

One night in the saloon, several men were boasting about how much weight they could carry. The doctor claimed that he could carry 500 pounds of sugar across the main street from corner to corner—chuckholes, mud and all—and never falter. The saloon keeper took bets and banners were made for the event. Five hundred pounds of sugar were delivered from the big mercantile store at Lane City and the contest was on. Ten other men tried and failed. Doc's turn came and he won and collected the money.

In 1908 he bought a new car for trips to Ruth, Reipetown, and Kimberly. About a month later, coming down from Ruth, he stopped on the railroad tracks while he and his three friends made a comfort stop. An ore train came around the curve and smashed the car. Nevada Northern refused to pay for the car since it was stopped on the tracks and no one occupied the car at the time of impact. Doc claimed that the engineer had plenty of time to see them had he not been asleep. Railroad officials met with their lawyers and informed Doc that he had no case.

Doc's lawyers said he would tell his story in court. Then Nevada Northern's lawyers asked, "What about the other three men involved? What would they say?"

Just then Doc piped up and said, "They'll swear to anything I say—they were drunk!"

He so charmed the railroad investigator that they awarded him money for a new car and some damages—and he promptly spent his new fortune entertaining them.

Dr. A. P. Lagoon's colorful character and charisma earned him love and respect from Ely's citizens because this one man realized the need for human warmth, pathos, and humor in the frontier mining towns of early Nevada.

First Church

In 1912 the three year old McGill Methodist Church began to raise money for a permanent building. Nevada Consolidated donated land and some of the building materials. Later wooden siding was put on, as well as a malthoid roof. That first church building is summed up in this poem written by a former member, Mrs. Thelma (Brownie) Ireland.

THIS CHURCH

It started first in people's hearts;
They wanted for their young
A Sunday School, so met in homes
For prayer, and hymns were sung.

A seed was planted and it grew;
The flame of hope was fanned,
It warmed the seed and before long
A church of God was planned.

Donated labor built this church;
Food sales and perseverance,
United effort with one goal
And with no interference.

The church bell came from Hamilton,
It was not needed there;
The deacon proudly rang it,
To invite the town to prayer.

So much work went into this church;
So many earned a crown;
We should be grateful for those folk
And never let them down.

They built with diligence and hope
Without a selfish gain;
Let not indifference, apathy
Make their work prove in vain.

The Kinnear house on the "Charmed Circle" was well-landscaped and had a commanding view to the west.

The Charmed Circle

by Ressie Walls Read

John Charles Kinnear was a veteran of Nevada mining for a half century and most of it was spent at McGill. In 1957 after retiring he wrote a book entitled, *"Fifty Years in Mining–1907–1957."* The book states that when Kinnear arrived in McGill, in 1910, he found a town far removed in character and a far cry from the boisterous, rip-roaring, gun-toting camp of Goldfield. McGill was a company town. It was young and progressive, with one dusty main business street with raised wooden sidewalks.

The town was sectioned off. The "Charmed Circle," where elite lived such as general manager and those of superintendent status, and a row of houses for assistant superintendents and those of equal rank were the only houses with bathrooms. The townsite itself was divided into Upper Town (Middle Town was built during World War I), Greek Town, Austrian Town, and Jap Town, as these areas were then called. Single employees lived in malthoid (tar paper) cabins in Lower Town.

The Kinnears moved into a three-room cement house in Upper Town. These houses were not modern. The toilets were out back, little buildings, like duplexes of proper size, joined together for neighborly convenience. Boards used in the walls that separated the privies were made of green lumber. The lumber shrank and these little outhouses got to be quite cozy affairs. On each side of these little houses was an addition for coal—all of this stained a dreary brick red.

The little cement house was of no comparison to the beautiful general manager's house they moved into around 1930. Originally it was a plain, two-story grey cement structure but in a few years it became one of the most attractive homes in Nevada.

Tall, black wrought-iron gates mark the entrance way leading up broad steps to a porch supported by red brick pillars. Artistic teakwood doors open into a spacious reception hall with walls of genuine walnut panels, and a wide stairway to the upstairs rooms. A large living room with a beautiful fireplace adjoins a smaller sitting room with a charming hooded, corner fireplace. The formal dining room is also furnished in walnut panels; the rest of the ground floor houses a large, very modern kitchen and servants rooms.

Upstairs, four large bedrooms with lavish connecting bathrooms, a central hall, and a sunroom span the entire width of the house. The third floor consists of one large hall which could be used for a ball room. There is a porte-cochere on the north side of the house and also a side entrance. The structure was surrounded by beautiful grounds enclosed by a high, red brick wall with massive weathered wood gates, light posts, cobblestone walks, and a greenhouse. Landscaped with trees and shrubs of every type and a profusion of flowers for every season, this lovely house looks across broad Steptoe Valley and the mountain range to the west.

In this delightful setting furnished with perfect elegance and charm, the family lived and entertained graciously. There were formal dinner parties, Christmas and New Years open house parties, luncheons, teas, childrens' birthday parties and church groups' meetings.

A memorable affair was the beautiful garden party honoring Mr. and Mrs. Kinnear on their Golden Anniversary in 1957, a tribute to the popularity and high esteem they held in the community.

Several families lived in the house after the Kinnears moved to New York, but now the house stands silent, cold and dark, the garden neglected and overgrown, with a "For Sale" sign in the window.

The phrase, gone with the wind, seems most apt for the passing of this era, though fond memories of the elegant life in the "Charmed Circle" of a western mining camp remain.

The evolution of McGill's principal thoroughfare is shown in these two views. A local delivery wagon is parked in front of principal businesses of the town in 1909. The Copper Club and the cafe down the street later became the post office and a furniture store.

Memories of McGill 1917 to 1922

by Georgia Shaver

When the nightmare in Europe suddenly became real, the United States entered the war in April 1917 and the effects were soon being felt in McGill. Aside from many young men going off to fight, the Red Cross formed chapters in the counties to ease the suffering of the boys over there. Our mothers went to meetings wearing distinctive dresses and nurses' headgear while they made bandages and rolled them, knitted socks and squares which were sewn together to make robes and blankets, and helmets to wear under the soldiers' tin headgear. School children lent their support to the war effort by buying "thrift stamps." These stamps sold for a quarter each and were posted in a little book issued at school. They were redeemable for full face value in 1923.

At school, we marched in single file to the strains of military marches played on a phonograph at the top of the steps. Our teacher was of German parentage, which made some of the parents suspicious of her. One day, she shook a boy for being sassy and, in the process, scratched his cheek. That afternoon his mother stormed into the room and called the teacher a "dirty Hun" for daring to touch her son.

When recess came, we flew out to get a place on the giant strides where we defied gravity and broken bones for the thrill of flying around in a circle. Horizontal bars, swings and hop scotch occupied the rest of our time. How we survived all those bruises and bumps, I'll never know!

When the big flu epidemic hit in the winter months of 1918, the school house doubled as an emergency hospital. Cots were set up, flu patients were moved in and doctors were able to attend to many more people that way. People on the outside were required to wear surgical masks for protection. Kids thought them handy for keeping faces warm while sleigh riding. Schools, churches and the movie theater were closed during the epidemic.

Segregation was part of early McGill with the lower paid men living in upper townsite. Except for A row and B row—they were called rows instead of streets—the houses were very cheaply built with no studding between the inner and outer walls. With no bathrooms or inside toilets, there were only three rooms—kitchen, bedroom and living room. A "two holer" out back was joined to a coal bin for each house. There were no grass, trees or fenced yards; just bare dirt. We played in the shade of the house, digging holes in the ground, deep enough to put our arms down in the coolness. We used rocks to make outlines of play houses, and to throw at telephone poles and at each other when tempers flared. Salaried men and their families occupied the "cement houses" on A and B rows.

In "middle town," where First, Second and Third streets are now, stood a few scattered houses next to a large area which was surrounded by a board fence. This was the site of circuses, dances by the grade school children and public gatherings and the May Festival, complete with a queen of the May and winding the Maypole.

On the lower or west side of Main Street was the Greek community. The Japanese people lived just north of the flume which crossed above the main road. Still farther north and also above the highway, was Austrian town. There were a lot of people who lived in Greek town who weren't Greek, and Austrian town had more Serbs, Croatians and Slavs than Austrians. The Japanese were not mixed with other nationalities. And from all of these communities came fine, law-abiding, wonderful people.

The movie theater bordered the north part of the business district, with a stationery store close by. Two dry goods and grocery stores bearing the names "Goodman-Tidball" and "Louis Cononelos" were doing business then, just as now! There were pool halls along Main Street, but the one known as the Greek pool hall was of special interest to the younger generation. Sometimes, in passing, we would hear strange, exotic music coming from within. We could see the upstretched hands holding handkerchiefs as the men danced to the strains of Greek music.

To the south of the Greek Church was the bakery where Gus Assuras and his brother, John, baked wonderful bread and rolls. There was only one doctor, one dentist and an eye doctor who came to town once a year from Goldfield to attend to our medical needs. When it came to culture, Chautauquas—early day community concerts and speakers—came periodically and were usually held in the second floor auditorium of the school house; piano and violin recitals were also popular.

One afternoon a fire started in the south end of the concentrator, or mill, as we called it. It spread so rapidly that all efforts to control it were in vain. Finally, the firefighters stood helplessly and watched it burn. The intense heat was felt four hundred yards away and when it burned itself out, there was nothing left but tangled girders and twisted steel.

The following year, a new, modern concentrator was built, restoring a vital link of McGill's prospering industry. The mill and some of the aforementioned businesses are still operating today, reflecting the perseverance and hardiness of McGill's veritable "melting pot" citizenry.

The bars and dance halls of nearby Reipetown also were amply staffed with women, and beer and whiskey were found in abundance. Note the men fighting.

On the South Side in '23

by Effie O. Read

Eastern Nevada was recovering from a slump after World War I, when the McGill concentration plant burned to the ground in July 1922. The company beat all records in restoring it to activity.

There was soon an upward movement of wages in iron, steel and copper. Statistics reported that wages were 16 percent higher than in 1915 at the beginning of the war. Immediately Nevada Consolidated Copper Company began adding to its forces, both at McGill and at the mines. Bars of copper could be seen stacked for shipment. There was a scarcity of men for the job openings, and even the daily train with its plush passenger service did not bring in enough men to fill the job vacancies.

The Lincoln Highway was the main artery of travel as well as a topic of contention and discussion. It was being routed through Ely and the U.S. Government would pay 80 percent of the cost of paving the main street of Ely. Up until that time Ely's main street was mud, rocks, dust and board sidewalks. The sprinkling wagon with its rear spray settled the dust on one side of the street while going one way and on the other half on its return. Mayor J. H. Gallagher was advocating the floating of bonds to pay the remaining one fifth of the cost of paving.

Those were the days when one might see an athlete running on the streets, climbing the hills or jumping rope on a side street. It was a period when boxing was popular in Ely. Many hopefuls came to Ely to train in its high altitude following the footsteps of the great Jack Dempsey who, after his first fight at the Bijou hall, decided to make the big time in New York.

The Indians complained that there was a crazy man living on the hill above the courthouse who slept with only a blanket, went around almost naked all day, doubled up his fists and struck at nothing but the fresh air.

The Bijou hall was used for dances and with so many mines in the district, part of the hall was filled with men. Ladies carried printed programs with tiny pencils attached by an elaborate colored cord and tassels. These programs had at least four dances left open as gestures of courtesy for strangers who vied for these dances.

Death Valley Scotty was showing himself about town, dropping half dollars and quarters on the sidewalk for the youngsters' enjoyment. He was routing the elaborate furnishings from Europe which were freighted through Ely and explaining his wonderful program of construction on the remote edge of Death Valley, keeping it as much of a mystery as possible.

Prostitution became a necessary evil and the red light district at Ely was one of the most tremendous spots in the West. Three blocks of buildings were in operation with units only large enough for a door and window. Furnished with a bed, dresser and place for a trunk, they were called cribs.

A rig and driver met the girls as they arrived on the six o'clock train. Many girls who thought they were coming to Ely for a legitimate job became scared and ruined. From the depot they could see the flood lights over a large steam bath advertisement high on the Alamo Hotel where the girls lived. They were then lured on to dancing and finally prostitution work. Many became disillusioned and took their own lives. Only short notices in the news told their story.

The girls were allowed on the streets only between two and four in the afternoon and the hasty messengers, usually Chinese on bicycles with trays of food on their heads or large packages from the business houses, hurried toward the red-light district to make their deliveries. No respectable woman ever walked on the north side of the main street of Ely because that side belonged to the honky-tonk girls.

Speak Easy But Prudently Bootleg Days in White Pine County

by Effie O. Read

When the Volstead Act became law on June 30, 1919, corruption and bootleg gin was soon widely spread in White Pine County.

An old kettle, a copper worm or ordinary piece of pipe, and a thermos bottle cap for a condenser served as a beginner's equipment. The more elaborate stills in the county were constructed of mash vats shipped by rail, taken to the hide-out, and assembled on the job. Business boomed for plumbers, tinsmiths and carpenters. Shell white gasoline was in demand for the cooking process but some used an ordinary coal range. Brewer's yeast at times became a premium, and white sugar and corn were the grocer's best sellers. However, United States Commissioner J. H. Gallagher, long time mayor of Ely, didn't get rich in his grocery business because when his sales increased on these items he was likely to investigate.

A gallon of moonshine whiskey could be produced at a cost of eighty cents to $1.50; but it sold for not less than $10 and the girls at the red light district would pay $15. If the bootlegger could obtain government green labels and cap his wares properly he could get $40 per gallon, his product duplicating the first class bottled in bond.

The charcoal process for removing the fusal oil and proper aging were most important. One bootlegger admitted that the most difficult part of his trade was transporting the barrels up the mountain side at North Creek to hide them in a cave where the "shine" was aged at least one year. For immediate sales he would strap a twenty-five gallon barrel on each side of a donkey and walk the donkey to the top of the mountain; upon return the whiskey was considered well aged.

Ely became a beehive of speakeasies and beer parlors, with such places as The House of 69th, Joe Venutti's Bluebird Rooms, the Oasis, Copper Club, Pullman Bar, Senate, and Josie's Beer Parlor.

Then there was Whispering Pat who sold his unaged bootleg for four dollars per gallon. His money purse was a cloth, ten-pound sugar sack. When prohibition agents knocked him over, the water company learned that he was not paying a water bill. He had backtracked from his dugout into the street and connected with the city main.

Four barrels of liquor stolen from a certain gentleman who had stored it away for the dry spell brought the owner a paroxysm of grief. Being able to smell booze at a great distance he soon located the stash, except thirty gallons which had leaked out in the transfer. High-jacking became a business with some, but bootleggers fortified themselves with an armed hide-out man who watched the highway. Pistol shots were warning signals of approaching vehicles.

Ely's elite, the Four Hundred, used the University Club for its parties and dances. One night they were extremely gay and learned that all of their bootleg scotch had been consumed. They immediately dispatched a member to find their bootlegger who could furnish choice scotch. The bootlegger was out of town but they found his helper at the place, keeping watch.

Now the helper knew that Charlie Johnson prepared the scotch by using sheep dip, but what he did not know was how much. Johnson very carefully took a broom straw, dipped it in the sheep dip and whisked it around in the container; but he overestimated by using about a tablespoonful.

Next morning the telephones in Ely were busy. The Four Hundreds were ill with cramps and dysentery. Naturally, the Four Hundreds were very careful to get the proper bootlegger after that episode.

Moonshine was the proper nomenclature because they worked at night. High on the Snake Creek Range, bootleggers established themselves at a crystal spring where water-cress stalks were as delicious as celery. There was only one road to the spring and it had been constructed especially for this haven. Friends bringing food and supplies at night time had certain flashes with car lights to warn those at work.

At the old Taylor ghost town a huge chicken farm was used for camouflage. The moonshiners would laugh hilariously about the drunken chickens whose feed was entirely of the bootleggers' mash. Pigs got plenty high on bootleggers' mash too. At Douglas Canyon, across White River Valley from Lund, there were also several stills in operation. Out in the valley one could look up into the sky and watch the crows and even small birds flying drunk after feeding on the throw-away mash.

Prohibition died unofficially on April 7, 1933. Closed door speakeasies were deserted and the new legal beverages were greeted with gusto and respect while bootleggers scrounged for another means of survival.

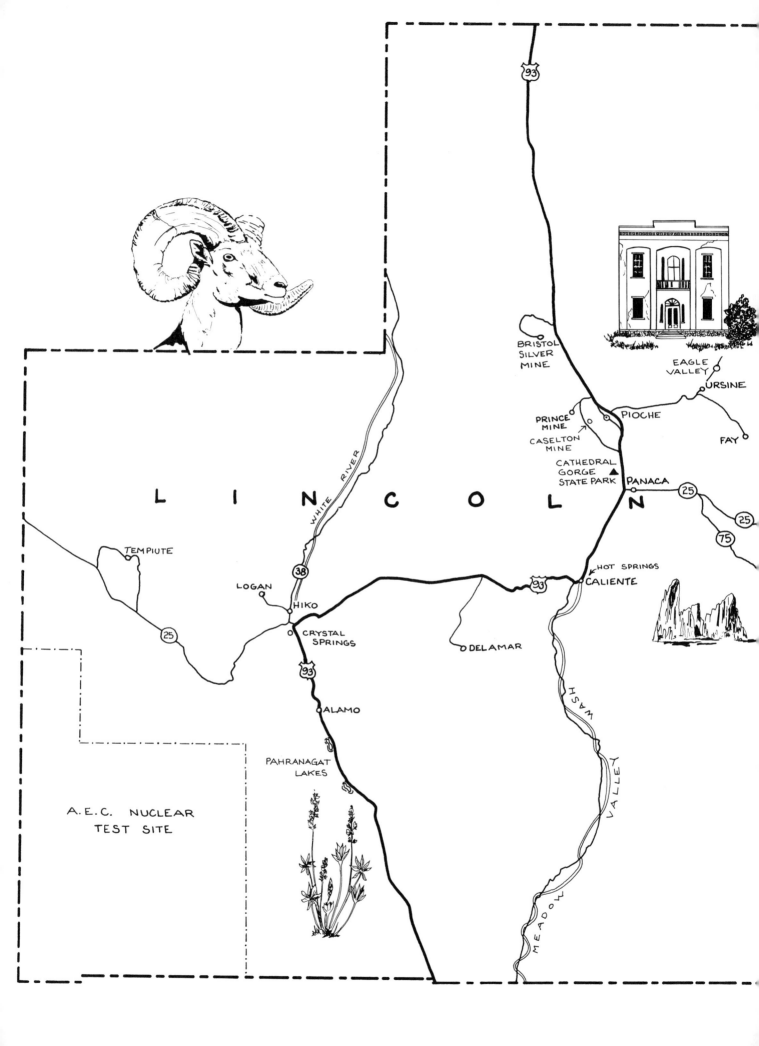

93

BRISTOL
SILVER
MINE

EAGLE
VALLEY

URSINE

PRINCE
MINE
CASELTON
MINE

PIOCHE

FAY

WHITE RIVER

CATHEDRAL
GORGE
STATE PARK

PANACA

25

L I N C O L N

25

75

TEMPIUTE

38

HOT SPRINGS

CALIENTE

LOGAN

93

HIKO

CRYSTAL
SPRINGS

DELAMAR

25

93

WASH

ALAMO

A.E.C. NUCLEAR
TEST SITE

PAHRANAGAT
LAKES

MEADOW VALLEY

Lincoln County

Valley of Lakes

by Joe C. Cathcart

The history of Nevada's Pahranagat Valley has its roots, as does so much of Nevada's history, in man's never ending quest for mineral riches. It began in 1865 when Standish Rood, famous for his continual search for new horizons in mining, left New York City on a mining expedition. In May of that year, Rood found himself in Salt Lake City where he met several of his former prospecting friends. They informed Rood that, with the help of the local Indians, they had discovered a new mining district which they named Pah Ranagat—an Indian word for "Valley of the Lakes." Rood accompanied them back to the Pahranagat Valley, arriving there on the 14th of June 1865.

It was from Rood that Eastern investors received the first description of the new mining district of Pahranagat. Rood's account was attractive, glowing and optimistic. He said that fuel was abundant, material for furnaces inexhaustible and that agricultural resources were sufficient for a large population. "The local soil hardens when heated and is an excellent material for building ore smelters."

Rood's account appeared in a mining company prospectus in New York in 1866. The same document reported assays running from $300 to $1,600 worth of silver per ton of ore. Mining companies were soon formed and prospectors rushed to the area. The Pahranagat Valley had been discovered.

The district's boundaries were approximately forty miles long and three miles wide, encasing a beautiful valley with mountain ranges on both sides. To the east the high, perpendicular bluffs of the Hiko Range separated the valley from southwestern Utah. The Pahranagat Range to the west was about eight miles from the valley and it was assumed that these mountains held the area's mineral wealth.

In the middle of the valley a fertile strip of land, about a mile wide, enclosed five crystal lakes: Upper Pahranagat (made up of two smaller lakes), Lower Pahranagat Lake, Crystal Springs Lake and Maynard Lake. These lakes were connected in a sort of chain.

At the southern end of the valley the men discovered a mountain range composed of crystalline salt and varying in height up to about 300 feet. Rood described these mountains as "glistening in the sunlight like burnished steel, at first giving the appearance of mountains of virgin silver."

Pahranagat was only 85 miles from the Callville settlement on the Colorado River and it was assumed that machinery, supplies and freight could be transported from San Francisco up the river to Callville. This journey was estimated to take 15 days and freight would cost approximately four cents per pound as opposed to the ten to thirty cents per pound, being paid by mines that needed to ship supplies and equipment overland.

The mountains would also supply ample timber and natives were peaceful and domestic, raising their own crops at the Maynard Lake Indian encampment.

While filing claims, it was discovered that the survey boundaries of southeastern Nevada were inaccurate and that portions of the district might actually lie in Utah or Arizona. These states all laid claim to the wealthy, new area and the issue was hotly contested. Finally, in 1866 Congress ended the "land war" and allowed the State of Nevada to annex thousands of square miles from both Arizona and Utah, giving southeastern Nevada its present day unusual configuration.

The twenty-six silver leads of the Pahranagat Valley quickly became twenty-six small mines. William Raymond, after purchasing several squatters claims, built the first mill and laid out a townsite. Raymond named the town "Hiko," an Indian expression meaning "white man's town."

By the end of 1866, Hiko and the area around it had attracted a few hundred residents but by 1871 the mining activity west of Hiko had already begun to die out.

The town of Crystal Springs was founded just a few miles south of Hiko; originally the townsite had been a fresh water source for a nearby Indian village. Crystal Springs became a stage stop and the first Lincoln County seat. This honor, however, lasted for less than a year; then the county seat was moved to Hiko.

*Logan City
c. 1905*

*Abanboned
Hiko mill
(opposite)*

Logan City, twelve miles northwest of Crystal Springs, was founded in 1866 and acquired a post office in July of 1867. The Silver Canyon mining camp was four miles north of Logan and the Crescent mining camp and mill was two miles west of Logan. By 1871, the Crescent Mill had been dismantled and later reassembled at Tempiute, a silver mining district approximately 35 miles northwest of the Pahranagat Valley. Tempiute later became more noted for its tungsten ore than its silver.

Lawlessness ran rampant throughout the valley during this period with cattle rustlers and horse thieves headquartering here. This soon gave way, however, to the notorious gun-play of Pioche.

Pioche mining activity, which began during 1868, increased dramatically when the county seat was moved there from Hiko in 1871. Guns were the only law in Pioche during this period and the town became infamous for its many homicides. The population of the city was more than 7,000 by 1872 with dozens of saloons and red light districts adding to the chaos.

During the 1880's and 1890's the "Valley of Lakes" was a small peaceful ranching community. In 1893, when Delamar began to open up, ranchers sold produce to the new gold camp two mountain ranges to the east. Pahranagat was generally overlooked by miners, but the nearby Groom mine shipped some ore.

This century's first decade saw all kinds of increased activity. Several railroads began to survey the area. The S.P., L.A. & S.L. (now the Union Pacific Railroad) began construction during 1901–1905 and the new towns of Caliente and Las Vegas were founded along the line. Mines began to reopen. The modern age had come to Lincoln County.

Delamar Sunsets
by Corrine Walker

It was in the early 1890's when wealthy Frenchman, Captain Joseph Rafael De La Mar began development of the rich mining camp in the Delamar hills.

Delamar boomed from 1895 into the twentieth century, finally becoming a ghost town at the beginning of World War II.

The names of the adjacent mines originated from hopes and experiences of men or meaningful events that took place. An example is the "Hog Pen" mine where the hogs uprooted the earth in their pens to uncover gold-bearing rock. The big Glory Hole looked as if a giant hand had gouged into the mountainside. These and many other mines furnished the ore for the mills and gold bullion that was then shipped to San Francisco.

The tailings from the mill ran through the livery stable and manure in the corrals absorbed the gold. Three men discovered this while cleaning the corrals and shipped it to a Salt Lake smelter. This is still talked about as among the most unusual gold shipments from Nevada.

Delamar was known to many as the "widowmaker." Several dozen women were widowed by her. Because water was scarce, the crusher was run almost dry and created a fine dust which contained silica. The deadly dust was inhaled by the men, causing silicosis and ultimately death. The dreaded dust also pierced lungs of women, children and animals. The tailings were the children's main playground where

302

Tales of Old Delamar

by Wayne Lytle

In the western mining camps everything had to be brought into town by team and wagon and whiskey was no exception. But many a whiskey barrel would suddenly leak on its freight wagon journey. These barrels would withstand the trip by wagon to the railroad or shipping dock, all the rough handling in each transfer, and never leak a drop. But give them a few miles on the way to their final destination, and half of these barrels would leak. The freighter would simply write "leakage" across the bill of lading and deliver the barrel.

My father, Freel Lytle, told me about this phenomenon. Every freighter had a horseshoeing kit which included hammer, nails, rasp, horseshoes, and so on. If he were lucky enough to get a barrel of whiskey on his load and was a drinking man, he would tap one of the barrel hoops up a little bit, drive a horse nail in through a crack between two staves, set a bucket under the drip, mark the bill of lading "leakage," and have a pleasant trip with good whiskey to drink and pass around.

One time the Delamar mill was shut down and they were waiting for parts; after they arrived in Caliente, the freight wagons just didn't show up. Swindler sent Freel out in the buckboard to see if he could find them. He found them alright, with a half a bucket of "leakage" whiskey, their teams tied to the wagon wheels, and all drunker than hoot owls. Freel found the small part needed most, threw it into the buckboard, dumped the whiskey in the dirt, and told them, "If you don't straighten up and get this stuff into town by noon tomorrow, I'll see that you don't get another freight contract from the Delamar Company." They just barely made it by noon the next day and you never saw a sorrier bunch of bleary-eyed men and half-starved horses in your life.

Slavonians constituted a considerable portion of the labor force at Delamar. Pete, also a Slavonian, was shift boss at the Magnolia tunnel which had been driven into the hill on a wide ore vein. The ore became better as the drift progressed. Five hundred feet into the hill, a gold streak showed up in the vein. The excited Slavonians plotted and schemed, then carried out lunch buckets filled with the best high-grade found. Pete took charge of this secret operation. He bought some ore sacks which would hold the loot until the group had about a ton of high-grade ore, worth several thousand dollars. Pete rented a team and wagon, took a few days off and left during the night hauling the ore to a train at Caliente and then went to Salt Lake City with it.

But he tried to sell it to a milling company that had been running sample tests for Delamar right from the

they built sand castles and walls. Women contracted dust in their lungs from the wind that blew across the tailings.

Water at Delamar had to be hauled to all houses except one where it was tapped. In this house lived the "last rose of Delamar," Agnes (Hannie) Horn, who had been there since childhood. Her husband was one of the young men felled by the dust. She was one of the camp's first settlers and among the last to leave. She was buried in the cemetery, beneath a rose bush that had once bloomed at her window.

Another woman poetically reflected on her hometown:

Oh, to see the sunset once more,
    Over the rocks and rills at old Delamar
No other place on earth could be
    As well loved by you and me.
Cabins built high on the hill
    And the din caused by the old mill
Winding road all of rocks
    Sweet little urchins with holes in their socks.
Smiling women, tired men,
    Oh how happy the world was then
Oh for the days that used to be
    When there were good friends for you and me.
But now it's a lonely place to be
    For it is a ghost town now you see
I'm going back, just once more
    To see the sunset at old Delamar.

In 1904 Caliente sprang up as a rail center and Delamar gold was hauled to there for rail shipment. The etching depicts teamsters unloading gold bars. The store (below) was the principal mercantile business of Delamar.

start. As soon as that ore was on their dock, the head miller called the sheriff. Pete took the rap and didn't squeal on the others. After about six months, he died of miner's consumption in the Pioche jail.

Freel was a teamster for the superintendent at the Delamar mining camp.

Periodically two gold bars were produced, then hauled 30 miles to the railroad agent in Caliente. Freel hauled the valuable bars in a buckboard. The small bar was worth about $120,000 and the larger bar, with more impurities, was worth about $90,000.

When the gold was ready to go, Freel would hitch up his team, throw a couple of grain sacks, a saddle, or anything ordinary over the bars and head for Caliente. He often did this on other assignments so the special departures attracted no attention.

There was never a robbery attempt, as Freel explained: "All gold is different. If anyone tried to take that gold and sell it, they would have been arrested by the first assayer they tried to sell it to. All assayers knew Delamar gold when they saw it."

When a guard named Turner was assigned to accompany the shipment, Freel gave this description: "They gave him an old lever action carbine of some kind, and he went with me on every trip. He wasn't much company because he stuttered so much that it was hard to understand him. Besides, he was half deaf. We made some pretty dull trips with that gold."

One day the gold arrived at Caliente just as a passenger train stopped for lunch. The news of the Delamar bullion spread quickly. The people crowded around the wagon and Freel couldn't get through with these two bars. This was Turner's chance to earn his keep. He crawled off the wagon with his old rifle, aiming the barrel at the people, stuttering, "G G G G G it B B B B B ack, or I I I I I'll SH SH SH SHoot Y Y Y Y Ya."

Turner attracted enough attention to himself so that Freel could get the gold into the station, get a receipt for it and send a telegram to Delamar. As soon as they received the telegram, his responsibility was over. Nobody ever did try to steal those gold bars—and Freel hauled many millions in gold during the six years he worked there.

Nigger Johnson came to Delamar in about 1898. He was a good practical nurse and worked for old Doc Dennison in the hospital. You could tell he had survived many experiences with sickness and death.

Years ago when a man got very sick, somebody always sat up with him. One of the miners was stricken with pneumonia, the Delamar dust always helping that along. Johnson and Hank volunteered to spend a night with the sick man. The evening was uneventful and the patient seemed to be resting under the watchful eyes of

Hank, at the foot of the bed, and Johnson, at the other end. Things were so quiet they both dozed off. Just after midnight Hank woke up and said "Hey, Johnson, how is he?"

After a minute or two he replied, "Dis end up here plum daid, how dat end down dere?"

Tikapoo

by Wayne Lytle

Being Tikapoo's squaw was not Fawn's idea. Tikapoo was an old man and Fawn was barely twenty years old. When Tikapoo's first squaw died, he made a deal with Fawn's father, trading two horses for the young squaw. Now Tikapoo only owned one old, lame animal that couldn't travel.

As autumn came, Fawn became very restless in Little Spring Valley, so she took Tikapoo by the hand and they started south toward Eagle Valley. It was quickly evident that Tikapoo couldn't travel any distance without becoming exhausted.

A day later, Ike Mathis was riding through the Spring Valley canyon, when his horse suddenly jumped to one side. Ike found a pile of brush covering a groaning Tikapoo. A large stone laid on his chest and two small bowls of food and water were near his head. Ike finally mounted the old man on his horse and took him to Eagle Valley.

With no broken bones, Tikapoo was soon his usual self. The local people made a tepee for him, fed him and Tikapoo became quite happy.

The younger children enjoyed taking food to Tikapoo. Maggie Lytle Warren, who spent all of her life in Eagle Valley remembered his reactions very well: "Old Tikapoo would laugh and clap his hands like a little child when he would see one of us coming with food."

One of the cowboys remembered seeing Fawn on her way north, evidently determined to find a younger man.

The older boys would visit Tikapoo in the evening hours and listen to his many tales and experiences. One night Tikapoo pointed to the moon and forewarned, "When moon straight up in sky, Tikapoo yauquay." Yuaquay, meaning to die, the boys assured him, "No, Tikapoo. You're alright. You won't die." The conversation shifted to other things and the boys left feeling better about it.

When morning came, the boys rushed to Tikapoo's tepee. His body was cold so Tikapoo had been dead for several hours. The moon was just setting in the west.

Watered Milk

by Wayne Lytle

In the 1870's Pioche emerged as a city of considerable importance because of rich silver mines. Just before 1890 many trees were planted along Main Street; they had matured considerably by 1918 when this picture (below) was taken. The delivery wagon burdened with household items made runs from Pioche to nearby Atlanta.

Two shrewd businessmen, Glisson of Rose Valley and Warren of nearby Eagle Valley, both sold raw milk in Pioche from wooden barrels. Both would resort to fisticuffs and other means of self protection if the occasion demanded. Both were known to consume huge quantities of liquid other than milk.

Sometimes both arrived in Pioche on the same day with their milk wagons, increasing the already stiff competition. On one occasion when Warren was alerted by a passing horseman that Glisson was also on his way to Pioche, he prepared for a showdown.

After both peddlers had covered the residential areas, they met on Main Street with their teams and partly full milk barrels. Reviewing his scheme over drinks in a nearby saloon, Warren then stepped outside and loudly announced, "Glisson waters his milk!"

Glisson protested but Warren plunked $50 on the headboard of his wagon and boomed, "Fifty dollars says you do!" While Glisson hastily placed his bet next to Warren's, one of the latter's friends secretly dumped a small can of water into Glisson's milk barrel.

The argument raged loud and strong, Glisson offering a free drink of milk to anyone in the crowd. Then he impulsively dumped the milk into the street. As the milk flowed, three fish went flopping down the street. Warren gathered his winnings while Glisson left Pioche muttering to himself, vowing to get even with Warren if it were the last act of his life.

So They Dug Frank's Grave

by Walter Averett

Delamar was still riding the gold boom in 1906, when excitement stirred the camp. Her name was Nell Monroe. She wore gabardine pants with high-topped lace boots, and soon became known as Cowboy Nell. She and her husband took the town by storm, attending all the social affairs and making friends everywhere.

One of their new acquaintances was young Sanford, a sampler in the assay office. When the time was right, Monroe worked the conversation around to his real purpose for visiting Delamar.

"You know, Sanford, there's lots of money to be made, and not as a sampler."

Sanford thought about it. "How is that?"

"Think of the money they keep in safes in the stores here. It's possible to open several of them in one night."

"You haven't looked at the buildings, have you? Every one of them has heavy iron shutters locked over the windows at night, to keep someone from breaking in. If you did get in and get the money, you wouldn't dare leave town, or everyone would know it was you. The law would be right after you."

"I happen to know how to get those shutters off, without making any noise. And what if somebody else turned up missing?"

"You mean somebody else will disappear, and wait for you somewhere?"

"He'll disappear, for good, but he won't leave town."

Monroe explained: "One of the stores keeps a man inside at night, and we don't want to miss that safe. Besides, he can be our missing man. That fellow at Miles' store. . . ."

"That's Frank Pace! He's a friend of mine!"

"Which comes first, friendship or money? Or maybe you'd like to turn up missing?

"Well, he sleeps in the back room of the store, and he has the combination to the safe. We'll get into the Nesbitt's store, then Wirtheimer's, then Samuelson's, and blow the safe in each one as we go. Then we'll stop at Miles' store and you'll wake him up, telling him you want to make up a lunch. When he lets us in, we'll wait until he opens the safe, then we'll kill him. . . ."

They had already dug Frank's grave, bit by bit, under the floor of their cabin.

And things might have worked out that way, except more help was needed to handle those iron shutters. The new recruit was a Pinkerton man, on Monroe's trail from Montana where he was wanted for murder. William Hanks, the Pinkerton detective, recognized Monroe by the plugs in his teeth. Hanks secretly notified Deputy Henry Leach of the impending crime and arrangements were made for the capture of the robbers. Armed guards would catch the Monroes red-faced and empty-handed.

The night was black as the four slipped up to Nesbitt's store. With long, sharp chisels covered with thick rubber sleeves, they quickly cut the hinge pins and noiselessly lowered the shutters. Cowboy Nell and the Pinkerton man watched outside while Monroe and Sanford climbed inside. Just as they reached the safe, one of the guards got nervous and ordered, "Stick 'em up!"

Monroe was shot in the leg and Sanford had jumped out the window, thinking he had escaped. Hearing a shot fired, Nell whirled on Hanks with, "You dirty s.o.b." She tried to shoot him, but he threw his arms around her and all she could do was fire into the ground.

When Sanford went to work the next day, he was arrested. Frank Pace and Jack Monahan transferred the three prisoners to Caliente to turn them over to the Deputy Sheriff. At the trial in Pioche, Sanford turned state's witness and was released. The Monroes went to prison, with nothing but time to consider what should have been done differently after they had dug Frank Pace's grave.

Burial of Sport Watkins

by Effie O. Read

Without a doubt "Sport" Watkins was Pioche's most noted eccentric. He lived among the hills of Lincoln County soon after the turn of the century. Seeking new paths but not necessarily great fortune, he became a regular fixture on the streets of Pioche. He had a slouch hat to shelter his straggling locks, hat and locks that seemed to have weathered and bleached together. He wore a faded blue shirt and his worn levis covered a pointed posterior which someone described as "So pointed, one could almost hang something on it."

He had a wide, worn leather belt doing double duty when he carried a revolver, which wasn't often and he had a wooden leg and always carried a cane. With each step his baggy britches would slip up and down as the wooden leg was short. This let his red flannel underwear show and bunch up around his waist and the ladies of the town thought that surely sooner or later his belt would fail in its purpose.

Sport worked irregularly. He mined a little, fed cattle in the wintertime and pumped water for cattle at Fifteen-Mile. He was a night watchman at Bristol for years. He lived in an old log cabin at Rose Valley where he was a hired hand for the Devlins. The Fogliani girls told how lonely it was while living on the ranch in

Northern Spring Valley and how their father needed a man to visit with, and how glad he was to see Sport Watkins drive up with a bay horse hitched to a shay, fitted with thills, or shafts.

He'd hold a job for a while but soon he'd be seen on the streets of Pioche restlessly walking from one saloon to another, drinking until he became helpless. Sometimes he was lifted from the gutter with his coat so frozen to the ground that it had to be torn from the ice. Every holiday saw him dead drunk.

Sport was indeed quite a drinking man. One Fourth of July, the young men of the town decided, when Sport was dead drunk again that day, they might just as well give him a burial.

He was soon stewed to the gills, so the men went out looking for a coffin. They found a large packing case, just the right size. They lifted him gently in and placed his head on a pillow. With hats off and heads bowed they sang, "Nearer My God to Thee." With a couple of ropes they started to lower him over an embankment when someone decided they should have a grave or at least a hole for the coffin. They delayed the burial long enough to push an old privy down the hill a yard or so. Then they proceeded to lower the corpse over the embankment and it was placed over the privy hole.

Thinking to give Sport a good scare, boards were placed over the coffin and a few pebbles were dropped on it now and then. In a short time he did awaken. The boards on top came off with a bang. He was screaming, "Get me out of here, get me out of here, I ain't dead yet. By Gad, Loui." The perpetrators of the practical joke stood off at a distance laughing raucously at the discomfiture of their victim.

Sport thought it a poor joke and began exploding, "You, you—. You'll be sorry for this. You'll see. I'll live to see every one of you buried. By Gad, Loui" and, ironical as it may seem, his malediction came to pass.

Our Family at Fay
by Myrtle Damrow Bliss

Mining towns have always been fascinating and fun places for living. Although Fay merely remains a memory, life in the mining camp, from 1912 to 1920, was lively and exciting.

Our learning days were spent in a fair-sized school house with teachers from other states who owned priceless possessions from the outside world. Miss Doll, one of our teachers, would make marvelous fudge in a beautiful, exquisite chafing dish.

When my brother and I were still small, our parents would take us with them to the dances. The children would then be bedded down in back of the stage while the place rocked with music till the wee hours of the morning. Surrounding mining camps, Goldsprings and Deer Lodge, would sometimes get together with us to see the circus in Modena, Utah.

As in all mining towns, there were fights and brawls. Once a young man was killed quarreling over a bill he owed the saloon keeper. The covered corpse lay out in the street all day while the officer in charge waited for the sheriff's arrival from Pioche. My father, Milton Damron, was the constable at Fay who made the arrest.

Modena, sixteen miles south of Fay and the nearest railroad depot, served as our post office and supply station. Mail was delivered on horseback or in buckboards and supplies were transported by wagon.

After George Moody moved away, Dad and Mother took over the post office and company store. The event of the week was mail time since I would then hear news, the latest gossip, and many stories from old-timers.

During the fall months, if the pine-nut crop was good, several bands of Indians would move in to gather the nuts. Shrewdly they traded pine-nuts for flour, bacon, sugar and other groceries and my father would then sell the pine-nuts. We stocked Jamaica Ginger, a flavoring with about 85% alcohol content and the Indians would buy all we had. Then there would be loud celebrating around the Indian camp fires while the potent ginger lasted. My mother was frightened by their boisterous noise and wouldn't leave the house until the festivities were over.

Though we worked hard and long hours, there were also lighter moments when we laughed, sang, coasted and danced, for at Fay our family frolicked.

Early in this century Pioche, in this view looking east, was a placid mining community which depended on nearby ranches to sustain its business district. The two-story wooden buildings on the left are the Deck and Price hotels. Over the hill emerges the Lincoln County courthouse.

A School Boy's View of Prince

by Arthur H. Dietz

Our family moved from Utah to Prince in the spring of 1915 when a friend wrote that work and housing was available. My father, a mining engineer, experienced the hardships of many other miners, with mines closing down because of poor ore bodies and financial troubles.

Mercur, Utah was such a town. Leaving a comfortable home, furniture, and friends was a heart-breaking experience.

The journey to Prince was real adventure. We were routed out of bed to catch the 3 a.m. train at Stockton, Utah, for the thriving rail center of Caliente.

I wanted to stay in Caliente since there were locomotives all over the place. Big ones, little ones, all belching smoke, blowing whistles, ringing bells, what a sight! But dad insisted on taking the next train to Pioche.

We rode from Pioche to Prince in a boxcar, sitting on packing boxes. My mother, used to the very best, complained, but Dad assured her that it would be a short trip to our new home.

The train finally stopped in Prince near the bunk house. The boxcar floor was high off the ground, with no ladder to get down. Spectators, all men, advised jumping, but Mom, with her long skirts, refused. Finally she wrapped the long skirts around her legs and jumped into Dad's arms.

We had dinner at Tom's Chinese boarding house and then walked down the hill past the company store to our new home, a black tar-papered abode with three small rooms. The outside toilet was convenient, since it was only about a hundred feet or so from the rear of the house. To make everything complete, running water from a faucet was not fifty feet from the back door.

My mother took a long look and commented, "Well, it's not much but we'll try to make it liveable."

The neighbors came to get acquainted and offered their help. The people next door had a new baby to show off. They were Ray Stevens' family whose wife, Birdie, was the daughter of one of the Prince Consolidated owners.

309

The town was a typical mining camp of that era—a wide, level spot surrounded by sagebrush. Actually, it was built along the sides of a wide wash, where the flood waters drained.

The mine office, with a room for the Prince post office, was centered near a row of houses. The arrival of the mail was a ritual. The oldest Baker boy, son of the mine mechanic, rode his horse three miles over the hills to Pioche with the outgoing mail, then returned before noon with the incoming. People gathered at the office early to spin yarns, gossip, and visit. When Baker arrived on the gallop, the natives' day was complete, whether they got any mail or not.

The only store in town was the one owned by the mining company. The store carried a few items of clothing, occasionally a few vegetables and cheese, some canned goods, always-tough meat, and lots of beer and liquor which was served in the back room.

Activity for the miners centered around Chinaman Tom's boarding house, and the company bunk house. A most memorable experience was the chiming of the dinner bell as it summoned the miners to break bread. The cook would use a steel rod to clang the sides of a huge triangle, fashioned from a long drill bit by the mine blacksmith, which could be heard across town.

The bunk house was equipped with a shower bath which we frequented to wash away the black dust blowing from the ore bins. Each leg of the bunk house beds stood in a can of coal oil to keep away bed bugs and other pests.

The company barn stood across the road from the bunk house. A few saddle horses and a beautiful team of matched black horses were kept there. Ralph Jarvis, the teamster, often let me drive the team to the mine with him. He would haul dynamite and, when delivering caps, he rode alone.

The one-room school house was furnished with only a few double desks and two students at each desk. Our teacher had a fairly easy time with only twelve pupils on three or four different grade levels.

A pipeline carried air from the compressor house at the Prince mine to Castleton. Suspended on crossed timbers a few feet above the ground, it passed close to the school, and sometimes we would walk home from school along the pipeline rather than down the road.

Coyotes were common near Prince. One bright, moonlit night we counted five of them howling at the moon, hardly fifty feet from the house. My dad raised chickens and built a coop out of crates from the grocery store. The coyotes would reach between the slats or climb the fence until we encased the coop with chicken wire. No one ever killed a coyote—people accepted them as a part of that great wilderness.

In the early summer of 1915, the residents watched a strange caravan approaching from the direction of Pioche. Four canvas covered wagons drawn by teams of horses stopped near our house and the drivers jumped down, each carrying a pitchfork. Welcomed by the crowd, they told their story. They were farmers from the Mormon settlement Panaca whose cherries and peaches were ripe but they had no market for their fruit since they were not allowed to peddle in Pioche. In desperation, these farmers loaded their wagons, armed themselves with pitchforks, and started out. Authorities could not stop that group of determined farmers who sold most of their load in Pioche and still had plenty left for the people at Prince. Grateful for the fresh fruit, Prince citizens shared lunch and cold drinks and invited them to return the following year.

One summer evening, Ray Stevens took me for a ride on the company railroad "speeder" to inspect some track up near the mine. It was a nice trip until Ray decided we had gone far enough and turned back.

Mr. Lee, one of the shop workers at the mine, had a few cows which he turned loose to feed along the railroad right of way. On our return trip, one of the cows, frightened by the "speeder," jumped on the track in front of us. We hit it broadside and were both thrown off, suffering cuts and torn clothes. The "speeder" went one way and the cow another. The

Cowboys are preparing for a round-up on the Delmue Ranch. The engine (at left) ran between the Prince mine and the town of Pioche, hauling ore.

cow was badly cut, one long horn broken off and, after a few minutes rest, got up and limped away. After a lot of hauling and tugging, our vehicle was back on the track and once the fan blades were straightened and the dirt cleaned off the engine, we left for home.

On the Fourth of July, 1915, our neighbors and my parents decided on an all day picnic. Since no autos, except postmaster Robb's Ford roadster, nor buggy horses were available, we decided to take the repaired "speeder" with a railroad hand car hitched on to it. It was a beautiful day so we traveled past Pioche to Delmue's ranch, not far from the railroad tracks.

Mrs. Delmue and some of the menfolks welcomed us and showed us around the house. A large gun rack in the center of the front room displayed several lever action rifles and much ammunition which once had been necessary to fight off marauding Indians and outlaws!

Resuming our trip, the tracks soon passed through some deep cuts in the canyon walls and that was our picnic site. We feasted on sandwiches, cake and cans of meat loaf. However, the ice in the lemonade had melted, so we drank it warm.

After lunch we continued on to Panaca, a tiny farming settlement. At a small store we bought ice cream cones—a welcome treat on a hot day. We returned to Prince in the cool of the evening, with fond memories.

Small pine trees grew on the flats west of town, and when the pine cones burst with ripe nuts, we would gather them with the neighbors. We quickly learned—never climb a tree to get the cones. The trees were dripping with pitch and no matter how careful we were, pitch was all over our clothes, on our hands and faces, and even in our hair. We were a mess. Back home we were scrubbed with coal oil and sent to bed.

A neighbor showed us how to heat the cones in a small covered pit. The nuts were warm and delicious and the whole neighborhood had a feast.

Tracks leading to the ore bins crossed the road near the bunk house and were connected to the main line with a hand operated switch. Once, when a few of us were walking along this track, we wanted to act like real railroad men and open the switch. It opened easily and we shifted the track to one side but we were unable to close the track. It just wouldn't budge, so we panicked and ran for home with the switch half open.

When the engine, at slow speed, came to pick up cars, it gently jumped the track and traveled only a short distance on the ties. A work crew was hastily called over from the mine and they worked the rest of the day sweating, swearing and jacking the engine back onto the track.

I watched them later in the afternoon and over-heard that they thought the switch might have been tampered with by some small boys. But thinking the switch was too heavy for children to operate, they blamed it on some disgruntled worker. I appreciated those kind words and they made a lasting impression with me.

311

School Daze

by Ruth Bradley Wilkinson

I first began to appreciate life after living in a mining camp, teaching school and making my home in a flimsy tent.

The year was 1940. After finishing two years of college, I had to select a place to teach. City jobs were offered to me but the prospect of adventure in Nevada mining country prevailed. The only thing I feared, without justification, were the Indians.

I traveled by train to Caliente and caught a ride to Alamo. From there a guide brought me to Tempiute.

"This is the place!" announced the guide. That remark sounded familiar enough. "This is the place" did someone say? Maybe this *was* the place—but *is* the place, no! Maybe I should have looked around more. Maybe this is only the outskirts of some town, or the *outer* outskirts. My guide insisted, "This is the town. Tempiute!" No need arguing. My years of schooling had given me a slight inkling that maybe I wasn't always right.

There I was surrounded by tents and not even a feather for my hair. My floppy picture hat and thin silk hose were definitely not appropriate in those surroundings. Walking through town, I saw a door crack open every now and then. The tents didn't have windows. Once or twice I heard a giggle or a snicker, but definitely no war whoops. We approached a combination of three tents built together. "This is the boarding house," said the guide. But I could tell that by the odors, and I only thought to myself, you are so right! "Mrs. Hyde will take care of you now," said my guide who never made a comment on the sixty mile trip from Alamo. He now made a hasty retreat and I followed the odors into the boarding house.

"Well, the new teacher. I declare! Have you been in the school house yet?" asked Mrs. Hyde.

"No—I—" "It's that tent down in the corner. It's the only one that the company can spare. It has a few holes in it, but they plan to build a schoolhouse out of wood soon. They expect more men out with families—that is, if you stay."

My numbed brain was taking in so many things, but finally it got to "if you stay." If I'd stay—I had to. Hadn't I turned down a school by my home town to come to Nevada for adventure? As I recalled my mother's last words before I left, "Remember, you have to stick it out." Ah,—the mortgage on the old homestead, and no heroes within miles, I didn't suppose, to offer me help. There were plenty of villains—no doubt!

"Where—will. . . ."

"Where will you live? In one corner of the schoolhouse, and you can eat right here." Mrs. Hyde's bright eyes were really taking in my reactions. In one corner of a 14' × 16' tent—I'd lose myself. "I charge a dollar a day—payable when and if you get your check."

"Well, let's make with the hash." Did I say that? It wouldn't have been Mrs. Hyde.

"Come in. Do come in. Everything is about ready."

So I entered my first boarding house. It had long tables with long benches. Everything looked clean and cheerful.

"My four daughters," said Mrs. Hyde.

"Hi," they all said in unison.

"Howdy," I found myself saying.

"Are you really going to stay after seeing the joint?" came from one of the girls.

"Raeola, set the table and shut up!"

Just as the table-setting was finished I saw Mrs. Hyde push a stray lock from her eyes and clang a bell. A group of men came rushing in. I soon discovered no end seats, so me and my long legs, we hoisted over a bench. Then I looked around—possibly 45 men I counted. I began to wonder if I couldn't cook my meals in one corner of that tent. "Men," piped up Mrs. Hyde, "This is Miss Bradley, our new school teacher. Please help me make her feel to home."

Immediately a rush of food came my way. It was good, and I ate like a horse. Two or three men, close around, started talking to me. It didn't take me long to find out that all the men were married but six. Some of them spoke of bringing out their families if I stayed. I found myself picturing three tents built together for the schoolhouse. "We play horseshoes right out in front every night. Drop around, if you'd like to play."

"Sure thing."

In a whispered voice I heard Sam say, "I wish they would make this coffee stronger and slice the cheese thicker they put on my sandwiches. I dropped a piece down a crack in the mill floor today and couldn't get it out." I soon found out that Sam could joke about anything. He said he had taught school 'till they passed a law that teachers had to be able to read and write.

After supper I dropped down to see my place. In one corner was a bed and across the other, in the back of the tent was a rope for my clothes. A wash-stand and a wood heater were up in front, and seven desks were arranged in between. My trunk would arrive in a day or two, and everything would be all right. But I felt a lump growing in my throat. I felt a couple of salty tears roll down my cheek, but just then I heard the clang of horseshoes. Hurriedly I brushed the tears away and walked up to the horseshoe set-up. I was asked to join a game. One man offered to show me how to hold the horseshoe. I decided not to tell him that my father had taught me all kinds of sports, including horseshoes. He was very proud of his teaching, and I soon forgot my homesickness. One of the Hyde girls called for us to come up and sing.

Come up and sing—this was really the life—horseshoes and singing for entertainment. I glanced at these men as we walked to the boarding house. So these were the rough and tough miners I'd heard so much about. They were going to the boarding house to sing.

Mrs. Hyde was playing a popular tune, and the girls were singing. Mr. Hyde was seated in a comfortable-looking chair reading last week's edition of the paper read at camp. The mail didn't come in too often. After an enjoyable interlude of singing, we sat down and talked a while. They heard most of my life's story to that date, and I heard some of theirs. One man had real tears in his eyes when he talked about his wonderful family. He hoped they'd come out now that there was a teacher here. I was beginning to think I was quite important and also wondering if I were really good enough to be a teacher. It looked like I'd better be.

"Well—nine o'clock. Time to hit-the-hay," John spoke up.

"Good-night, everybody."

"Good-night."

We all walked out, and I headed for my corner in the tent. The lump had gone, and I felt right at home. One man called out, "You're all right, teacher."

I remembered that, "You're all right, teacher," in the night when the storm started. The roof had a few leaks, and although I was wondering how I'd bathe in a wash basin I wasn't ready for a shower. I had to move the cot three times.

Morning arrived, and the sun came out, and I forgot the storm. I heard the breakfast bell and dashed up to eat. The air smelled so pure and fresh.

"How are you this morning, Miss Bradley?" one of the men asked.

"I really feel great. This is a grand climate up here in the hills. I always wondered why they put mines up in the hills."

Some of the men looked at me a little puzzled and a few others laughed out loud.

"Good luck!" the men called as they rode off to work after breakfast. That brought me back. I dashed down to school to straighten up the few books they had in a small book-case. Promptly at 5 minutes to 9 I stepped out and with an old cow-bell rang the warning bell. I felt very important doing it. The Hyde girls came running down and three Koyen children, old enough to go to school, came over from their house. The boy had the words "Dead-Eye-Dick" written on his belt with shining nail-heads. He spit a couple of times before entering. I was relieved to notice it wasn't tobacco.

When all seven were seated, for a moment I felt a little frightened, but finally I cleared my throat and started the welcoming speech I had been preparing all summer. It went over all right, so I decided my summer's work wasn't wasted. I had a list of things to do during the year. We started in, and I'm sure we did most of them that day. After school I made up my first school schedule and read the first note written about me. Decided not to read anymore.

Later there were many other "first days" of school for me but that day in the tent classroom at Tempiute will always be the most memorable.

Tempiute, an old silver camp of the 1860's, came back in 1940 as a tungsten camp centered around the Lincoln mines company operations. School was held in the brown tent.

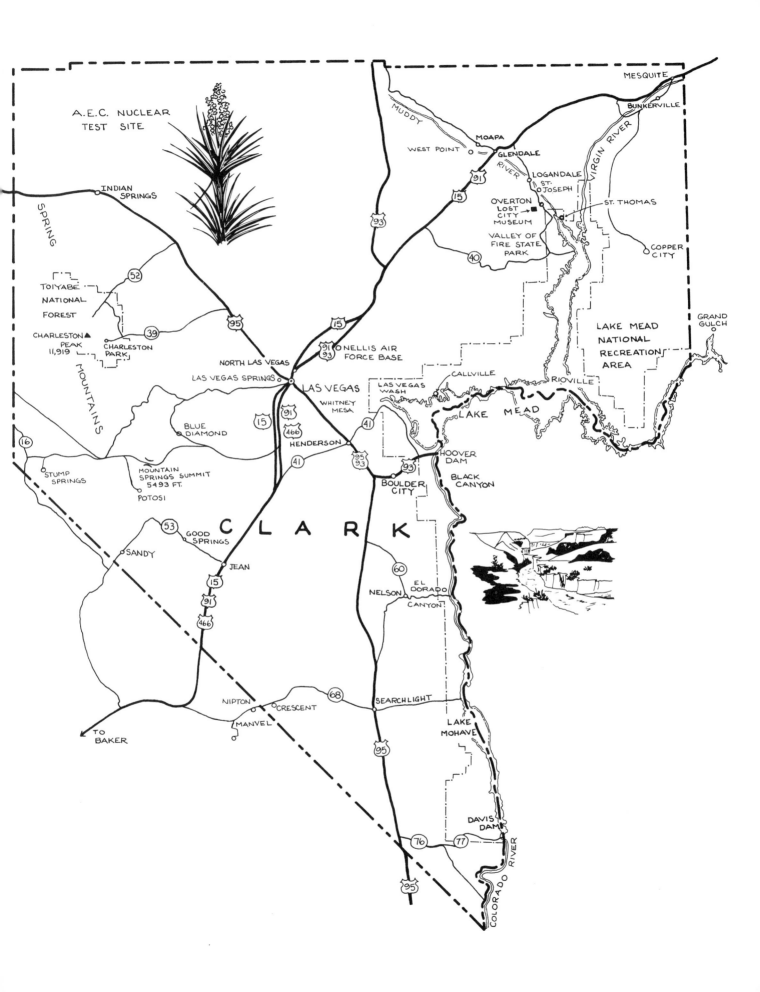

A.E.C. NUCLEAR
TEST SITE

INDIAN
SPRINGS

SPRING

TOIYABE
NATIONAL
FOREST

CHARLESTON ▲
PEAK
11,919

CHARLESTON
PARK

MOUNTAINS

52

39

95

NORTH LAS VEGAS

LAS VEGAS SPRINGS

BLUE
DIAMOND

15

91

466

WHITNEY
MESA

LAS VEGAS

15

91

466

HENDERSON

41

MUDDY

WEST POINT

MOAPA

GLENDALE

RIVER

91

LOGANDALE
ST.
JOSEPH

OVERTON
LOST
CITY
MUSEUM

ST. THOMAS

VIRGIN RIVER

15

93

VALLEY
OF
FIRE STATE
PARK

40

COPPER
CITY

MESQUITE

BUNKERVILLE

LAKE MEAD
NATIONAL
RECREATION
AREA

GRAND
GULCH

CALLVILLE

RIOVILLE

LAS VEGAS
WASH

41

LAKE MEAD

16

STUMP
SPRINGS

MOUNTAIN
SPRINGS SUMMIT
5493 FT.

POTOSI

95
93

41

HOOVER
DAM

BOULDER
CITY

BLACK
CANYON

C L A R K

53

GOOD
SPRINGS

SANDY

JEAN

15

91

466

60

NELSON

EL
DORADO

CANYON

NIPTON

CRESCENT

MANVEL

68

SEARCHLIGHT

95

LAKE
MOHAVE

TO
BAKER

DAVIS
DAM

76

77

95

COLORADO RIVER

Clark County

First in Vegas Valley

by Frank Maggio

In preparing my book, *Las Vegas Calling*, research led me to the fascinating possibility that Las Vegas Valley was first seen by a courageous teenager whose exploits have gone unheralded, unrewarded, and almost completely unheard of. While his exciting story was not overlooked by historians, it was not given its proper prominence in works dealing with man's epic struggles to conquer the West.

The discoverer was Rafael Rivera and the events of his story take us back 145 years. With diaries and records as guides, all facts point to Rivera as being the first white man to enter Las Vegas Valley.

In late 1829, Rafael Rivera was a scout for Antonio Armijo, trail boss of a Mexican trade caravan that pushed out of Albiquiu, New Mexico on a hazardous journey to probe the desert and mountains north and west of that Spanish colony to determine a feasible route of commerce to Los Angeles. The group of about sixty Spaniards equipped with horses and a team of pack mules embarked on their journey on November 7, 1829.

Only one known contemporary document relates the details of the caravan's long dangerous trek through barren, gameless desert lands. This document is the extremely brief diary of Antonio Armijo, the caravan leader.

Armijo was not the most honorable of men. As a matter of fact, he was a rogue with a temperamental and stubborn streak, but he was a courageous and intelligent leader.

Wisely, his caravan traveled during the cool winter months. The desert heat from June to September would have been unbearable. In spite of the comfortable weather, however, it was rugged going. They pushed on through areas of southcentral Utah and the northwestern corner of Arizona, heading south along the west bank of the Virgin River and into present-day Nevada southward to the point where it joined the Colorado River, about 70 miles directly east of present Las Vegas. The entries for the rest of the journey from the Virgin River to Whitney Mesa in Las Vegas, are the most intriguing and mysterious portions of Armijo's diary.

According to Armijo's records of December 25 through January 6, Rafael Rivera got lost in the Virgin River area and was gone for 12 days. "We hit the Severo River again, from which point the reconnaissance party went out. . . . At the same river the reconnaissance party rendezvoused. . . . Again at the (Colorado): Citizen Rafael Rivera is missing from the reconnaissance party of the day before. . . . Stopping: on this day the reconnaissance party went in search of Rivera. . . . Stopping: reconnaissance party returned and did not find Rivera. . . . At Yerba del Arroyo, at which point the reconnaissance party goes out in search of Rivera."

Armijo leads us to think that his experienced and daring outdoorsman is lost. The next entry reads: "Stopping: waiting for the reconnaissance party. Citizen Rivera returned and announced that he had discovered the villages of the Cucha Payuches and the Hayatas. . . ."

Rivera must have made elaborate preparations for his solo scouting trip or he never would have made it. He carefully accumulated adequate provisions from the supply burros—dried meat, beans, horseshoes, hobbles, grain, warm clothing, water and other necessities. He took enough to cache supplies for his return journey. When all was ready, he rode southwest from Armijo's caravan through the vast, inhospitable desert.

From the debouchure of the Virgin River into the Colorado, he continued along its north side to where the Las Vegas Wash comes in from the north. At this junction no rider could travel farther because the Colorado turned sharply into deep and frightening Black Canyon, now the site of Hoover Dam.

Rivera traveled due west toward present-day Henderson where, from an elevated area he gasped at his first panoramic view of The Meadows. Lush green Las Vegas Valley lay before him. It was January and looking due west he could see the welcome sight of the snow-capped Mount Charleston in the Spring Mountain Range. This was good. The snow indicated that there would be plenty of water and, equally important, game would roam the foothills. He hobbled his horse

and left it to graze by the wash, while he rested and studied Las Vegas Valley.

He could not help but notice that the terrain from the wash to the Spring Mountain range was a patchwork of variable paths. Some beckoned, others were uninviting. It was nature's way of telling him which way to travel.

To the southwest, there was a lava rock plain that stretched for more than ten miles. This lava bed is located along the Henderson cutoff looking westward to the freeway. It would have been impossible to ride through there because a horse's hoofs would be worn to the quick in a matter of a few miles. Also there was no sign of feed in that direction.

The only route to follow was along the wash. Due west was the course of least resistance, since traveling along dry washbeds is a common course of travel. The wash angled westerly in two directions, the left arm extending directly to present-day Whitney Mesa (site of Southern Nevada Vocational Technical School).

From the mesa, Rivera plainly saw the lava rock bed extending to the south. Looking west, he could see the sun go down behind Mount Potosi.

The rider then headed due west. At the base of the mountains he found the bubbling waters of the "little Spring of the Turtle" (Cottonwood Spring, in Blue Diamond). He and his horse feasted and watered, and then he pushed westward to discover Stump Spring in Pahrump Valley and also Resting Springs, near Tecopa, California.

His tremendous courage did not give out here; he continued to press on to the Amargosa and Mojave Rivers. (The Mojave River in the Barstow area is 153 miles west of Las Vegas.) Elated, the jubilant explorer rushed back, with good news of his newly found route, to Armijo and the caravan that was camped at the Las Vegas Wash. He had made an incredible round trip.

Significantly, Rivera's intrepid journey welded a critical link through southern Nevada in what soon became the famous Old Spanish Trail. In his separation from the caravan for 13 days, he covered 506 miles, averaging 43 miles daily in very cool weather. This was a fantastic round trip journey for a young man who was "lost" and not familiar with southwestern terrain.

Noted historians have confirmed Rivera's primacy as trail blazer. Le Roy Hafen acclaims Rivera as the "pioneer scout of the Antonio Armijo caravan which in 1829–1830 was opening a trade route from Santa Fe to Los Angeles. . . . He deserves high honor as the first white man to see and explore the Las Vegas region."

In commenting on the phenomenal ride, Elbert Edwards gives this graphic account of the hardened young scout: "Alone, with only his horse for physical and moral support, he had traveled over hundreds of miles of desert wastes and through the lands of strange and unknown Indian tribes. He had sought out life-sustaining water holes and mentally mapped out a route along which to lead his companions to their destination. . . . He was, without doubt, the first caucasian to look upon and traverse the Las Vegas Valley. His name, however, was hidden for more than 120 years. . . ."

For decades, others have been credited with discovering Las Vegas Valley. Francisco Garces reached the areas of the extreme southern tip of Nevada in 1776, but whether or not he even entered Nevada is in serious dispute. In that same year Francisco Escalante led a small nine-man party to southwestern Utah, but he, too, failed to enter Las Vegas Valley. Jedediah Smith blazed many trails, but the nearest he came to Las Vegas was about 75 miles, in November 1826.

In 1829 the Kit Carson-Ewing Young party travelled in the vicinity of the Mojave River, in the modern Barstow, California area. Fifteen years later Kit arrived in Las Vegas with John C. Fremont. There is no mention in Fremont's extensive journals that his scout,

The terrain in the picture at left looks much the same today as it did when Rivera crossed it 145 years ago. The setting is in the Cottonwood Springs area. "Vegas" was then situated in the midst of a vast, inhospitable desert as shown on this map of 1850. Nomadic Indians roamed the area.

Kit Carson, knew Las Vegas, though Fremont praised his scout's knowledge of other areas familiar to him. Fremont came to Las Vegas Valley 14 years after Armijo's young scout arrived here.

Who was first in Vegas Valley? Southern Paiutes had visited the valley for centuries, camping out at Las Vegas Springs. These nomads roamed the area, making temporary dwellings near the springs in wintertime. But the first non-native was, without a doubt, Rafael Rivera.

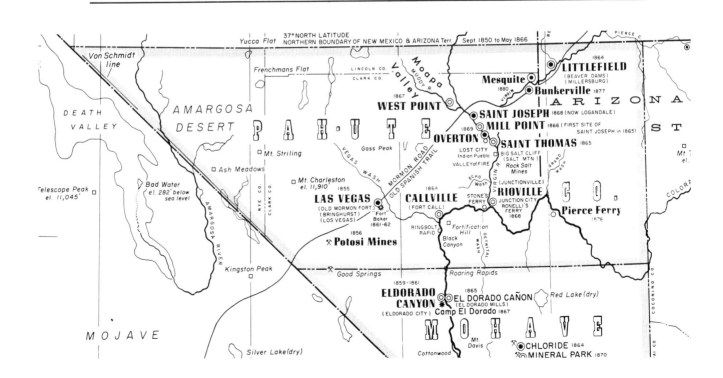

The Lost County of Pah-Ute

by Donald Bufkin

Twelve thousand square miles of present day Nevada, the equivalent of an area larger than the State of Maryland, was once the northwestern portion of Arizona territory. The expansive tract of land embraces all of Clark and parts of Lincoln and Nye counties.

It is not inconceivable that, but for the legislative wiles of Nevada's illustrious Senator William Morris Stewart aided by his colleague Senator James Warren Nye in the mid-1860's, Las Vegas might today be one of Arizona's principal cities rather than the Nevada gambling capital.

The land which later became Pah-Ute County was part of New Mexico Territory from September 1850, until the creation of Arizona Territory on February 24, 1863. During this period of better than twelve years only two settlements of any consequence were attempted. The first and most noteworthy, although not successful, was a Mormon colony at Las Vegas (The Meadows), a favorably located camping and watering site on the Spanish Trail from Santa Fe to Los Angeles, and on the Mormon Road from Salt Lake City to San Bernardino.

The colonists, led by William Bringhurst, president of Las Vegas Mission, arrived at the site in June 1855, 36 days after departing from Salt Lake City. The settlers constructed a "fort" and began farming and stock raising with some attempts in 1856–57 to work the rich lead-silver deposits at Potosi, 25 miles southwest of Las Vegas. After nearly two years of struggles with the elements and the constant Indian thievery, most of the Mormons left the mission in March 1857. A few who remained were recalled in 1858 during the Johnston Army troubles in Utah.

The other settlement was one entirely different from agricultural Las Vegas. In the winter of 1857–58, Captain George Alonzo Johnson proceeded up the Colorado from Yuma in the river steamer *General Jesup,* reaching El Dorado Canyon. In 1861 the first promising ore specimens were discovered. Claims were located, sporadic mining began, and a camp of several hundred flourished in the canyon.

The Territory of Arizona was organized in February 1863. The first territorial legislature created Mohave County out of the northwest part of Arizona. It was during the second legislative session in December 1865 that the act creating Pah-Ute County was approved. The enactment specified Callville as the county seat and the governor appointed the necessary county officers.

The history of settlement in the northwestern corner of Arizona Territory lying generally north and west of the Colorado River was, except for mining in El Dorado Canyon, coincidental with Mormon attempts to consolidate a corridor of communities between Utah and California.

As early as 1849, Mormon leaders envisioned a State of "Deseret" and took the first steps to make the hope a reality. At a convention held in Salt Lake city in March 1849 a constitution was adopted, a provisional government organized, and boundaries proposed which encompassed all of what was later Utah and most of present Arizona and Nevada, along with generous portions of other states.

Congress was asked later in 1849 to admit this expansive region as a state. The dream, at least on this grand scale, was short-lived for on September 9, 1850, the proposed area was divided into the Territories of Utah (even the name Deseret did not survive) and New Mexico, and the southwestern portion was included in the State of California.

With the territorial organization of 1850 denying full realization of Deseret and the corridor to the sea for the Mormon brethren, a belated modification of the concept was implemented. Late in 1864 Anson W. Call was dispatched to the head of navigation on the Colorado River to locate a favorable site for a riverport and to build wharves and warehouse facilities for the transfer of goods and passengers traveling on the Colorado River between points farther inland and the Gulf of California seaports of Guaymas and Mazatlan, Mexico.

The site became known as Callville. Indications of its initial success are noted in the Salt Lake *Daily Telegraph* of November 24, 1865, not quite a year after the founding of the town. The newspaper story credited the Pacific & Colorado Navigation Company with maintaining riverboat service via the steamers *Esmeralda* and *Nina Tilden* between Callville and the mouth of the Colorado river connecting with ocean vessels to San Francisco.

Waning activity at Callville in 1867 was apparent when the county seat was lost in October. The Colorado River also contributed to the eventual demise of the town. Navigation had been hazardous at best and impossible when the river level was low, thus Callville was without inhabitants by June of 1869.

Other Mormon settlements founded in Pah-Ute County enjoyed a greater measure of success and permanency by their reliance on a traditional farming economy. The Virgin and the Muddy Rivers offered the most favorable agricultural development and missionary activities among the Indians. The western reaches of Pah-Ute County contained no major river valleys. Only Las Vegas, first inhabited in 1855, and the Potosi Mines, worked sporadically after 1856, existed in that desert area.

Prophetically fearing that action adverse to Arizona might be taken by Congress in response to proposals to alter the boundaries of the western states and territories, a joint resolution of the Arizona Territorial Legislative Assembly was approved on December 28, 1865, asking that the boundary lines between California, Nevada, and Arizona be fixed by government survey.

Reference was made to rapid settlement in conjunction with the rich mineral deposits and growing agricultural wealth being developed as necessitating a solution to the vague boundaries then in existence.

Foreboding of possible changes was also apparent by the organization of Lincoln County, Nevada, in February 1866. Carved out of large and sparsely settled Nye County, the act creating Lincoln County provided that should boundaries of the State of Nevada be extended in the future to the east and to the south, then the boundaries of that county were to be similarly extended.

Nevada had achieved territorial status when separated from Utah in 1861. In July of 1862 it had gained one degree (approximately sixty miles) of area along the entire length of the common boundary with Utah. On October 31, 1864, Nevada attained statehood and was represented in the Senate of the United States by James W. Nye, the ex-Territorial Governor of Nevada, and by William M. Stewart, the able and forceful Comstock mining lawyer. Upon assuming their seats in the Senate both men immediately began to work for boundary extensions in southern Nevada.

Nevada's acceptance of the Congressional Act of May 1866 had extended the jurisdiction of Lincoln County over most of Pah-Ute County and created a state of confusion that was to continue until 1871. The overlapping county governments, coupled with ill-defined state and territorial boundaries, made conditions exceedingly difficult for the residents of the disputed area. Apart from the Arizona-Nevada situation, a similar confusion existed between Utah and Nevada in the area.

In understandable sympathy with the plight of the Mormon farmers in the Virgin and Muddy River valleys, the Utah body established Rio Virgen County on February 18, 1869. The intent of the Utah legislature was, however, to attempt the extension of Utah jurisdiction over the disputed area in response to requests of the inhabitants, most of whom had originally emigrated from Utah. Saint Joseph was designated the seat of Rio Virgen County and appointments were made to county offices.

In the same month Utah established Rio Virgen County, Nevada's legislature passed an act placing all tax transactions on a coin basis, a condition Mormon settlers found impossible to meet.

Early in December 1870, a boundary survey showed that Virgin and Muddy River communities were indeed in Nevada. Two months later the sixth Arizona Territorial Legislature repealed the act which created Pah-Ute County and thereby relinquished any lingering claims on the disputed area. The Mormon farmers secured the permission of the church elders, Brigham Young himself acknowledging the gravity of the situation, to return to Utah, leaving their towns and farms to the mercy of Lincoln County's tax collectors. On February 20, 1871, James Leithead, leading a large group of farmers and their families, departed from Saint Thomas, bound for Utah, following the same route along the Virgin River toward Saint George, over which many had come seven years previously. Only the family of Daniel Bonelli remained, concentrating farming and commercial enterprises at Rioville near the junction of the Virgin and Colorado Rivers, later known as Bonelli's Ferry.

The Mormon exodus retarded settlement and development in the area for more than a decade. A few of the original families returned after 1881 to take up farming and re-establish community life, this time as acknowledged citizens of Nevada.

John N. Goodwin, the former Arizona Territorial Governor, and at the time Territorial Delegate to the House of Representatives, said in resisting the passage of the first bill to extend Nevada's southeastern boundary at the expense of Arizona:

"There is no natural connection between those Territories. This portion of the Territory of Arizona is part of the watershed of the Colorado River. All streams running through the Territory empty into the Colorado. The people receive their supplies up the Colorado River. . . . All their connections and business are with the Territory of Arizona. Now, if they were annexed to the State of Nevada they would be obliged, in order to reach the capital [of Nevada] either to go round by San Francisco or to go up nearly to the point of the overland mail route before they could get into the route leading to the capital. . . . It is separated from that State by a portion of the great desert [a reference to Death Valley]."

The argument of the delegate from Arizona was to no avail and the bill was approved on May 5, 1866, upon the condition of acceptance by the State of Nevada. The Arizona Territorial Legislature twice protested by petitioning Congress to rescind its action, but the legislature of Nevada accepted this federal gift by an act passed on January 18, 1867. This action, however, did not end the existence of Pah-Ute County and the *de facto* Arizona authority over the area in question.

As evidence of continued association with Arizona Territory, Pah-Ute County was represented in the Arizona Territorial Legislature as late as 1868.

The Last Indian Raid

by Alberta Perkins

On a bright, warm winter morning, February 20, 1866, the largest and possibly the last successful Indian raid in southern Nevada took place near St. Joseph on the Muddy River.

The Mormon settlers, who lived in an area called The Island, had just come through a harsh winter without great losses. There was a hint of spring in the air as they looked over the natural pasture that the Lord had provided for them.

The native grasses grew in abundance, and although not as good as in summer, it was plenty good enough to winter stock on. The Island, comprised of several hundred acres, was too wet and marshy to farm but was adequate for both winter and summer grazing. The banks were steep on all sides and only the spot next to the settlement could be forded—an important consideration for the safety of the settlers.

The farming area, a sandy bench, was high and dry and more healthy than the mosquito-infested low lands.

On this February day, several men went to find a cow that had strayed. A few cows were kept close to the settlement for milking but on that morning no stock could be seen.

Suddenly they came across a bridge that had just been constructed, but by someone outside the settlement. "All our horses are gone, too," shouted the men as they raced on foot to spread the alarm.

Although a runner was sent to St. Thomas and a party of ten men took up the trail by foot, they soon realized that they were no match for the mounted Indians. Tracks led up the valley to the California crossing, then west toward Las Vegas Springs.

A group of horsemen from St. Thomas had caught up with them and continued the chase. They soon came across the first of many butchered animals. Although they searched for days, not one of the animals was found alive.

How could this happen? According to historians, the Indians acted out of character. The Southern Paiute had been described by John C. Fremont as the "lowest type of Indians in the American West." Their diet consisted of lizards, grasshoppers, grass seeds, mesquite beans, and anything else they could catch or gather.

This group of primitive Indians, on foot, crept up to the Island, built a bridge strong enough to hold livestock, and then stole horses and seventy head of cattle right from under the settlers' noses.

The raid almost wiped out the settlement and brought about such a furor that family records of the pioneers include letters dated as much as 25 years later to Washington, D.C., requesting compensation for the losses. The guilty parties left the area, never knowing that they had participated in the last Indian raid in southern Nevada.

This 1925 Pahute pageant depicted the life of ancient people who inhabited the area now known as Lost City. The Pahutes were very apt in the parts they played in the pageant.

Brigham Young in Nevada

by Elbert Edwards

Few men in history have had greater influence on the political, economic, social and spiritual affairs of men in a given area than has Brigham Young in the Great Basin region during the period white men first began to occupy this area. Nevada was included within the sphere of his forceful leadership.

The growth of the Mormon Church during the 1850's resulted in planting colonies in favorable sites within the Great Basin. Mormons led in the settlement of Carson Valley in the extreme western part of then Utah Territory which, within a very few years, developed a thriving agricultural and pastoral economy.

Similarly Young ordered the settlement of Las Vegas, then in the extreme northwestern part of New Mexico Territory. However, anticipation of trouble with Washington officials led to an evacuation of these settlements in the fall of 1857.

In 1858, fearful that a renewal of Mormon persecution would force another exodus from their established homes, Young sent well organized exploring parties into the interior of the Great Basin in search of new home sites. These expeditions provided the first exhaustive exploration of the vast desert areas of the southern part of present Nevada and led to the establishment of Panaca, southern Nevada's first permanent settlement.

The ever growing population of Utah, with the attendant problems of supply transport from distant places led the president of the church to seek new routes and new sources. In 1864 the dynamic Young directed the construction of Callville on the Colorado River, at a point only thirty miles east of Las Vegas, in order to utilize the river in the development of a system of transportation.

In conjunction with the river system there was to be established a line of settlements to provide service to the travelers who came by the river headed for points in Utah. To serve this function, and also for the purpose of cotton production, president Young directed the settlement of the Muddy Valley.

Accordingly, on January 8, 1865, a small wagon train formed a circle on a flat near the confluence of the Muddy River with the Virgin. The resulting community was named St. Thomas. Subsequently other settlements were made at different points along the valley to be named St. Joseph, Overton and West Point.

By act of Congress, taken in 1866, the newly created State of Nevada was expanded to include these southern communities. Prior to 1870 the location of the dividing line was one of controversy. Lincoln County officials demanded taxes from the settlers of Meadow

Valley and along the Muddy River and the Mormon colonists resisted, pending an official boundary survey.

While Young had sent hundreds of colonists into the southern desert areas, and had received regular reports from the missions through the years, he had never visited these outlying settlements. In 1870 he decided to do so.

To be visited by the president of the church was the greatest honor that Mormon communities could hope for. As he approached the small community of Washington in southern Utah, a local unit of cavalry, an artillery company and martial units escorted him into St. George; there the entire population greeted him. Little flower girls, dressed in white, scattered green branches before his carriage and tossed spring blossoms as he passed.

With the announcement that he intended to visit the communities on the Muddy and Virgin Rivers also came the word that he wished to cross the Colorado River and explore northern Arizona. A member of Young's party wondered who could furnish a flatboat capable of carrying a wagon and team across the Colorado.

Here was an opportunity for special honor. St. Thomas and St. Joseph had no martial bands or uniformed militia, but they could provide a flat boat for

321

the convenience of their beloved president. Such was the word that was sent back by Bishop James Leithead.

That there was no timber within sixty miles over a country with no roads and scarcely any water, made no difference. Teams were sent to the mountains for logs. When they arrived a saw pit was erected in a small grove of cottonwoods that was large enough to provide a little shade. The logs were then smoothed and whipsawed for the frame, siding, and floor inside and out. The planking was then hauled the 25 miles to the Colorado River where it was assembled, caulked, pitched and launched, ready to ferry the president and his party across the river.

But, disappointing to the laborers, the boat was not to be used. The barren deserts of the Arizona side of the river, across from the mouth of the Virgin, offered nothing to challenge Young's curiosity. Disillusioned, Bishop Leithead wrote, "All that labor and expense was thrown away so far as we were concerned."

The completion of the boundary survey proved the communities in question were well within Nevada and the Lincoln County Sheriff prepared to enforce the collection of back taxes, payable in gold. President Young, now aware that his Nevada followers operated exclusively on a barter system and could not meet the demands for specie, released them from their mission. Again Nevada experienced an economic setback in the exodus of these industrious settlers.

The church's advocacy of the United Order under Young's administration led Edward Bunker and Dudley Leavitt to shepherd a small group of members to establish Bunkerville on the broad flats of the Virgin River in 1877. This stable agricultural community was later supplemented by another called Mesquite, just across the river and to the northeast of the older community.

Nor were the lands of the Muddy Valley to be idle for long. In 1880 Mormons returned to the old town sites and acquired the land rights. The dedication of the new settlers to the principles of the church has, through the years, contributed to the development of Nevada.

Fight for Survival
by Kenley Reese

The history of the Virgin River communities of Bunkerville and Mesquite is a tale of men against the river. Since the first settlers came to the valley in 1877 and set up camp on the southeast side of the river, in the vicinity of Bunkerville, the struggle between man and river has remained the central theme of survival. The conflict began on the first day the irrigation canal was started.

That first summer the new settlers saw what the future held for them, losing their dam three times before the meager, burned-up crops were harvested that fall. Yet the 27 people knew if their first crops failed, many of them would not see another year. Desperately, feverishly, they turned to the task of replacing the dam with tons of rock, trees and brush, but each time the river swelled and swept away their labors.

The sandy riverbed bottom was ever widening and shifting. The river had to be dammed across the entire channel, since water at low tide had to be diverted into the canal. Rocks sank in the quicksand, and the trees and brush were carried away. Yet, when it was possible to get any semblance of a solid dam, it would hold until the river had filled the ditch canal with silt, sand and floating debris, only to be torn away, doubling the work of establishing an irrigation system.

After every major flood, the men held conferences to decide whether or not to stay and battle the river again. Despite the backbreaking labor and the knowledge that the destruction might be repeated over and over again, the settlers voted to stay.

In 1880, Mormons from Panaca, Pine Valley, and St. George, Utah, colonized the Mesquite Flat, the land directly across the river from Bunkerville.

The first canal in Mesquite drew water from the river two and a half miles east of the Arizona border, making the canal about six miles long. The task was so difficult that it was impossible to plant crops that first year, but by the second year a thin, burned out crop was harvested. By May 1882, there were fifteen families in Mesquite. The canal was extended to the lower end of the flat, and optimism grew.

Then on a bright, hot day in late June, the seven and a half miles of canal was broken and swept away. The small band tried to repair the canal and rebuild the dam, yet the floods kept up.

Many of the men, standing in thick water for days, came down with chills and fever. Eventually the water was again controlled but the hopes and optimism ebbed with the closing year. By 1883, following another damaging flood, the settlement was abandoned and the river raged as the sole owner of Mesquite Flats.

Meanwhile, in Bunkerville, the struggle went on. The flood that crushed the last resistance in Mesquite took its toll, sweeping haystacks, large chunks of farm ground, and domestic animals down with the bulging waters. Yet always, as before, the hardy band on the southeast side of the river hung on.

Two years after Mesquite was abandoned, Dudley Leavitt moved his five wives and fifty-one children onto Mesquite Flat. At least ten strong young men were in the family, conditioned by the severity of pioneer life.

It took six weeks to lay the foundation for the dam. It was built of three-sided log "pig pens" loaded with heavy stones, corner to corner, and bank to bank, across the river.

Things went well for a year or two, yet the constant deluge from the raging river broke dams and filled ditches. The backbreaking labor in the blistering heat, and knowing that it was a regular cycle, were enough to discourage this second attempt. The family moved further up the river where wresting a living from the fallow ground appeared to be more promising. Mesquite Flat was barren again.

Between the years 1890 and 1895, many newly married couples migrated from Utah to Bunkerville and it soon became evident there was not enough land on the southeast side of the river to support the growing population. Several of these young men, with a desperate need for a place to live and with nothing to back them save the vigors of youth, crossed the river to Mesquite. For the third time an attempt was made to defeat the restless river.

In March 1894, this handful of men began the arduous task of rebuilding the old canal. While working one afternoon, two men came into the valley. No one knew where Mr. Seymore and Cap Smith came from or where they were going but the two men stayed and helped with the project. Finally, when the water was

out on the land, Cap Smith financed the entire project of fencing a 15 acre plot and a building lot in town for each man in the small group. Then Seymore and Cap Smith quietly got into their saddles and rode away.

By the fall of 1897, other families joined those first few settlers. Out of desperation for their families and to give them some hope for the future, the men stood and slugged it out with the ever raging river.

During the Christmas holidays in 1909 a heavy snow fell, blocking the summit road to the north. The last two days of December turned exceptionally mild and warm rains even fell in the higher elevations.

Word came over the new telephone line that homes in Nevada were in danger of being destroyed. Men from the valley helped to evacuate the families.

The flood raged all New Year's day, hurtling along objects that depicted the disaster further up the river—chickens, sheep, cows, haystacks, even rooftops. The brown, turbulent water told the story of entire farms washed away. After the waters ebbed, silt and muck covered everything, yet the settlers still hung on.

In 1932, a new highway through the valley was almost completed when the first heavy storm came early that fall. Flash floods filled the barren washes, damaging fields and fruit trees, leaving farm ground covered with gravel. A temporary bridge was washed away and about 200 tourists were stranded, so the people opened their homes to them.

That night a dance was held in the open-air hall. Despite the flood damage and the never ending task of rebuilding, the raging waters failed to dampen the atmosphere. Deep in the minds of the valley people, the question had changed from "Should we stay on?" to "How can we do it better?"

*Manvel stage
set to go
to Searchlight*

Gunwoman

by Captain R. A. Gibson

In 1903 I managed Jim Harland's stage and freighting outfit at Manvel, California, a station on the Santa Fe Railway, just over the Nevada border from Searchlight. One day I was busily loading lumber and mining timbers onto two long-line or jerkline outfits when I noted a two-horse wagon was approaching on the Nevada road. The wagon piled high with furniture made the wheels wobble from side to side and the squeal from the dry axles could be heard from afar. The wagon had been repaired with "Mormon tie-rope" (bailing wire) in many places and similarly the tires were held to the felloes.

The driver wore the usual desert Levi's and a blue woolen shirt, and pants were tucked into expensive riding boots. He had several weeks' growth of beard, was extremely dirty, and had the usual six-shooter worn by all desert men. He wore it on his right leg, strapped down ready for action. The woman was short and heavy and wore a two-piece khaki suit which was badly in need of soap and water. She also had a shooting iron strapped around her waist and a 30-30 Winchester Rifle rested across her knees.

The man spoke then, saying, "My name's De Vito. I'm a skinner and looking for a job with your outfit. What are the chances, and are there any old shacks in town where we can shake down for a few days, in any case?" I told him that one of our 16-animal team skinners had quit only the day before and that if he was a good driver, he could show up at the corral on the morrow.

His wife spoke up then, a rasping voice which reminded me of the sound of rasp on a horses' hoof, saying, "Bob is a damned good skinner, don't drink and isn't afraid of anything or anybody 'cept me and I wouldn't hurt a fly unless. . . ." Here she was interrupted by a small boyish voice from the rear of the wagon, "You'd better be nice to my 'maw' or she will kill you. She killed a man in Arizona and that's why we had to get out so fast—the sheriff was after us but 'maw' was too cute for the law and here we are in California."

The woman then jumped to the ground, grabbed the boy, and gave the poor lad a thrashing, and I stood by mute because of the ferocity shown. She then threw the sobbing boy back into the wagon with the same cold-bloodedness and told him that if he ever made another crack about her or Arizona, she'd skin him alive!

I told them of an empty shack near the butcher shop. As she drove away with her husband, she yelled, "Just forget what you hear and what you think and we will get along fine—hope my little fit of anger won't make any difference about the job."

They moved into the little wooden shack and Bob was waiting when I arrived at the corral the next morning, shaved, boots polished and ready to begin his new job as skinner. I pointed out his 16 horses and he set to them at once with the curry comb and brush. He had soon finished with this job, harnessed up, and was ready to take his wagons up to the lumber deposit by the time I had finished getting the other wagon train away for its long drag to Searchlight.

Bob became a very good skinner and everyone liked him. His team, though working hard, looked fine and sleek like horses from a riding stable.

The only reference Bob ever made to our first meeting was after he had been there several months. He said "I can never thank you enough for having overlooked what my old woman said and did that day we arrived. I do hope my work is satisfactory because I am very happy here and want my kids to have schooling, which they never will get if I have to keep moving along."

I was happy to inform him that he was the very best skinner we ever had, adding, "Don't worry about what your wife did or said, it has no bearing on you and your work."

I saw Mrs. DeVito nearly every day and, although she always wore her six-shooter, she made no trouble and got along well with the few women of Manvel. She remarked many times that she was happy, once stating that she was sorry her terrible temper made it necessary to move about so much.

The DeVito's had two children, a little girl about five who had hidden that first day, and the seven year old boy who had gotten himself in dutch. Their playground was the corral.

One day while passing Doc Murdock's house, I saw them in one of the cedar trees behind the back porch, a tree that Mrs. Murdock carefully took care of. The children were high up in the tree and were throwing down small twigs which they broke off, so, I admonished them to get down. They did so at once and trotted home. Mrs. Murdock, who had come to the door, said "Thanks Gib. I had hoped they would get down without my having to scold them."

I went on back to my office and had only been there for a few minutes when I heard a shot and the shrill scream of a woman. I rushed out the back door and ran towards Murdock's as fast as I could, sure that something had happened between his wife and Mrs. DeVito. When I got there Mrs. DeVito was sitting astride the fallen wife of Dr. Murdock and was beating the poor old lady over the head and face with the butt of her gun. I bowled the DeVito woman over just as Mrs. Munro, the butcher's wife arrived. Mrs. Munro, powerful as any man, caught Mrs. DeVito and literally dragged her to her shack while I carried the unlucky Mrs. Murdock into her house for first aid. I immediately found the doctor's laboratory and gave what first aid I could, using carbonic solution to cleanse the wounds on the head and face and pouring a little listering into the chest wound to note whether the bullet had penetrated a lung.

Just then Mrs. Munro came in and when I told her my fears that the right upper lung had been pierced, she said, "Get your horse, Gib, and scour the hills for the doctor. He's prospecting somewhere out north but find him quick, for God's sake, or he'll return a widower."

I ran to the corral, saddled up, and for the next hour rode the tops of the hills looking for the doctor and his grey pony. I was about to give up when I spotted the doctor and his horse descending a long valley. I lost no time in getting to him, explained what had happened and told him to ride as he never rode before if he would see his wife again. I did not try to keep pace with him but came in about two miles behind the doctor, proceeding directly to his house where all the townspeople were gathered.

The doctor was operating on his poor wife and several of his neighbors were doing odd chores such as heating water and handing the doctor the instruments he called for. The job was finally completed and the people ordered home. I went into the house and asked if I could be of any service but was told that nothing more could be done. I took it upon myself to warn the doctor that he must not take revenge on Mrs. DeVito, as she was angry enough to kill him but he refused to listen.

I went over to the sheriff's house but found that he had been away for several days. Thinking that the Justice of the Peace was next in command, I ran over to his store only to be told that he was taking no action until the sheriff returned. This refusal made me boil over so I wired the sheriff at the county seat, mentioning that the deputy was away and the J.P. would take no action. One of our jerkline teams had come in that afternoon and just before the team was outspanned, the butcher and about ten men came to borrow the outfit. I found that they were going down the line to an old mining camp where years before they had sported a small one-cell iron jail and they proposed bringing it back to Manvel to house the DeVito lady.

They returned just before dark. While they were unloading the cell, Mrs. DeVito walked up with her 30-30 and asked, "What are you going to do with the cute little doll house, boys?"

I spoke up, "They aim to have this ready for you when the sheriff or his deputy arrive and if I were you I'd go over to the J.P. and give up."

She snarled like a wildcat and said, "There aren't enough men in this burg to put me into that mousetrap." She then raised her rifle and told the gang, "Get the hell back to your own wikiups and be dam' quick about it." She turned on me then and said, "I thought you were my friend. You've been dam' good to Bob else I'd let you have it; now 'git' before I forget all that."

I *got* since there was no use arguing with an angry armed woman who had already shot a man in Arizona for less reason. That night the men of the town met at the post office to talk it over, finally deciding to await the arrival of the sheriff or his deputy. Everybody was asked to keep an eye on the lady and not to let her get away, even if we had to form a vigilance posse to arrest her.

The next day Bob came into town. I met him at the

corral to be the first to tell him what had happened. Struck dumb, he cried saying, "I've been so happy here, the first decent job I've had for ever so long, and now I've got to pull up stakes again because of my wife's rotten temper." I was sorry for him. He was so decent and I hated to think of losing him as a driver. I took care of his team and he went home to his wife who continued to pace back and forth in front of their shack. I finished caring for the horses and went over to see Dr. and Mrs. Murdock.

As I came around the corner near the shack I heard Mrs. DeVito saying, "Drop that gun doctor, you dam' sawbones, and *git* before I drill that empty head of yours." The doctor, who probably figured that she meant what she said, started for his house on the double and I followed him. He told me that while Mrs. Murdock was badly beaten up, he felt that she would pull through if no complications set in. With this information I went over to Bob's house and asked him to take a walk with me since I had something serious to discuss with him.

I told him I had wired the sheriff who would no doubt come with several deputies to make the arrest and unless he could control his wife, somebody might get killed. I could not see any other way out unless he hitched up his own team, loaded his furniture, and made a getaway into Nevada. He realized that I was right. We returned to his house and told his wife what we decided. She cussed a bit, but realized that they had better "git goin" because she did not propose being taken by anyone and put in that "mouse-trap."

I helped them load their belongings and no one was the wiser until the following morning when someone noticed that the "bird" had flown.

That very afternoon, just before sundown, the sheriff and two deputies came in with their horses on a special train and, hearing that the lady had started for the border, mounted their horses in hot pursuit. They caught up with the slow-moving outfit just after it had crossed the Nevada line, with Mrs. DeVito sitting in the tail end of the wagon. She thumbed her nose to them and said, "Go on back to your alfalfa patches boys, I'm in Nevada now and by the time you take out extradition papers, I'll be somewhere else. Adios!"

Duel at Copper City

by Walter Averett

It was in 1905, near Cedar Basin, when Matt Reese followed a string of copper float to discover the Lincoln mine. Soon the inevitable tent mining camp appeared and the small community became known as Copper City.

Harry Gentry, who owned a store in St. Thomas, owed a bill for supplies to the Moapa store run by Fremont Cobb. As Gentry did not have adequate funds to settle the account, Cobb accepted part interest in some claims at Copper City in payment.

At the same time, developments at Copper City prompted Brigham Whitmore to send Jack Ward to prospect the area. He staked a number of claims, including some on ground surrounding the Cobb property. The two were fated to clash.

It was rumored that there was a deliberate plot to get rid of Cobb or Ward, or both, as Cobb began to be told, "Ward has you fenced off and you can't get to your mine." In truth, he did have to cross Ward's property to reach his own.

Cobb was supposedly a retired U.S. Marshal while Ward was described as a good-hearted fellow who caused no trouble. Still, it was said Cobb was afraid of Ward and purchased an automatic pistol for protection.

One evening in the early summer of 1906 or 1907, Ward and several other men were drinking. Someone shoved a gun in Ward's hand and told him, "Here, you take this up to Cobb's tent and have it out with him." He thought it over and decided to "go over there and fight Mont Cobb a duel to get this straightened out."

Cobb, his wife, Nettie Mills, and a man named Culver were eating supper when Ward arrived and called for Cobb to come out. A witness stated, "I happened to be outside and saw old Jack wobble over there. He came up to the door and said, 'Who wants to see Jack Ward over here?' Culver replied, 'Why, nobody.' Jack said, 'Well, somebody said they wanted to see Jack Ward and let's settle up here. I came over here—now we'll fight like men. We'll step off ten yards and shoot it out.' "

Culver went outside to try to talk Ward out of his anger. He put his arm around Ward's shoulder and said, "Jack, come on away with me. There's a woman in there and you don't want to cause her any trouble." Ward threw Culver's arm off saying, "Jack Ward's a gentleman, and he never insulted a woman in his life, but you tell Cobb that if he wants to settle this now he'll come out and we'll step it off."

Culver again tried to stop Ward who told him, "Don't put your hand on me; I'm all right." He turned to look at Culver and saw Cobb come to the door, saying he didn't want any trouble. Ward started to raise his gun and Cobb fired, killing him.

Some people wanted to lynch Cobb on the spot, but he was taken into custody for trial and released on grounds of self defense. Ward was buried at St. Thomas and Cobb returned to his home in Pasadena, California.

When the cemetery was relocated thirty years later prior to its being flooded by the waters of Lake Mead, one coffin broke open and revealed the body of a man dressed in Levi's and a black shirt. A cemetery helper exclaimed, "That's Jack Ward! Those are the clothes he was wearing when he was shot."

The "duel" was really in vain, since Copper City was abandoned soon after the incident.

Las Vegas Christmas
by Harvey Hardy

After spending most of 1905 working seven days a week, 12 hours a day as superintendent of a small mine near Goodsprings, I decided to take a short Christmas vacation with a friend who had recently come west from Boston. The two of us decided it would be good to see Las Vegas on Christmas Day.

I had some money on deposit in the general store which was open every day of the year, Christmas not excepted. I went in the store and told Sam, the owner, that I wanted fifty dollars. Sam gave me the money and then said, "What you going to do with it?" Sam owned the store, the saloon, the boarding house, the feed corral, and ran the post office so that he did all the business in the town and it was all conducted on a credit basis with accounts paid monthly. Cash was seldom used in the town unless it might be to buy a drink in the saloon.

I explained that Harry and I had decided to go over and take a look at the new town of Las Vegas. Sam studied a couple of seconds and then he said, "Have you got a gun?" I said that I had one but it was up at the mine. Sam said, "You wait." He went back into his living quarters and returned with a gun, a Smith and Wesson .38 with pearl handles and a bright shiny nickel plated frame.

Handing the gun to me he said, "Now put that in your belt and be d--m careful. That's a tough town over there and they tell me they get a man for breakfast pretty near every morning."

I thanked him, put the gun in my belt, and Harry and I started out to walk eight miles down to Jean, the station on the new railroad, where we could catch a train that would get us into Las Vegas about noon.

I found Las Vegas very different from what it had been when I saw it the preceeding January. The town had only been in existence since May when the lots in the township had been sold at auction. Much had been accomplished in those seven months. There were some brick buildings up and many of lumber construction though many people were still living in tents.

Our first move was to find a place to stay. The "big tent" was said to be the best in town so we went there, registered, and were assigned a room, or rather a space. The hotel really was a big tent with a wood floor and canvas hung up to divide the spaces. Our space contained a double bed and a wash stand, complete with a basin and a pitcher of water, but it was clean and that was important.

After lunch we walked around town, which didn't take very long. Harry, having recently come from a Boston winter, was much impressed seeing young fellows playing tennis in their shirt sleeves on Christmas Day.

In the evening we went to a Christmas entertainment in a church—complete with a Christmas tree, Santa Claus, and little bags of candy for the children. The church was in a permanent building so that it would appear that the town had not neglected the spiritual side in its rapid development.

After the church entertainment the only place that offered any alternate form of entertainment was the notorious Block Sixteen, so we went up to take a look.

The Clark Road, called the Salt Lake Route, was completed in May of 1905 and the lots in the townsite were sold at an auction. The lots were sold with restrictions that prohibited the establishment of saloons, gambling houses or sporting houses on any of the lots except those in Block Sixteen.

Senator Clark evidently intended that Las Vegas should be a model town. But it wasn't long till the smart boys found a loophole in the restrictions. They found that a hotel could have a bar and the bar could have

On Christmas Day 1905, 8 months-old Las Vegas was already an emerging town that had two-story brick buildings and long warehouses. The town still had plenty of tents but they were being replaced by wood-frame dwellings. The streets were carefully oiled and graded, and stores and shops of all kinds flanked both Main Street and Fremont Street. At left a water-wagon, drawn by four mules, will dampen the dusty streets and provide water for other uses.

gambling and this led to the building of saloons in the business part of the town with a few rental rooms upstairs giving them a hotel classification. The Senator's good intentions were thwarted.

That Christmas night when Harry and I reached Block Sixteen, it was running full blast. The bars were crowded, the games of faro, roulette, craps, blackjack, and poker were all running with their attendent dealers and boosters. Standing room around the heating stoves was at a premium for the December nights in Las Vegas can get pretty chilly.

But to the present generation whose idea of a western bar room scene has derived from the Hollywood movies and TV westerns, the place would have been a great disappointment, for there were no charmers with short skirts and bright smiles wandering among the customers, there were no lady card dealers, and there were not even any lady customers.

I was born and raised in the West and wide open gambling was no novelty and not very interesting. But Harry, coming from a very proper Boston suburb, found it all very new and exciting and he wanted to see it all. We went from one end of Block Sixteen to the other, visiting all the saloons and gambling houses enroute.

Along about midnight in one of the joints, while Harry was trying to solve the mysteries of roulette and I was having a drink with a couple of newfound friends, a big fellow tapped me on the shoulder and said, "Come on over here out of this crowd. I want to talk to you." I followed him over to a more quiet corner and he said, "You boys seem to be strangers here. Where do you come from?" I explained that we had just come over from Goodsprings that morning. He then wanted to know where we were staying and after I told him that we had a room at Squires Big Tent he said, "The reason I am talking to you like this is because I am the night watchman in this town and the only law here. I don't want to see any trouble so I am going to give you some advice. There are a dozen fellows here who have seen you boys spend a little money and they have been following you around. Any one of them would be glad of a chance to knock you in the head for a dollar. So when you go home stay in the middle of the road all the time and don't go near any bushes."

I thanked him for his advice and said that we would do our best to follow it. Later I learned that the big fellow's name was Sam Gay and when Clark County was formed and Las Vegas became the county seat, Sam Gay was elected sheriff.

Some time after midnight, with Harry's roulette problem still unsolved and my newfound friends somehow lost in the shuffle, we decided to call it a day and go to our hotel.

Across the street from Block Sixteen was a vacant block with a wagon road angling across it towards our hotel. As it was a short cut we followed it. About the

middle of the block the road passed between two mesquite bushes. When we were almost up to the bushes a man stepped out from each of them and advanced towards us in a very unfriendly manner. No words were spoken but we had no doubt as to their intentions. Now of course we had a few drinks during the course of the evening, but I had not had enough to make me forget that I had Sam's gun in my pocket. When I pulled it out and presented it towards our prospective assailants the nickel plating on the frame paid off big. Its flash in the moonlight left no doubt as to its identity. Our two friends faded back into the bushes and we proceeded to our hotel unmolested, but were we thankful to Sam for his foresight and his gun!

The next day we waited around for a train that would take us back to Jean. That night we got bunks in a tent and the next morning after breakfast we walked the eight miles back up to Goodsprings where I left Harry and continued another four miles up to the mine.

An important part of Las Vegas' early development was the drilling of artesian wells. "Pop" Squires, through his newspaper, encouraged farming in Vegas Valley.

The Great Booster
by Janice Haupt

Soon after the distinguished-looking Charles "Pop" Squires stepped off the train at Las Vegas depot in 1905, he soon found himself immersed in the social and economic problems of a new fast growing desert village. Through economic foresight, he helped plan Las Vegas' first water company, power and phone, its first bank and other enterprises.

It was an exciting time in Las Vegas during the first building stages, but there were many problems. Within two weeks after the town began, it was invaded by many thousands of flies, attracted by the corrals and the inadequate privies at the rear of every tent home. Many of the new citizens found it unbearable and left. The townspeople called an emergency meeting and voted to pass a popular law requiring metal enclosed boxes for every privy in town. The group feared the rule would be unenforceable, since the nearest law enforcement agency was in the county seat at Pioche. Pop volunteered to undertake the job, and did it.

It was also Pop who took the first city charter for Las Vegas to Carson City. He was delegated to try to get the legislature, then in session, to pass it, and to get his friend Governor Oddie to approve it. On March 16, 1911, the legislature passed the Las Vegas City Charter and that same afternoon the governor obligingly affixed his signature, making it law.

On this same trip to Carson City, Pop took a large box of almond and fruit tree sprigs, in full bloom, to Governor Oddie's mother at the Governor's Mansion, where Pop was a guest. Mrs. Oddie was having a dinner party that evening and used the beautiful spring blossoms for a centerpiece on the long dining room table. The guests included members of the legislature, state officials, and of course, Pop. The dinner table was blazing with lights and warmth. The glorious blossoms from the old Stewart ranch in Las Vegas opened their petals a little wider. Suddenly there was a buzzing sound that grew louder. The women covered their heads with the tablecloth and the men began fighting a savage, buzzing insect until somebody made a lucky slap and downed it. A big bumblebee, feasting on the

The leading hotel in early Las Vegas was the Navajo, whose rooms had doors and windows with canvas shades. The panorama (below) attests to the importance of the railroad; the train station is at far left, while the business buildings erupt from the sage-covered townsite. Sunrise (Frenchman) mountain looms in the rear.

nectar of the blossoms in Las Vegas, had taken a rest in the heart of the flower and was imprisoned until the room's warmth again opened the petals and turned him loose.

Many people of the Southwest believe that Pop, more than any other man, was responsible for the building of Boulder Dam. He constantly envisioned a great dam on the Colorado River, giving much of his time and effort to promote the building of it. For about fifteen years, while editing and publishing the Las Vegas *Age,* he campaigned for the dam. As a Colorado River Commissioner, he made many trips to Washington, D.C., to appear before Congressional leaders and committees. Herbert Hoover, Secretary of Commerce at the time, became a good friend of Pop's, and together they urged action on the Boulder Dam project before the House Committee on Irrigation and Reclamation. No one was happier than Pop when his dream of a great dam on the Colorado River became a reality.

Pop Squires will be remembered as an impeccably dressed gentleman with a boutonniere in his lapel—a pioneer business tycoon, a man of boundless energy, and an eternal optimist. He was a friend to everyone—presidents, senators, governors and, especially, the people of Las Vegas.

LABORDAY 1917 - GOODSPRINGS NEV

Jean and Goodsprings

by Leonard R. Fayle

The town known as Jean was originally placed on the maps and construction specifications of the San Pedro, Los Angeles and Salt Lake Railroad as "Goodsprings Junction."

By following the road of the railroad construction crew, my father, George Arthur Fayle, in the winter of 1904, brought his nine horses and two ore wagons to Goodsprings Junction. He had been hauling ore from the silver mines of Calico, now a ghost town twelve miles east of Barstow, to Daggett on the Santa Fe Railroad. He came to southern Nevada with a little encouragement and financial help from his aunt and uncle, Samuel E. Yount, who were operating a general merchandise store in Goodsprings, a settlement in the hills seven miles west of the new railroad. The Younts had bought their store from Mr. Joseph Good who headquartered his cattle raising operation there. Goodsprings was formerly named "Good's Spring" after the cattleman.

My father's reason for coming to Goodsprings Junction was to take advantage of the mining boom forecast for the Goodsprings area with the advent of the railroad, for it was known that there was considerable mineral wealth in the nearby mountains. The previous nearest shipping point was the town of Manvel, on the Santa Fe Railroad, a two-day trip each way by wagon.

In February, 1905, the rails of the San Pedro, Los Angeles and Salt Lake Railroad were joined by crews working from each direction, at a point midway between Jean and Las Vegas.

Father already had built a corral for his horses, a tent store, and underground cellars for storage of miners' dynamite and perishable foods such as potatoes, hams, and bacon-sides. A post office was soon established and given the name of "Jean" in honor of my mother, the first postmistress.

In 1910 and 1911 the Yellow Pine Mining Company bought and installed the narrow gauge railroad that the Quartette Mine of Searchlight no longer needed.

The narrow gauge railroad brought the ore from the Yellow Pine Mine, four miles northwest of Goodsprings, to the company's mill in Goodsprings where there was water for processing, and then carried the ore concentrates to Jean for shipment on the railroad to eastern smelters.

The other mines in the area sent their ore by wagon or truck to Jean for loading on the railroad. These shipments were usually factored by the firm of Yount and Fayle, who bought the ore and sold the miners their supplies, then sold their ore to the smelters.

At Jean, there were many burros that the small mine operators used to get their ore to the loading platforms on the floor of the valleys where the roads were located. There were men who owned several burros and pack saddles with bags or boxes who carried the ore off the mountains, and carried supplies up to the mines for a fee. Many of the old trails and footpaths are still visible today as they wind their way through the desert brush up the canyons and around the steep cliffs.

In 1912, my father turned the ore hauling part of the business over to Dan Potter, who brought his family to Goodsprings, and whose children were in the same age group as my brother and me.

My father had bought a half interest in the Goodsprings store. Thus, from 1912 to 1915 both stores operated under the name of Yount and Fayle, and our family moved from Jean to Goodsprings.

There my father expanded the business, but first secured a two bedroom cabin on the premises for sleeping quarters for the family. A kitchen was not needed for we ate in the boarding house, along with the mill hands and miners. Then he built the Pioneer Saloon (still standing and in operation) and made an office of the former saloon that adjoined the store. This old saloon building was pushed away from the old store about 50 feet and a new store building was erected between the two. These buildings were torn down a few

years ago for the building materials they contained. Only the concrete floor remains. In 1915, construction began on a new hotel. On one of his occasional visits to Goodsprings, Sam Yount, seeing the hotel under construction, objected to this enterprise—advising my father that he had seen too many mining camps flourish and then fail, and he said that the boom Goodsprings was enjoying would end with the cessation of World War I. Thus the partnership of Yount and Fayle ended.

Although the hotel was a landmark in town, a comfortable place to stay with its steam-heated rooms, and a good place for the mill hands and miners to eat, it was a financial failure from the start. It had been sold and leased many times since my mother sold it and the other properties to the Yellow Pine Mining Co. in 1922, and finally the hotel burned to the ground.

As Sam Yount had predicted, with the ending of World War I, there was no longer a need for lead and zinc as war material, hence the price of the metals dropped, mining became unprofitable, and Goodsprings joined the ranks of Nevada's dead mining camps.

A holiday crowd at the Fayle Hotel in Goodsprings enjoyed a full of festivities. Now the hotel is gone, and few old landmarks are still left at Goodsprings (below).

Temperance Town

by Charles "Pop" Squires

Strange as it may seem in these days of resort hotels and gambling casinos, Las Vegas started as a "temperance town."

J. Ross Clark, President of the San Pedro, Los Angeles and Salt Lake Railroad, was also President of the Young Men's Christian Association in Los Angeles and a prominent churchman of that city. When the question arose of permitting the sale of liquor in the new railroad townsite of Las Vegas, Clark's wishes were deferred to and the answer was a very prompt "No!"

So Thomas E. Gibbon and C. O. Whittemore, in whose hands had been placed the management of the Las Vegas Land and Water Company, took up the task of devising the means whereby the sale of liquor could be legally prohibited in Las Vegas. They hit upon the simple and seemingly fool-proof scheme of writing a "no liquor" clause into all contracts and deeds for the sale of lots in the new Clark's Las Vegas Townsite. This clause, naturally, raised vigorous objections on the part of would-be lot buyers.

In spite of the uproar, all contracts of sale and deeds for lots in the Las Vegas townsite contained the clause prohibiting the sale of intoxicating liquors on the property; except in a building devoted exclusively to hotel purposes, or by a drug store on a doctor's prescription; or the sale of liquors in wholesale quantities in connection with a wholesale liquor business, or the serving of liquor with bona-fide meals.

The penalty for violation of the liquor clause was reversion of title to the property to the Las Vegas Land & Water Company. This condition did not apply to lots in Blocks 16 and 17. Those Blocks, between First and Third Streets and Ogden and Stewart Streets, immediately took on the character and activities of the "red light" district and became most valuable property.

Some of those who had bought lots in the heart of the new city planned to open saloons. However, most of the liquor business of Las Vegas was at first confined to Blocks 16 and 17.

John Wisner was one of those fearless spirits who had been operating a saloon in the nearby McWilliams townsite for some months prior to the auction sale. He had bought lots on Main Street, just north of Fremont (where he later built the first Overland Hotel) and opened the first real saloon in Las Vegas.

Wisner was promptly warned by the Las Vegas Land & Water Company that his title to the lots was forfeited. John ignored the warning and after argument, the company brought suit to revert the title under the clause in the contract with which John had purchased the lots.

In October 1905, the suit, Las Vegas Land & Water Company vs. John S. Wisner, came before Judge Brown in the court house at Pioche. Frank R. McNamee and C. O. Whittemore appeared as attorneys for the company and Hugh Percy of Las Vegas and Henry Nisbett of San Bernardino represented Wisner.

The jury, after a trial lasting several days, brought in a verdict against Wisner on four of the points at issue and in favor of Wisner on two points. This, of course, settled nothing, but served as the basis for more legal jangle down through the years. However, no title has ever been reverted to Las Vegas Land & Water Company through the liquor clause in deeds and contracts. Anyone who wanted to start a saloon immediately provided a room or two for rent and called his saloon a "hotel."

Down through the years there remained a cloud on the title to property in Las Vegas because of that liquor prohibition clause in the original Las Vegas Land & Water Company deeds. In spite of the fact that the company never made any further attempts to revert the title to lots because of the clause, there remained among attorneys the fear that somehow, sometime, that liquor clause might lead to expensive litigation. It did happen in some cases that attorneys for financial concerns were reluctant to approve loans on property with this prohibition in the title.

To clear up all this suspicion the Las Vegas Land & Water Company years later made a recision of that clause in an instrument in which they recite the terms on the clause that, "Now, Therefore, In consideration of One Dollar and other valuable considerations, agree with each person or corporation owning lots in Clark's Las Vegas Townsite that they will never bring any suit to enforce said liquor prohibition clause."

That declaration was filed in the office of the Recorder of Clark County on April 2, 1948. Since that date, we may safely assume, Las Vegas has not been a temperance town.

Ghost Orchard

by John Harrington

Early advertisements attempting to lure settlers to Las Vegas dwelled on the potential fertility of this valley; and with the Union Pacific Railroad providing transportation, a few hardy settlers arrived with the hope of transforming the arid desert into productive farmland. One of these visionaries, a man with an iron-like will, was Edwin G. McGriff.

After having scouted Las Vegas in 1912, he moved his family here in 1914, living for a year at Las Vegas Ranch. McGriff was a man tempered by adversity—locusts had wiped him out in the late 1890's and financial disaster had struck him down in 1910. Yet, he was willing to start all over again with the challenge of dry-desert farming.

McGriff was in his early fifties when he decided to pioneer southern Nevada. Acclaimed as the father of the Utah fruit industry, he had breathed life into the first major Utah orchard. He had planted more than 27,000 peach, apple, cherry, plum and apricot trees and had tended more than 72,000 grape vines before an over-extension of interests brought financial ruin. His Utah experience proved invaluable in Las Vegas.

McGriff arrived in Las Vegas with his wife Olive, his daughter Della, and a symbolic cast-iron bell that had tolled during the long years of hard work in Utah. From 1915 to 1920, he leased the land that became known as the McGriff ranch from C. E. M. Beall, finally purchasing the property in 1920. He immediately planted orchards and vineyards that soon thrived under his tender care.

Desert heat and lack of refrigeration restricted importation of fresh fruits into Las Vegas. And so Las Vegas residents of the 1920's and 1930's frequently visited McGriff's orchard to purchase fruit. McGriff-packed fruit was often the only fresh fruit to be found in Las Vegas' limited grocery stores. In addition, the Union Pacific Railroad purchased fruit for its dining car service, and boxes of succulents traveled both north and south by rail.

Ultimately, his horticultural efforts were doomed since markets to the south were more easily supplied by southern California farmers while northern markets were too distant. He did tame the desert lands, but not the marketing problems. His success was due in part to advanced horticultural skill, aided and abetted by the unique artesian basin which underlies Paradise Valley. The McGriff ranch was the site of two copious artesian wells. The main well drilled by John F. Evey, who had originally patented the McGriff property in 1911, was a typical miracle of the desert. The drilling crew had hit

Artesian well, Paradise Valley

Ed McGriff and friend in orchard c. 1920

hard rock and quit for lunch. They returned to find water flowing in abundance and at the surprising temperature of 90 degrees.

The early wells gave a more lasting name to the McGriff ranch and the road which runs adjacent to the property. Also the warm water was piped into one of Las Vegas' first naturally heated green houses. Now Las Vegans are more likely to know the McGriff ranch as the Warm Springs ranch just west and south of Paradise and Warm Springs roads.

When Ed McGriff died in 1938, the death knell for the orchards was struck. The property was purchased by William S. Mason (of Mason jar fame) with hopes of turning the ranch into a millionaire's retreat, but by the late 1940's it had become Roy Rogers' Warm Springs ranch. Even as late as 1952, remnants of the orchards were still producing. The well was still flowing, feeding a delightful swimming pool that Mason had built, but neither Mason nor Rogers carried out their visions. At the end, the old iron bell that Ed McGriff had salvaged from his orchards in Utah—the bell that had chimed the lunch and dinner hours for ranch workers across two states and two centuries—stood alone and mute. Today the old McGriff place is a ghost orchard.

El Dorado Doctor

by Arda M. Haenszel

In the spring of 1919, prohibition was in and gold mines were on the way out, but it was with a feeling of adventure that my father, Dr. Allen L. Haenszel, decided to move his family to Searchlight and serve as the only physician within a sixty-mile radius, roughly the area between Needles, California and Las Vegas. He served the medical needs of not only the town itself, but also the small communities of Nelson, Barnwell, and Crescent, and the residents of numerous isolated mines. At the Techatticup mine in Eldorado Canyon, the management arranged with the employees to pay "hospital fees" for regular services of the doctor. Consequently, every week my father boarded the Cashman stage for the trip to the canyon, maintained office hours at the plant that afternoon and the next morning, and returned with the stage the next afternoon. A small, one-room cabin was provided for the doctor to spend the night.

In the Eldorado district there was small-scale or intermittent activity at the Rand, Wall Street, and several other claims, but Techatticup was the main producer, running 24 hours a day in three shifts. They supported two small settlements: Nelson, where there was a general store, and Techatticup. The Cashman

brothers, Harvey and James, who owned the Searchlight garage, ran a weekly truck stage from Searchlight to Eldorado Canyon.

Spice was added to our first weeks in the area when we were told that not long before our arrival a renegade Paiute named Queho had murdered a family in Eldorado Canyon and had not yet been captured. Rumor had it that in his flight he had stopped over with Indian Mary, a quiet, harmless old Chemehuevi who lived alone in a little cabin at the foot of Daugherty Mountain on the north edge of Searchlight, and that he had forced her to shelter him and give him supplies. But it was never proved, and Mary kept mute.

On one occasion there was an accident at the Techatticup mill, and my father had to make an emergency trip. We did not own a car, and a hasty search revealed that the only vehicle available for use was an old Ford chassis belonging to a youth who tinkered with it as a hobby. It was said to be in running order, but it was a mere chassis with only a front seat in the way of comforts, and lacking even floor boards around the pedals. Since my father did not know how to drive, and there was no one else to take him, my mother volunteered. I was taken along, because, as my mother said, if anything happened on the way, she at least wanted all of us to be together. The route entered the Eldorado Mountains diagonally from the southwest and approached Nelson over a notorious hill, at that time a stretch of very steep, narrow shelf road considered somewhat hazardous under normal conditions. Not far out of Searchlight my mother discovered that the Ford, though fully equipped with four feeble cylinders, lacked brakes. My father had to help it up the hill, pushing a few feet at a time. Then I would quickly bring up the rocks for him to put behind the wheels to prevent it from rolling backward. At the summit we all took a deep breath and started down the grade. Speed records were broken as we coasted brakeless around the curves and down through Nelson, eventually coming to a stop at Techatticup. My mother maintained the utmost coolness and composure, showing signs of fear only after she had brought her family safely through it.

On another occasion my mother and I accompanied my father on one of his regular weekly trips to

Techatticup, and passed the night with him in his little cabin. It was just big enough inside to hold a three-quarter bed, a chair and a table. There was not much sleep for the three of us in that abbreviated bed, but the dinner at the company boarding house that night was great. The usual Chinese cook presided over the kitchen. He was famous among miners all over the region for his apple pie, and after tasting it, we agreed with them. The most vivid impression was the noise of the stamp mill. It was a good-sized mill with many stamps which pounded continually, night and day. The loud, penetrating sound had a curious quality, an uneven rhythm, and it echoed back and forth from the walls of the canyon.

It was on this same visit, I believe, that my mother and I were given a guided tour of the mill and cyanide plant by Bert Calkins' son Louis, the owner of the Ford chassis, who at that time was working the night shift at the plant. He explained the cyanide process of extracting the gold from the ore. It was refined on the spot and shipped in gold bricks via the Cashman stage.

We left the desert and these many experiences in 1923, to return only after many years.

Two Story Man

by Larry Strate

It was 1907, just two years after the property auction at "Clark's Las Vegas Townsite" that Las Vegas' first "skyscraper" was built. It was located on the north side of Fremont Street and had two stories. This building told much of the life of a pioneer—John S. Park, banker and Mason.

Park was the son of Kentucky pioneers. His youth was typical of those days—some schooling, and a lot of working. His early employment at the family-owned Madison County Bank in Richmond, Kentucky, was the beginning of a banking career. Many years thereafter he was associated with Farmers Bank at Fort Smith, Arkansas.

Following a substantial financial loss in Florida, he wandered restlessly until he moved to Chicago. There Senator William Clark's railroad representatives chose him to establish a bank in Las Vegas, and he accepted the offer.

So it was at age 53, when most men are willing to accept their life with little change, John S. Park faced westward. He and his wife arrived in Las Vegas a few months before the first lot sale on the townsite in May 1905. His son, a dentist, relocated his practice in Las Vegas the next February. The bank occupied only desk space in the newly opened Kuhn's Grocery Store—a one-story frame building amidst a group of tent structures located near the present intersection of Main and Fremont Streets.

During his tenure with First State Bank, Park had many titles; he also had many jobs, including janitor. His thrift paid off—this was one of two banks that did not use script during the panic of 1907—and as Las Vegas grew, so did First State Bank. He began to acquire bank stock and in a few years had gained control for himself and his family. He directed the bank until 1927 when he retired, having held all positions from cashier to Chairman of the Board of Directors.

Among his residences in Las Vegas was the Kyle Ranch property, some distance north of the downtown office. Since no municipal transportation existed, he drove an electric automobile—the first in Las Vegas. He also pioneered the development of electric power and telephone service to the Las Vegas community.

The second floor of the First State Bank building tells story number two of John S. Park's life. The beginning of any city is not an easy or quiet time. It is most generally associated with violence, noisy construction, traditional rough work and very little relaxation. As in other towns it was a natural assumption that the establishment of a Masonic Lodge in Las Vegas would contribute to law and order. As early as July 1905, there was sufficient representation to warrant asking for authority to establish a Lodge. Not so, it was decided, and the delay moved into 1907. Then a group of 15 resident Masons made application before the Grand Lodge of Nevada. Park headed the movement. With the granting of dispensation, John Park was named Worshipful Master.

Quarters were found through Park's efforts, on the second story of the First State Bank building, and he furnished them comfortably. The 110 by 40 feet building now housed the Lodge upstairs, and a grocery store and bank downstairs, and a stage used for opera performances.

In a city's development, there are individuals who contribute much and shape its destiny. John S. Park was such a man. A painting of Park hangs in a place of honor in Las Vegas' Masonic Temple. Had there been a multi-story skyscraper in 1907 in Las Vegas, John S. Park could have matched it—story for story.

The Last Paiute Chief

by R. A. Gibson

Old Chief Tecopa—I say old because he was just wrinkles and squint—lived around the turn of the century near the railroad station at Manvel, 15 miles west of Searchlight. He would meet each train that would come north from Goffs on the Santa Fe Railroad main line.

Tecopa would always have his own little story to tell. If he saw a man wearing high boots, he knew that he was a mining engineer and had money. Tecopa especially liked three-buckled boots better than two-buckled boots, believing that the richer engineers had more buckles.

He would walk up to an engineer getting off the train and say, "Me Chief Tecopa, Paiute Indian. . . . My people great friend of '49ers. Me fight Shoshone many time to help white man. . . . Cough! Cough! Cough! Dr. Murphy he say me gotten tuberculosis. Cough! Cough! Cough! Me 106 years old. Pretty soon die. You got four bits?"

He would always wear a full dress suit, an annual gift of a Los Angeles banker. His tall stovepipe hat with rosette, white shirt and tie, and full dress suit of striped pants and ornately designed swallow-tailed coat made him a striking figure.

I saw him leave on the train in 1903 and was very surprised a week later to see him return wearing the same old suit. For many years the banker would meet Tecopa in Los Angeles and then take him to the Turkish bath, the barber shop and to a tailor to outfit him in new clothes, for his old clothes would be stiff with dirt. Once Tecopa was all slicked up, the banker and his two beautiful daughters would show off the old chief to the residents of the city.

But on his last trip to Los Angeles in 1903, he found that the banker was not around. He called at the bank, where all the tellers knew him, and one of them said, "Hello Tecopa, how. . . ."

"Cough! Cough! Cough! Me fine. Got tuberculosis. Where Mr. Dittman?"

"The boss is in Europe."

"Europe? Me no sabe him where'bouts."

"Maybe thirty days east," said one teller. "Come back next fall."

"Huh? What 'bout new outfit? Suppose you buy?"

"No, I have no orders to outfit you, Tecopa. Sorry."

Feeling sorry for the old Chief, the teller took $2.50 and slid it across the counter to Tecopa, hoping that he would leave.

"Ugh! Heap big money store! $2.50. You keep-em."

The old man hung around the bank and was getting in the way. Finally, a teller called for the police to take care of the chief for the night. In recalling this, Tecopa told me:

"Big man . . . fine blue suit come take me fine big hotel . . . strong hotel, iron on windows, doors . . . no body get in . . . fine room sleep in . . . plenty fine grub: bacon and eggs, potatoes, bread, plenty coffee, three times every day . . . fine big hotel."

"Big man put Tecopa on train . . . no suit . . . long time Mr. Dittman no come to Los Angeles . . . me old man . . . 106 years old. Cough! Cough! Cough! Dr. Murphy say tuberculosis . . . pretty soon die . . . Maybe so. You got four bits?"

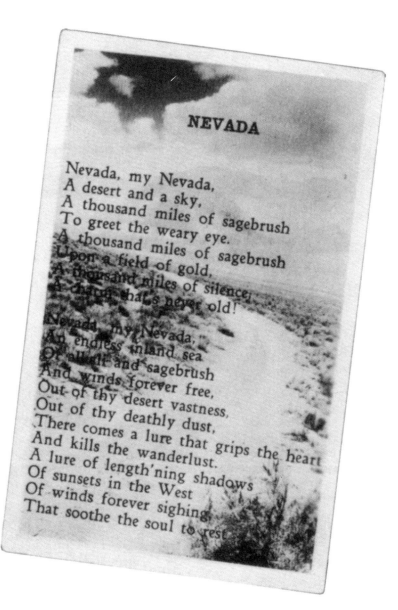

NEVADA

Nevada, my Nevada,
A desert and a sky,
A thousand miles of sagebrush
To greet the weary eye.
A thousand miles of sagebrush
Upon a field of gold,
A thousand miles of silence,
A desert that's never old!

Nevada, my Nevada,
An endless inland sea
Of alkali and sagebrush
And winds forever free,
Out of thy desert vastness,
Out of thy deathly dust,
There comes a lure that grips the heart
And kills the wanderlust.
A lure of length'ning shadows
Of sunsets in the West
Of winds forever sighing
That soothe the soul to rest

336

Burro King

by Joyce Jones

Although the waters of Lake Mead covered St. Thomas and the surrounding area in 1937 after Boulder Dam had been built, they failed to cover the legend of the Burro King, Frank Getchel.

Frank was a young man when he left the Ozarks and came to the Gold Butte mining district in about 1907 to make his fortune. Mining in the area was at its height. Grand Gulch was booming and Frank found his calling in raising burros to sell to the miners who worked small prospects high in the mountains.

Very protective of his herd, Frank eventually found the number of animals increasing as his sales decreased. After World War I, mining came to a virtual standstill, but by then Frank had claimed all the animals in southern Nevada, both wild and tame.

Even when donkeys were rounded up in Overton, Frank would come to claim ownership of them; and when he would walk up to an animal to lead him away while others had to rope it, Frank's claims were generally upheld.

Among the few things that made Frank angry was for the local people to ride his stock. He was constantly after the children, both boys and girls, to leave them alone. Youth being what it is, and temptation being there, the burros were often ridden, even under threat of punishment. At the sight of Frank or hearing his loud voice shouting his one phrase of profanity, the children would head for the brush with little chance of being caught.

Years passed by and with the coming of prohibition Frank made good wine, usually fig, as he had fig trees on his lot. One time the son of a prominent citizen got high on the wine. The father had Frank arrested, and as a result he was sent to Carson City for a year. At first, he said he was put in with a bunch of "God darn" kids who teased him and called him "Burro John," but soon he was put with the rest of the bootleggers and got along fine. In fact he liked it so well that when his prison time was up he refused to go. Finally a guard told him that he was needed at home because his burros were being sold for chicken feed. This was actually happening.

After his release from jail, he had to do assessment work on his mining claims. He walked to Jumbo Basin. When asked what he was going to eat, he said he had left a piece of bacon and a bag of beans hanging in the tunnel. At other times he did not burden himself with packing food and often went days without eating.

In later years he located a placer claim three miles southwest of St. Thomas. On it was a small spring which Frank called health water. He pushed an irontire wheel barrow from the spring to St. Thomas with a five or ten gallon bottle of his mineral water. He managed to sell some of it in Las Vegas also.

With the formation of Lake Mead, his property was to be well within its area, but he steadfastly refused to sell his "fountain of youth." He became even more frugal than ever. To save wear on his shoes, he often carried them, and to make sure that they would wear evenly he often wore them on the wrong feet.

One spring morning, when Frank had not been seen for a few days in St. Thomas, Harry Frehner drove to the spring and found him dead. Some said it was from an overdose of his own spring water. A friend in Las Vegas paid for his burial and assumed ownership of his property until Lake Mead inundated the site. The burros are all long gone. But there are still those who remember the eccentric "Burro King of St. Thomas."

St. Thomas in near abandonment c. 1938

The Legend of Lorenzi Park

It was September 1911, when David Lorenzi arrived in Las Vegas, population 800. He had originally come west for health reasons. Later he tried his lot at mining in Arizona, but now he wanted to buy a farm and settle down as he had plans to marry in the following year.

The train was two miles from town when some land caught his eye. It sloped to a high knoll and was covered with heavy brush and mesquite trees. Water had to be near, he thought, with all this vegetation—most important in this desert country. After looking over other parcels of land he decided to buy that which he had first seen from the train window. There was a spring on the property—just as he thought there would be, but since the spring wasn't adequate for the irrigation of crops, Lorenzi had to drill a well.

He cleared the land, leaving a few mesquite and willow trees. He found an old wild grapevine interwined among the mesquite. Removing the trees was quite a job, then the vine had to be braced and an arbor built under it. This vine, estimated at 500 years old, was judged to be among the oldest in the United States.

Lorenzi later put tame grape grafts on the trees. They looked like bandaged thumbs when he wrapped old white bed sheets around the grafts. It was a sight to see with the different varieties of grapes growing on a wild vine.

After his accomplishments he sent back to Arizona for his fiance, Julia Moore. Her parents brought her to Las Vegas and they were wed in 1912. He had started a new business in town called "The Oasis," a sweet shop serving light meals, which supported them until the farm could produce. Fruit trees, grapes, cantaloupes, tomatoes and alfalfa were planted and produced well on the rich soil.

Being a dreamer, he decided to build a resort for the townspeople. Speaking of his plans for a desert spa, people thought him mad and didn't believe he would finish it once construction was under way. With a team of mules and a drag line he dug out the lake's contours. An island in the center of the lake was connected to the bank by a bridge and weeping willows were planted there and around the lake.

By 1921 the project was completed. With ducks swimming on the lake and swimming and boating activities, this was truly a gem in the middle of the desert. A large picnic area was cleared with cottonwood trees for shade. A million acres of dirt had been leveled and shifted from the desert area when the resort was opened.

The spa had its own electric power plant, though in later years power service was obtained from Las Vegas, at which time the small ranches hooked onto the same power line at no cost.

A swimming pool, 90 by 115 feet—the largest in Nevada—boasted of a fountain with electric lights. With the pool for swimming, the lakes were then stocked with blue gill, black bass, croppies and Louisiana frogs which grew to two feet or more. The first time visitors strolled around the resort at night, they couldn't imagine what they were hearing. The sounds of the frogs sounded like cows bellowing.

A second lake was next constructed with another well drilled to supply it and a dance pavilion erected beside it, extending over the water on concrete pillars. Every Wednesday and Saturday night it was open to the public, featuring local and out of town orchestras.

When President Franklin Delano Roosevelt signed the bill to build Hoover Dam, the town went wild with excitement. Locals poured into the resort and celebrated for three days and nights. After the dam and Lake Mead were built, Lorenzi supplied 50,000 fingerlings to stock the lake with fish.

Lorenzi's paradise continued to flourish. Rodeo grounds and a race track were added and a hall was built on the island for Sunday band concerts and moving picture shows in the evening. A dog racing track was never completed because the state wouldn't grant a license.

On July 4, 1931, the fireworks finale displayed the "Sinking of the Battleship Maine." When it exploded, the sailors dove into the water. Flaming pieces dropped onto the water and the dry grass and shrubbery, catching them on fire. Spectators formed a fire brigade and extinguished the flames. This was the finest display of fireworks ever shown in Las Vegas.

Lorenzi, the promoter, sponsored bathing beauty parades down Fremont Street, dance contests with gold coins awarded for prizes, boating and swimming races to kick off the fun and excitement for holiday festivities.

After a number of owners, the park was sold to the city and re-named "Lorenzi Park," to honor its founder. The wishes of the old dreamer and builder were finally answered.

The original home of the Lorenzi family was made out of cross ties from the old railroad track that Lorenzi rode into Las Vegas. The fireplace in his home was made of petrified wood that he discovered in the petrified forest in Nevada. The unique hearth was an item in "Ripleys Believe It or Not" column in the *Los Angeles Examiner*. However, the home and dance hall were demolished when the city claimed the Lorenzi Resort, but the spirit of an adventurous young man still prevails.

Depression Pioneers of Boulder City
by Phyllis M. Leavitt

It was a hot, dry June day in 1930. In the blue shadows of evening we arrived in Black Canyon. The rugged terrain surrounding the camp was covered with gray brush and greasewood and black porous lava rock pushing through the sun-baked earth. Here I was to take my place among the housewives who had followed their men to the dam construction site. We had left Payson, Utah, a depressed area with no available jobs, and had come to the construction camp of Boulder Dam. This area we would call home for the next six years.

Cooking was done over an open fire with a black skillet and dutch oven. Brush and driftwood provided fuel. Breakfast usually consisted of bacon, eggs, or flapjacks with canned milk and syrup. My husband built a wooden box to hold our perishable foods. Two feet wide and about three feet high, it was covered with wet burlap and served as our first ice-box. After breakfast the camp was set in order. We carried water from an old railroad car. I washed our clothes on the scrubbing board in a round tub, and ironed them with flat irons heated on the fire. We bathed in an old tin wash tub. Our drinking water, stored in ten gallon milk cans, was hauled in by a trucker at no cost to us. A coal-oil lamp with a reflector hooked on the tent wall was used for lighting.

The children around the camp seemed to fare better than anyone. They enjoyed running and playing among the rocks but had to be watched carefully because of the many hazards including tarantulas, scorpions, snakes and open mine shafts.

To keep the big, hairy tarantulas and poisonous scorpions from climbing onto the beds, my husband filled four empty coffee cans with coal-oil and set a post of the bed in each. If a pest were able to reach the top of the can, it would fall into the oil and drown. Another precaution was to tuck the bed covers tightly under the mattress.

The women in the camp were all extremely friendly and a pioneer spirit prevailed. Every family tried to look out for one another and to make the best of the hardships. The intense heat was probably the hardest condition to endure. Daytime temperatures of 100 to 115 degrees became tolerable by frequent dips in the Colorado River. The heat at night posed a different problem. We moved mattresses outside of the tent to take advantage of any cool breeze that might come from the canyon. The heat would cause us to perspire profusely, and by morning the dye from the mattress was imprinted on our backs.

After a few months of living in Black Canyon, my husband gathered enough scrap lumber to build a small one-room cabin 12 ft. wide and 27 ft. long. How wonderful it was after living in a hot tent! A man who was leaving Boulder City sold us a used coal cook stove with four lids and a little oven. What a happy day for me; I was so overcome with emotion, I sat down and cried for joy.

Saturday was special because everyone went into Las Vegas, thirty miles away, to buy supplies for the week. Our old car had gasped its last breath when we first arrived, so we were at the mercy of helpful neighbors to give us a lift into town with them. We bought our groceries at the Sewell Market on Fremont Street. Bread was 10¢ a loaf, margarine 19¢, sugar 10 lbs. for 49¢, eggs 15¢ a dozen, a pair of shoes cost a dollar, and unbleached muslin was 15¢ per yard. All day long we shopped, played a game or two of Bingo, or visited the El Portal Theatre which was then showing the new "talkie" pictures. Supplies that we forgot to buy would have to be borrowed from our neighbors or we would go without until the next week.

When the townsite of Boulder City was established, we moved our cabin to Avenue L. We then

*napshots
*om Depression
*hoto album

hooked on to the city sewer and water, and life became more comfortable. My husband enlarged the cabin by adding two rooms and built a dresser, wall table and a kitchen cabinet with three drawers. I ordered a washing machine, a kitchen table and four ladder back chairs from the Sears catalogue. In spare moments I sewed curtains, sheets, and pillow cases, and all clothing for my little girl.

Many men were getting tired of their own cooking, so we decided to take in boarders. This venture proved to be quite an undertaking because the construction of the dam was now in full swing and men worked around the clock. Our six boarders worked three different shifts which meant that I had to prepare seven meals each day. Soon after feeding day shift men at 6:00 a.m., I prepared breakfast for the graveyard men coming off shift. At 9:00 a.m. the swing shift men would eat. Lunch and dinner also had to be prepared for the shift workers, as well as my family. I baked about eight loaves of bread every other day, in addition to hot biscuits and pies. The table was set with just plain good food that men like, mainly meat, potatoes, and gravy, corn bread, cakes and pies.

My husband had several jobs during the six years that we lived here. His first job was that of a laborer at the dam, for which he received $4.00 per eight hour day. He then worked as a cement washer and was paid $4.50. Soon he graduated to the job of a high scaler and earned $5.60 a day. He also worked as an orderly at the Boulder Hospital and as a gardener on the grounds of the administration building. He delivered mail and helped build the first LDS church in Boulder City.

We had neighbors from all over the United States, Hawaii, Alaska, and Australia; many were engineers at the dam. We worshipped in different religious denominations such as LDS, Baptist, Methodist and Pentecostal. Several families of the latter faith lived near us and we were awakened many nights with their bonfire services.

I had plenty of good company, especially from Utah. It seemed as if everyone I ever knew in my entire life came to visit the dam. I would provide old army cots for them to sleep on the lawn, feed them, visit the dam with them, and send them on their way.

In the fall of 1936, Boulder Dam was completed and only a small crew stayed on. As hundreds of construction workers left, many thought that the Boulder Dam boom was over and that Las Vegas, the small oasis in the desert, would revert to a railroad village. We packed our belongings and returned to the greener pastures of Payson where my husband might be able to find another job, without giving any thought to what would happen to the land we pioneered.

Gigantic 727-foot high Hoover Dam truly ranks among the world's great engineering feats. The dam fulfills two major functions, in flood control and in generating electric power. Incidentally, it also affords a "bridge" across the Colorado River. Construction started in 1931 and less than four years later more than 4.3 million cubic yards of concrete had been poured into the awesome hole at Black Canyon. The magnitude of the dam, as seen from the downstream side, is strikingly portrayed in these photos. The nearly completed dam (above) shows the lower coffer dam and water diversion tunnel beyond the catwalk. A man-made Niagara is formed by the twelve-stream waterfall from the Arizona side.

Colonel Bob

by John Beville

For the people who have made their mark on the Nevada scene, their memories are kept alive by the stories told about them. Colonel Bob Russell, host at the Apache Hotel at Second and Fremont Streets, lawyer and dentist, was one of those men.

When the Las Vegas Rotary Club held its meetings in the Old Frontier Hotel, someone scheduled a lecture on an African safari. This was all Bob needed to set him off. He went to the kitchen early where he secured the services of a little colored boy. From a towel he fashioned a turban around the boy's head, bringing him to the lectern. Here Bob went into a diatribe about how this boy had been his gunbearer on a lion hunt in the darkest jungles of Africa.

However, Bob reckoned without the diabolical fiendishness of one Allye Lawson, no mean practical joker himself. Allye, too, made a trip to the kitchen. For five dollars he bribed a huge black woman, an Aunt Jemima type, to aid him in a plot.

Just as Bob finished his fable about the lion hunt the woman came screaming from the kitchen exclaiming that Bob was her long-lost husband, a deserter who stole from her their only son . . . the little gunbearer. As Bob turned his head to see what was going on she planted a solid kiss smack on his lips. It was the first time Bob was utterly stopped in his tracks. He sat down without another word.

During the hot summer months while Bob attended the weekly meetings, temperatures were too high for Bob to leave his dog in the car. The dog was his constant companion, accompanying him at hunting, fishing, marketing, the works: health regulations to the contrary. The two of them used to take nocturnal strolls in the darkness of Shadow Lane. Two friends of mine told me of walking one night down Shadow Lane and seeing an eerie sight. In the distance, nearly ground level, too low for either the Headless Horseman or Tinker Bell, moving back and forth across the road was a mysterious light.

Soon Bob approached along with his dog, who carried a flashlight in his jaws. When confronted with this, Bob explained, "The dog is getting old and can't see the road. I trained him to carry the light so he can see where he is going and where he has been!"

As song leader, Bob always occupied the head table. Reluctant to leave his dog in the car, he trained him to sit quietly beneath his chair.

As I was leaving the meeting one day, a visiting Rotarian from Riverside called me furtively aside.

"Are you a regular member of the Las Vegas Club," he asked. I admitted it.

"Tell me," he went on, "What is the significance of the dog at the head table?"

"Oh that," I replied. "The dog is a member in good standing and we are likely to run him for president any day."

The poor guy mumbled something and groped for the exit.

Magic Theatre

by James M. Greene

In the heart of downtown Boulder City is the theatre which has been an institution in the town since 1931.

Earl Brothers owned Boulder City's theatre when it was the only air-cooled building in the fledgling Boulder Dam construction camp. He was a uniquely human man and his business filled many of Boulder City's needs in unusual ways.

In the early days of construction many graveyard shift workers tried to sleep in their homes during the torrid daytime hours of summer. They placed wet towels or sheets over themselves to be cooled by evaporation; at best this method worked for maybe an hour or so. Earl's movie matinees were the ideal times for restful sleep so the workers could be fit for their next work assignment.

During World War II, Brothers donated three rooms above the theatre to the Red Cross for workrooms. The ladies of the city knitted soft covers for the tender stumps of amputees and prepared clothing packages for the war-weary needy overseas.

Every year on Halloween night the Boulder theatre had a free midnight show after the witches and goblins had fled to the never-neverland of children's sleep. Earl followed the same custom as Father Time wrote the final words on the old year and presented Boulderites with a new one.

The most subtle use of the theatre's magic took place when the parents who worked three shifts and seven days a week had to get their children out of the house for the visits of Santa Claus and the Easter Bunny. Earl arranged for free movies starting in the morning and running through the evening for the children of Boulder City. When the children returned to their homes, the magic was performed—aided by a cooperative theatre owner.

Norman D. Nevills

by Florence Lee Jones

Running the rapids of the Colorado River and its tributaries has become a favorite but competitive sport in recent years, but in 1938 it was both daring and dangerous.

Norman D. Nevills was the first to guide women through the treacherous waters and bring them out alive. He was sharply criticized before starting the 666-mile trip for endangering the lives of the passengers, including botanists Dr. Elzada Clover and Miss Lois Jotter, and for adding the hazard of women passengers to the expedition.

Nevills also pioneered the use of three plywood boats, the "Mexican Hat," "Botany," and "Wen," which previously had not been put to a rough-water test. The boats, 16 feet long and five feet wide, were constructed with seven air compartments, so they were unsinkable, and weighed 1000 pounds when loaded. Two eight-foot oars and a spare were provided for each boat. The women sat on coils of rope with a boatman, but they did walk the shoreline on the worst rapids.

The 1938 trip was essentially a scientific expedition with Nevills, a trained geologist, focusing upon river navigation and archeology along the canyon walls. Dr. Clover and Miss Jotter collected more than 300 different botanical specimens; Eugene Atkinson, University of Michigan zoologist, studied the animal life; Don Harris, United States Geological Survey engineer, took water samples for silt studies; and W. B. Gibson of San Francisco made the first photographs ever taken of the sheer canyon walls and colorful vistas of the river country.

The boats and six voyagers left Green River, Utah, on June 20, 1938, and arrived at the junction with the Colorado River three days later. Near the confluence of the two rivers, they docked at the head of Cataract Canyon in mid-afternoon to search for a large

In Las Vegas painted frame houses were common (left); the theatre still is open in Boulder City, a town founded in 1931 and still possessing many of its original buildings.

The Nevills scientific party is shown as it entered the quiet waters, below Grand Canyon, in the area where the Colorado River becomes Lake Mead.

rock bearing the inscription "First Steamer, Major Powell, 1869," left there by the famous first Colorado River traveler. While the women photographed the landmark, the men went to inspect Rapid Number One, where high waves indicated trouble. Suddenly the "Mexican Hat" came bounding over the water, oars in place, making a solo trip with one-third of the expedition supplies. The boat shot through three of the worst rapids on the river before it floated quietly into an eddy, having kept upright throughout the rough ride.

This was the first of many exciting experiences for the river runners, who made several portages of the boats, fighting off rattlesnakes in the nighttime camps, and the rising of the river by several feet in one night, as the annual spring floods began. The arrival of the party at Lee's Ferry was delayed by these incidents, and an airplane had been sent out to search for them, so word of their safety could be reported.

When the party arrived at Lee's Ferry on July 8, there was a big assemblage of people to greet them, and Dr. Clover and Miss Jotter were hailed as heroines for

their daring adventure. They had secreted facial creams aboard the boats, so they could protect their faces under the glaring sun, but they were as tanned as the men in the group.

The expedition members rested for five days at Lee's Ferry, then started the run down the lower reaches of the Colorado River. The women ignored the opportunity to return to civilization and plunged ahead with the others. A new passenger, Emery Kolb, who had run the river in 1911 and 1923, became a "hitch-hiker" and lashed himself to one of the boats so he could take motion pictures through the canyons.

The boating party experienced many thrills in running the treacherous rapids in the next three weeks, until they passed Separation Rapids and floated serenely into Lake Mead on July 29.

Such a trip as the Nevills party made never can be done again. In the meantime, Glen Canyon Dam has been built and Lake Powell has been formed, so that many of the rapids of the Colorado River have been tamed forever.

344

The Inn and gas station are shown as they looked around 1925. It took two years to build these structures out of abandoned railroad ties. The highway in front of the Inn was not oiled until 1937.

A Resting Place

by Ann Brauer

From 1903 to 1906, George and Belle Latimer's Indian Springs Ranch was a popular overnight stop on the long, dry wagonroad from Las Vegas to Beatty. The ranch, with its free-flowing spring and tree-shaded ponds, is situated about 40 miles northwest of Las Vegas.

On one occasion in 1903, the Latimer's dinner guest was Emmet Boyle, later to become governor of Nevada. During the meal, Belle frequently walked to the window sniffing distastefully at the evening air. Finally Boyle inquired about her strange behavior.

"Them damn dogs has dug up Wild Bill again!" she exclaimed.

Wild Bill, known as Bad Bill to the Indians, had been a foreman at the ranch. Cruel and unfair in his dealings with the Indian helpers, he worked the Indians for a season, then drove them away at gunpoint without paying them. Coachie Seegmiler was one victim of Bill's cruelty during the summer of 1903. Several versions of the story have developed, making difficult the assimilation of the facts—but the following account seems plausible.

During a two week absence of the Latimers, Bill broke the arm of Coachie's mother and refused to pay Coachie his wages. Then Bill threatened to kill him if he should try to leave the ranch.

Coachie waited until Wild Bill was taking a nap on the front porch. Quietly, he crept into the kitchen and lifted a loaded gun from the rack. As Wild Bill slept, Coachie crept close, aimed, and pulled the trigger. In fear, he fled to his parents' home in Moapa.

When the Latimers returned home about a week later, they were greeted by a deadly stench. The best burial they could manage was to scrape Wild Bill's remains into a gunny sack and lower him into a small grave.

Wild Bill's rest did not turn out to be final. The dogs discovered his resting place and dug him up. The Latimer's buried him a little deeper, but on the night of Boyle's visit, the dogs once again succeeded in finding the remains. Dinner waited while Wild Bill was once again laid to rest.

Coachie was later arrested, given a speedy, emotional trial, and sentenced to hang. The Moapa Paiutes were enraged. They threatened an uprising in which white men throughout southern Nevada would die if the sentence were carried out. Another less emotional trial was held, resulting in a six year sentence for Coachie.

The recorded history of the Indian Springs Ranch began in 1876 when Charles Towner "bought" the land from Whispering Ben, a Paiute. Towner, however, failed to deliver the promised 100 head of cattle. Nevertheless, he acquired legal ownership of 640 acres and the valuable springs.

Throughout the years the ranch has seen prosperity and decline. Beginning in 1905 it was a stop-over from Las Vegas to the mines near Beatty. In 1903 Montana Senator Clark bought the ranch for use as a watering and rest stop on his proposed railroad line from Las Vegas to northern mines. The railroad was completed in November 1906. Clark then leased the ranch to caretakers who provided passenger service.

In 1910 Ira and Alice MacFarland leased the ranch and bought it shortly thereafter. They worked hard to clean up the area. Junk and garbage were removed, the barns relocated to a site away from the house, trees trimmed and new ones planted, and lawns and gardens established. They remodeled the house, cleaned and enlarged the ponds, built bridges, and stocked goldfish. All the while they continued farming. MacFarland cleared pastures and kept cows, horses, pigs and chickens. He located Whispering Ben and brought him, with his family, back to the ranch to set up an irrigation system.

Mrs. MacFarland was a beloved hostess. A gentle Eastern lady, her home and hospitality reflected her upbringing. Her table was set with crystal, china and sterling, and meals were served by ''Old Jimmie,'' a mild-mannered Indian who dressed in a white coat and cap for the occasion.

By the end of World War I the railroad had been torn up, the rails sold to China, and the ties pushed aside to accommodate an automobile road which was paved in 1934.

Shirley Caples bought the Ranch in 1940, making it into an artist colony. Writers and painters came to the ranch to live and work for varying periods of time. Walter Van Tilburg Clark lived there while he wrote much of *The City of Trembling Leaves*.

Mrs. Caples continued to improve the ranch. Once again the landscaping was improved and expanded and more rental houses were added, including two adobes. She also had a modern home built for Alice Mac-Farland, now widowed.

When the ranch was sold in 1951, it began to decline. The lawns and gardens were neglected, and many of the large trees cut down. Reeds overgrew the untended ponds. But in 1954 when Fred and Nevin Bartley bought the property, restorations were begun. The new owners cleaned the ponds, replanted lawns, gardens and trees, and modernized the rental units. Soon the ranch was again a garden retreat in the middle of an arid, often harsh desert.

By 1941 the station was a regular stop for Death Valley tourists and Reno-bound motorists who had left Las Vegas. The business had modernized with the addition of cabins that had kitchenettes.

Nellis Air Force Base

by Binnie Douglas

On November 22, 1975, Nellis Air Force Base celebrated America's Bicentennial by opening its doors to its host city. The 65,000 Las Vegans who attended the open house and spectacular air show were greeted at the gates by airmen dressed in colonial costume. The 18th century dress combined with the historic aircraft displayed on the field gave the visitor a heightened sense of the history which the base represents.

Nellis Air Field came into existence on January 25, 1941, when the city of Las Vegas leased the property to the U.S. Army Quartermaster Corps for the development of an aerial gunnery school. The southern Nevada site had been chosen not only for its ideal flying weather but also because 90 per cent of the area to the north was public domain wasteland available at $1 per acre and suitable for bombing and gunnery ranges. The little town of Las Vegas, eight miles to the south of the new air field, waited anxiously for the establishment of the base to augment its population of 8,422 and boost its economy.

Interaction between the base and the city, which the Las Vegas Chamber of Commerce had hoped for, began almost immediately. As the first B-17's arrived in 1942, so did an influx of young men who spent their paychecks in Las Vegas casinos and restaurants. During the height of World War II, 600 gunnery students and 215 co-pilots graduated every five weeks from Nellis. The only recreation available to these 18 and 19 year-old airmen was in downtown Las Vegas which included, at the time, a red light district near North First and Second Streets. The base commander did not want this fact included in the young men's letters home and so Las Vegas officials ordered the district shut down.

The field was deactivated in early 1947 after the end of the war, only to be reactivated in 1949 as the Las Vegas Air Force Base. It served as a pilot training wing and increased in importance when jet fighter pilots trained there for the Korean War. In 1950, students at Las Vegas High School recommended that the base be renamed in honor of 1st Lt. William Harrell Nellis, a fighter pilot and Las Vegas High graduate, who was killed in action over Luxembourg on December 27, 1944.

The Las Vegas economy was not all that was affected by the presence of hundreds of young men just eight miles from the city. Las Vegas high school students watched the invasion with mixed emotions. Impressionable school girls found the airmen glamorous, cloaked with the excitement of the times. For them, the young men brought a cosmopolitan atmosphere to the tiny desert town. The high school boys viewed them as competition.

The next quarter century saw Nellis develop into a major arm of the Tactical Air Command and home of the world-famous Thunderbirds. A powerful economic influence on southern Nevada, Nellis' 8,019 military personnel and 1,151 civilian employees in 1975 brought a combined payroll of $86,000,000 to Clark County. More than 1,100 airmen are currently enrolled at the local university and upon completion of their tour, one out of every five Nellis service people eventually becomes a permanent resident of the area.

Colorado River Boatman

When the United States government attempted to tame the Colorado River with the construction of Boulder Dam, Murl Emery already had been operating his boats on the river, prospecting its banks and tributaries. In the 1920's, while the Bureau of Reclamation was operating its test drilling crews out of small rowboats, Murl was running the river in a thirty-foot boat of his own design using Locomobile or Pierce-Arrow Engines.

Born in southern California, Murl's family was usually on the move. Finally they settled in Cottonwood Cove, where his father ran the ferry "Arivada," mainly patronized by bootleggers running their "white lightning" to Arizona.

Murl recalled, "Sheriff Sam Gay had Clark County so wet that moonshine sold for only a dollar a gallon. . . . Over in Arizona Sheriff Bill Mahoney had Mohave County so dry that good squeezings were $50 a gallon. Our ferry was the Arizona Connection."

At one time Murl made a trip a hundred miles upstream through treacherous rapids and ten miles into the Grand Canyon, claiming to have been the first to accomplish this feat. The Las Vegas *Age* reported in 1929, "The occasion for his making this trip was an offer by two millionaires to guarantee the value of his boat if he would take them to parts which had not been visited by a motor boat before. He satisfied their desire for excitement and the unusual, for the two gentlemen felt fortunate to get back."

Long before Boulder Dam was built, Murl opened the river to tourists. Known as the "Boulder Boatman," he took such passengers as Herbert Hoover, governors, congressmen, and others through the hereto unknown beauty and grandeur of the Colorado.

Government surveyors working on preliminaries for the dam construction, camped at Emery's landing in Black Canyon at the mouth of Hemenway Wash. The Emery's converted their small three-room cabin into a messhall and store, and provided tents and sleeping quarters for the workmen.

Before the Six Companies built roads down into the canyon, Murl ferried men and supplies in three shifts around the clock. Until the tunnels were completed and the river diverted, the men went to work by boat. By the time the Six Companies had homes and a commissary built for the crews, a town of three hundred people lived on the river bank where Murl's store supplied them with their needs.

When the dam was completed and Lake Mead began filling up, Murl carried the first sightseers to the damsite. As the lake expanded, the trips became longer until they reached into the lower Grand Canyon as far as Emery Falls.

In 1940 Murl left the lake and returned to his river, building a house and boat dock at Nelson Landing below the dam. Here he decided to experiment with fish and built ponds to utilize the cold water coming out of the dam from Lake Mead. He persuaded the newly established Department of Fish and Game, which he was instrumental in forming, into stocking the ponds with trout.

That first year the fish grew so rapidly that Murl knew he was in the right business. Fishing news travels fast and soon Nelson Landing prospered as a booming resort, providing boats, bait, gasoline, food, cabins, and boat pilots. Guides would run the fishermen up or down the river (up into the colder water for trout and down to warmer water for bass) and drop them off at their favorite fishing spots, and to facilitate locating spots Murl painted mile markers on the river bank which are still in use today.

The river was not Murl's only interest in Nevada, as all his early life had been spent in the mining camps where his father was a stationary engineer and hoist man. When Murl retired, he remembered all the tales he had heard around the camps and began revisiting the old mining areas. For the past fifteen years Murl has toured the state trying to locate and preserve the little stamp and ball mills the prospectors used.

At his home in Nelson he has created what he called an "outdoor museum of mills" that were actually used in the early days. The collection includes an original arrastra and a two-stamp "high-grade" battery stamp mill built in Tonopah. Murl believes, "If it has

anything to do with Nevada's early mining, let's save it"—and he does.

Sight-seers, students, old-timers, or just friends spend a while looking and listening, hoping that Murl will start up the little two-stamp mill and pan the crushed ore to proudly display the colors from the bottom of the pan.

Listening closely to Murl Emery's fond recollections and exploits as a Colorado "River Rat," his love and loyalty for Nevada spark in his heart like the glittering ores of the mines and the glistening waters of the mighty river.

Murl Emery passed away in 1981.

At left is the site of Hoover Dam as it looked in the late 1920's. The steep Black Canyon walls are dramatically shown. The mud dredger is doing preliminary work in the Colorado River.

ROULETTE GAME AT BANK SALOON TONOPAH NEV OSBORN

The central Nevada mining boom camps of Tonopah and Goldfield were the focal point of speculation, banking and gambling, early in this century. High stakes roulette were played at the popular Bank Club in Tonopah (above). At the unidentified club in Goldfield (below) poker was a favorite pastime; the faro bank, dominated by women, attracted many male spectators. Current train schedules, north and south, as well as mining stock quotations are posted along with advertisements on the chalk board on the right.

Gambling

History of Chance

by Frank H. Johnson

Nevada may have a worldwide reputation for its gambling ways, but it can't lay claim to having added anything really new to the games at which ever-venturesome mankind can win or lose a buck.

It may have changed and glamorized some of them, but the basics have remained the same for so long that even the experts tend to disagree over the issue of origins.

Take roulette. Some claim it was invented by French scientist Blaise Pascal while he was on a monastic retreat. Others assert M. Pascal expended his time developing a perpetual motion machine utilizing a ball and a wheel which he only incidentally happened to call roulette.

Some give an anonymous French monk the credit; others a monk from Tibet. Perhaps roulette came from China. There are advocates of that theory, too.

In any event, it surfaced about 1655, and the proliferating wheels haven't stopped turning since, except during an occasional police raid where they were found to be spinning illegally.

Although Nevada has yet to produce a truly new game, it has not been immune to changing fads and fancies.

The Nevada Gaming Control Act has a section listing the more common games which may be licensed for use in casinos. The first two are faro and monte and the fourth is keno.

All three games were popular "back when," with faro the most popular of all. When the mining camps were booming, there wasn't a sawdust saloon that didn't offer their delights.

Today, only keno remains, and even it is a far cry from the Chinese lottery traditionally run by the Celestials who fringed the camps in substantial numbers.

What happened to monte? The kind played with a 40-card deck (8's, 9's and 10's removed) is still played illegally in some parts of the country, but is apparently too dull or too suspect to entice players in today's Nevada.

There isn't any need for speculation as to the fate of Three Card Monte, a game traditionally played with the two red aces and the queen of spades. The operator of such a game is no more suspected of benevolence than the manipulator of a shell game, and perhaps less so inasmuch as it is easier to mark a card than a pea.

Faro is a different story. Another relic of the murky past, it probably originated in Italy and probably was named after the Egyptian pharaohs during the reign of Louis XIV. Those are good guesses, anyhow, although not exactly the sort of information one would pass on to the American Kennel Club in hopes of qualifying the family mutt as a true blue blood.

What is more certain is that faro was played on the Mississippi riverboats, with wagers ranging from the coin of the realm to slaves and entire plantations, then moved along with the country's westward migration.

In Nevada and elsewhere in the early West, a painted tiger often signified the houses offering the perilous joys of faro bank, a game based on guessing not only the rank of cards pulled from a dealing box, but whether they will be "winners" or "losers," according to the sequence of their appearance. It was almost inevitable that the phrase "bucking the tiger" would attach to those patronizing the establishments.

Nevada is currently out of both painted tigers and faro, but the catchy "bucking the tiger" still lives on, particularly among the set to whom the phrase "twenty-three skidoo" still holds meaning.

Faro might have lived on, too, had it been a little more challenging to the player or a little more lucrative to the casino. At the end, which was not too long ago, the die-hard traditionalists among Nevada gamblers were paying independent operators to run the game, which has the fatal effect of offering almost dead even odds when played without hanky-panky.

Replacing and surpassing faro as Nevada's trademark game has been craps, a genuinely American version of a pastime which may have developed in Europe.

Craps is played with dice, and dice, or reasonable facsimiles thereof, have been found fashioned from bones, shells, seeds, rocks and animal teeth dating back thousands of years. The South Sea Islanders played with dice in ancient times, but then so did Eskimos,

Africans, American Indians and just about every other race or culture which might want to claim a piece of the historical action.

Chuck-a-Luck, featuring dice in a wire mesh container and a variety of possible bets, mostly bad, was almost the symbol of the Nevada gambling hall in times gone by. It was not exactly a generous game for the customer, but, then, there are those who will risk at least a modest wager on the proposition a beer bottle thrown into the air just might not come back down again.

It is perhaps significant that Chuck-a-Luck originated in England as Sweat-Cloth, and showed up in the United States about 1800 as plain, old Sweat.

A number of games that have been licensed in Nevada, such as the Oriental fan tan and pai-gow and the Greek and Jewish barboot, never really caught on beyond a handful of ethnic afficianados. They have simply come and gone, and may come back again if the demand warrants.

One problem, at least with pai-gow, a game played with domino-type tiles, is that it is almost impossible to learn without playing, yet is almost impossible to play with a learner in the game.

One card game consistently on the Nevada scene is poker. The concensus is that it originated sometime during the Eighteenth Century, although there are purists who contend it dates back to a Fourteenth Century Persian game known as as-nas.

The origin of the name "poker" can create a debate among those who fret about such things. Some think it came from the French "poque," others from the German "pockspiel," and still others from the Hindu "pukka." The redoubtable game authority John Scarne holds out for pure Americana, contending the name was born on the Mississippi riverboats, where the term "poke" was applied by pickpockets to a gentleman's pocketbook or wallet.

Stud poker and draw poker are the varieties most commonly licensed in Nevada today. The old saloons tended to call their poker according to the way patrons called their drinks. Thus, gin poker, whiskey poker and rum poker. Two of these games, at least, became rummy and gin rummy. If a game named whiskey evolved, it did not gain any noticeable prominence.

However, for the great majority of Nevada's visitors, the most popular game isn't a game at all, but a device—the slot machine.

It might be argued that man was born to shoot craps, though this is not a subject to pursue too deeply.

There are all kinds of games that can be played with dice, including Monopoly, but the version known as craps, if one is to believe historians who are into that sort of thing, began with an English game called hazard, which is a corruption of az-zahr, which is, or at least was, the Arabic name for dice.

Many Englishmen who played hazard referred to it as "crabs," which is the name it bore when it turned up in New Orleans about 1800. There, the American blacks found "crabs" to be an enjoyable way of distributing and redistributing the wealth, whatever there was of it, and adopted the game wholeheartedly, albeit with a slight change in pronunciation.

The modern Nevada version is considerably more refined than the type played on Army blankets, and is called "casino craps."

Nevada's most popular card game—in fact, the world's most popular card game—is blackjack, or 21. Both the French and the Italians claim to have invented it, with the French having a slight edge in believability inasmuch as its name is derived from the French vingt-et-un. Besides, the claimed Italian progenitor is a game known as seven and one half, which incorporates the king of diamonds as a joker and is thirteen and a half points short of the magic number everybody always is trying to make at the casino tables.

The English call the game, or a variation of it, pontoon, and the Australians have a close cousin called Van John.

Another relative of 21 is baccarat, a fashionable diversion for the really high rollers which is commanding an increasingly important role in Nevada casinos.

Baccarat is another oldie whose origins are subject to disagreement. Most experts tend to believe it is of Italian extraction and that it migrated to France about 1490. The Encyclopaedia Brittanica thinks otherwise, and grants France full credit for the game.

Whatever the case, baccarat took its own sweet time in reaching Nevada, although it has long been the most popular gambling game in Europe and South America.

Baccarat's first cousin, chemin-de-fer, showed up in Nevada in the early 1950's and hung on until about 1958. The big difference between the two is that the player in chemin-de-fer (or shimmy) gets a chance to bank the game, whereas the house assumes that role in baccarat. It was evident in Nevada, at least, that the players found the banker's role a dubious honor, for baccarat made it big and shimmy barely got off the ground.

Baccarat pits are customarily draped with heavy velvet, ponderous security guards and self-imposed mystery. However, the game is not nearly as intricate as its surroundings. Two hands are played, one for the bank and one for the players, and the side totalling closest to nine wins.

Keno, of course, came to Nevada with the Chinese who were imported to work on the railroads and in the mines. Since the winners are based on the draw of twenty numbers from a total of eighty, a purist might suspect keno was a form of lottery. Lotteries are forbidden by the Nevada Constitution, but Nevada has chosen not to consider keno a lottery, and the federal government, in an administrative ruling governing the purchase of tickets for advance games, agreed many years ago there can, indeed, be a non-lottery lottery.

At one time keno was called "race horse keno," and each of the eighty numbers represented one of America's better known thoroughbreds. The practice fell out of vogue, probably because of the time and effort attached to calling names as well as numbers as the winning ping pong balls were drawn.

Visitors to Nevada's casinos can still place a bet on the Big Six, or Wheel of Fortune, which edged its way into respectability from carnival beginnings, but the Chuck-a-Luck game of pioneer days is a thing of the past.

MGM, Las Vegas

1895 Fey Liberty Belle, forerunner of today's casino slot machine.

1906 Mills Liberty Bell was developed from the Fey Liberty Bell.

c. 1907. Caille, 2nd largest manufacturer of slots, replicated the Mills Liberty Bell.

The Fabulous Slots

by Marshall Fey

The "Liberty Bell" is not only symbolic of the Bicentennial year, it is also representative of the slot machine. During the industry's early years slot manufacturers named their machines after the famous Philadelphia landmark. For many years slot cases were embellished with cracked Liberty Bells and some were even decorated ornately with the Statue of Liberty. Appropriately, the largest payout obtainable on the first Liberty Bell machines was earned by lining up three bell symbols. Today the bell award, surrounded by cherries, oranges, and plums, remains the only surviving payout from the early slots. From the name Liberty Bell also evolved the generic term "bell slot machine," a designation for categorizing the popular slot machine.

Since the inception of the original bell machine, a product of American inventive ingenuity, the United States has been foremost in the manufacturing of coin operating gambling devices. For approximately seventy years, this country has been exporting slot machines to the far corners of the earth. Today Japan, Australia, England, Belgium, and Denmark have entered the manufacturing field, but our nation still remains the principal slot machine producer.

In 1895 an ingenious three reel gambling device was created in San Francisco. The inventor, Bavarian-born Charles Fey, dubbed his machine the "Liberty Bell" in honor of America's famous symbol of freedom.

Fey placed his first Liberty Bell machine in a San Francisco saloon and it was an instant success. In 1897 Fey opened a shop on Market Street, where his staff handled the manufacturing and servicing of the machines and the operation soon expanded as far south as San Jose, across the bay, and to the cities in central California.

Fey refused to sell or lease his Liberty Bell machines; instead he operated and serviced his exclusive enterprise on a percentage basis. Since gambling devices can not be patented the inevitable occurred in 1906. Catastrophe struck Fey's private operation when one of his precious machines disappeared from a Frisco saloon. The machine reappeared in the Mills Novelty Company factory in Chicago, a contemporary manufacturer of other types of coin operated machines. Rumors of the astoundingly successful Liberty Bell machine had excited Herbert Mills' entrepreneurial determination to produce a bell slot of his own.

In 1907 Mills introduced his own facsimile of Fey's

machine and attempted to capitalize on its popularity by naming it the Mills Liberty Bell. While the machine's case differed from Fey's, the name and basic mechanism were the same. (The essential functions of the original bell n echanisms still remain identical to the mechanical machines of today.) Mills began to mass-produce bell machines and soon became the largest manufacturer of slot machines in the world. (In the past decade Mills has relinquished this distinction to the Bally Manufacturing Corporation.) The bell slot machine had spread from San Francisco to the eastern United States and was on its way throughout the world.

In the United States puritanical laws were constantly impeding the legal operation of the slot machine. Though gambling was first legalized in Nevada in 1869, the mood of the era at the turn of the century was for general reform. Gambling and drinking were thought to be the decadent evils of the day. In 1910 Nevada succumbed to this do-gooder movement and outlawed all forms of gambling. The San Francisco *Post* reported this incident by stating: "With the closing of the gambling houses in Nevada, one of the worst relics of the wild and wooly west has passed out." Games of chance continued operating in this state, illegally, and authorities were paid to look the other way.

As the gaming industry grew in subsequent decades, so did the sophistication of the slot machine. The original Liberty Bell machine, with three reels containing ten symbols per reel, presented possible payout combinations totaling one thousand ($10 \times 10 \times 10$). By the time the casino era had arrived, the standard machine, now with twenty symbols per reel, had a greatly increased payout combination of eight thousand ($20 \times 20 \times 20$).

By adding a fourth reel the possible permutations soared to an amazing one hundred and sixty thousand. Fortunately for the player, the modern slot had grown more generous than its ancestral Liberty Bell. The average payout percentage has increased from seventy-five on the original bells to over eighty-five on today's more liberal machines.

Electricity made possible a new concept in slots that would revolutionize the industry. In 1963, the Bally Manufacturing Corp. of Chicago introduced a machine, though basically mechanical, that had an electro-mechanical circuitry which enabled multiple coin play. It also contained a motor driven hopper to make possible automatic payout of jackpots.

Among the many new machines these new innovations made possible were the five reelers, the five line pay, and the fifteen coin multiplier. A decade later, the Jennings Manufacturing Co. of Reno developed a machine with a completely transistorized circuitry that may introduce a vast possibility of future machines yet to be conceived.

c. 1911. Watling, 3rd largest manufacturer of slots, also copied the Mills machine.

The three reel slot in the twenties, designated as Bell slots, were often adorned with liberty bells.

1968. Bally, today's largest manufacturer of slot machines, named their first four reel machine "the Liberty Bell special"

Father of Modern Nevada Gambling

by Don Stubbs

If a few cantankerous ranchers on the upper Humboldt River hadn't been so stingy about sharing their precious water, legal gambling in Nevada as we know it may never have come into being at all! It was disgust over having to see his downstream ranchlands go thirsting—while upriver stockmen hoarded all the water behind their solid dams—that prompted Phil Tobin to seek a seat in the legislature and thus right this watery wrong. The matter of legalizing gambling was the farthest thing from that 29-year-old cowboy's mind. Thus, in 1930, as Nevada and the nation groped for some way to climb out of the depths of depression, Phil M. Tobin was elected to an assembly seat from Humboldt County.

Gambling seemed destined to cling to its place in Nevada history. Legally, it had been an on-again-off-again proposition: territorial laws against gambling were repealed by the newly-formed State of Nevada in 1869 and a basic backroom industry slowly evolved until after the turn of the century. But legal gambling, then with a generally seedy image, poor controls, and tabbed as a spotty and inadequate tax revenue producer, fell prey to organized reformers and was again outlawed in 1910. From that time until the Great Depression, games of chance were illegal, but they continued on, in saloons and backrooms, until Tobin decided to take drastic and positive action.

It was called "the Wide-Open Gambling Bill," officially known as AB 98, and it legalized all gambling games. Restrictions were few: children were not allowed to take part or loiter in areas where gambling was going on, and game operators had to provide a description of the premises where their wheels and tables were placed. The bill also contained a schedule for allocating tax revenue to the state, counties, and municipalities. One glaring oversight was the omission of a provision for effective enforcement.

Tobin singlehandedly authored and sponsored AB 98, but he had to round up a lot of sympathetic help in both houses to push the bill through. Committee meetings and hearings were formidable obstacles, as were hostile church groups, temperance leaders, educators, and the usual gaggle of self-righteous soapboxers who crowded the Carson City hearing rooms. But the year was 1931; the state was in severe financial straits; pioneers, ranchers, miners and gamblers still carried a lot of sway; and three-quarters of a century of non-stop gambling all combined to apply the pressure needed to put Phil Tobin's bill on the statute books.

After the Committee on Public Morals finally reported the measure out, the assembly passed it 24 to 11. It ran into even less opposition in the senate, which said "aye" 13 to 3. Governor Fred Balzar—who supported the controversial bill from the start—signed it into law March 19, 1931.

"Wide-open gambling," now fully legal, got off to an uncertain and faltering start. The action, such as it was, was centered in the north, mostly around Carson City and Reno, which saw the old yet new business with a suspicious eye. Local governments quickly restricted the geographic locations of gambling halls and saw to it that the games were operated cleanly and conservatively. Las Vegas, then little more than a railroad depot and travelers' stop, was not yet even a gleam in the developers' eye.

Phil Tobin has not seen Las Vegas since 1942. He says he cares little about the huge development of the Strip, which had its own faltering beginning in 1940. Reflecting an attitude common—then and now—to many northern Nevadans, Tobin is a die-hard Separatist. He views the northern and southern sections of the state as having little in common, and, only half-jokingly, offers a plan where Nevada could be cleanly divided into separate sovereign states by an east-west line drawn somewhere in the vicinity of Tonopah. But Tobin is a hard-line realist in viewing the importance of gambling to the economy of the state. The impact of the industry's modern revenue picture strikes him even harder than a less-seasoned observer. A few rickety roulette wheels and even-odds Faro bank games added only a few dollars to government and industry coffers for decades. Now, with casino winnings regularly topping the billion-dollar mark, Tobin readily concedes the gambling (politely termed "gaming" these days) industry is the unshakeable cornerstone of Nevada's economy.

But what about Phil Tobin? Picture the man who was architect of a system, itself not altogether held in the highest esteem, which is unique in the U.S. Phil Tobin is as reasonable as a human being can be. Raised in the inoffensive environs of Winnemucca; tutored and experienced in the great American outback; associating with none other than reasonable people (except those who would withhold his river water), Tobin appeared on the lawmaking scene in Nevada as a pillar of common sense. His efforts in legalizing gambling were attempts to exercise cool control over well-established fact, rather than throw the state open to unbridled exploitation.

His entire life has been spent on the open range, and he has owned three ranches at different times. He still works for the C-2 Cattle Company in the Quinn River valley in Humboldt County, "doin' whatever I want to, mostly." But it gets cold in that country in the wintertime so Tobin usually spends the chilliest part of the season with his son Phil Jim, daughter-in-law and two grandsons at their home in Reno. That time of year also affords him time to visit southern California, usually Catalina Island, and a chance to visit the horse tracks—his only gambling weakness. Phil Tobin claims his accomplishment of helping to legalize gambling never led to any gainful involvement in the industry. His interests, financial and otherwise, have always been with the land and the cattle business. As for others who gamble, Tobin frowns on the man who would whittle away life savings at the tables; he approves even less of those who would attempt to legislate morality. Harry Truman once said that "if you can't stand the heat, stay out of the kitchen." Those are Phil Tobin's sentiments exactly—even if ol' Give-'em-hell-Harry *was* a democrat!

Phil Tobin (1902-1980)

Dealer's Choice

by Phyllis Darling

August 15, 1945—VJ Day; America was one vast celebration. The juke boxes were playing "Kiss me once, and kiss me twice, and kiss me once again" and thousands of newly returned soldiers were enjoying the comforts of home after years overseas. When the parties had ended, the long-awaited reunions had been held, and home-cooked dinners made C rations just a horrible memory, the G.I.s took a closer look at postwar America to see what opportunities it held for them.

One of these young men, an ex-Army Air Corps flier, stood on Santa Monica Boulevard in Los Angeles that August and gambled on his future with the flip of a coin: heads he would go to Alaska, tails he would go to Las Vegas.

Two days later, Al Courtland was introduced into one of Las Vegas' most popular low-cost housing areas —the park benches at the Union Pacific Railroad station. Finding the accommodations a bit cramped, even for an ex-tail gunner, he moved into the Windsor Hotel

on Fremont Street.

In the free-wheeling, post-war period of the late Forties, there were no dealer's schools and no break-in periods. Would-be dealers simply walked into a casino and if the boss took a liking to them, they would soon be sitting at a table, playing with house money. This was called shilling—the first step in becoming a dealer. Though Al didn't know the difference between a hardway six and a natural seven, he walked into the Golden Nugget and asked for a job as a shill. His short-lived career ended abruptly when Al threw the dice off the table on his first throw.

Out on the street again, he tried his luck as a 21 dealer at the old Las Vegas Club. That job lasted four months and by that time Al fell into the routine of a Las Vegas dealer.

In those days working arrangements were quite informal. When the eight-hour shift broke, dealers who wanted work lined up in the casino and the boss chose the next crew. Dealers who were not selected ran to the next casino in time for another lineup. Those who wanted to work around the clock made rounds every eight hours.

The pay was $8 in cash at the end of every shift. The tips, or "tokes," seemed more than adequate to Al because at the time a shot of whiskey cost 25¢, a hamburger at Wimpy's 12¢, and a movie 14¢. Wimpy's, the dealers' favorite restaurant, was across the street from the El Dorado Club (now the Horseshoe) where Al found steady work.

As a left-handed dealer, Al faced one of the many superstitions of the old-time Vegas gambler that left-handed dealers brought bad luck. Moustaches, beards, the color red, and pipes also fell into this bad luck category. One steady customer at the El Dorado crap tables took the term "keeping the dice cold" literally— he kept his dice in the ice box. The bosses were not immune to superstition either; one boss, believing that salt was unlucky, poured six shakers into the pockets of a player who had hit a winning streak.

In the Forties women worked as 21 dealers and even as crap dealers. However, in the Fifties, big-time gamblers brought their prejudice against women dealers with them. By 1955, not one female dealer remained in the casinos.

The dealer's fortunes changed and grew with the city. When the focal point of Las Vegas gambling moved to the Strip, so did the dealers. By 1950, Al Courtland was a 21 dealer at the first Las Vegas Strip hotel—the El Rancho Vegas. In 1953 he moved to one of the first glamour hotels on the strip, the Sahara. Today, the ex-flier who made his Las Vegas debut on a park bench at the railroad station is a casino manager in Las Vegas. Al had parlayed a flip of a coin into a thirty-year winning streak.

The First Strip Hotel

by Jim Daley

Back in 1939, a charming, colorful promoter decided to construct a hotel on the highway to Los Angeles, just three miles from downtown Las Vegas. Tom Hull, operator of southern California's Hull Hotels, started what is today's famous Las Vegas Strip.

The El Rancho Vegas—inviting and spacious with its neon windmill, marked a new fun and recreation concept. Red tile roofs, white adobe bungalows, and a beautiful pool paradise formed the setting for Las Vegas' first casino and show room. Ballard Barron was the casino boss, and dealers would disappear fast if they became too friendly with the gamblers. Garwood Van and his band played dance music between shows. An early star was comedian Frank Fay, and Sophie Tucker sang "Pistol Packin' Mama."

It was a quiet inn during the day, but come dusk patrons would crowd in while the neon windmill and bright lights would get the silver cartwheels rolling. Transients, tourists, and celebrities all gathered for an unusual and exciting time, but good accommodations were hard to come by. All staff and chorus girls would occupy one room, while Hull ordered six of his traveling executives to occupy his suite. Late arrivals were advised to grab a chaise at the pool or try Boulder City, thirty miles south.

Some of those signing the guest register were Andy Devine, Lana Turner, and Linda Darnell. Howard Hughes checked in, then as elusive as he is today—reserving a table for thirty in the Rancho Room, he would host a lively party but would never appear himself. Bugsy Siegel established headquarters at the El Rancho while planning the third Strip hotel, and movie chain mogul D. W. Griffith was already building the Last Frontier two miles further out.

The railroad brought in most tourists of that era, since air travel then was limited to only one airline serving southern Nevada. Western Air Lines, Las Vegas' first air service, offered flights on DC-3 jets which would often have to remain overnight in Vegas, much to the delight of casino pit bosses.

Tom Hull was like a cat with nine lives. He had many ideas and tried them all. One night he turned the large cafe into a bingo parlor, only to decide thirty-six hours later to convert it back to the cafe. He kept managers in a state of confusion. He owned other hotels, including the Santa Monica-Miramar and Hollywood-Roosevelt. Hull was one of the first to employ the Spartan Executive plane to speed him about, and early day pilot Paul Mantz kept him on the move. Hull was not only the daddy of the Strip, but the originator of the luxury motor hotels as we know them today.

Although the El Rancho Vegas is gone, travelers can still find El Ranchos in Fresno and Sacramento—a tribute to the foresight of Tom Hull, builder of the Strip's first hotel.

Against a backdrop of brown sandstone walls laid by New Mexico Zunis, this Las Vegas crowd of about 1947 is enjoying Ramona Room brunch. A virtual Las Vegas "Who's Who" is in this picture. Here was the town's social center where most banquets were held, in addition to wedding receptions; especially popular was the Sunday hunt breakfast. Talent scout for the Ramona Room was Maxine Lewis, who brought in such notables as Liberace, Vincent Lopez, Arthur Lee Simkins, Birney Cummins, and Phil Spitalmy's all girl band.

At his first arrest

Bugsy Siegel
by John F. Cahlan

Benjamin Siegel was known to his associates in Murder, Inc. as "Bugs" because of the tremendous rages which possessed him any time he was crossed. The general public referred to him as "Bugsy," a lowly but feared hit-man of the mob. But many Las Vegans admired him as the man who brought world-wide recognition to their community in efforts to create an entertainment capital of the world.

When he came to Las Vegas posing as a legitimate businessman, he was addressed as Benny, Benji or Mr. Siegel. He despised his nickname and tried to erase the gangster image associated with the name "Bugsy."

Siegel made his first public appearance in Las Vegas at a Chamber of Commerce meeting in the old Biltmore Hotel then situated on the northeast corner of Main Street and Bonanza Road. He announced his plans for constructing a new, plush resort hotel backed by financial investors of a noted Eastern distilling firm. What he neglected to disclose, however, was the fact that the company was owned by the mob.

The El Rancho Vegas and the Last Frontier Hotel were prospering on what is now known as the Strip and despite World War II, these two businesses were doing exceptionally well. Travel was restricted because of gas rationing and most of the "swingers" had been drafted, resulting in a national slowdown in the resort hotel business.

However, Benny was certain that southern Nevada would host many people visiting the enlisted men stationed at the nearby Army Corps Gunnery School and those soldiers training in the desert east and south of Las Vegas.

Benny believed that proper accomodations would attract such visitors and top echelons of the armed services to stay at the hotel. With the unlimited financial backing of the mob, he knew his concept of the Flamingo Hotel could become a reality and be a profitable venture as well.

But Siegel faced real problems. Building materials were in short supply because construction was limited to such purposes which could aid the war effort and officials did not believe that one new hotel in Las Vegas could contribute anything to assist in winning the war.

However, Benny was shrewd and, though the public didn't quite understand his success, knew that certain people could be swayed. He had to find someone in Washington who might be able to move the War Production Board to relax regulations so his materials could be supplied. Senator Pat McCarran of Nevada was chairman of the appropriations committee and had the kind of juice Benny liked. When the senator received information regarding Siegel's plans and discovered that the voters of southern Nevada were whole-heartedly in favor of them, he spent a great deal of time convincing officials that some sort of construction was needed to house the "thousands of people in the southern Nevada area who are aiding the war effort and need satisfactory living quarters in order to continue their work."

Everyone conveniently "forgot" that the satisfactory living quarters for those engaged in the war effort would come complete with a gaming casino and all the other accoutrements necessary for a first class hotel and resort.

When Siegel applied for liquor and gaming licenses, present rules and regulations were not in effect making it much easier to meet the requirements. In those days the county commissioners constituted the investigative body and their recommendations were

Spirit of a Gambling Town
by Sam Bowler

From the dust of the desert it rises and rises
A town of glamour of games and surprises,
Of lights that go twinkle, twankle and twang
And machines that go whirr, flutter and bang.

And to this fantasia all curious come,
Whether tourist, or traveler or seeker of fun
To try out their luck, with a buck, or some change.
Through dawn, through dusk, through night they remain.

With cameras and lenses, and meters for sun,
Snapping off pictures one after one,
Pointing and shooting with kliks, klickles and klings
Each trying to photograph all assortment of things.

Around every corner leaps electrical flickers,
Reds chasing blues, spiraling-yellows as kickers.
Each timed in rhyme, in rhythm, and more
Creating a huge flashing symphony score.

With the jingle of silver, the crackle of cash
A winner's sharp laughter, a loser's faint gnash,
It's a whole other world, swirled and stirred
Where the chatter of dice can always be heard.

Oranges, lemons, cherries and plums
Spin in precision with hisses and hums
Coming to stop with clunks, clangers and chimes
Sometimes, if lucky, spitting a jangle of dimes.

The wheels that extend on spindles of glitter
Rotate with flashes as they clatter and clitter
In a medley of motion of blares, blurrs and blinks,
But slow to a silence in a matter of winks.

Kings and Queens, and Jacks of-all-trades
Clubs over hearts and diamonds on spades,
They're thrown on the tables with flips, flaps and flings
Causing wide-saucered-eyes from the money this brings.

Numbers that come in all shapes and sizes
Some that go down and up and cross-wises,
Are painted with colors, and covered, and curled
Analyzed and systemized in this make-believe world.

From the dust of the desert it rises and rises
This town of glamour of games and surprises,
An unbroken echo of wild, wondrous things
That linger forever in the depths of your dreams.

usually accepted by the state tax commission, which then approved and issued gambling licenses. Benny relied on some of his local friends to influence the commission since one of the commissioners was not entirely convinced that Bugsy was the type of individual who should be operating a casino. The commissioner was a pioneer in southern Nevada and was not eager to see a known eastern gangster come in and wreck the operations of the county. Subsequently Bugsy's friends arranged a meeting with the official and at the next session of the county board the recalcitrant commissioner eagerly made the motion for approval of the licenses.

The Flamingo was unveiled in all its glory with an opening celebration that was the most elaborate ever held in Las Vegas at that time. The black tie affair was by invitation only and guests included the movie crowd, Siegel's backers and associates and the news media. The lavish stage production copied the show format originally introduced at the El Rancho Vegas, but the stars of the Flamingo show were of much more prominence than the budding stars which graced the stage of the El Rancho and Last Frontier.

The story of Las Vegas' newest luxury hotel made international headlines and Siegel, his partners and the locals soon proclaimed this venture a smashing success. The Flamingo became a haven for those who mingled in high society circles while Bugsy Siegel's association with the gangster element came to an abrupt halt. While sitting on the divan in the Beverly Hills residence of his girl friend Virginia Hill, Bugsy was fatally shot between the eyes by a mysterious gunman. The murder has never been solved; however, speculations are that Benny became a marked man when he took over the Flamingo and failed to maintain accurate books.

Las Vegas prospered and Benny's work had not been in vain. Nor did Siegel found Las Vegas; he merely discovered the hidden lode and publicized it worldwide, attracting tourists and promoting interest for the entertainment capital of the world.

Family Operation

Among Nevada's casino operations thrives a family business that defies the other corporate structured hotel-casinos of downtown and the Las Vegas Strip. Yet, the first impression of its enterprising patriarch, Benny Binion, does not smack of a multi-millionaire's image. He holds no office hours. In fact, he has no office. He conducts business on the spot—whether in one of his restaurants or on the stools of the gaming tables. His integrity and honesty require no secrecy or heavily guarded documentation and such staid qualities have built a flawless reputation for this legendary figure of Fremont Street.

Above all, Binion is a gaming innovator. He first introduced the highest limit crap game. Anyone can bet $5,000 flat and take $10,000 on double odds while playing $5,000 place bets on any number. His pit bosses are allowed more autonomy than those in larger hotels and the relationship between employees and management exemplifies staunch loyalty and understanding.

Binion recalls that "twenty years ago people would come to town, broke and really down; we'd give them a job and they still keep coming back." Some have moved on while others still work in his club.

The Horseshoe Club is owned and operated exclusively by the Binion family, headed by Benny, his wife Teddy Jane, and their sons Jack and Ted. When the club opened in August 1951, it was the first hotel and casino in downtown Las Vegas to sport carpeting on the floor throughout the building.

Against the judgment of neighboring casino owners, Binion remodeled the three-story structure

At left, Benny keeps a close look on the action during the World Series of Poker. The million dollar display draws more than 600 people daily.

"Lazy people don't gamble," is one of Benny's favorite quotes. He has spent a lifetime studying human nature.

during the early 1950's and business immediately improved. However, in 1953, Binion was forced to sell the club to Joe W. Brown, a New Orleans gambler who originated the $1 million cash display still present in the casino.

In 1958 Brown sold out to a group of investors including Jack Binion, "Doby Doc" and Ed Levinson. Levinson then became president of both the Fremont Hotel and the Horseshoe.

When the Binion family bought out Doc and Levinson, Benny again regained entire control of the Horseshoe.

Though Binion's long-time friend Joe Brown loaned him the money to display the $1 million, Binion conceived the idea while visiting the nation's capital. He noted the long lines of people waiting to tour the Federal Treasury and thought that a huge money exhibit would attract tourists in Las Vegas. Encasing one hundred $10,000 bills in a giant horseshoe, Binion then watched as visitors flocked to have their picture taken beside the now-famous display. Benny now owns the display in its entirety. This tremendous attraction is an expensive project with insurance costs amounting to $3,000 annually and loss of revenue from interest totaling more than $80,000 per year, but it is also viewed by an average of 600 people every day of the year.

The annual World Series of Poker is perhaps Binion's greatest innovation, for that event insures world-wide publicity for Las Vegas and the Horseshoe. In the early 1970's Binion asked, "Why not a World Series of Poker?" for a unique gamblers' reunion.

Oddsmaker Jimmy the Greek told Benny that he could promote this series as a sporting event and sent news releases to thousands of publications. Now the card game has been firmly established as a yearly

showdown, pitting renowned poker players against each other and their bulging purses. The $10,000 buy-in is available to all comers willing to gamble on a chance of winning all-or nothing at all. The game continues until all contenders "bust out" with the remaining player declared the champion.

Publicity about the game has attracted famous "Amarillo Slim" who won the series only once; Johnny Moss, who plays steady as a rock and has won three times; other prominent poker players are Brian Roberts, Joe Bernstein, Texas Jack Strauss and Crandall Addington.

Benny Binion often expresses his personal philosophy with a favorite slogan such as "I cherish not my winnings. They do not stay with you." Apparently this is a blatant contradiction when it comes to the casino mogul for he has wisely invested his fortune. But then he also states that "I grieve not my losses" and this may account for the Binion prominence in the gambling field, because nobody and nothing has managed to keep Benny down for any length of time.

But there was one winner who completely shattered Binion's business ego—momentarily at least. It seems that, several years ago, a carpenter charged Benny $1800 for a job when he really had completed only about $300 worth of work. Binion paid the man in full but persuaded him to play the tables and parlay his earnings. Escorting the carpenter to the bar, Binion sat beside him and ordered several free drinks. Finally the worker played cards; but his luck was better than Binion's and he cashed in more than $5600 in chips. Seldom, if ever, does Binion get mad at winners, but he was angry that his plan had failed and backfired. At a later time, when another player won almost $500,000,

the biggest payoff ever hit at the Horseshoe, Binion scarcely gave it a second thought.

He loves to see players gambling with high stakes and has mastered the art of handling high rollers. Should a big spender ask "What's the limit?" Benny calmly replies, "Let your first bet be your limit."

One of Benny's most memorable anecdotes tells about the three men who flew in from Dallas and gambled for three hours. They had told their wives they were going to a picture show. By the time they left to catch the flight back home, they had won $96,000 on the Blackjack tables.

Binion recalls one interesting experience when an ambulance pulled alongside the curb on Fremont Street one night about 4 a.m. Two men helped a lady into a wheelchair and a nurse accompanied her into the casino. After about four hours' play they wheeled her back to the waiting ambulance which had been standing by in case of emergency. Mystery still shrouds the identification of the lady and whether she came from a local hospital or nursing home.

For the past few years Binion's buddy, long-time personal friend Chill Wills, has been acting as the Horseshoe's host and has been featured in the club's television advertising. Binion was Wills' best man when the veteran star was married at the first celebrity wedding hosted at Benny's place in 1973.

For relaxation and exercise Binion rides the trails on his expansive Montana ranch where he raises cattle and horses. 250 sections of land encompass the 160,000 acres of the Binion empire and the excellent, uniform quality of beef he serves to his Las Vegas customers has been bred and produced under Benny's close, personal supervision on his spread.

But Las Vegas is and always will be this man's home. He has yet to spend an unpleasant moment at the Horseshoe and sees a bright future ahead for the gambling mecca. He firmly believes there is no limit on the fabulous prospects of the state of Nevada. "With faster transportation and improved air travel, tourists from neighboring states come and play and are able to return home that night," explains Binion.

With professionals like Benny Binion, the future of Nevada's gambling and tourism seems indeed headed on a collision course with success.

"Mr. B," as he is affectionately called, is flanked by his two sons, Teddy (left) and Jack. Both are executives in this family operation.

Guardian of the Games

There he is, walking among the gaming tables and looking at the games in progress, answering with dignity players' questions about everything—gaming procedure, floor shows, credit. He is always dressed in a sport jacket or business suit. He is forever congenial, never abrupt, smiling, and greeting customers with enthusiasm: "Hello Mr. J. . . . Glad to see you. I have missed you here. You've been away too long." This man is the casino executive, the floor public relations man, the hotel's initial contact with old and potential customers.

What makes this man on the floor a success for the casino? After all, the glittering neon and the expensive hotel facades generally look alike. The *real* difference is the man behind the tables—the floorman—who realizes that the kindness and constant attention to the players spells the difference between a successful casino and an ordinary one.

"Win or lose, the player must leave as if he has been treated with respect," says Mort Saiger, a 33-year veteran of the Las Vegas Strip and a successful casino executive. "The customer must come first. . . . He must be treated so royally that he would want to return soon."

This may extend to an offer to help a player who might, for instance in Blackjack, try to split his fives when a dealer has a seven or an eight showing. Courteously, the floor man might say, "I'm sorry, sir . . . May I suggest that rather than splitting 5's, doubling down is a much better play." In that situation, the customer should double down to vastly improve his chance of winning. This treatment almost never embarrasses the player.

The personal touch Mort gives his Frontier Hotel customers on the floor is borne out by the volume of mail that he receives from all over the world. "You have been very thoughtful and generous to me with your many gifts of kindness," wrote a man from Minnesota. "The information you gave me about Blackjack was most helpful," a London customer recalled. In Los Angeles a customer declared, "Thank you for the show and the gift of the two books—an unexpected surprise."

Obviously, Mort takes a personal interest in his customers. He finds out their personal tastes . . . makes them feel at home. "I inquire about their hobbies, what sports they follow, even their tastes in music," declared Mort, who himself is a lover of opera and the classics. He introduces customers to his friends, takes them to dinner, or invites them into the casino lounge for conversation over a cocktail.

Most important of all, the floorman must never

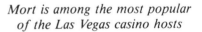

Mort is among the most popular of the Las Vegas casino hosts

begrudge the lucky player, whether large or small. "There must be winners in order to have players. . . . As long as we get the play, and as long as the customer abides by the house rules, we are happy to see a winner, and wish him to come back."

Almost all casino floormen start out as dealers; they do not rise from the ranks of hotel administration. Mort's advancement within the Frontier Hotel is typical.

In July 1942 he began as a steward at a downtown club which soon folded. Three months later he was running the stables at the newly completed Last Frontier Hotel. He took guests for rides, did the banking, and brought the mail from the new post office in downtown Las Vegas.

After working the stables all day, Mort dressed in the evening to help with the shows. He worked the lights and assisted the show producer.

This was a satisfying life for Mort, but when he married Reba in 1945 he needed more money. The management then made a Blackjack dealer out of him.

Ever thoughtful and businesslike, Mort worked up quite a clientele who always asked for him when they came into the casino. Seldom a month went by that he did not sell at least a few score rooms for the Last Frontier.

In 1952 Mort went across the street to work at the Desert Inn as a dealer and finally as a floorman. But in 1969 he returned to the Frontier, this time to a new modern hotel which had replaced the ranch style Last Frontier on the same site.

The job of casino floorman has not changed much in the last thirty or forty years. The rules of most games have stayed essentially the same. Aggressiveness, diligence and sincerity are all traits that lead to executive capacities. Casino operations are more sophisticated now with increased salesmanship and junkets to bring planeloads of players to the hotel.

In 1942 Mort remembers his boss saying every night, at about 2 a.m., "All right, boys, this is the last roll. . . . We are going to close." Now there is play around the clock, seven days a week. The last time casinos closed were during the Kennedy and King funerals. Slot machines and tables were covered with white sheets for about two hours.

Truly, the floorman is a key man in the casino operation. It has been said that the actions of men are like the index of a book—they point out what is remarkable in them. The casino floorman points out what is remarkable about a hotel.

Young Mort rides along with star William Bendix along the dirt shoulder of U.S. 91 (now the Las Vegas Strip), in about 1942.

A Warm **WELCOME**

...and refreshing friendliness typify the gay greeting that awaits you at the
Last Frontier, the most distinctive hotel in fabled Las Vegas. At the friendly Frontier,
all the color of a bygone romantic era is combined with the ultimate in
resort luxury to bring you "The Early West in Modern Splendor."
Located in the heart of the far-famed "Strip," the Frontier maintains casual
informality through sun-splashed days and exciting nights, boasts the
world's finest entertainment and food rated the greatest
by the most discriminating gourmets.

Hotel LAST FRONTIER

Entertainment

The Origins of Casino Entertainment in Nevada

by Paul A. Leonard

Night club entertainment has become big business in Nevada and especially in Las Vegas, acknowledged as the entertainment capital of the world, and in the Reno-Tahoe area of western Nevada.

Practically every current great name in the field has appeared either in one or the other of the two areas and most of them in both.

When did this influx of the nation's "big names" in entertainment start in Nevada—and where?

If a resident of Vegas were asked the question it's an almost sure bet the response would be, "Why here in Las Vegas, of course." A Renoite would guess his own "Biggest Little City" or maybe Tahoe was the birthplace of the big-time shows.

Little would they know about it.

For neither of the two large cities of Nevada can claim the honor.

While they were tinkering around with third-raters 35 years before the nation's Bicentennial another city in the Silver State stole the march on them.

It was Elko, with a population of about 4,000, that started it all. Or rather, one man in Elko did it.

His name was Newton Crumley, Jr., and when he made his daring plunge he had just turned 30 years of age.

Crumley's father had long since purchased the old Commercial Hotel at the intersection of Fourth and Railroad Streets in the heart of Elko. It was a prosperous business when "old Newt" put his son in charge of the hotel.

By the end of the 1930's plans were completed to enlarge the hotel and an annex was built immediately west of the Commercial. Only two stories high, it was, nevertheless, considered a fine addition to downtown Elko. Most of the ground floor was given over to a large room, simply called the Commercial Lounge.

"Young Newt" had some new-fangled ideas about promoting business in a hotel with gaming—and one of them was to bring in entertainers. The "lounge" was just large enough to stage a floor show.

The junior Crumley started slowly, engaging first a routine female dancer. She packed the joint.

Such success stimulated the enterprising young hotel operator—and he hit upon the idea of going first class.

Crumley, an excellent pilot, had recently completed his flight training with the Army Air Corps at Randolph and Kelly Fields in Texas. Perhaps it was that high-flying that provided him with the impetus and daring that brought him and Elko into the big-time.

In any event, he engaged none other than Ted Lewis and his band for a full week.

When this startling announcement hit the local papers it shook the residents of Elko and Elko County. The gist of their reaction was, "What's that Crumley kid doing, hiring one of the top bands and names in show business—and for a whole week?"

It was the general feeling that the brash young man would send the Commercial Hotel into bankruptcy.

That wasn't the way it worked out—not at all.

So, to Elko on April 26, 1941 came Ted Lewis with his musicians, his famous intermittent cry, "Is Everybody Happy" and a lithe young black man who mimicked the noted band leader as he went into his gyrations, featuring his famous top hat, to the band's rendition of "Me and My Shadow."

To say that Lewis brought down the house is almost understating the situation. The Commercial was packed to the doors every performance.

Although unverified by the management, it was rumored Lewis and the band spent more at the tables than the $12,000 tab—so much more, in fact, Lewis came back for a repeat at little or no expense to the Commercial.

In any event "young Newt" was joyful over his gamble and in ensuing months he booked, from time to time, many more of the famous entertainers of the day. These included Paul Whiteman ("the king of jazz"), Jimmy Dorsey, Sophie Tucker, Carl Ravazza, the Ritz Brothers, Chico Marx of the Four Marx Brothers, Phil Harris, Henry Busse, Ray Noble and Lawrence Welk —the latter before he became a national figure in the entertainment world. Others who appeared were

Rowan & Martin, Kay Stevens, Wayne Newton, Bob Crosby, Vicki Carr, Sophie Tucker, Alan Jones.

After Crumley had demonstrated the importance of big-name "draws," Las Vegas and Reno-Tahoe picked up the cue and booked star attractions.

As the clouds of World War II deepened the big name policy was dropped. Pearl Harbor came, and by that time Crumley was flying fighter planes enroute to becoming a colonel and commandant at Minter Field, Bakersfield, California. After the war he returned to operate his hotel.

The big time came back to Elko for a time in the 1950's as Crumley vied with Red Ellis, co-owner of the Stockmen's Hotel, as the pre-eminent gathering place in northeastern Nevada.

The man who brought Nevada entertainment of age died February 11, 1962 in a plane crash about thirty miles north of his birthplace of Tonopah. He and E. J. Questa, president of the First National Bank of Nevada, were killed when the plane wings iced up and the craft plunged to earth, snuffing out the lives of two of Nevada's most prominent residents.

Elvis * Wayne * Liza
That Superstar City
by Bill Willard

Las Vegas entertainment and gambling bears all the scratch marks of a love-hate stand-off. The combination seems likely to weather many a storm despite all of the put-downs and criticisms over the years.

There were times in Las Vegas—calamitous times indeed—when the least cross-eyed look, or a negative thought spoken or written about our most important products was certain to bring forth wails of anguish from our own press and whatever publicity people or press agents abounded. Defense was the order of most any day.

Over the quarter of a century, during which time Las Vegas has risen in favor with all manner of people high or low, national or international, there has evolved the smug attitude of something which has arrived.

This is the entertainment capital of the world.

This hasn't been a gee-whiz town since the fertile Forties, which was the Model-T decade spawning the Fabulous Fifties. That's when Las Vegas took off and 25 years later scarcely a sign of a descent is anywhere evident, either in gross gambling wins or star entertainment.

There are certain weaknesses revealed in future star bookings, just as there were 25 years ago. There was that group of top resort hotel bosses that met in the early part of 1950 to declare a moratorium on further hotels built in Las Vegas, until the populace caught up with the five Strip hotels, El Rancho Vegas, Last Frontier, Flamingo, Thunderbird and Wilbur Clark's Desert Inn.

The Las Vegas *Sun* printed insert sections April 23, 1950, to hail the opening of the Desert Inn the following evening. The banner headline of the first section read: "Vegas Looms As Resort Capital With Completion of $3,500,000 Desert Inn."

In September of 1950, the *Sun* headlined: "Golden Slipper Saloon and Gambling Hall Opens in Last Frontier Village."

It didn't take long for panjandrums of the Golden Nugget downtown, Guy McAfee, Buck Blaine, Art Ham and buddies to send out a quiet word to Bill Moore, Ballard Barron et al about a slight word infringement in the casino's title. It was immediately changed to the Silver Slipper.

The popular Club Bingo had been converted into the Sahara and the Sands flung open its doors on December 16, 1952, with a four-day entertainment blast headed by Danny Thomas (he played sick with laryngitis to allow a host of headliners to cavort over the extended opening) and an influx of press from just about every eminent publication in the world.

Entertainment? The Last Frontier Village adjacent to the Silver Slipper catered to everyone in the family—"from the kiddies to the grownups. Sure to delight the youngsters is the full-size merry-go-round, scooter ride and miniature railroad train. In addition, there are the pony rides during seasonable weather." Not to forget Last Frontier Stables, where all stars and entertainers gathered faithfully each week for the "Sunday Morning Breakfast Ride" out past Hoot Gibson's D-4-C Ranch to the mesa or beyond to Red Rock Canyon via horse or stage coach.

Ten years after all of this innocent fun and games, western style, Last Frontier Village had all but vanished in the wake—or for the sake—of asphalt. By now, this petroleum product was replacing the natural desert tundra, for travel by car was chugging ahead rapidly and Las Vegas was on the map, just a quick bypass on Route 66 over Boulder Dam, and there was your real live Sodom & Gomorrah with plenty of free parking.

Las Vegas had boomed and busted a bit as the Riviera became the first high-rise hotel on the Strip, nine stories and so-o-o-o metropolitan with an almost lobby, a raised section overlooking the casino. Liberace opened the showroom; a Liberace only half glitter and glam, the other half semi-formal as he plied the 88s of his special concert grand, accompanied by good old brother George, and a most elaborate candelabra. The entertainment world was shocked to learn that Liberace was paid $50,000 a week for this engagement, tops so far in the accelerating rush of weekly stipends which had begun earlier with the battle of Marlene Dietrich (Sahara) and Tallulah Bankhead (Sands) for $25,000 per. Both won.

The bust was the Royal Nevada, squeezed between the New Frontier (new owners tossed out any reference to "last"), and the burgeoning Stardust. Recession had begun late in 1953 when proverbial cannonballs could be fired through some showrooms. Witness Jack E. Leonard's crack to a meager batch of ringsiders at El Rancho Vegas, "Look at this—enough customers to fill a Jaguar."

It was a high rising decade, not only in building on the Strip and downtown, but in prices to attend the headline events in major showrooms. The Sixties began with but a mini-minimum charge in the showrooms, around $2.50 per person, and rose to an average of $10 as the Seventies came in. Then the minimums became maximums, shooting as high as the ill-planned Frank Sinatra week at Caesars Palace in early 1975 when management forced a $40 minimum as business suffered and Sinatra hit the roof. Bar drink prices also rose in many of the posh palaces as tourists sought relief in lounges, but were also confronted with set minimums or one or two drink minimums which weren't too reasonable in themselves.

In the Fifties the lounges began as a plan to aid casino traffic, to keep people around the gaming area and not let them wander too far before hitting another table, wheel, or slot. The Last Frontier in the old Gay 90's section first featured special entertainment, the Mary Kaye Trio, and credit producer Eddie Fox for that. Down the Strip at El Rancho Vegas, Steve Gibson Redcaps and Damita Jo warbled on a small raised stage adjacent to the bar and then came the big lounge move across the Strip from El Rancho when Bill Miller enclosed the area off from casino confusion to become the Sahara's Casbar. The hottest act during those early years was Louis Prima and Keely Smith.

Booked into the Casbar in 1960 by Stan Irwin was an act that billed itself as Don Rickles & The Franklins. Rickles was one of the few to graduate from a lounge into the main showroom. Shecky Greene was another and Wayne Newton sent brother Jerry packing and, as a single-o, became the workhorse of the Howard Hughes stable as the now wealthy Arabian steed fancier locks up more than forty weeks a year between the Sands Copa Room and the Frontier's Music Hall— and at $150,000 a week! But it is a myth that lounges are propagation points for mainroom talent, especially headliner status. As a matter of fact, it is the other way around. Many a star of the Fifties could only find work in lounges in the Sixties and today we note some of the former mainroomers of the last decade presently working in whatever lounges exist.

Consorting with the devil titillated millions. During the Fifties they came to find hoods in Vegas and find them they did—or thought they did. These were the fantasies of losers, who arrived in droves to toss money away and be entertained in the bargain. During that far away innocent time, the price of entertainment was what the visitors chose to make it and no forced extras. It was—no cover or minimum—come as you are— howdy partner and our handshake is all we need to seal the deal.

What a busy epoch was the decade of the 60's!

Columnist Joe Delaney pegged it very well in a Las Vegas *Sun* piece at the end of the Sixties, on December 29, 1969. He wrote that "Howard Hughes has to be the most important 'happening' in Las Vegas, if not to the state of Nevada, during this decade."

Another down cycle or bust period occurred ten years after the business droop of the Fifties and into this vacuum stepped the vast Hughes machine in 1966, headed by a once-upon-a-time free and easy Las Vegas playboy and rounder, a billionaire who had to get rid of somewhere around $174 million or hand over most of it to the IRS. Hughes directed his empire from atop the Desert Inn, which hotel had fittingly begun the sharp

LAS VEGAS
NEVADA

daytime sun · nightime fun

One way Las Vegas publicized itself was by circulating many kinds of colorful brochures, each depicting what was in store in fun in the sun Las Vegas.

up eventually owning the hotel, later spinning off into Caesars World, Inc.

But the Sahara and Sands were filled, battling it out for year-end business with Dietrich at the Sahara and the following personages at the Sands all headlining the first anniversary celebration: Danny Thomas, Frank Sinatra, Billy Eckstine, Vic Damone, Billy Gray, Patti Moore & Ben Lessy, Jimmy McHugh & Songstars, a typical Jack Entratter splash.

The battle was enjoined between Sahara show producer Bill Miller and the Sands showboss Entratter, but Miller had the edge by being billed over Dietrich—"Bill Miller presents . . ." The same Miller and syndicate bought into the sinking Royal Nevada in October 1955.

Miller brought in "Guys and Dolls," starring Robert Alda and most of the New York cast. Right after the musical closed in late November, Phil Spitalny and His All-Girl Orchestra headlined.

But then late in December 1955 *Daily Variety* reported, "Royal Nevada represents an investment of $7 million and if it folds it will be the second Las Vegas hotel folded within three months, the other having been rise in Las Vegas fortune 16 years before. At the end of the decade the difference in the Las Vegas economy was apparent as the *Sun,* on the same page as Delaney's roundup of the past ten years, showed a cartoon of Hughes and a graph of Nevada economy on the rise from before 1967 through 1969. With this chart were paeans of praise to the lone arranger who had acquired Strip hotels, two airports, a television station, golf course, mines and other hunks of real estate. "Las Vegas began a new cycle of growth coupled with business stability," the caption ended. . . .

There was plenty of blue chip wheeling and dealing as Del Webb International bought the Sahara, built the Mint and took over the Thunderbird, followed by Hughes' purchase of the Desert Inn, Sands, Frontier, Castaways, Landmark and El Rancho Vegas property (that resort, the first on the Strip built in 1940, burned down June 17, 1960). Parvin-Dohrmann expanded from the Fremont to take on the Riviera and Aladdin and the Tropicana operating corporation was picked off by Trans-Texas Airlines which had about half of its stock owned by Minnesota Enterprises. Denny's restaurant chain sought to buy Caesars Palace, but Lums wound the interracial hotel, the Moulin Rouge, which shuttered recently.

"It's also still a touch-and-go operation at the Dunes, even though that hotel's now under operation

372

of the Sands Hotel management. The engagement of Maurice Chevalier, who opens tonight, will probably be the test of whether or not the Dunes can make the grade financially."

The downtown skyline disproved any notion of recession or bust in 1956 as the first highrise in that section opened with Eddie Levinson and Eddie Torres handling boss and entertainment chores respectively of the new Fremont. The whomping noise heard nightly in the late '50s from the hotel's Carnival Room was from a kid brother act known as Wayne and Jerry Newton and that was entertainment enough to draw casino loads of bettors.

A Las Vegas nitery review in *Variety* of April 25, 1956 stated, "Accent is on pitch and pull for this batch of acts. The nitery is pitching the local debut of Elvis Presley, but the pull will be in Freddy Martin's smooth music-making, and word-of-mouth churned up by Shecky Greene's unbridled comedy. . . .

"Elvis Presley, arriving on the wave of tremendous hoopla, fails to hit the promised mark here in a desert isle surfeited with rock'n'rollers who play in shifts atop every cocktail lounge on the Strip. The brash, loud braying of his R & B catalogue, which albeit rocketed him to bigtime, is wearing in these surroundings. The applause, moreover, comes back edged with polite inferences. For the teen-agers Presley is a whiz; for the average Vegas spender, a bore. His musical sound with a combo of three is uncouth, matching to a great extent the lyric content of his repertoire."

News item: "Four Las Vegas Niteries Threaten to Drop Shows as AFM Ups Scale 20%."

Hassle between four Strip hotels and AFM has been going on for some time with the tooters seeking a 20% scale hike to $150 per week. Hotels have declared flatly they "cannot and will not meet" the union demands.

"We'll do without music if necessary," one hotelman declared today. "And if that means curtailing our shows entirely, okay, we'll do it. Las Vegas wasn't built solely on shows and music."

The travails of the mid-Fifties certainly had an effect upon the Sixties. The Lady Luck had been built and opened shortly after the Tropicana, with the Lady Luck's name changed to the Hacienda upon the entrance of Doc Bayley on the scene. The Tropicana started out with a cloud overhead as to money backing and ownership when the famous Frank Costello note turned up later with digits from the hotel's counting room.

All of this ownership business became more of a problem as the Sixties moved onward. From boss structures headed by hard-fisted gamblers who learned their business the hard way—dodging the feds for years —almost the entire Las Vegas hotel-casino business

segued into corporations. Corporation regard for entertainment was usually centered upon the matter of fact consideration of the bottom line. Every nook and cranny of the resort must pay for itself, or if the casino take had to be proportioned, the investment would have to eventually pay off.

As for sheer growth in every aspect of entertainment and gambling enterprises, the Sixties decade was incredible. Conservatively, more than 600 acts or productions, including headliners in main showrooms, lounge combos, name orchestras were bought by entertainment chiefs as come-ons for gambling action, repeating many times and at many hotels. This number excluded individuals such as dancers in the production spectacles such as the Lido, "Folies Bergere" and "Casino de Paris" or tab musicals and less pretentious shows that dotted the Strip all during the ten years from "The World of Suzie Wong" at the Riviera in 1960 to "Minsky's Burlesque '69" at the Aladdin.

Kirk Kerkorian became one of the big tycoons, purchasing one fourth interest in Western Air Lines; bought the Flamingo through his wholly-owned Tracy Investment Corp.; acquired control of MGM and absorbed the defunct Bonanza corner, adding on acres and acres for the brutish, overpowering MGM Grand which opened in December of 1973. Without doubt, the Grand is the big news of the current decade.

The peak of entertainment was achieved in January 1963 when Frank Sinatra's clan descended enmasse upon Dean Martin at the Sands Copa Room and literally tore the joint apart. Clansmen were Joey Bishop, Sammy Davis Jr., and Peter Lawford. There were numerous other sudden appearances onstage for about three years and the tales told of the ad libs and other schtick trotted out are legion, plus many apocryphal accounts as each super-achiever attempted to grab off the most yocks with bits of funny business. Sammy Davis, incidentally, was not a total headliner in those years. The billing read "Will Mastin Trio, starring Sammy Davis Jr."

Howard Hughes and Frank Sinatra were never the best of buddies. So, it was no earthshaking news when Jack Entratter's famous clan began departing the Sands and the major brouhaha of the decade occurred when Hughes cut off Sinatra's credit at the hotel. Casino executive Carl Cohen gave his own version of how a heavyweight always goes to the jaw and soon Caesars Palace headlined The Man. Martin ankled over to the Riviera where he became a 10 percent "owner" (at entertainment executive Ed Torres' sufferance as it turned out) and Davis worked fewer and fewer dates at the Sands running out his contract, eventually winding up with his name on the Tropicana marquee. "Sammy Davis Jr. presents . . ." and finally being bought out of his Hughes pact by Caesars Palace for a sum whispered to be $500,000. Sammy still owns an interest in one of the Tropicana sub-corporations, however. And Dean was shown the door at the Riviera when his demands became too excessive, but he picked up a juicy deal with MGM for starring in some films and opening the Grand at the close of 1973. He has been Grandstanding as top star of the hotel in week-long gigs since then and is certainly the top draw not only in the main showroom, but in the casino as well.

Halfway through the Seventies, another down cycle penetrated Las Vegas, although there was no cause for dire alarm insofar as gambling income is concerned. The fiscal year ending June 1975, showed enormous gains considering the recession, inflation, energy problems and general economic blahs nationally. Casino take was $729 million which meant a contribution of $38,200,000 to the total of $55,200,000 in percentage fees collected by the state.

Contrast this to figures of 1950 when the Las Vegas area gambling revenue paid into the state treasury was $1,348,501, extolled in big headlines then as "largest ever."

The Seventies beheld the triumphant return of Elvis Presley to Las Vegas. He became the king, one of the alltime top draws into the huge International, then later the Hilton showroom.

He now was ELVIS.

He was the first of the Superstars, Vegas variety, which meant first name only on the marquee. There were Barbra, Sammy, Liza, Engelbert and Wayne, fortunately blessed with first names to identify with immediately. Consider The Man, the Champ of Las Vegas, Frank Sinatra, who prefers last name only from time to time—Sinatra—equally as viable among the Superstar crowd.

Even Las Vegas can claim its own superstatus among all cities, upper bracket stardom, perhaps Mega-stardom. All the jetsetters, the insiders, highrolling junketeers now simply refer to it as VEGAS.

Since World War II entertainers have been the principal reason for the average of 35 million annual tourists who now visit Nevada. They are the lure, the magnet, the essential ingredient in Nevada's gambling industry. "The Man," Frank Sinatra—whose fans span generations—and Ernie Kovacs were representative of the burgeoning Nevada show business scene in the early 1950's. Louis "Satchmo" Armstrong (top, opposite) receives the "Golden Mouthpiece" award at a special presentation at the Flamingo Hotel. Congratulating the trumpet king are Ella Fitzgerald—the first lady of song—and Duke Ellington, late great composer of contemporary jazz music. Entertainment Director Bill Miller stands in the background.

The topper of the 40's and 50's, ribald and generous Sophie Tucker, was one of the warmhearted greats of show business. Joe E. Lewis ("E" for Everglades), the great comedian, bon vivant of the night club circuit, typically bubbles "it's post time," 1945–1965. Yes indeed, that joker was wild.

Nat King Cole epitomizes the romantic balladeer. He was a Nevada entertainment leader through the 1950's until his death in the mid-1960's. The "schnozzola," Jimmy Durante—"Everybody wants to get inta da act"—has been a Nevada star for three decades, beginning after World War II.

The split between the Dean Martin and Jerry Lewis comedy team brought two great individual talents to Nevada's resort stages. Louis Prima (below) "the Chief," truly the "last of the wild" of great all-time Nevada entertainers, started in Vegas lounges and effervesced on to stardom.

Sammy Davis Jr. packed them in at the Sands Hotel at the peak of his career singing, dancing and clowning.

Liberace, a $600 a week act in the 1940's, now commands a top price at the Las Vegas Hilton and at the Sparks Nugget. Judy Garland's heart-tug was her daughter Liza (opposite left), now a top attraction at the Riviera Hotel. Wayne Newton emerged from a chubby lounge star of the late 1950's into the midnight idol of the 1970's at Reno, Lake Tahoe and Las Vegas. Elvis was a Las Vegas Strip reject of 1955–56 but today he is one of a very few superstars who can fill the huge Hilton showroom to capacity.

From the left: Lionel Hampton, Tommy Dorsey, Charlie Barnett, Louis Armstrong.

Entertain Them . . . But

by Mildred M. Wilson

The old cliches "That's entertainment" or "The show must go on" have had special significance for black entertainers in Las Vegas. In a town whose livelihood has depended largely upon pleasing masses of tourists, these performers have survived the test of time and demonstrated that they also possessed a product that was marketable and almost invaluable. For more than thirty years black entertainers have played a major role in the economic growth of Las Vegas.

Blacks were among the early settlers of Las Vegas in 1905, pursuing their own dreams and goals. The common denominators in those days were mining and transportation, and blacks lived, worked, and socialized with the white community.

The late 1920's brought an economic boost to Las Vegas. Planning began on the Boulder Dam project, but as the town grew in size, its people changed their attitude. Where once there had been harmony, the dam project brought a rift in race relations. Housing, restaurant accommodations, and job discrimination developed. This lack of racial harmony continued through the 1930's and into the 1940's.

In 1942 black entertainers arrived to work at the resort hotels. Even though job discrimination was still prevalent in Las Vegas, a variety of comedians, singers, dancers and musicians were hired. Ironically, they were contracted with the specific instruction to entertain the patrons of the hotels but no social mingling in the hotel was permitted.

The Last Frontier was one of the hotels that figured prominently in the early employment of black entertainers. It provided food service in the back of the hotel on picnic tables, since the performers were not afforded the usual hotel or dining accommodations. The hotel also provided a taxi service because housing was unavailable in areas other than "old town," later to be called West Las Vegas.

One veteran resident, who migrated to Las Vegas from Poland, recalls that, in addition to his regular duties as a lighting technician, he also served as a taxi driver. As he states, "I would wait after each night's performance and, in the hotel's Chrysler station wagon, drive the entertainers to rooming houses on Jackson and Monroe Streets."

One of the most prominent houses that lent support to the black performers was owned by a long-time black resident. Known as Harrison's Guest House, it was constructed around 1935 on North F Street. It was reputed to be one of the first private houses built in "old town" and boasted of nine rooms, two baths, and a guest house in the back.

The conservative exterior of the stucco structure was enhanced by a small porch. A glider and assorted chairs on the lawn beckoned one to relax and black performers enjoyed the camaraderie of their peers. They took snapshots of each other—a favorite pastime, or chatted with admiring neighborhood fans who hung over the winding fence seeking autographs.

The interior of the house had a cozy living room. The warm colors of the Persian rug and patterned wallpaper complemented a roomy sofa and assorted chairs. There was an array of pictures and mementos. A desk was tucked conveniently in a corner between two windows, thus permitting a writer sunlight on either side of him. Guests, including Sammy Davis, Jr. —then a part of the Will Mastin Trio—Lena Horne, and Arthur Lee Simpkins, would often relax in this room and either take a nap on the roomy sofa or engage in lively conversations.

One of the extras that the Harrison Guest House offered was a small, comfortable guest house situated at the back of the main house. Especially suitable for performers with families, it often served as home for Pearl Bailey and her family.

The generosity and sympathetic support of "old town" residents might be equated with the military USO clubs of the 1940's. Much like alienated soldiers in a strange land, these black performers were contracted primarily to entertain, often far from their families and familiar surroundings. Landlords, such as those who operated the Harrison Guest House, provided reinforcement and a home away from home.

Residents of "old town" also endeavored to accommodate the black performers' social needs. The Moulin Rouge, which opened its doors in 1955, soon became a popular spot. Black waiters, cocktail waitresses, dealers, and croupiers came from various parts of the country to work in the club. Here the performers could relax, gamble, and socialize. After their own performance at a hotel, they would often come to the club and re-create their acts for black patrons.

By 1958 the black performers recognized that they possessed a commodity that was essential to the economic well-being of Las Vegas. They urged that their black friends and fans be offered better treatment, and entertainers refused to sign contracts without assurance that all hotel facilities would be available to them and their crews. A major interracial conference of influential and concerned civic leaders, hosted by the Moulin Rouge, followed shortly thereafter. This provided further momentum to fair employment practices among the hotels with reference to blacks in general.

After 1958, attitudes toward black performers changed in Las Vegas. Once a gravel road with one hotel, the Strip has now many luxurious hotels and casinos, and black entertainers freely engage in all accommodations that each offers. At one time Sammy Davis, Jr., had to pay his employers to place a bet for him because he was not permitted to play in the casinos. Today, his services not only command a high salary, but he owns a large share of a popular Strip hotel.

An enforced open-housing law, passed in 1971, also precipitated major changes. Prior to then Stanley Morgan, leader of the famed Ink Spots, suffered injustice by having his Rancho Manor home damaged by a dynamite blast. But the new law enabled other black entertainers, including the Mills Brothers, Billy Eckstein, and Joe Williams to purchase homes in Paradise Valley, Rancho Circle, and other fashionable parts of Las Vegas.

The Moulin Rouge was located on Bonanza Avenue, in West Las Vegas. It is now part of a motel.

Indian cowboys performed many chores at Nye County's Blue Eagle Ranch, including the branding of calves. The rodeo scene (below) is on the site of Ely's airport.

Potpourri

Nevada—I Love The Name
by Norman Kaye

You can still hear the bantering
Of the skinners of yesteryear
Their voices ring shrilly in the desert night
So eerie, yet loud and clear

They speak of the dusty wagon trains
the heroes that would come and go
The Indian's plight, and Mexicans too
And death in the Donner snow

Spitting out names like Pizen Switch
Gave them a sense quite unique
A form of flying in the Ruby range
With highs up to Wheeler peak

They speak of the mines and the ore fields
Of Nevada of yesterday
Where Comstock, Goldfield, Gabbs and McGill
Gave wealth so rich men could play

The faro banks of the early gambler
With fast guns and ill shuffled decks
Where quite a few won all they played for
While other who did, lost their necks

The balance came in with the Mormons
And all other religions too
A gift of God, equity, with dignity
A spiritual lift on the avenue

The immigrants, ranchers, freighters, and merchants
All part of our history's scene
The ingredients that made it all possible
To live the American dream

To live and know that Nevada
Was more than a passing state
With its shadowy deserts, valleys and mountains
It could never be less than great

And great is what Nevada is
And that's quite easy to see
A place unlike anywhere else in this world
The home for you and me

Ins and Outs of Rustlers

by Don Bowman

In the late 1950's the dramatic capture of a Nye County rustling ring took place. The gang of rustlers was not large as they had hardly gotten started, and their capture was mostly the result of bad manners.

The trouble started in Tonopah where a couple of cowpokes were cooling their tonsils in the Mizpah Saloon one day. They had been tippling for quite a while, when hunger pangs developed. They decided that some good fresh beef should be the main course of their next banquet; so, they gathered up a couple of jugs of their favorite bourbon and headed for the rangeland delicatessen that sided the Smokey Valley highway.

By the time they arrived in the range, their appetites were really whetted. When their red-rimmed eyes spied an old cow not far from the road they could almost see Grade A stamped on her forehead. Ol' Slim dragged out his 30-30 Winchester, and with one sure shot, hit this old cow right in the front leg. Then he proceeded to use up the rest of the magazine of bullets trying to finish her off.

A quick inventory produced no more bullets, so they decided to car-kill the cow 'cause the gun didn't shoot worth a darn anyway. After a wild chase, the cow finally got knocked down by the pick-up which by now had a broken headlight and a slightly puckered bumper.

The boys then bailed out with their butcher knives and proceeded with their knowledge of the finer cuts. Slim took a snort out of the jug and told Shorty to grab a hind leg and rear back on it while he skinned the cow. Shorty grabbed it and reared back at a 45 degree angle. His load of booze shifted, he lost his idea of where upright was, and he turned loose of the leg as he toppled over on the ground.

Well, Shorty had that leg pulled back quite a ways, and when he let go, it flew forward like a bent sapling, cracking Slim right between the eyes, breaking his nose and his glasses. Slim took this as a personal assault, and the ensuing argument led to a scuffle, then to a full scale war. When neither rustler had a shirt left on his back, they stopped to catch their breath and have another drink. While they were resting, who should show up but the rancher who owned the cow which by this time looked like the aftermath of a train wreck.

In their whiskey-dimmed brains, Shorty and Slim decided it might be smart to make things right. So, they told the cow's owner that they were going to pay for the beef anyway, trying to talk their way out of the scrape.

The rancher finally agreed to take payment whenever they could get the loot, and climbed back in his pick-up to leave. The two meat packers now decided since they had purchased this beef, they deserved a little service in return, so Shorty piped up, "Hey, you sorry S.O.B., aren't you going to help us load her?"

At this, the rancher's small thread of patience snapped like an overstretched rubber band, and he roared off for town to get the sheriff. Audacity got results.

Anyhow, it all ended with our two boys cleaning streets for the county for quite a while. After this they wouldn't even eat poached eggs . . . let alone poached beef.

Near as I can tell, they broke just one rule. . . . With red meat, drink red wine. Emily Post says it's a breach of etiquette to combine "Old Doublejack" Bourbon and beef!

Nevada

by M. Burrell Bybee, Sr.

I

The trample of feet to the westward,
  The trample of feet in the sand,
The hordes trample into the sunset
To struggle and fight for land;
The hordes from the dense, crowded cities
  In search of a home in the west.
They came, and they altered the landscape
  Sometimes I think not for the best.
But there's one spot the crowds did not trample
  That God in his mercy left free,
And he called it the state of Nevada,
  So it's dear old Nevada for me.

Chorus

The land of the cowboy and miner
  The land of the coyote and deer,
The land of the sagebrush and pinyon,
  Where the sun shines each day of the year.
A sample of God's first creation
  Where all of his creatures are free.
It's rough and it's tough, but I like it,
  So it's dear old Nevada for me.

II

The meadows in wide-spreading valleys,
  The canyons in mountains so high,
Where the mountain trout plays in the brooklet
  And the snowcaps are kissing the sky;
Where the cattle's still roaming the ranges
  With the antelope, elk, and deer.
It's one spot that never changes
  It's just nature's own souvenir.
The last of the unconquered wasteland
  Where men live their lives with a zest
And a man is a man who can take it—
  The last frontier of the west.

Walker Lake Fish

by Estelle Moore

Walker Lake was once truly a fisherman's paradise with its great variety and large number of fish. People at Schurz and nearby Mason Valley can still remember the huge cutthroat trout from the lake that used to go many miles up Walker River into the mountains to spawn, giving sportsmen along the river some fine catches.

A ten-pound cutthroat wasn't at all unusual and some even grew to twenty-seven pounds or more in size. Then in the 1930's Weber Reservoir was built on Walker River a number of miles above Schurz and these fish were unable to go up the river to spawn, causing their number to diminish greatly.

The plentiful Sacramento perch was one of the fish most preferred by fishermen and they were easy to catch. A big white silver trout (sometimes as large as ten pounds in weight), which fishermen called the "silverside," was quite a fighter when on the line. The bass was also a favorite.

And then there were the lowly carp! None of the locals cared to eat carp, even when their food supply was low, but for about five years during the 1920's a very active commercial carp fishing industry existed at Walker Lake.

Two middle-aged brothers, M. J. and Cass Sapp, lived in a little one-room house on the lake about nine miles south of Schurz. During the winter, when the weather was cold enough, they would cut big ice blocks from the river above Schurz to store for use when shipping their fish in the summertime.

The brothers, though small and wiry, were diligent fishermen and they did much heavy work. They had

two large rowboats about 18 feet long (stored up on shore when not in use) to seine, or net, carp. They used one boat at a time, loading the net on the stern in a pre-folded pile and rowing to a chosen fishing spot. They would tie one end of a 100 or so foot long rope to something at the edge of the lake and then row out into the lake until they reached the end of the line. The net would then unfold itself into the water as the rope pulled it out of the boat. The rower would take the craft on a semi-circular route, spreading the 300 by 10 foot net about 100 feet out from the shore, then going in toward shore to begin drawing in the fish.

The Sapp brothers were proficient fishermen, sometimes getting in as many as three catches of several tons of fish in one day, and once in a while it would be so large that they had to let some fish out in order to bring it in. Each netting might number hundreds of carp averaging 10 or 12 pounds in size and sometimes reaching 20 or 25 pounds.

They would keep the fish alive in a large holding pen in the lake near their home and when the time for shipment arrived, they would then ice them down in large fish boxes approximately 5 by 2 by 3 feet in size and take them over to Schurz on their old Model-T truck. There the fish would begin their trip by rail to the Bay Area in California, where they were much prized by the Jewish population.

The Sapps employed local labor to aid them in their work, but they did most of the fishing themselves. Their business might have gone on for many more years had the older brother not lost his life by drowning, near the north end of the lake, when a sudden storm swamped his boat. The hip boots he was wearing helped to drag him down and his body was never found.

W. J. Sapp remained on the lake for some years afterward to operate a boat concession, renting rowboats to fishermen.

Another businessman seined carp from Walker Lake for three or four years about the same time the Sapps were there. His market for the big fish was in the Los Angeles area, where they were transported by truck. This gentleman had quite a successful operation going, but he became a little greedy. One day when the authorities were examining his fish, ready for shipment, they found the top layer of carp covered a large number of illegal trout. He was fined and evidently did no more commercial fishing in Walker Lake after that.

Youngsters and serious fishermen alike had no trouble catching fish from a boat, often just using droplines, or from the shore of the lake in those days, but now the perch, bass, "silverside," and even the carp are gone because of the increased salinity of the water. The average size of the remaining fish is smaller today, and the only cutthroat which fishermen catch now are believed to be the ones planted by the Fish and Game Department.

Ghost Town Landmarks —
Desert Storms and Vandals
by Theron Fox

If Mother Nature's perpetual onslaught does not level desert landmarks, she usually gets a helping hand from a few unscrupulous vandals or through official neglect. These pictures shown how they work together.

Shown at right is the famed Withington Hotel at Hamilton, the county seat of White Pine County beginning in 1869. For several years it was Nevada's largest hostelry. It was built of native stone, although some say that stone used for construction was hauled as ballast in a sailing ship from Wales around Cape Horn, and then transported over the Sierra to Hamilton on ox-drawn wagons. It makes for a good story.

The first photo taken in 1956 shows how the building looked just before the end. Left standing now are a few mere crumbling walls and two inside vaults, whose sides and ceilings are still intact.

Desert elements did not get a full chance at the Eberhardt Mine vault near Hamilton (opposite page). When photographed in 1956 the vault was still intact, protected by a huge iron door and casing. Inside the vault was an old safe; though still in good condition it could not be removed through the only door. Desert scavengers found a way, however, and removed the door and casing, demolished the walls and away went the safe.

When the elements or the vandals did not rip things apart, official neglect sometimes entered the picture. The rear of the Belmont court house was left open when

the wall was torn down to take out the jail block, which was removed to the new jail in Gabbs. The wall was never repaired, and the pictures show what happened subsequently with the caved-in and fallen wall. Most of the bricks were carried away for souvenirs.

A new roof was put on the courthouse in 1975. Work has already started on new floors for the building and full restoration is anticipated under a three-phase program among county, state and federal agencies.

Poor Little Pupfish

by Jim Yoakum

Early settlers and visitors to Nevada told stories of a tiny fish that swam through hot water springs in southern Nevada. They were tough, those fish, for at times the waters were very hot, and some springs were saltier than the ocean. There was another story that they lived in water left in the hoof prints of wild horses. Commonly called the "pupfish," its scientific generic name is *Cyprinodon*.

When mature they are only one to two inches long, hardly the size of an adult's little finger, and live primarily on algae.

In the water they dart here and there, like fleeting hummingbirds. The males take on beautiful blue and purple colors during the breeding season, but the females are slimmer and mottled with brown. During the time of breeding each male vigorously defends his territory, generally an area only two feet in diameter. He chases away other males but welcomes a female to lay her eggs among the algae.

Pupfish thrive in springs, ponds, streams, and small rivers. An adult male requires water no deeper than an inch and can live the year around in an area less than two feet wide. Water temperature fluctuates tremendously in the desert environments, from 72 to 112 degrees and some pupfish hibernate through freezing winters buried in mud. Experiments have proven that they can live in waters six times saltier than the ocean.

This adaptability to survive in extreme environmental variables has allowed the little pupfish to exist for eons. However, during the past half century man has caused the extinction of two pupfish subspecies, and seriously threatens the survival of three more.

There are many ways man has threatened the pupfish colony. Stocking pupfish waters with exotic (that is non-native) species such as bass, carp, goldfish, tropical fish, frogs, and crayfish, endangered the pupfish through competition for living space. Another way is to change drastically his environment by diverting waters for irrigation purposes, covering springs and piping the water for domestic use, or to pump out underground water so that springs dry up and the fish perish. The latter has been the most serious problem during the 1970's. Will the pupfish survive until the next century? The future looks bright. Wildlife biologists have recently formed "recovery teams" to identify problems of survival and make recommendations to ensure perpetuation of the species. In addition, Eagle Scout groups have dug new water sources; conservation organizations have bought lands and waters; exotic species have been eliminated; and protection fences have been built around crucial tiny springs.

For centuries the Indians and pupfish lived in southern Nevada and California without interfering with each other's existence. Then the white man arrived. He exterminated two kinds of pupfish unintentionally. But some races of pupfish still exist, and like the pupfish, today's concerned scientific man may learn new ways to adapt to environmental changes to aid his own survival.

Restless Houses

by Harold O. Weight

From the great days of Virginia City through wild uranium rushes, mining camp "boomers," stampeding from strike to strike, have been glamorous figures in western fact and fiction. But who recalls the sagas of the boom camp buildings—the mills, stores, saloons, schools and homes that rose magically while the fevers raged? Many of these were as footloose as the humans they sheltered.

We had a personal experience with one such migration in the 1950's, when we stopped at Mina to yarn with our friend Carl Sullivan, old-time prospector-boomer-miner, and one-time Mineral County supervisor.

"Sully's somewhere between here and Rawhide," Mel Sinnott, then owner of Mina's general store, told us. "You can't miss him. Probably can't even pass him —he's hauling a house."

"House trailer?" I asked.

"House," said Sinnott. "Sully hoisted it onto his truck and took off. He's starting a new community at Dead Horse Wells."

Dead Horse Wells, at the western edge of Rawhide Dry Lake, was an important watering place for freight teams from the 1880's, when it was on the route to Candelaria, through the Rawhide boom. In the 1950's, the Nevada Scheelite Mine was booming only a few miles to the north, and increasing numbers of miners and mill men had no place within 20 miles where they could cut the dust from their throats. Sully had decided to become a public benefactor by establishing the Dead Horse Saloon—which he already had arranged to lease to insure himself prospecting and mining funds.

Dead Horse Wells was about 55 miles from Mina, with the last 24—from the Gabbs highway—unpaved, dusty, washboard, and plentifully supplied with ruts and chuckholes. We more than half expected to find a disabled house somewhere along this stretch. But, when we reached the wells, Sully was just doubling the size of his community by easing the transported building onto its new foundation.

"Kidnapping houses won't make you popular in Mina," I said.

"Building's mine, legal and paid for," Sully said. "That's more than can be said for a lot that have drifted around Nevada. And if I remember, this particular house was hauled into Mina from Candelaria. Probably Candelaria got it from Columbus or Aurora or Bodie."

Probably it did.

Few boom buildings could expect to enjoy any sort of sedate and stable history. Sometimes entire towns were abandoned abruptly and inhabitants, lacking even stage fare, walked out empty-handed. Impossibly high freighting costs meant furniture left in homes, goods on store shelves. But towns so abandoned seldom succumbed to the elements or vandals. If another camp was within reach, buildings were moved wholesale. If not, individual buildings were appropriated through the years by surrounding mines or ranches. Or sometimes, decades later, another excitement would explode not too far away, and an old camp would be stripped rapidly.

Thus fared Columbus, mill town for the ores of nearby Candelaria. Founded in the 1860's, with its first mill freighted piecemeal from Bodie, abandoned in the '80s, it was left almost intact because of 20 cent a pound freight charges. It remained largely intact until the Tonopah silver strike, in 1900. Then Columbus was robbed of everything but adobe and stone, to make the new town sprout.

Belmont, while still very much alive, also supplied Tonopah with transfusions for growth in 1901. But the Belmont *Courier* editor made a plus out of a minus,

House moving Gold Creek 1911

388

Moving a house at Rawhide

explaining that the buildings dismantled hadn't been occupied for years, anyhow, and the town looked better with them gone.

Goldfield has known the ebb and flow of migratory houses from the day of its birth. It took from Tonopah, then gave back. Buildings went to Beatty, to Gilbert, even to far off Las Vegas.

Rawhide, Nevada's last big boom, collected buildings from Fairview and Wonder, but later it lost a large number to Fallon. Departures there, as elsewhere, often were illegal. Allan Patterson, who had moved his assay office from Wonder to Fairview to Rawhide, left there of necessity for a job in Jerome, Arizona. Offered $250 for the Rawhide building, "Pat" sent the requested authorization for the man to move the structure. He, in turn, showed the authorization to Sheriff Gene Grutt and vanished with the building, without paying.

The most ambulatory building of which we have record is the old Montgomery hotel—pride of early Beatty. It left Beatty to follow the Pioneer boom. Pioneer "lasted short," and the Montgomery traveled

Mornin' On the Desert

(Found written on the door of an old
cabin in Southern Nevada.)

Mornin' on the desert, and the wind is blowin' free,
And it's ours, jest for the breathin', so let's fill up, you and me.
No more stuffy cities, where you have to pay to breathe,
Where the helpless human creatures move and throng and strive and seethe.

Mornin' on the desert, and the air is like a wine,
And it seems like all creation has been made for me and mine.
No house to stop my vision, save a neighbor's miles away,
And the little dobe shanty that belongs to me and May.

Lonesome? Not a minute! Why I've got these mountains here,
That was put here just to please me, with their blush and frown and cheer.
They're waiting when the summer sun gets too sizzlin' hot,
An' we jest go campin' in 'em with a pan and coffee pot.

Mornin' on the desert — I can smell the sagebrush smoke,
I hate to see it burnin', but the land must sure be broke.
Ain't it jest a pity that wherever man may live,
He tears up much that's beautiful that the good God has to give?

"Sagebrush ain't so pretty?" Well, all eyes don't see the same,
Have you ever saw the moonlight turn it to a silver flame?
An' that greasewood thicket yonder — Well, it smells jest awful sweet
When the rain has been a-shakin' it — for its smell is hard to beat.

Lonesome? Well, I guess not! I've been lonesome in a town,
But I sure do love the desert with its stretches wide and brown.
All day through the sagebrush here the wind is blowin' free,
An' it's ours, jest for the breathin', so let's fill up, you and me.

on to Tonopah. In 1947 it returned to Beatty as a store, completing a round trip which took more than 35 years.

For generations brick and stone ghost towns of the "earlies" resisted the wanderlust of their wooden brethren. Then old used brick became popular for modern buildings, and a sadder kind of migration decimated them. Mark Twain's old town of Aurora—which one day might have become a Williamsburg of Nevada—was a prime sufferer when some of its most beautiful and historic buildings were demolished for their bricks.

Today developments which may be of a temporary nature depend almost entirely on mobile housing. But until this is universally true, boom camp buildings probably will continue to follow booms.

Carl Sullivan stated the case well as he lowered his Dead Horse Wells addition into place:

"In a progressive state like Nevada, you can't expect houses to sit around and deteriorate when there's a boom on elsewhere. Just like us old Nevada boomers, they're plagued with restless feet."

The Tree That Made Nevada's Silver

by Ronald M. Lanner

If silver was queen of Nevada's resources, the ubiquitous pinyon tree was her lady-in-waiting. With-out the charcoal made from the resinous wood of this nut-bearing desert pine, Nevada's ores would not have been smelted.

Pinyon, producer of the nutritious pine-nuts that were the winter staple of Great Basin Indians, was also the preferred source of firewood in the Comstock Lode area.

As the Comstock played out, and further discoveries were made in central and eastern Nevada, the need for fuel became more intense. The days of easy silver were over; instead of rich lodes, the new silver was found in chemically-complex ores that had to be smelted. Cordwood did not deliver enough heat and Nevada had no coking coal; with no railroads to bring coal from afar, the answer was charcoal.

Charcoal is made by burning wood in airtight kilns designed to gradually and systematically exclude oxygen. A skilled coal-maker learns to control the moisture content and size of the logs with which he charges his kiln, the rate of combustion, the burning temperature, and many other fine technical points. While a pound of pinyon wood produces 8,000 British thermal units, a pound of pinyon charcoal yields 13,000 B.t.u., and it weighs only a third as much while taking up but half the space.

Skilled Italian and Swiss-Italian *carbonari* made charcoal in masonry ovens or great pits in the ground that held up to 100 cords of wood. They took pride in their well-honed axes, and in their ability to chop a tree right down to the roots. In 1873, Rossiter W. Raymond described the charcoal made by Italians at Eureka as

Ward Charcoal Ovens now under a state park.

the best product available. Superior to charcoal made in Utah, the Eureka product was also used in Little Cottonwood, just a few miles from Salt Lake City.

Mining began in Eureka in the early 1870's and, within a few short years, the Eureka Consolidated, the Marcellina, the Phoenix, and the Richmond companies built smelters nearby. By 1874, thirteen smelting furnaces were in operation, and in 1878 there were sixteen, requiring a staggering amount of charcoal. The Nevada State Mineralogist reported in 1873 that the thirteen Eureka furnaces had a daily capacity of 595 tons of ore using 30 bushels of charcoal per ton of ore, so if all these furnaces worked at capacity, they would have consumed 17,850 bushels of charcoal daily. Charcoal was the biggest expense in the smelting operation, even greater than labor costs. There was constant grumbling about the prices demanded by the *carbonari*, and the smelter owners looked to a future when railroads would bring in coal from the vast deposits of southern Utah.

Black clouds of dense smoke from the furnaces, heavily scented with fumes of lead and arsenic, were constantly depositing soot, scales, and black dust, giving Eureka the aspect of an industrial town in Pennsylvania's coal region.

But outside the city the effects were even more severe and long-lasting. A typical yield of pinyon wood was ten cords per acre, and a cord made about 30 bushels of charcoal. So the furnaces of Eureka, working at capacity, devoured over 530 cords of pinyon, the product of over 50 acres, in a single day. After just one year of major activity, Eureka's hillsides were bare of trees. By 1874, the wasteland extended 20 miles from town; and by 1878 the woodland was nowhere closer than fifty miles from Eureka, every acre picked clean by the *carbonari* or domestic foragers. Now charcoal pits were fed with logs from neighboring counties with 600 *carbonari* employed to supply the Eureka market.

Even in the isolated Delamar District of southeast Nevada, a one-company operation, contracts as large as 10,000 cords were let. Woodcutters and their families moved into the woodlands, migrating further from the smelter as the hills were cleaned off.

Near Como and Dayton, the deforestation of their hills and the destruction of their nut-groves often brought Indians into conflict with white settlers and miners. The influx of Italian coal-makers and the employment of Chinese woodcutters soon created anti-foreign violence and labor strife, culminating in the 1879 "war" at Fish Creek.

The smelters are gone now, and the air is clear again. The hills, once stripped of trees, are again covered by woodlands. Few people come to collect pinyon nuts or gather firewood, and the trees that once supported Nevada's economy tower silently over the desert ranges.

Little Brown Nut

by Mary K. Miller

Native Nevadans have memorable recollections of the centuries-old ritual called pine-nutting which was first introduced in this area by the Paiute Indians.

Unlike the Indians, we no longer depend on pine nuts as a staple food but still gather the precious nuts with just as much determination. Donning our oldest and grubbiest clothes and gathering our equipment, we head for the hills surrounding the East Gate area, hunting for scrubby little trees called pinyon pines. Our gear included a canvas tarp, a long hooked pole, an old cushion to kneel on, and a container for the nuts.

The "nut pines" are very hardy and can easily endure Nevada's extreme climate. The trees will grow in the poorest, shallowest soil with very little rainfall and produce pine nuts for several hundred years. Scattered throughout the West, there are nearly 8 million acres of pinyon forest in Nevada alone.

In the early fall, most of the cones are still green. The best time to go pine nutting is after the first frost, when the cones dry out and open up releasing the ripe nuts. When a group of trees heavily laden with pine cones is located the ritual begins. A tarp is spread under the tree and with the long hooked pole, the branches are shook until the pine nuts drop into the canvas. Cones that drop are gathered in burlap sacks and then beaten with a stick, knocking the nuts out of the opened cones to the bottom of the sack. This procedure is easier and much cleaner than picking the nuts out of the pitch-covered cones with your hands.

There are a few hazards which may discourage pine-nutting beginners. Watch out for the pine needles, especially if you are in a sitting position. While under a tree, do not raise up suddenly or you may strike a hard limb and get a big knot on your head and a glob of pitch in your hair for life. Children should always wear whistles around their necks, for it is almost certain that one or two of them will get lost among the trees. When everyone has gathered as many nuts as can be carried, the hand-cleaner is brought out and we all see the skin on our hands once more!

The Indians prepared the nuts in several ways. They made a soup by boiling them in water, or they ground them until fine, then sieving the mashed nut-meats through a meshed winnowing basket so the final result is like fine flour, this is then mixed with water and kneaded like bread dough and consumed in this form.

Most Nevadans, however, float the nuts in water to separate the bad ones that rise to the surface. Then they put some of the nuts in a shallow pan, sprinkle with water and salt, roast for about twenty minutes in 350 degree oven and then thoroughly enjoy them.

*Pine-nut
harvest
c. 1878*

Even if a pine nutting expedition proves fruitless, one can still experience nature's wonders so abundant in our state. There are the beautiful multicolored reds and yellows of the autumn leaves on the quaking Aspens, the wonderful pungent smells of juniper and sagebrush, and the fresh, clean air breezing in from the snow capped, rugged Sierra ranges. You can really learn to appreciate what Nevada has to offer and what should be preserved for generations to come.

Personally, I'm just nuts about our Silver State!

Prospector's Heaven

by Laura Bell

When Jack Cassidy and his pack burro, Dolly, gave up the ghost at a dry water hole, Jack headed for the pearly gates with hopes as high as if he were bound for a new strike on earth. Finding the gates unexpectedly ajar, he quickly urged Dolly through the opening.

"Come on," he commanded. "Pick up them feet. Feller'd think you didn't know you was squeezin' into the Promised Land by the skin of your teeth. Tain't once in a thousand years feller gets a break like this, slippin' into Heaven and no questions asked."

He was overcome by the rich prospect before him. "Gee-min-ee, ain't that a bear though!" he exclaimed. "Looks like it's all in place."

He was pulling the pick out of Dolly's pack ready to do some digging when St. Peter hurried out through a private doorway. Obviously upset, his flowing robes awry, he approached Jack in consternation.

"Here, here, my good man! What are you doing here? Why, nothing like this has occurred before in all the centuries I have been gatekeeper!" He stepped in front of Jack, regarding him in sorrowful silence as he shifted his wings and laid his hand on his long white beard.

"Gee-min-ee!" said Jack. And as the silence lengthened he thought, "Waitin' fer me to bust the ice, I guess."

Respectfully he addressed the Saint, "Figgered I'd like to get a look at them hills." He jerked his thumb over his shoulder. "Looks like they are highly mineralized."

St. Peter shuddered. "I can allow no more prospectors in Heaven," he said firmly. "Those who have already gained their reward have dug up the paving stones with their picks and washed bare the celestial hillsides with their placer operations." He folded his wings tighter in a gesture of finality and turned toward the gates.

"Come, my man. You must retrace your blasphemous footsteps immediately."

Jack followed St. Peter dejectedly. "Ain't got a show in the world," he whispered to Dolly. But he hung back, nevertheless, trying desperately to think of some way to stay in this prospectors' paradise. Dolly hung back, too, walking close to her master.

392

St. Peter, feeling the resistance, turned to Jack in righteous wrath. "Permit me to remind you that your presence here is entirely unsanctioned. Even if you were not a prospector it would be my duty to send you back through the gates." And he muttered an aside to himself, "Would to Heaven I could get the rest of them out."

Jack's quick ear caught the words. He brightened. "Hey, wait a minute," he said. "If I get them birds out, will you let me stay?"

St. Peter eyed him suspiciously. "You are suggesting the impossible," he said. "You must understand that once a man is officially admitted into Heaven he leaves only by his own free will and desire. There is no other place to go except Hell and there is a prejudice against that region."

Jack chuckled and slapped his thigh gleefully as his idea expanded. "Them birds'll forget their prejudices once I get at 'em. Them and their Irish buggies and their boo-rows will beat it out so fast it'll make your head swim!"

St. Peter was incredulous. "They have been seeking gold all their lives, and now they have found such quantities—"

"That don't make no difference," Jack cut in excitedly. "I'll have them pilin' over each other trying to be the first ones out."

St. Peter paused at the exit gate. "If you are certain you can accomplish this you may consider yourself as entered into Heaven."

There was a fanfare of trumpets as Jack turned Dolly around, his face beaming. "Gee-min-ee, I feel better," he said. "Nothing like making it legal." He thanked St. Peter and he and Dolly set off toward the hills. Before long they came to a couple of prospectors operating a windlass on what they told Jack looked like a good chloriding proposition.

Jack picked up a chunk of the material they were dumping and squinted at it through his ore glass. "Boy, that's the real McCoy!" he exclaimed. "Any ground open around these parts? I'd light here like a bee on a blossom."

"It's a funny layout," said one of the prospectors. "High grade makes all on the surface. We thought if we could get some depth on 'er we might open up another ore shoot."

Jack suddenly remembered his promise to St.-Peter.

"Sa-ay, if you go deep enough you're a cinch to strike it rich, all right!"

The two chloriders looked at him questioningly.

"Ain't you birds heard about the big strike down in Hell?"

"No. When?" they yelled in unison.

Jack elaborated. "Day before yesterday. Feller found a pothole full of nuggets big as walnuts. Still prospectin' for the source last I heard."

The chloriders let go of their windlass as if it were hot. In less time than it takes to tell it they had their burros packed and were hastening toward the pearly gates.

Jack looked around hopefully. "Now, if the rumor will jest spread in Heaven like it would on earth—"

He hadn't long to wait. Soon prospectors with their outfits could be heard rushing in from all directions. Jack guffawed again and, tilting backward, slapped his thigh. "Jest like I figgered. Them birds don't never change. Jest can't resist rushin' to a new strike, no matter how good a thing they got to work on."

The victims of Jack's ruse rushed past him, running with their wheelbarrows, whacking their burros, shouting the news to him, "Big strike down in Hell! Bigger'n Tonopah. Richer'n National."

They clattered out through the pearly gates, leaving Jack surrounded by stillness and a faint haze of gold dust. Dolly gazed wistfully after them and Jack had to push her to get her started off towards the mountains.

"Git along," he urged. "We got the whole diggin's to ourselves. Let's get some corners up before somebody else comes along."

St. Peter, who was nearly swept off his feet by the exodus, peered out through the pearly gates after the prospectors hurrying down the high road to Hell. Then he closed and locked the gates with a sigh of relief. Rubbing his hands and looking pleased he exclaimed, "That Jack Cassidy certainly knows prospectors. Now he can enjoy the gold here at his leisure."

He had disappeared through the door to his quarters when Jack and Dolly, panting in haste, skidded to a stop at the pearly gates and Jack shouted for St. Peter. As the saint appeared he called urgently, "Hey, open up them gates. I got to thinkin' about the rumor of a strike down in Hell and I believe there's somethin' to it, after all."

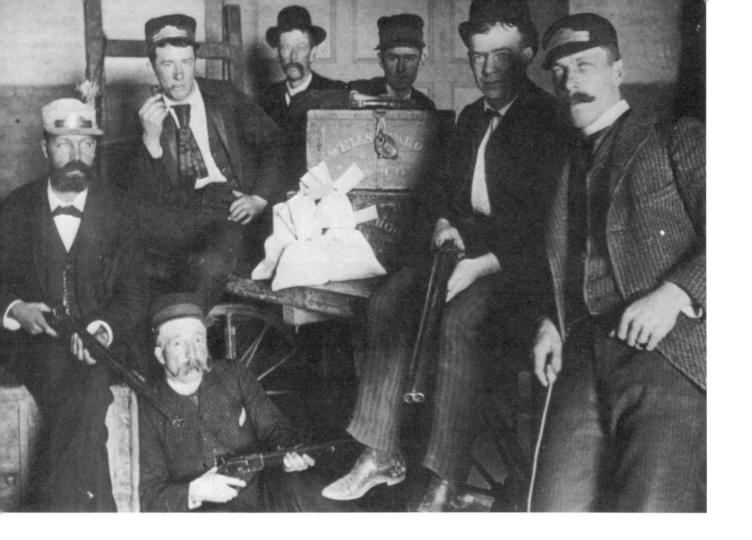

Reno Wells Fargo agents in 1890

Gold bars at Goldfield bank, 1907

Business and Industry

Nevada Banking History

by Jordan J. Crouch

Can you imagine stopping at a bank to cash your paycheck, finding that the bank consists of two whiskey barrels with a couple of planks to form a counter, and that you have to pay a service fee of one dollar to cash that check, regardless of the amount? Laborers on the Central Pacific Railroad (now the Southern Pacific) who were building the crossing over the Sierra mountains did just that at the first bank in Reno. The check cashing idea was conceived by the Bender brothers when they became aware that these workers had no place to cash their paychecks.

Banking began during the Comstock days of Virginia City, when the Wells Fargo Express and Banking Company opened in 1860. There were no banking laws to protect banker or depositor; in fact, Nevada wasn't even a state.

By 1863, with several banks now established in Virginia City and nearby Gold Hill, the Virginia City Bankers Association was founded.

Many historians credit two reasons for Nevada's statehood in 1864. The first was financial—the wealth Nevada could pour into the federal treasury to finance the war between the states; and the second was political —President Lincoln was assured two Senate votes needed to pass the Emancipation Act.

By the turn of the century banks were popular all over the "Battle Born" state, leaving their marks in business history. The first decade of the 20th century was one of the most important eras in Nevada history, and certainly a most important one in Nevada banking. On May 17, 1900, James Butler and his wife staked their first claim in the Tonopah district, and two years later, Marsh and Stimler staked their first claim in Goldfield. The rush to Virginia City and the Comstock Lode from 1860 to 1875 was not as large as the influx of people to the Nye and Esmeralda Counties strikes. Twenty-six banks were handling transactions during the first five years of this bonanza. Goldfield business leaders, George Wingfield Sr. and U.S. Senator George S. Nixon contributed greatly to the success of Nevada's

banking history and national figures such as Bernard Baruch, Charles M. Schwab, John Hays Hammond and Tex Rickard were attracted to Goldfield.

It was at Tonopah, about 1910, that the story made the rounds that a banking company was suspect of being in bad shape. Customers began to withdraw their cash from this bank and they would take the money down the street to a saloon keeper whom they trusted and who had a large safe. The saloon keeper would give a receipt to the depositors. At night when the safe was full, he would take the money up the back alley, into the rear door of the bank.

The next day the bank would have a new supply of "fresh" money to pay off new withdrawals, and this went on for several days. When the depositors found the bank willing to pay them off, they didn't want to draw out their money and word quickly spread. Soon people were presenting their receipts to the saloon keeper for their money and returning it to the bank. At night the banker would bring the money down the alley to the saloon keeper, so he could pay off, with "fresh" money, others who presented their receipts. These people would then take their money back to the bank. This points out how versatile banking was in the young 20th century!

On November 16, 1902, the oldest bank now operating in Nevada was formed in Reno—the Farmers and Merchants Bank, organized by Richard Kirman who later became governor and Walter J. Harris who authored much of Nevada's banking legislation. The following year the bank was nationalized and named Farmers and Merchants National Bank. This bank is now known as First National Bank of Nevada and is still headquartered in Reno.

In 1905 a First State Bank was organized in Las Vegas, then a small railroad town. The bank's first president, J. Ross Clark and his brother William Andrew Clark, had led the building of the railroad. Clark County, with Las Vegas as its county seat, was later named for J. Ross Clark and the First State Bank is now part of First National Bank of Nevada.

December 5, 1908, forty-eight years after the first bank was opened at Virginia City, the banks organized the Nevada Bankers Association in Reno and made the first concerted effort to draft a comprehensive banking law. Fourteen state and seven national banks were represented.

Stirred into action in the early 1920's by two bank robberies, the Nevada Bankers Association offered rewards of $1,000 for the capture of any bank robber alive, and $2,500 reward "to the person who shall lawfully kill any person in the act of robbing or attempting to rob the bank."

During the great depression of the early 1930's many banks closed their doors. As banks suffered when the mines gave out a generation before, they suffered now because the market for livestock vanished and ranchers could not meet their loans. One Reno bank, headed by Walter J. Harris, posted a sign in the bank's window during the 1933 bank holiday, stating, "If you have money in this bank and want it, come and get it."

Somehow, banking survived those exceedingly trying days of the 1930's, followed by trying times again during World War II. Today there are eight banks in Nevada; four state and four national banks, with one hundred and twenty branches scattered throughout the entire state into practically every village and hamlet.

If those early pioneer bankers of a century ago, with their humble beginning and "shoestring" capital, could see the Nevada banks of today, with more than two billion dollars in combined resources, thirty-five hundred employees, investments in buildings and fixed assets near a hundred million dollars, with loans near a billion and one half dollars, with computerization, foreign transactions, and almost every form of banking unknown to them in early days, one feels confident they would, after their initial shock of perception, be extremely proud that they had a part in the beginning and development that brought Nevada banking to where it is today.

A Wise Indian

An Indian who lived at Stillwater owed a merchant a food bill and went into the store one day to pay the account. After doing so, he asked for a receipt. In vain, the merchant told him that one was not necessary.

"Me must have to show me owe you nothing," said the Indian. "Me go to heaven and the Lord ask Injun if he pay his bills. Injun said yes. Lord ask Injun where is receipt. What Injun do? Can't go all over hell to look for you, so want my receipt now!"

The Nevada Test Site

by David Jackson

A facility which has played an important role in national defense and the economy of southern Nevada is the Nevada Test Site (NTS). Operated by the Energy Research and Development Administration (ERDA), the NTS is used as a field laboratory for the development of nuclear weapons and nuclear explosives for peaceful purposes.

Many other research programs requiring a remote location and established support facilities are conducted at the NTS. Thousands of southern Nevada residents have worked at the NTS and in Las Vegas since its establishment in 1951. The payroll during this period exceeds $1.5 billion and goods and services purchased in Nevada exceed $500 million. Many of the scientific and industrial businesses in Las Vegas have resulted from the establishment and continued programs at the NTS.

The area was occupied by Paiute Indians in 1849. More recent historical use of the NTS mainly com-prised mining, grazing and hunting. Two inactive mining districts, Oak Spring and Wahmonie, lie wholly or partially within the borders of the NTS. Oak Spring District occupied part of the northeast corner of the test site and included at least two on-site properties, the Climax Mine and the Crystal Mine, when the NTS was established. According to one authority, exploration of the area started as early as 1905 (probably for gold and silver ores), but it was not until 1937, when tungsten ores were found, that serious development started. After 10 years of co-use during the period of atmospheric testing at the NTS, the mining claims were acquired by the government and the owners reimbursed.

The principal mining activity in the Wahmonie District was at the Horn Silver Mine, located in the southwest portion of the site. Prospecting started in the area before 1905, but it was only in 1928, when silver-gold ore was discovered, that there was significant activity. Wahmonie, a mining camp of 1500 people, grew up within a few weeks, but by the summer of 1929, the ore body was depleted and the town abandoned.

Extensive geologic investigations made by the U.S. Geological Survey using samples from ex-

The Handley event canister is being lowered down hole at Pahute Mesa. The Handley test — more than one megaton — was conducted in March 1970. The platform at right is a cable chute that guides the timing and firing and diagnostic cables down hole without crimping them with a sharp right angle turn. On opposite page is an underground surveyor.

Camp Mercury, located 65 miles northwest of Las Vegas, is headquarters for the U.S. Atomic Energy Commission's 1,350-square-mile Nevada Test Site. Mercury provides office space, overnight living quarters, utilities, mess halls, recreation facilities, a motor pool, laboratory facilities, and administrative offices for test organization personnel. In the distance is the Spring Mountain Range.

ploratory drill holes, emplacement holes, and tunnels in the areas used for nuclear testing have revealed no mineral deposits which would be economically recoverable considering today's mineral requirements.

It is known that the NTS area was used for cattle grazing and that waterholes were developed and cabins and corrals built at several points on the site.

After review of known information about fallout, thermal, and blast effects, it was determined that under careful controls, an area within what is now the Nellis Air Force Range could be used for relatively low-yield nuclear detonations with full assurance of public safety.

Originally 680 square miles, were set aside for nuclear testing on the Air Force's Las Vegas Bombing and Gunnery Range (as it was then known), approximately the eastern half of the present Nevada Test Site. The predominant features of the area are the closed drainage basins of Frenchman Flat and Yucca Flat. The main Control Point (CP-1) remains located on the crest of Yucca Pass between these two basins. This area was formally turned over to the Atomic Energy Commission by Public Land Order 805 dated February 18, 1952. Originally referred to as the Nevada Proving Ground, the site soon became known as the Nevada Test Site. Additions to the area were made to the west in 1961 and the Pahute Mesa area and Desert Rock area were added in 1965 to provide its present size of about 3,500 square kilometers (1,350 square miles).

Although the NTS was originally selected to meet criteria for atmospheric tests, it also has proved satisfactory for underground tests. In the years previous to the selection of the NTS, there had been searches for other areas suitable as alternative sites. For tests of the yields considered in this environmental statement and for those of somewhat higher yield, the NTS continues to be the most suitable area and provides an established facility in a location remote from population centers. The geologic media at the explosion sites permit the placement of nuclear devices at sufficient depth for proper containment and control of radiation. The water table is relatively deep and water movement is very slow. Weather conditions permit a year-round testing program.

Construction of the Nevada Test Site facilities began on January 1, 1951. Operation RANGER was the first series of tests for which the NTS was utilized. The first test, code named ABLE, was a one-kiloton device which was airdropped and detonated on January 27, 1951, in Frenchman Flat. This was the first of a series of five tests in Operation RANGER.

After 1951, succeeding nuclear test series were carried out alternately at the Nevada Test Site and at Pacific test locations. Testing at that time was conducted on an intermittent task force basis at both the Nevada Test Site and in the Pacific and continued in that mode until October 1958.

On October 31, 1958, the United States and Russia entered into a voluntary test moratorium which lasted until the USSR resumed testing on September 1, 1961. After resuming its test program at the NTS on September 15, the Atomic Energy Commission revised its scheduling philosophy from an intermittent activity to a steady state of operations.

From 1951 until early 1962, all nuclear tests at the NTS were under the management of the Albuquerque (New Mexico) Operations Office. Because of the significantly increased activities resulting from the resumption of weapons testing in the fall of 1961, the Nevada Operations Office (NV) was established in Las Vegas on March 6, 1962. NV was assigned the AEC's responsibilities for nuclear detonation programs at the NTS, as well as at all other United States test sites.

The portion of the Atomic Energy Commission concerned with the design, development and production of nuclear weapons became a part of the Energy Research and Development Administration (ERDA) when it was formed on January 19, 1975. ERDA's prime responsibility is the research, development and demonstration of new sources of energy for the United States.

The first full-scale nuclear detonation which was designed to contain all radioactivity underground, was fired at the NTS in 1957 in a sealed tunnel. Since late 1962, the United States has conducted all of its nuclear weapons tests underground.

Six nuclear cratering tests were conducted as part of the peaceful applications (Plowshare) program. The first and largest, the 100-kiloton SEDAN, opened a huge alluvium crater in Area 10 roughly 340 meters (¼ mile) across and 98 meters (320 feet) deep on July 6, 1962. The BUGGY experiment, conducted to the south of Buckboard Mesa in Area 30 in 1968, employed five nuclear devices, each having a yield of about one kiloton, fired simultaneously to produce a ditch (simulated canal) 77 meters (254 feet) across, 261 meters (865 feet) long, and 20 meters (65 feet) deep. One small device (SULKY) with a yield equivalent to 92 tons of TNT (not kilotons), buried 90 feet in basalt, failed to produce a crater.

Although the major effort at the Nevada Test Site has been in weapons-related testing, the experimental program has included a variety of nuclear and non-nuclear events wherein the ERDA laboratories, as well as other government agencies, have taken advantage of the facilities available, the climate, the remoteness, and the controlled access to the test site.

The 1,527-foot BREN Tower located in Area 28 at the NTS comprises a flexible radiation study facility where a variety of experiments have been performed since 1962. The facility was constructed for the AEC's Division of Biology and Medicine (now ERDA's

Division of Biomedical and Environmental Research). The acronym BREN refers to the Bare Reactor Experiment—Nevada. This facility has been used to conduct neutron and gamma ray interactions over a variety of geometric configurations in air, ground, shielding materials, shielded vehicles; and with tissue equivalent simulations, electronic components, and live organisms. A 14-MeV neutron generator (presently located at the Oak Ridge National Laboratory) was once mounted on the side of the tower. It was capable of being hoisted to seven different levels where power and control cable hookup stations are located. A control bunker housed the accelerator controls and instrumentation for the various experiments. Access to the upper levels of the tower is provided by a two-man personnel cage on an eight-ton capacity freight elevator. In the past, meteorological sensors have been installed at various elevations in support of both operational and research activities. The tower also has been the site of laser scintillation experiments, small missile launch tests, and a complex series of sonic boom experiments.

A herd of range cattle has been maintained on site since the mid-1950's and an experimental dairy farm in Area 15 has been operated since the early 1960's. Levels of radionuclides in these experimental herds are monitored as part of the routine radiological surveillance program. Data from experiments with animals taken from these herds are being used to improve human-dose prediction models and to furnish information on the effectiveness of protective actions which may be taken to reduce the amounts of radionuclides getting into human food under various contaminating situations.

In addition, beginning in FY-1974, the Nevada Operations Office became responsible for the custody and administration of the geographical area and the facilities at the Nuclear Rocket Development Station (NRDS) which before that time had been administered by the Joint NASA-AEC Space Nuclear Systems Office (SNSO). The NRDS occupies the southwest corner of the Nevada Test Site and contains some $140 million of specialized facilities and twenty experimental reactor/nuclear engine/nuclear furnace tests have been conducted in this area since 1959.

Operations control center, Mercury

402

At left a mushroom cloud rises above Yucca Flats at Nevada Test site in 1958. At various times NATO and Air Force observers have witnessed testing ten miles from ground zero. Since July 1962 all operations have been underground, requiring drill rigs. The big hold equipment (above) dwarfs normal oil field gear; it is capable of drilling holes up to 120 inches in diameter and 6000 feet deep. This drill string will weigh about 300,000 pounds when fully loaded. At center a drill rig is being placed over an encampment hole. The rig will be moved away from the hole immediately after the test to prevent it from being damaged by collapse of the subsidence crater.

Las Vegas' Wing Fong

In the summer of 1939, 13-year old Wing Fong left Thailand for his new home in the western world.

His uncles owned the Silver Cafe in Las Vegas and welcomed Wing to growing southern Nevada. Unable to speak the language, the schoolboy used Chinese and English dictionaries to translate his lessons and to learn the language. After school and during summer vacation, Wing worked in his relatives' restaurant learning the rough basics of owning and operating a business.

Located at First and Fremont Streets, the Silver Cafe catered to the family trade. The proprietors of the cafe never turned down a hungry but broke gambler, establishing a moral precedent which was to be young Fong's guiding characteristic throughout his life. The cafe served as an after-the-game rendezvous spot for the Little Leaguers and offered volunteer fire department members free meals.

The Silver Cafe honored meal tickets or coupons which were issued to workers on the Union Pacific Railroad and many other companies. Employees received $5 meal tickets so they at least had guaranteed food should they lose the rest of their pay on the gaming tables. The cafe offered 25 cent breakfasts and 35 cent dinners with additional discounts for regular customers.

While pursuing a college education, Wing continued working at the Silver Cafe during spring and summer recesses. Upon graduation in 1950, he joined the firm of Pioneer Distributing. Fong then realized the hardships of racial discrimination. Unable to procure employment on his own, even with a college degree, Don Ashworth helped him get the job with the distributing company. Wing later worked for the Las Vegas Bottling Company until he opened his own grocery store on South First and Gass.

He remembers well the many times a customer came in and started feeding the one-armed bandits. Wing tried desperately to stop her from playing the machines but she would continue until all the money was gone and she was unable to purchase her staples. Fearing her husband's wrath she would then be afraid to go home but Wing always packed her some goods hoping she had learned her lesson. Such experiences have prevented Wing Fong from becoming a gaming executive. "I just don't have the heart to take people's hard-earned money in return for nothing, even worse, I could not bear to watch them lose every cent in a frustrating attempt to recoup their losses."

Humane customer relations have played an important role in Fong's business ventures and have always assured him of loyal customers.

Howard R. Hughes Industrialist

The late Howard Hughes stands head and shoulders above others who have amassed fortunes in America. He proved that accumulating wealth was insignificant. His foresight brought into actuality what otherwise would have been hoped-for accomplishments of the far future. Success was his only victory. His legacy to mankind will benefit untold generations to come.

Time was his greatest enemy. He dedicated his life to progress and security for his country. As a patriot he had no peer. In later years he preferred privacy, not to reflect on past glories, but to accomplish the goals to which he had dedicated himself. He employed the best brains and talent, and spared no expense to produce what he sought. Almost to the end his mechanical wizardry was inventing, innovating and perfecting necessities which kept America in the foreground.

But time ran out.

There was another side to Hughes. The public is aware of some of his philanthropic endeavors, like the Howard Hughes Medical Institute of Miami which disburses $1,000,000 annually to scientists and technicians. His pledge for $1,000,000 made possible the medical school at the University of Nevada at Reno.

Little is known, because of his insistence for anonymity, of the countless deeds of kindness and concern that meant the difference between life and death. Hughes, in keeping with his philosophy, spared neither time, effort nor expense to aid a fellow human being in distress. Like the obscure scriptwriter's wife who was stricken suddenly with polio. One of the two iron lungs in the world at the time was flown 3,000 miles to rescue the woman, who today is alive and a happy mother to her children. On another occasion, a newspaper reporter covering a Hughes story, was seriously injured in a plane crash. Little hope was given for his survival. But Hughes had prominent doctors flown in to handle the case. The reporter is back covering the news.

As a movie producer Hughes was the perfectionist, a stickler for detail and was downright obstinate in turning out flawless products. There were spectaculars like "The Outlaw," "Hell's Angels," and "The Front Page," which he brought to the screen; but very few people are aware that he also was awarded an Oscar for a silent movie.

Hughes displayed the same energy when he came to Nevada in 1967. He soon acquired seven hotels and casinos, 1,200 mining claims, airport operations, an airline, a television station and a golf course.

The acquisition of the Landmark Hotel depicts

Howard Hughes' nature. The property, a "white elephant," had lain dormant for five years. Hughes' chief of operations kept urging his boss to allow the property to go into bankruptcy and then purchase it for a "song." Hughes demurred. It would have meant tremendous losses to contractors, sub-contractors, concessionaires and shop-owners, some of whom had every cent they owned invested. Hughes paid for the hotel with the condition that all creditors be paid in full. It is in operation today, with more than 1,000 gainfully employed.

Long after Hughes was firmly established as an aviation pioneer, he continued to pound out one safety measure after another. He designed his own H-1 racer and established trans-continental and around-the-world records, for which he was awarded Harmon and Collier trophies and a Congressional Medal. He designed the flush-rivet fuselage, a power-driven landing gear and the bell-shaped engine cowling. Then came his pressurized all-weather Constellation that revolutionized civilian travel.

With the coming of World War II, Hughes developed the XF-11 warplane and on the drawing board designed improved machine guns for B-17 bombers. During and after the conflict he kept turning out military hardware at a steady pace.

With the advent and progress of electronics, his companies went into production of the Phoenix air-to-air and the Hellfire air-to-surface missiles. His visionary gift of scientific understanding for future necessities was the brainchild for new materials and new products. His unmatched concept led to the development of the laser, communication satellites and highly classified weaponry.

The scope of his foresight knew no bounds and his perception accepted no barriers. The areas he covered ranged from undersea to outer space. He knew and sanctioned every detail of sophisticated equipment invented, discovered or created by the scientists he employed, from infra-red sensors to electro-optical systems.

The marvel of Howard Hughes was his driving determination that never slowed or ceased, to provide the best know-how for improvement and perfection. His efforts played a large part in keeping America's military second to none and U.S. citizenry more comfortable and safe than anywhere else in the world.

As recent as 1968 the world's largest communications satellites were launched after being turned out at a Hughes plant. They were capable of carrying more than 5,000 two-way telephone calls and 12 color TV broadcasts—simultaneously. Two weeks later he produced a multi-plexed passenger entertainment and service system, described by experts as one of the most significant extensions of space age technology for commercial aircraft.

The Hughes 3-D radar was introduced as the only system for a restricted frontier area with the speed necessary to react. Then came an all-electronic memory device to speed, simplify and make most efficient computer information; a laser rangefinder for U.S. Army's Sheridan tanks which fired a light beam at 186,000 miles per second for computing range to score a direct hit on the first round; a radar system electronic extension of a fighter pilot's visual and mental facilities for F-15 superior fighter; AWG-9 airborne weapons control system for Navy's F-14 planes; a polymeric coating for electrical wiring that insulates from excessive heat; an Army tank-killer to penetrate enemy armor more than a mile away; and an Earth Resources Technology Satellite to measure and manage the natural resources upon which mankind depends for existence.

Howard Hughes was a man devoid of ego. Praise flustered him. He had no time for reflection. He was geared to go forward, to ameliorate the human race. He was truly a great American.

In his role as genius, visionary, inventor, mechanical wizard, humanitarian, movie maker, and patriot, his mission was accomplished.

It was a job well done.

Henderson in 1942

Industrial City

by Ben Sweet

"Basic Townsite," the company town which was to become the community of Henderson, was born on September 3, 1941, when McNeil Construction Company signed a contract with Basic Magnesium Industries to construct a magnesium processing plant at an ultimate cost of $173,000,000. This plant would be the largest producer of metallic magnesium in the United States with the raw material, brucite, being shipped from Harry Springer's mine at Gabbs.

Henderson was selected as the new factory site because of good water supply from Lake Mead and abundant power from Hoover Dam. Rail connections already existed via Union Pacific's Boulder City branch from Las Vegas.

It was meant to be a temporary town not expected to survive the end of the war.

By December 31, 1941, Defense Plants Incorporated had assured the construction of 1000 residences and work was started in January of 1942. A crash construction program began with imported British technicians and blueprints. The first factory delivered its first bomb in 1942, and the tenth and last plant opened in 1943.

On January 10, 1944 the new "Henderson Post Office" was dedicated in honor of Nevada Senator, Charles W. Henderson.

By then the new town had become Clark County's third city after Las Vegas and Boulder City. Oldtimers recall it was a moralistic company town with no gambling or hard liquor.

There was a movie house and bowling alley in the new town. Gambling and booze were available at the nearby "Pittman Strip," now part of Henderson proper, and in Las Vegas or Railroad Pass.

When Germany finally signed the terms of surrender in 1945 after the European Phase of World War II, B.M.I. had already been cutback for more than six months; most of the 14,000 employees had moved away and more than half of the houses were left vacant. Henderson was fast approaching ghost town status.

Federal agencies owning the property considered dismantling the plants for scrap. But Senator Pat McCarran persuaded the government to sell the industrial complex to Nevada. The state located new industry to occupy the plants and Henderson's future was secured.

The new owners formed a subsidiary, Basic Management Incorporated, to supervise the common property, including water, power, most of Henderson's original townsite housing units, and the extensive railroad yards. For a time BMI operated its own switching railroad before leasing the tracks to Union Pacific.

At this time, under the Reconstruction Finance Corporation, an effort was made to utilize the vast facility that was the B.M.I. and on May 21, 1945 Stauffer Chemical Company assumed the operation of the Caustic and Chloride plant at B.M.I. project.

Three days later it was announced in the Las Vegas *Review Journal* that a contract had been signed by Western Electro Chemical Company and the federal government to produce solid propellants for the embryo guided-missile program. With this program some 500 new residents moved into the then empty houses of Henderson.

In October, 1946, RFC relinquished custody of the B.M.I. project and R. Julian Moore came to Henderson as assistant to Richard H. Greenberg, comptroller for the southwestern division of the War Assets Administration. In a few months Moore became Chief Custodian and Maintenance Officer of the plant.

Since those days of World War II Henderson grew steadily, faltering at times, but it has become a clean, pleasant community with a small town atmosphere with current population at about 16,000.

The Henderson industrial complex thrives today with Titanium Metals, Kerr-McGee Chemical Corporation, Stauffer Chemicals, and Flintkote Corporation; all are manufacturing modern chemicals, lightweight aircraft and spaceship parts, and building products. Business is so good Union Pacific sends two trains daily to Henderson delivering supplies and carrying finished products to market.

It is a good record for a desert town that was enlisted for temporary war duty and then mustered out.

Bankers Named George

by Dennis Pletzke

The two financiers who made the greatest impact in Nevada early in this century were George Wingfield and George S. Nixon. They became most successful and powerful mine owners and bankers.

George Wingfield worked for a few years as a cowhand around Winnemucca, then moved to Tonopah in the spring of 1901 just as the rush to that camp was beginning. Starting as a dealer in the Tonopah Club, Wingfield soon controlled the gambling concession there. From gambling he turned to mining and within a short time obtained a foothold in the Tonopah and Goldfield mines by astute purchases and by negotiating a number of successful grubstake contracts. Somewhere along the way he made the decision to join with Nixon in trying to effect a consolidation of all the Goldfield mines.

Together they gathered in the largest share of the profits from the mines, which, throughout the region, produced about $250 million in gold and silver. Upon Nixon's death, Wingfield became the main controller of banking in the state, as well as the owner of hotels, including the Riverside of Reno, cattle ranches and other properties. Until bankruptcy overtook him during the Great Depression, Wingfield remained the economic, and perhaps the political, overlord of Nevada.

One authority on twentieth-century Nevada history has written that "The real capitol of Nevada was Room 201 in the Reno National Bank Building, Wingfield's main office and headquarters for his henchmen, the lawyers George B. Thatcher and William Woodburn." This may have been so, but no good evidence has been produced to prove it.

Nixon started his career in Nevada as a telegraph operator on the Carson and Colorado Railroad, but in 1884 accepted a position as clerk in a Reno bank. Two years later he organized the First National Bank of Nevada at Winnemucca and within a few years had become an important financial figure in the state. He became acquainted with George Wingfield in the early 1900's, probably at Winnemucca, and when the boom started at Goldfield the two pooled their resources to establish the organization which soon came to control the fortunes of the Goldfield area.

Nixon had already established himself as the boss of Winnemucca when Wingfield called him to the richer fields of Tonopah-Goldfield. The extent to which he controlled the town was indicated in a letter from the District Attorney of Winnemucca, Clarence D. Van Duzer, to Francis Newlands in 1899:

"Mr. Nixon is a cashier in a bank, a stock man, runs a saloon and hotel, has gone into the merchandise business, is an insurance agent, and sells stock, cattle, wool, etc. on a commission and monkeys with mines. . . .

"Nixon is strong and powerful with his friends and a large element who support him because they fear him. He is all powerful in the County and I find myself continually, where my duty calls on me to act as I have been taught to act, openly and honestly, in opposition to him. . . .

"Nixon is foreman of the Grand Jury now in session. Victor Bouton stole fifty head of cattle and sold them to Thies. Thies knew they were stolen cattle yet he bought them and I have proof that Bouton rode Thies horses while doing the stealing. I have six indictments against Bouton. There is strong feeling in this County on the Cattle Stealing owing to the publicity of it. Yet when it comes to indicting Mr. Thies who is a director of the First National Bank we meet the opposition of Mr. Nixon who naturally desires to protect his friend."

Nixon, more experienced in banking than mining, sold his mining holdings to his associate for $3 million. Concentrating on the expansion of his banking interest, he took control of banks in Tonopah, Carson City, Reno, and Winnemucca, as well as extensive real estate holdings. At the time of his death in 1912, he was worth an estimated $35 million.

George Wingfield

George Nixon

407

Bob Griffith

Two Griffiths

by Florence Lee Jones

The name of Griffith has been synonymous with progress in Las Vegas for more than seventy years. The saga started with Edmond W. Griffith (1862–1932) and has been embellished by his son, Robert B. "Bob" Griffith.

The capsule description of his life often given by Bob tells the story: "I've been lucky to come to a new town as a boy and grow up with it."

Already a successful contractor in his native Canada and in California, Edmond Griffith was in Salt Lake City in 1904 constructing the city and county building. There he met the aggressive U.S. Senator William A. Clark of Montana, who was completing plans for the San Pedro, Los Angeles & Salt Lake Railroad. Having acquired the 1800-acre Las Vegas Valley Ranch from Mrs. Helen J. Stewart, Clark established a new town and division point of his railroad on his new property. The Senator offered Griffith the job of building the roundhouse at Las Vegas, and he accepted.

Griffith returned to Pasadena to purchase supplies for his new enterprise in the desert. He left his 5-year-old son in the Brookside School for Girls, a residential facility for young children, where Bob had been enrolled since 1903, upon the death of his mother.

When the historic auction of lots in Clark's Las Vegas Townsite was held on May 15, 1905, Griffith purchased the southwest corner of Fremont and Second Streets, establishing a cornerstone of the future Griffith holdings. He also bought a lot at 113 South First Street, where he opened a store dealing in hardware, furniture, household articles, and prospectors' supplies, including burros. To meet a community need, Griffith went to Los Angeles and enrolled for a brief course in embalming, qualifying him as Las Vegas' first undertaker.

Bob joined his father in Las Vegas in June, 1905, living in a tent with him, and benefitting from his father's efforts in helping to establish the first school and the first church in the new town. When the roundhouse was completed, Griffith contracted to build business structures and houses in Las Vegas. In 1911, he built his own two-story business building at Fremont and Second streets, where the Golden Nugget casino now stands.

In the summer of 1915, Griffith opened a campground resort in Kyle Canyon, Mt. Charleston, after having done most of the work on a road leading into his Charleston Park property. He offered "an auto service" to transport Las Vegans, as few residents then owned cars. He promoted development of a paved road between southern California and southern Utah, via Las Vegas, then known as the "Fremont Trail."

Griffith was elected to the Board of City Commissioners in Las Vegas in 1915 and to the Nevada Assembly from Las Vegas in 1916. Two years later he was named to the Nevada Senate and was instrumental in having the assets and the roadbed of the Las Vegas-Tonopah Railroad purchased by the state. The roadbed then became the first highway connecting Las Vegas with northern points of the state.

The first city park in Las Vegas resulted from his persuasion of the Las Vegas Land and Water Company to deed 31 acres of land to the city to be used as an agricultural fairgrounds. This land extended from Stewart Avenue to East Bonanza Road and from North Second to North Fifth Streets.

Starting a family tradition of interest in the Colorado River resources, the elder Griffith was named in 1920 by Governor Emmet Boyle as a member of a committee of Nevada citizens to safeguard the interests of Nevada in negotiations for development of a dam on the River. In later years his son was to be chairman of the Colorado River commission developing the Southern Nevada Water Project.

After completing his education in the Las Vegas schools, Bob went to Reno to attend the University of Nevada but interrupted his studies for several months to help his father complete a contract on a new school building in Las Vegas. After being graduated in 1923 from the University, he married Ruth Atcheson.

Bob started his business career in partnership with his father in the contracting business in Las Vegas, but in 1925 he was appointed as postmaster of Las Vegas and served until 1930. Following the example of his father, who had been a charter member of the Las Vegas Chamber of Commerce, Bob joined the Chamber and served on a committee which investigated the need for an adequate water system for West Las Vegas, a controversial issue in Las Vegas at that time. In the late 1930's and early 1940's, as secretary-manager of the Chamber, he promoted the establishment of the Las Vegas Aerial Gunnery School, now Nellis Air Force Base.

Together with City Commissioner Al Corradetti, he expended his own funds to purchase the Van Rains Ranch, which had a large flowing well, so the water could be piped to the airfield. This timely action saved the military establishment for Las Vegas, because wells drilled there had not produced sufficient water for the installation and plans were afoot to halt the development.

For several years Bob was engaged in the refrigeration business and also owned and operated an automobile agency, as well as developing his lodge, dining room and cabins at Kyle Canyon. Meantime, he also aided community development projects and fostered nationwide publicity for the city of Las Vegas.

His diverse interests extended to serving for about twenty years as a member of the board of directors of the First National Bank of Nevada, secretary of the Shriners' Crippled Children's Hospital in Los Angeles, and president of the Clark County Taxpayers Association.

Perhaps Bob Griffith's greatest contribution to southern Nevada progress was made as a member and chairman of the Colorado River Commission while plans were developed and construction completed for the Southern Nevada Water Project, to deliver water from Lake Mead into Las Vegas Valley. He guided Nevada's participation in the $50 million project, which was completed on June 2, 1971.

What would Las Vegas and Southern Nevada be like today if the Griffiths, father and son, had not started with the town? No one ever will know, because their monuments are all over the valley as a tribute to two outstanding Las Vegans.

An hour from Las Vegas is Kyle Canyon, where Bob Griffith built a recreational complex with pavilion.

Warehousing and Nevada's Freeport Law

by Sonja Mosse

Ed Bender operated a successful warehousing business in Reno during the 1940's. As in all other states, shippers had to pay personal property taxes on the stored goods at the Bender Warehouse. An eastern shipper had just stored some goods destined for California when the assessment date caught him. Completely dissatisfied and unhappy with that arrangement, his complaint started Ed Bender thinking on a revolutionary idea.

Bender had read of many ocean freeports and decided that Nevada was ideally situated for an inland port. In conjunction with the Reno Chamber of Commerce, Ed worked out a bill which was introduced to the 1949 state legislature by Assemblyman Carl Fuetsch. It became law and amendments in 1953 and 1955 clarified the original bill. The way was opened for Nevada, and Reno in particular, to become a distribution center.

The freeport law was placed in Nevada's statute books but businessmen still hesitated to use the storage facilities, fearing the legislature would repeal the law and profit from the taxes derived from the expanding warehousing business. Therefore, in the election of November 1960, Nevada voters adopted a State Constitutional amendment which guaranteed the free port operation, preventing it from being changed at the whim of the legislature. As a constitutional provision, a change in the law requires passage of a repealer by two sessions of a legislature and a vote of the people.

Following passage of the law, another very important step had to be taken—this was the inauguration of a program to gain more favorable shipping rates for the Reno area. This long and winning battle was fought by Edgar H. Walker, freight and traffic expert of the Reno Chamber of Commerce. The Chamber's Transportation Committee sided with truckers, helping them resist pressures by California political and business interests who have struggled to raise freight rates since 1950 and destroy Reno's advantage.

The Freeport Law provides tax free warehousing on goods stored, assembled, disassembled, bound, joined, processed, divided, cut, broken in bulk, relabeled or repacked in transit through the state. There is no time limit to disrupt inventory control.

A further exemption is allowed Nevada's distributors in accordance with a public law passed in Congress. This legislation provides exemption from state income tax for those concerns whose only activity in a state consists of soliciting orders which are sent outside the state for approval or rejection and are filled for shipment and delivery from a point outside the state. In effect, this law restricts the powers of states to impose a net income tax derived from interstate commerce.

Merchandise stored in Nevada means loss of taxes and income to surrounding states, but manufacturers are pleased with the area because it puts them one day away from the rapidly expanding western markets. Most points in the state are only hours away from the teeming Pacific and northwestern cities and, as a result, shippers' volume has increased enormously, with some firms reporting a 50 percent jump in sales in their first year of operating from Nevada distribution centers.

Nevada's freeport localities are free of the congestion clogging large metropolitan areas of the West, yet major rail lines and transcontinental highways are close enough to provide low-cost shipping but fast deliveries either westward or eastward. In Reno 13 truck lines (seven transcontinental) have terminals. Five bus lines and two railroads serve the area. Within a 400 mile radius lie Los Angeles, Portland, Salt Lake

City, Boise, San Francisco and Sacramento. Shipments are made overnight to San Francisco, within 24 hours to Los Angeles, 48 hours to Portland and 72 hours to Seattle.

The Bender Warehouse Company, Nevada Transfer and Warehouse Company and Pacific Freeport Warehouse Company do most of the freeport warehousing in Reno and Sparks. In the past few years, warehousing has been booming in Las Vegas and it has also become a major new venture in the Elko area.

Nevada Transfer began in Reno in 1907 and now has half a million square feet of warehousing space in its Reno, Sparks and Las Vegas buildings.

One of the largest warehouses in Sparks, the Crane Company, services the northwestern United States from a modern freeport facility which is equipped with its own two-car spur track.

Frank Bender, pioneer in the Nevada warehousing field and Washoe county representative on the state board of economic development, claims that an average of 2½ million pounds of freight per month are moved across the Bender Warehouse loading docks. Huge cartons shipped in by rail and truck from all over the country are repacked into smaller parcels at the warehouses and then distributed to western points.

National concerns have their own warehouses in industrial parks which have been developed specifically to accomodate their type of facility.

The Sierra Pacific Power Company operates a unique industrial park system. Just five minutes from downtown Reno, their park is complete with wide streets, sewers, water, gas and electricity. It houses 12 firms with others under construction. Another industrial park near Verdi, 10 miles west of Reno, is also under operation and the power company has plans for a third park to accomodate special heavy industrial requirements.

Through active industrial development programs by the Department of Economic Development and the Western Nevada Industrial Development Commission, many firms have established their own warehouses and assembly plants and watched their sales and profits increase proportionately to their inventories.

Warehousing costs in Nevada are competitive with the rest of the country so that the savings in freight and taxes go right into the profit column. Lack of taxation on unsold merchandise totals up to a tremendous savings on personal property taxes, especially to California businessmen who store their entire inventories for western distribution in Nevada. Warehouse officials estimate that manufacturers who use the Nevada Freeport Law facilities can save about four percent, on an average, of the original cost of their products.

A prime example of effective use of the law is Bigelow-Sanford, Inc., a major carpet manufacturer.

The law and other Nevada industrial advantages prompted Bigelow to move its entire west coast warehousing and distributing center from California to Sparks. The company now takes advantage of the law to cut, bind and process raw carpets and at the same time can afford to maintain a large enough inventory to carpet 10,000 homes from its facility in Sparks. Not a penny of inventory tax is paid on the carpet that goes to markets in seven western states.

The three major factors which make northern Nevada a wonderland and "Reno—the hub of the West" can be attributed to the state Freeport Law, proximity to western markets and steady labor force. Manufacturers realized decreased distribution costs while service to customers is improving. Warehousing is not limited to east-west distribution because well over a million and a half cases of canned goods have been stored in Reno for future eastern distribution.

Utah recently entered the freeport warehousing field, but officials believe that this will not threaten Nevada's port industry, for Utah's legislature can repeal the law whenever it seems feasible.

Other states have the tax advantage but not the shipping advantages, while some states with shipping advantages are handicapped by their heavy taxing. So the warehousing business continues to grow in Nevada's inland ports, benefitting the entire economic structure of the state. As more warehouses are built and expanded, laborers, plumbers, electricians and scores of other workers are employed; some 100 jobs are created for every 100,000 square feet of warehouse space or manufacturing area opened.

The freeport law was boosted in December 1966 when Attorney General Harvey Dickerson held that a foreign corporation need not register with the Secretary of State to do business in Nevada because it stores its products in the state's warehouses or because some of these goods will be consumed in Nevada.

A U.S. Supreme Court decision, effective January 1976, could provide a booming new business to the southern Nevada area. This high court ruling allows states, counties and cities to tax imports stored in bond. Such legislation will have a shocking impact on industry because any imported product in its original container can now be taxed by states without freeport laws. Industry would avoid double taxation by using Nevada as an assembly or storage point, for manufacturers in other states would have to pay tax on the products' parts and again on the finished product.

Nevada could abolish its free port laws in favor of this new tax provision but the state's warehousing industry has been well established and continues to expand dramatically. However, with the court's decision, there will definitely be an exodus of manufacturers or warehousing from neighboring states to Nevada.

Nevada Railroads

by Art Rader

Major Nevada railroads are greeting the Bicentennial year with busy traffic schedules and booming profits. Nevada's three trunk lines are prosperous operations happily uninfected by the epidemic of insolvency which is wrecking eastern railroads and giving the industry a bad name.

The Union Pacific and Southern Pacific rank among the most profitable railways in America, and the Western Pacific is doing well.

The SP's predecessor, the Central Pacific, was the first railroad in Nevada, built during 1867–1868 along the Truckee and Humboldt Rivers.

The C.P. inspired construction of many feeder lines and hastened the economic development of northern Nevada. Many towns started or experienced their first booms with the railroad, including Reno, Sparks, Wadsworth, Winnemucca, Elko, Carlin, Wells, Lovelock, Battle Mountain, and Montello.

The S.P. purchased the C.P. in 1899 and still looms large in northern Nevada's economy where the diversified company operates 833 rail miles, 550 miles of truck lines, and 77 miles of pipelines. Warehousing, petroleum storage, and light industry are important markets served in the Reno-Sparks area. Mineral products reach market over branch lines.

Union Pacific was the second trunk railroad constructed across Nevada. It also had an ancestor, the San Pedro, Los Angeles & Salt Lake Railroad, built across southern Nevada in 1902–1905. The Salt Lake line founded the city of Las Vegas and fostered the Tonopah & Tidewater and Las Vegas & Tonopah connecting shortlines.

Although U.P. flourishes today as a land bridge between the Midwest and southern California, it has extensive local business in southern Nevada.

Branches serve mines in Blue Diamond, Johns-Manville near Lake Mead, Apex, and Pioche-Caselton. Farm and mineral products are carried over a branch through Moapa Valley. The industrial park in Henderson is reached by a busy line that continues to Boulder City. Warehouses flank the mainline through Las Vegas and North Las Vegas, where two more branches serve Nellis Air Force Base. Large rail maintenance and yard facilities grace the center of Las Vegas in the shadow of Casino Center.

Western Pacific was the last major railroad built through Nevada, constructed across the northern counties in 1907–09. The line generally parallels S.P., linking Oakland with Salt Lake City.

Proximity to S.P. has long inhibited W.P.'s growth. Its giant neighbor, longest and largest railway in the nation, captures the largest portion of traffic in areas shared by both lines. Yet imaginative management has kept W.P. busy and profitable.

W.P. has expanded Nevada markets in recent years. Warehousing and an industrial park are tapped at Stead, north of Reno. Gypsum is loaded at Gerlach and potato farms and mills near Winnemucca are serviced by the smallest of the transcontinental railroads.

Passenger trains have not vanished from Nevada. Amtrak, the government-backed corporation, operates daily passenger trains from Oakland to Reno and Winnemucca via S.P. and on to Salt Lake City via W.P. Special tourist "fun trains" operate periodically between Reno and Oakland and Las Vegas and Los Angeles.

The once-abundant roster of shortline railroads in Nevada has been depleted by the ravages of fate and changing transportation needs. Gone but for memory and a few remaining landmarks in the desert are fabled Virginia & Truckee, Carson & Colorado, Nevada Central, Eureka & Palisade, Tonopah & Goldfield, and a dozen more.

But some vestigial remnants of this railroad heritage survive as operating concerns in modern Nevada.

Linking the six miles between Empire and Gerlach in northern Washoe County, U.S. Gypsum operates a lonely industrial railway. The line hauls gypsum products from the company mine and mill at Empire to an interchange with W.P.

Operations over the road are powered by a solitary and diminutive 75-ton General Electric diesel locomotive hauling three or four cars.

Perhaps the shortest railroad in the world is operated by Nevada Power at its electrical generating plant near Moapa. A single diesel-electric locomotive labors at switching chores over a few thousand feet of company track, accepting coal delivered by U.P.

At Hawthorne, a large fleet of antique diesel locomotives trundle over 200 miles of rail at the U.S. Navy Ammunition Depot. The railroad owns extensive shop facilities and is busy hauling raw material for munitions into factories, switching ordinance to underground dumps, and carrying finished products to the S.P.

S.P.'s Mina Branch is the last operating remnant of the historic Carson & Colorado. The 130-mile long branch connects with the mainline at Hazen, near Fernley. The stretch from Fort Churchill to Mina duplicates the portion built by the C&C in 1882. The survival of the railroad vindicates the judgment of Henry Yerington and William Sharon, who built the C&C knowing it would develop an unpopulated area and generate enough traffic to stay in business. S.P. purchased the line in 1900.

Today the branch offers some of the most desolate and isolated railroading in Nevada. But business is brisk enough to require two trains daily. Copper from Mason Valley is carried out at Wabuska. The Navy

Depot is tapped at Thorne. Mineral plants operate at Mina and Luning. Ore from mines at Gabbs is shipped out at Luning, ore from Silver Peak serviced at Mina.

Between Kimberly, Ruth, Ely, and McGill in White Pine County, Kennecott Copper's company railroad has an aging fleet of first-generation diesel engines hauling copper ore from mine to mill. A section of this line is the only electrified railroad in Nevada.

Most famous of the surviving shortlines is Nevada Northern. The 150-mile long railroad was built in 1905 to haul copper from Ely to the S.P. at Cobre. It is still in business today doing the same job.

Although diesels long ago replaced steam, the N.N. remains a wonderfully antique railroad. Stations and shops in East Ely, Cherry Creek, and Currie retain turn-of-the-century atmosphere. Some of the rolling stock is of 1915 vintage. The last operating steam locomotive in Nevada still resides in the East Ely engine house, the proposed start of a new tourist railroad.

The Southern Pacific RR (opposite page) is the great northern Nevada trunk line, while in southern Nevada it is the Union Pacific RR.

Nevada's Bus-man

by Douglas McDonald

Sebastian Mikulich came to Las Vegas in 1913 as a service boy on the Union Pacific Railroad, delivering parts from the storeroom to the shops. His first business, the Las Vegas Transfer and Storage Company, was started in 1921, but this was soon replaced when he realized the potential for motor transportation in southern Nevada.

Sebastian started with two daily round trips between the Union Pacific station and the post office in Las Vegas, through the graces of Bob Griffith as Postmaster, in 1922. He also started service to Indian Springs and Wahmonie and began looking for other areas.

In 1927 he looked into the possibility of freight service to the new camp of Weepah, but stated, "I could see what was real mining and what was a joke."

When he serviced Wahmonie in a GMC truck, he loaded lumber first, then canned goods and stores, and finally put the extra passengers on top. "It only lasted about eight months, but people came like flies. They came on horseback, in wagons, and in cars, and there were about 1200 people there within months. It had a dance hall, saloons, grocery stores, post office, hotels, and shops."

By 1929, Sebastian had secured the mail contract to Tonopah and began service with a Ford pickup and a seven-passenger Buick with a baggage rack on top and a freight box on the rear. Later that year his Las Vegas-Tonopah operation serviced the towns of Las Vegas, Indian Springs, Wahmonie, Beatty, and Tonopah with a GMC bus built in Whittier, California.

After the state took over the old Las Vegas-Tonopah Railroad grade to use as a highway, Sebastian traveled a part of it in his runs.

The road was rough, and often spike fragments from the old railroad would cause punctures in the tires. Sebastian always traveled prepared though, and that included at least five gallons of water as well as tools. On one occasion, while north of the Johnnie turn-off, he noticed a red flag waving in a mesquite thicket. Thinking a camper was fending off mosquitoes, he drove on. The following day, on a return trip, Sebastian did not see any movement in the trees. He and his single passenger stopped and walked over to investigate.

Within the mesquite they found a man almost dead from dehydration. Wetting a towel from his spare water, and pressing it to the lips of the suffering man, Sebastian managed to get him to the truck. With the passenger sitting on him when he raved, and gently giving him small amounts of water, they managed to get him to Dr. Martin's six-room hospital at First and Fremont Streets in Las Vegas. He recovered, and went back to his geologic work, but it was in vain as he died of the flu shortly afterwards.

Many times Sebastian stopped to aid stranded travelers. And many were the times he was stranded himself. He always carried a shovel, pick, and burlap sacks to work his way out of a tight spot. "Sometimes on the trip up the road would be fine, but the next day on the trip south the road was gone and the car would be stuck. But it wasn't hard—I always got out."

There were also the little services. He delivered supplies to out-of-the-way cabins, a spool of thread to a housewife, or newspapers to out-of-touch prospectors. And always there was the coffee and apple pie at Bonnie Claire. "If I didn't stop, she would get awful mad."

His work and reputation for sticking to a schedule was such that in 1931 the Public Service Commission awarded him with a certificate for service. About the same time Sebastian started hauling freight for the construction of Boulder Dam. It was not uncommon to see a load of dynamite, powder, steel, lumber, or any of a hundred things being trucked out to the damsite or Searchlight or Eldorado Canyon.

In 1935 he acquired the first Flexible bus for his runs with one special feature—air conditioning. The bus had two engines in the rear, one for driving and one for the cooling unit. "These gave us a lot of trouble as they were the first to come out."

He fought for, and got, the franchise to Reno, "even though it cost me $50,000 in attorney's fees," and his business was incorporated in 1947 as the Las Vegas-Tonopah-Reno Stage Lines, Inc.

By 1954 he had the longest Star Route in the United States—470 miles daily—and in 1956 went to semi-truck and trailers. He acquired the Phoenix-Boulder City line, and the Virginia-Truckee stages, and express runs were extended into Oregon. The schedule between Reno and Las Vegas was stepped up to two daily round trips and modern equipment was purchased.

Starting with just one car and a truck, Sebastian Mikulich has built the L-T-R into the largest bus and freight line headquartered in Nevada. He was the earliest common carrier in southern Nevada; provided a much needed service when Nevada roads were little better than trails; and today offers a much needed service connecting the north and the south—all a tribute to one man—the Nevada bus-man.

Opposite are buses from late 1920's (top) and late 1930's

The first service truck (right)

The Longest Automobile Race in History

The longest automobile race in history, from New York to Paris in 1908, stirred the imagination and attention of the world. Here was a contest of man and machine in a supreme test of physical and mechanical endurance.

At 10 a.m. on February 12, 1908, six automobiles representing France, Italy, Germany and the United States lined up at Times Square as some 250,000 persons witnessed the start of the 22,000 mile treck (13,341 land miles) across the United States, Japan, Siberia, Manchuria, Russia, Germany and France.

The lone American entry was a four cylinder, 70 horsepower 1907 Thomas Flyer manufactured and entered by the E.R. Thomas company of Buffalo, N.Y., a stock model selected six days prior to the start of the race.

After 42 days of battling blizzards, snow drifts, mud and freezing temperatures, the Thomas Flyer arrived in San Francisco 11 days ahead of its nearest rival in the race.

The official route designated by race officials called for all contestants to travel by ship to Valdez, Alaska, from Valdez through Fairbanks, Tanana, Unalakeel and Nome, from Nome to East Cape Siberia by boat 150 miles. However, when this route was declared impractical the Thomas Flyer returned from Valdez to Seattle where it was placed aboard an ocean liner and shipped to Yokohama and later to Kobe. The Thomas continued 350 miles on land across Japan, then by ship from Tsuruga to Vladivostock, Siberia, and by way of Harbin, Tschita, Irkulsk, Omsk, Tomsk, Tiumen, Ekaterinburg, Nijni-Novogorod, Moscow, St. Petersburg, Berlin and to Paris.

The 8,280 miles from Vladivostok to Paris took 72 days. It was reported by the crew that the food was poor, the drinking water was scarce and they spent only five nights in bed during the entire trip cross trackless Siberia.

The Thomas Flyer triumphantly entered Paris at 8 p.m. on July 30, exactly 170 days out of Times Square, escorted by a cavalcade of automobiles and thousands of cheering Frenchmen.

Perhaps in years to come when space travel is commonplace, the New York-to-Paris Race will be looked upon as a primitive adventure, but in 1908 no one could deny this experience as proof of man's continuous ability, daring and ingenuity to overcome physical obstacles blocking the path of progress.

Harrah's Automobile Collection Restores the Thomas Flyer

Almost equal to the excitement generated by the New York-to-Paris Race in 1980 was the restoration of the Thomas Flyer by Harrah's Automobile Collection, Reno, Nevada shortly after this world-famous car was acquired.

The car was restored not to its original factory specifications, but rather to the condition that it was in when it arrived in Paris at the end of the race in 1908. The restoration, one of the most enthusiastic and enterprising attempted by Harrah's craftsmen, was completed in about six weeks and involved more than 40 restoration experts.

From 1912, when the Thomas Flyer was sold during the E.R. Thomas Company bankruptcy sale, this world-champion car remained in storage deteriorating throughout the passing years, and was in very poor condition when it arrived in Reno in 1964.

The biggest restoration problem involved "aging" the car to simulate the wear of the race. This process was accelerated by driving the Thomas Flyer literally through the sagebrush of the Nevada desert.

The late George Schuster drove the Thomas Flyer into Paris in 1908. In 1964, when Harrah's Automobile Collection started to restore the car, Schuster, then 92 years old, was invited to come to Reno to lend his first-hand experience and knowledge of the car, which proved invaluable during the restoration.

Sixty-seven years ago this Thomas Flyer made history. Today, the car once again occupies a place of distinction. At Harrah's Automobile Collection, it reposes on a red carpet platform several inches above the show room floor.

Specialized Hauling

From acids and ore concentrates to heavy construction and mining machinery, Wells Cargo's specially developed equipment transports practically everything that can be moved by truck. The company is particularly proud to be recognized by the U.S. Military as one of the foremost explosive haulers.

At the end of 1953, 49,476,737 ton miles had been traveled for the Army, Navy, Marines and Air Force hauling munitions, all with only two minor accidents. During World War II, Wells Cargo hauled 550 tons of magnesium and salt per day for a distance of 344 miles, the greatest movement of low grade commodity over that distance ever undertaken by truck.

Today Wells Cargo is involved in all kinds of specialized hauling throughout the world.

Historic Landing

On April 6, 1926 a small Swallow biplane lifted into the air at Pasco, Washington and its pilot pointed his frail ship toward Elko, 487 miles away, stopping en route at Boise.

The pilot was Leon Cuddeback, then chief pilot for Varney Air Lines, one of four predecessor companies of United Airlines. His cargo was 64 pounds of mail.

Cuddeback said his flight from Pasco to Boise was uneventful, although he flew only about 500 feet above the rugged Blue Mountains. On arrival, he was amazed at the interest in his flight. "I got to Boise, and there was the governor and thousands of people on the field," he recalled.

At Boise, he was supposed to switch airplanes but he couldn't get the other started. The Swallow, with an underpowered 150 horsepower Curtiss K-6 engine, was a balky machine. In desperation, Cuddeback had the ground crew refuel the first plane, and off again he went.

The flight to Elko was more eventful. "I got over the Duck Valley Indian Reservation and ran into a mean thunderstorm. I flew right down over a road, kept the wheels out of the sagebrush and plowed ahead until I came out of it," he said. "It was rough, with some hail." At Elko, he was surprised a third time by a large welcoming crowd.

Thus ended the first chartered service to Nevada by United Air Lines.

Joseph Kelley

Joseph H. Kelley started his gaming career on the *Rose Isle,* a gambling ship located off the southern California coast. Starting out as a dishwasher in 1932, he worked his way through the ranks even though his formal education had ended with the sixth grade. Times were tough when he finally emerged as a dealer, so Joe really appreciated the chance to work the financially lucrative "smokers" or one-night stands.

In 1941 Joe and his wife enroute to Reno detoured through downtown Las Vegas. There, the Kelleys met a large group of acquaintances from southern California who had moved to southern Nevada. Feeling at home among friends, Joe decided to stay awhile; he has been here ever since.

The Silver Club on First and Fremont Streets soon employed Kelley as a crap dealer, a position acquired through the "juice" of one of his transplanted California friends. After about six weeks Joe relocated at old Las Vegas club working for J. K. Houssels, Sr. When the Pioneer Club opened he moved again; it was considered a big thing to work for a new hotel. However, with the advent of World War II, Kelley—now a crap dealer at the plush El Rancho Vegas—was drafted into the armed forces.

In the service he quickly rose to the rank of sergeant, got busted for brawling, again earned his sergeant's stripes only to be demoted again to a single stripe private.

Back in Las Vegas after the war, he met Mort Saiger and returned to his experienced profession as a crap dealer at the Last Frontier. Finally he became a floorman at the El Cortez Hotel. Then in the late 1940's, Kelley and 19 partners leased the El Cortez from Houssels, Sr. A few years later the highly diversified partnership remained intact with only six partners, including Houssels, Sr. and his son Ike, Julian Moore, and Fred Morledge.

Early in 1954 Bill Moore conceived the idea of building a hotel and casino on the Boulder Highway. Kelley invested $5,000 and secured a 45 day option to raise the additional needed funds. The option ran out but it was extended and the funding was finally financed by the old Desert Inn group. On Memorial Day 1954 the Desert Showboat welcomed its first customers. The intial run of the Showboat produced mighty "slim pickins." One bankroll sustained both the El Cortez and the Showboat, and the latter would surely have gone "belly up" had it not been for Houssels, Sr. transferring necessary cash as needed in the new venture.

Diligence, consistency and innovations helped the Showboat to stay afloat in the rough waters. Kelley firmly stands on his philosophy that innovation is the secret to success. The Showboat was the first to keep track of slot machines through the installation of a computer, enabling management to quickly spot a faulty machine and make necessary adjustments. When the hotel switched to electronic slot machines, many players were leery of the new devices. Kelley realized that people are creatures of habit and that players prefer to stick with machines they are used to, so the change was made gradually. A similar method was used for introducing Blackjack "shoes." One shoe was introduced at one end of the casino, then the other end, one was phased into the middle, and so the transformation continued until all tables were equipped with four card decks. The change was so gradual that few players realized the difference.

With the addition of bowling lanes, the Showboat became popular as a one-stop family fun center. Unlike the major "Strip" hotels, this entertainment complex catered to the family and local trade. Its success is best reflected in their slogan "Our best reference is local preference."

Kelley later introduced professional bowling, casting the national spotlight on Las Vegas with the annual Showboat Invitational which has become the second richest and oldest tournament on the P.B.A. tour with a $100,000 cash purse. When the Showboat hosted the WIBC bowling tournament in September 1973, the contest attracted more bowlers than ever recorded in any single roll-off.

Pushing himself seven days a week and working long hours, Kelley knows it's time to climb into his airplane and get away from it all when he starts getten irritable. Once airborne, he can feel himself unwinding "just like a big ball of string."

"Las Vegas will continue to expand because entertainment, recreation, accommodations and food are still more reasonable than other vacation spots around the nation," believes Joe Kelley. And as long as this business continues to thrive, it will be largely the result of executives who dare to be unique and innovative; and as long as Joe Kelley adds his personalized touch to Las Vegas' atmosphere it will be most evident at the Showboat, the riverboat "gamble" which cashed in with its "Ace high"-Joe Kelley.

Collectables

Nevada Collectables

The collector of Nevadiana has a very real link with the state's heritage and establishes an intimacy with Nevada that can rarely be matched in other fields.

Dr. Elizabeth Thorne examined the basic purpose of the collecting mania: "Collecting is an attempt to limit the world you deal with to objects you can arrange so that you make a world where you're in charge. You become the god of the universe."

Many collectors pursue their hobby for its financial rewards, but the hard-core "addict" appreciates cultural and historical significance represented in his assemblage of artifacts or specimens, and most collectors gain a sense of security and achievement through their accumulations.

Personal reasons for hoarding items of intrinsic value are as varied as the categories of collectible objects. However, collecting generally is a sign of a scientific mind zealously evaluating and studying new discoveries. The collector then becomes a specialist in his field of pursuit and gains a sense of power and self-sufficiency. Many others who collect for mere aesthetic pleasure then become connoisseurs while some people benefit from the hobby as an emotional outlet for relieving tension.

No matter what the reason, collecting remains a positive experience because enthusiasts add beauty and order to their lives and display a devout interest in the world around them.

The collectors of Nevada paraphernalia have exposed a tremendous wealth of historical treasures once buried in the desert mining camps across the state or found in a forgotten attic. Glittering rocks, crumbling mining equipment, bottles of odd shapes and colors, hundreds of stock certificates, customized gambling tokens and incredibly colorful western and mining frontier literature have sparked a vivid interest in collecting unique Nevadiana.

The current collecting explosion as a national pastime has greatly influenced a prolific revival of treasure hunting among the rubble and dumps of the once prosperous gold and silver camps. With each new discovery—be it the remnants of a miner's cabin or supplies, whisky bottles from the many saloons, newspapers from "traveling" printshops, or scraps of letters and journals—the history of our state becomes more exciting, real and, most importantly, complete.

Old Bottles

by Grace Kendrick

The spooks of Nevada's ghost towns were forced to the skies during the 1960's as their haunts were invaded by bottle diggers. During that decade the quest for old bottles reached a feverish pitch that can be compared only to the early silver rushes. In the world of antiques, never before had an item boomed to such great popularity so quickly. Old bottles which previously had been considered worthless, turned into revered antiques as an estimated million Americans became avid bottle-collectors.

And it all started on the Nevada deserts. Collecting began on the city dumps of Tonopah and Goldfield. Ancient discarded bottles, some piled more than twelve feet high, awaited the collector to sort through them and take his pick. The thousands of perfume and toilet water bottles found in Goldfield's dump gave substance to the rumor that thirty ladies "worked on the line" each night during the heyday of that city.

The greatest glory hole of all was a vacant lot in Virginia City, two blocks downhill from the Bucket of Blood Saloon. Here the bottle-vein surfaced with "gin jugs," chinese "opium vials," and old black-glass booze bottles. At the discovery of "Hoboken of Rotterdams," lady's legs, and globular bottles 40 inches in diameter, more and more persons got the bottle fever—and more ruthless became their tactics. They sat like vultures on the balconies of the business district; with binoculars in hand they watched and waited patiently for the weary digger to abandon his claim for well-earned sleep. Then, the new addicts would move in with lanterns, gloves and earmuffs to take over the night shift and hijack the bottles.

The temptation to dig side-tunnels became irresistible and fortunately no one got in trouble except when a policeman arrested an 80 year-old lady for undermining the Virginia City street with a garden trowel. Bottle-rich garbage deposits were unearthed in Silver City, Gold Hill, American Canyon, Six-mile Canyon, and in the privy hole of the old townsite near the Sutro Tunnel.

In the eastern part of the state some of the most outstanding bottles were found, including a Success-to-the-railroad historical flask, a blue schoolhouse inkwell, rare San Francisco whiskey flasks, log-cabin bitters, and a brilliant green "La Cour's Bitters Sarsapariphere."

Soon the Nevada bottle collectors numbered in the thousands. They listened eagerly to the tales of the "old timers" to search out the early dumpsites of towns such as Elko, Yerington and Lovelock. The most difficult were Reno and Dayton because settlers of those communities used the rivers to rid themselves of their refuse.

History books were perused to locate little-known settlements such as Rabbit Hole, Como, Soda Springs, Thompson, Platina and Pizen Switch. Once again women walked beside wagons—Jeep Wagoneers this time—along the early trails and across the infamous 40-mile Desert.

Most bottle diggers feel that the most precious finds were these bottles which had been made for early Nevada businesses. The one that reached the highest monetary value is a brown whiskey bottle with raised lettering in the glass: "THOS. TAYLOR & CO.—IMPORTERS—VIRGINIA, N." Mr. Taylor, who had the bottles made about 1870, was one of the first distributors in the world to sell his whiskey in the now-familiar cylindrical bottle which holds one-fifth gallon.

Collectors were thrilled to find whiskey flasks bearing the names of dealers and towns: Oberfelder and Abadie of Eureka, Livingston of Carson City, Kane's Cafe, Sam Johnson's Bar, H. C. Heidtman and The Waldorf of Reno, Coleman and Granger of Tonopah, and a bar bottle reading "Compliments of the Season Exploration Mercantile Co., Goldfield, Nevada."

Collectors have been rewarded with discoveries of pharmacy bottles which record in glass lettering the existence of legendary Seven Troughs, Tuscarora, Delamar and Ruby Hill.

Other early drug store bottles showed up from Carson City, Goldfield, Gold Hill, Ely, McGill, Eureka, Reno, Tonopah and Virginia City.

Old "soda pop," milk, and beer bottles were cherished; especially ones carrying the names of Lovelock, Tonopah, Carson City, Elko, Goldfield, Ely, Eureka, Las Vegas, Boulder City, Reno, Virginia City, Winnemucca and Tahoe.

Today, the wealth of the dumps seems exhausted and the bottle fever has abated. But the collectors have contributed a wealth of color and realism with their valuable finds, enriching the glory and past history of the state of Nevada.

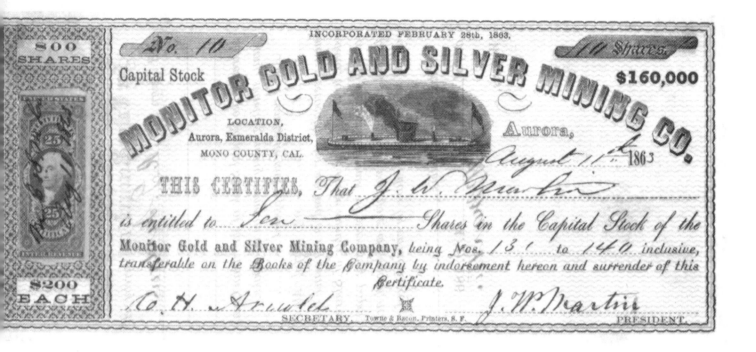

Obsolete Stock Certificates

by Clint Thomas Maish

At an auction near Reno the winning bid on one item was $360. Some people may have been amazed that a person would be willing to pay such an amount for a stock certificate, especially one from the Sutro Tunnel Company which had not been in business for nearly a century. This high bid illustrates the great interest in collecting Nevada stock certificates.

Since the discovery of the Comstock Lode in 1859, thousands of Nevada companies have issued stock certificates for mines, railroads and other businesses. In the early 1860's Mark Twain noted a great flurry of incorporations for Nevada mines and the resulting issuance of handsomely engraved certificates. By 1864, more than 700 companies had offerings for mines along the Comstock Lode. With each new mining boom came another cycle of stock promotions for the mines and associated industries such as railroads, mills, and tunnels. Stock exchanges were formed in Virginia City, Tonopah, Goldfield and Rhyolite; and when such formal arrangements were lacking one could always buy stocks in the saloons or in the streets. Every man had a pocket full of stocks and every man was in search of a bonanza.

Only a fortunate few purchased certificates in paying mines; most of the certificates were for "wildcat" promotions which, in some cases, were nothing more than a hole in the ground. Despite the continued losses from these purchases and the inevitable bust that followed the discovery of every bonanza, there were always eager investors in Nevada stocks. For those who lost out in the Comstock, there was the Esmeralda or the Humboldt, Reese River, White Pine, Bullfrog, or Rawhide.

Collecting obsolete stocks is a many-faceted hobby. Many collectors seek certificates depicting illustrations of mines, miners, allegorical figures or trains, and actual Nevada scenes. Others assemble their materials by locality such as certificates imprinted with the names of Aurora, Como, Treasure City. Another group treasures those stocks bearing signatures of famous mining personalities including William Stewart, John Mackay, Tasker Oddie and George Wingfield.

Imprint enthusiasts look for names of noted printing establishments like Britton and Rey of San Francisco or the American Banknote Company. The most desirable imprints are those produced in Nevada by the *Territorial Enterprise, Daily Union, Appeal,* or *Daily Inland Empire.* Also of interest are such colorful company names as the Avalanche, Golden Boulder, Miner's Hope or Water Witch.

The boundaries for collecting are almost limitless. No one knows how many different certificates exist and new ones continue to surface and often reap good prices. Those papers may not have been profitable for the original investors but they are a bonanza for the collector.

Postage Stamps

by Charles W. George

In all, there have been five U.S. postage stamps issued commemorating places or events in Nevada. The first was the "Boulder Dam" stamp, which had its first day sale in Boulder City on September 30, 1935; the "Settlement of Nevada," issued in Genoa on July 14, 1951; "Silver Centennial," first sold in Virginia City on June 8, 1959; "Statehood Anniversary" commemorative, issued on July 22, 1964, in Carson City; and the "American Wool Industry" stamp, released in Las Vegas January 19, 1971. These first-day covers, with suitable cachets, illustrate the colorful and interesting issues honoring Nevada.

Gaming Chips

by Phil Jensen

The forerunner of the modern gaming chip is the Spiel Mark or game counter, which in many cases were crude imitations of the United States coins with unusual captions on them. Since Nevada gambling was not legalized until 1931, even the oldest chips are relatively new. However, chips from the 1930's are still difficult to locate since most have been destroyed when a club closes, when a new issue of chips replaced old ones, or when casinos have been destroyed by fire.

Many chips are hard to identify because the operator was careful not to include much information on them. Generally speaking, chips in the old days had only the owner's initials on one side and the denomination on the other. This enabled the operator to use the same chip in several locations, or, in case the game was operating illegally, any chips seized in a raid would be virtually useless as evidence.

As the years went by and larger clubs opened, chips became more elaborate. Now there are multi-colored ones with names, locations, designs and pictures on them.

Some of the early chips were made in a variety of materials including rubber, glass, celluloid, bake-a-lite, wood and ivory. Most modern chips are made of a special mixture which is a well-kept secret by the manufacturer.

Acquiring chips can sometimes be a trying task. There are many current ones which can be bought right at the tables, but old, obsolete ones require much searching. The best way is to get a casino owner to dig into old junkboxes which every casino invariably has.

A large part of procuring old chips is making contacts with people who are in a position to get them. This is especially true in the smaller towns where a one day visit isn't long enough to turn up any choice items.

Just recently when the old Pioneer and Domino Hotels in Reno were torn down, the general manager of the Overland Hotel, who owned the building, found some of the old chips used in the Corner Bar Club and gave them to me.

Many casinos in Hawthorne and in other boom towns have long since closed their doors, having operated in the 1940's and 50's when there was much activity and numerous clubs. Today, old chips from these casinos are very hard to find. Winnemucca and Ely are the other towns which once boasted more clubs than they do now, and, finding old chips from these towns is very challenging.

Hopefully, I might find an old-timer who was shooting dice in one of those old casinos one day twenty years ago and dropped a few chips in his pocket for a souvenir. And maybe he'll give one of them up along with a story that invariably goes with it.

Books and Pamphlets

by Stanley W. Paher

The world of books is among the most remarkable creations of man, outliving nations, monuments, and civilizations. After an era of darkness, a new race builds on the old; new edifaces rise from ruined foundations. But in the book world are chapters that note these cycles of history. These volumes live on in eternal youth, still young and fresh as the day that they were written, still telling of deeds of men who were buried centuries ago.

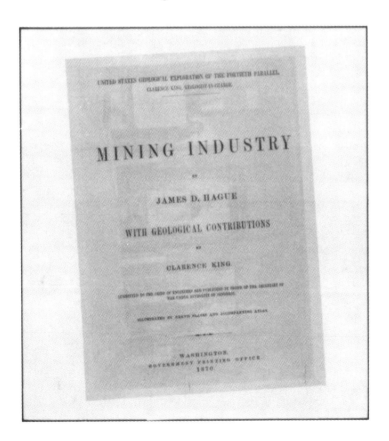

The world of the Nevada book collectors is a big one, and few can hope to encompass all of it. Such collecting requires specialization; some of the most-used categories are author, period, subject, or various combinations of these. An oft cultivated specialty is the limited edition volumes and Nevada imprints.

It is important for the collector to know what he wants. Since he cannot hope to amass all of the books ever written about Nevada, the collector must carve out a special niche, such as mining, agriculture, travel and exploration, outlaws and gun men, or biography. There are nearly 300 books of Nevada fiction and poetry.

Books on gambling are so popular that a special literary club had to be formed. There are cook books, archaeological studies, and books on Indians, transportation, education, hobbies, and various reference works and maps.

The collector should not ignore government documents, or "flimseys" such as broadsides and pamphlets. Many California books contain chapters and sometimes even entire sections pertaining to Nevada. The title might hide its contents. John Muir's *Steep Trails* has chapters on Nevada's forests, farms and ghost towns. Edwin Corle's *Listen, Bright Angel*, a comprehensive Grand Canyon book, has significant material about the area where the Colorado River meets southern Nevada. *Shorthand and Reporting* by Charles Sumner has refreshing Nevada material embodied in a biographical sketch.

The very heart of a magnificent Nevada book collection must contain many early editions issued before 1950 that cover a single phase of the state's history. Notable among these are William Wright's *The Big Bonanza*, Powell's *Nevada, the Land of Gold and Silver*, John C. Fremont's *Explorations . . .*, and Burton's *City of the Saints*.

Among the general state histories, these should be included; Thompson & West's *History of Nevada, 1881* (the 1st edition), Sam Davis' *History of Nevada, 2* vols., James Scrugham's *Nevada, a Narrative of the Conquest of a Frontier Land,* 3 vols., H. H. Bancroft's *History of Nevada, Colorado and Wyoming,* and Effie Mona Mack's *Nevada . . .,* published in 1935.

Many a specialist would make great sacrifices to attain an early Bancroft map of Nevada Territory, or those early booklets with colorful wrappers. Government and mining reports are highly coveted. A crazed book man might hawk his diamond cufflinks to obtain an early state directory or a report of the masonic lodge in Hamilton or the by-laws of the Young American Fire Company. Early newspapers, especially the pre-statehood *Territorial Enterprise* or *Reese River Reveille,* are important adjuncts to a Nevada book collection.

Collectable books crop up in the strangest places: at garage sales, junk shops, antique stores, used book marts, and of course Western Americana book dealers. Overlooked gems might be found in a forgotten attic or bureau drawer. Book dealers throughout the nation issue catalogs, and collectors pore over each issue to find books still lacking in their collection.

Book buyers might be categorized according to their habits and personal use of acquisitions. Some have as objective unusual book bindings which might blend with a room decor. Many handsome voluminous libraries are seldom used and the owner might be quite unaware of the contents of his books.

Other collectors stock their shelves with assorted but interesting Nevada volumes which reflect his taste and curiosity. He might glance through the pages without appreciating the knowledge and spiritual wealth. His mind is not yet prepared for integration with profound and literary riches.

But the man who totally owns his books reveres his worn, dog-eared editions as sources of immense reading pleasure. His blemished and notated pages show familiarity with the material.

The value of a good library is immeasurable, for good books are like wise old friends which can be turned to time and time again. Amid his books, the reader can fight the last Indian battle of 1911 at Little High Rock Canyon, travel with Mark Twain in *Roughing It* as he battled tarantulas, mine speculators, and mined for silver.

The reader can discover new trails with the pathfinder John C. Fremont, walk with California-bound emigrants in the days of '49, gallop through the sagebrush with the Nevada cavalry, ride in a Concord stagecoach, and rub shoulders with nabobs and miners alike in the old-time Sazerac Lying club.

Though a storm might rage, a pulp companion can permeate the reader with warmth and comfort. The harsh impersonality of life can be cast off as new characters, places and events unveil a world of excitement, interest and personal satisfaction.

Merchant Trade Tokens
by William V. Wright

One of the fastest growing branches of numismatics is the collecting of merchant trade tokens. Trade tokens were minted mainly to be used as cash or trade by merchants in their own businesses. Practically all were minted during the first quarter of the twentieth century, although a few businesses used them prior to 1900, and a few hardy souls are still using tokens in their day-to-day operations.

Trade tokens are popular with collectors because they are usually customized with individual characteristics. For example, a saloon token from Delamar may look like many other tokens to the casual observer, but it is indeed entirely different from the hundreds of thousands of tokens that were minted at the same time because of its cutomized, distinctive embossing.

The availability of merchant trade tokens, providing the opportunity to make new discoveries and learn about their history, contributes to the popularity of token collecting.

Some token collectors diversify their interests with some specializing in a "place" or "town" collection by procuring tokens from towns throughout the state. Others collect a representative group from all states, some assemble only bakery tokens; others are only interested in saloon tokens; and perhaps another will collect one token from every state or territory.

Collecting all tokens from Nevada builds an interest in the history of the state and gives ample opportunity to visit the most remote areas of the state. There seems to be a certain vicarious thrill in visiting Nevada ghost towns such as Bull Run, White Rock, Ferber, Lane City, Carrara, Bullfrog, Divide City, Skelton, Mazuma and Seven Troughs, all of which had issued tokens.

Nevada collectors have now catalogued tokens from approximately 175 different towns; not a bad showing since there were only 600 different post offices and a mere 400 communities permanent enough to publish their own newspaper.

Merchant trade tokens represent more than a simple hobby for collecting enthusiasts, for the historical facts and legends surrounding each token's existence keep the frontier image of Nevada vivid and alive.

GOING TO HUMBOLDT.

Mark Twain's Nevada

by Jeanne Elizabeth Wier

Bold indeed would be the pen that would attempt to delineate in their finer details the elements of that composite photograph which represents Nevada's greatest literator, Mark Twain. But it may not be amiss to indicate some of the frontier characteristics which struggled for supremacy throughout the long life of the subject of this sketch—characteristics which were never successfully overlaid or overgrown by the culture of the East. First in importance as in development was the strong radicalism and individualism of the man.

Next in importance to Mark Twain's Mississippi books is his "Roughing It," the story of experiences in the western mines and particularly in Nevada whither he came with his brother who had been appointed Territorial Secretary under Governor Nye by President Lincoln in 1861. Of this book he said, "It sells right along just like the Bible." For it was the story of the enchanted land of the West known through the East even at a much later time by the more famous name of California, and such Mr. Clemens himself calls Nevada in his famous letter to the California Pioneers at their banquet in New York in 1869:

SELLING A MINE.

TERVIEWING THE "WIDE WEST."

WORTH A MILLION.

WORTH NOTHING.

Literary

Elmira, October 11, 1869.

Gentlemen: Circumstances render it out of my power to take advantage of the invitation extended to me through Mr. Simonton, and be present at your dinner at New York. I regret this very much.

If I were to tell some of my experiences, you would recognize Nevada blood in me; I fancy the old, old story would sound familiar no doubt. I have the usual stock of reminiscences. For instance: I went to Esmeralda early. I purchased largely in the "Wide West," "Winnemucca," and other fine claims and became wealthy. I fared sumptuously on bread when flour was $200 a barrel and had beans for dinner every Sunday when none but bloated aristocrats could afford such grandeur. But I finished by feeding batteries in a quartz mill at $15 a week, and wishing I was a battery myself and had somebody to feed me. My claims in Esmeralda are there yet. I suppose I could be persuaded to sell.

I went to Humboldt District when it was new; I became largely interested in the "Alba Nueva" and other claims with gorgeous names, and was rich again—in prospect. I owned a vast mining property there. I would not have sold out for less than $400,000 at that time. But I will now. Finally I walked home—200 miles partly for exercise, and partly because stage fare was expensive. Next I entered upon an affluent career in Virginia City, and by a judicious investment of labor and the capital of friends, became the owner of about all the worthless wild cat mines there were in that part of the country. Assessments did the business for me there. There were 117 assessments to one dividend, and the proportion of income to outlay was a little against me. My financial barometer went down to 32 Farenheit, and the subscriber was frozen cut.

I took up extensions on the main lead—extensions that reached to British America in one direction, and to the Isthmus of Panama in the other—and I verily believe I would have been a rich man if I had ever found those infernal extensions. But I didn't. I ran tunnels till I tapped the Arctic Ocean, and I sunk shafts till I broke through the roof of perdition; but those extensions turned up missing every time. I am willing to sell all that property and throw in the improvements.

Perhaps you remember that celebrated "North Ophir!" I bought that mine. It was very rich in pure silver. You could take it out in lumps as large as a filbert. But when it was discovered that those lumps were melted half dollars, and hardly melted at that, a painful case of "salting" was apparent, and the undersigned adjourned to the poorhouse again.

I paid assessments on "Hale and Norcross" until they sold me out, and I had to take in washing for a living—and the next month that infamous stock went up to $7,000 a foot.

I own millions and millions of feet of affluent leads in Nevada—in fact the entire undercrust of that country nearly, and if Congress would move that State off my property so that I could get at it, I would be wealthy yet. But no, there she squats—and here am I. Failing health persuades me to sell. If you know of any one desiring a permanent investment, I can furnish one that will have the virtue of being eternal.

Mark Twain

In this touching welcome we doubtless have the real reason why Mr. Clemens never revisited Nevada scenes. He never forgot his early residence here and was to the last in communication with some few of the friends of his western life. But he never could be prevailed upon to come back.

"CAST YOUR EYE ON THAT!"

Virginia City

by Joseph T. Goodman

In youth when I did love, did love
(To quote the sexton's homely ditty),
I lived six thousand feet above
Sea-level, in Virginia City;
The site was bleak the houses small,
The narrow streets unpaved and slanting,
But now it seems to me of all
The spots on earth the most enchanting.

Let art with all its cunning strive,
Let Nature lavish all her splendor;
One touch of sentiment will give
A charm more beautiful and tender;
And so that town, howe'er uncouth
To others who have chanced to go there,
Enshrines the ashes of my youth,
And there is Fairlyand, or nowhere.

Who tends its marts, who threads its ways,
Are mysteries beyond my guessing;
To me the forms of other days
Are still about its centers pressing;
I know that loving lips are cold,
And true hearts stilled — ah, more the pity
But in my fancy they yet hold
Their Empire in Virginia City.

Unhallowed flames have swept away
The structures in which I delighted;
The streets are grass-grown, and decay
Has left the sunny slopes benighted —
But not for me; to my dimmed sight
The town is always like the olden,
As to the captive Israelite
Shown aye Jerusalem the Golden.

I would not like to see it now,
I choose to know it as I did then,
With glorious light upon its brow
And all its features bright and splendid;
Nor would I like that it should see
Me, gray and stooped, a mark for pity,
And learn that time had dealt with me
As hard as with Virginia City.

Valley Grave

Only a grave in the valley,
   There in the shifting sands,
Where the winds blow hot across the waste
   Of arid burning lands.
A pile of bones, a headboard rough,
   To mark the lonely spot —
Teamster or miner, I wonder which?
   Thirst, or a pistol shot?

Only a grave in the valley —
   And the winds of the desert bare
Sing their songs, a requiem,
   On the shimm'ring, stifling air.
The howl of the grey coyote
   Comes from yonder hill,
When the night is black and the hot winds dead,
   And the cactus gaunt and still.

Only a grave in the valley,
   Lonesome and desolate,
With headboard bleached and name obscure —
   One of the whims of Fate.
Who but God can tell us,
   The tale of the sandy plot?
Teamster or miner, I wonder which?
   Thirst, or a pistol shot?

*Desert well
Death
Valley
country*

Walter Van Tilburg Clark's

by Jason White

Excerpts from an unfinished novel.
Editing and commentary by Robert Morse Clark

The tentative title for this novel was *Jason White*. It might have been started as early as 1941, when Dad took a leave of absence from his teaching job at Cazenovia High School in upstate New York and, at the invitation of his close friend, Robert Caples, spent a year at a short-lived artist's colony on the Indian Springs Ranch north of Las Vegas. Most of it was written back in Cazenovia, after *The City of Trembling Leaves* had gone to Random House in late 1944. In an interview when that novel was published in 1945, Dad mentioned that another was well along. Sickness intervened, the family moved west again, and by 1947 work on *Jason White* had stopped.

What remains is an incomplete, handwritten first draft of more than 600 pages, done rapidly and lined with marginal notes for cutting and shaping in revision. The work might have been abandoned simply because it was growing too large to handle. Unlike the well-known, published fiction, the book meant to follow its central figure, Jason White, from his birth and boyhood in Maine to his death in the 1920's as a Nevada rancher. Moreover, the book was conceived as part of a multi-volumed chronicle of Nevada. The Gold Rock region, modelled on Austin and the Reese River and Great Smoky Valleys, would be a center. Links were to be made between separate books by the reappearance of characters as well as place names. Later in the manuscript than the passages selected, Jason meets cowmen from the cast of the previously-published *Ox-Bow Incident,* and one of these is a part owner of a Gold Rock mine.

The excerpts chosen, however, have nothing to do with these, and little to do with Jason, except as part of his education. They were chosen because, in limited space, they give Dad's fictionalized version of an all-too-common experience in Nevada deep-mining boom camps.

It is 1887. Jason, 21 years old, has been in Gold Rock for two years, working as a bartender and, though contemptuous of the mindless money-grubbing of the camp, as an occasional prospector. When the Black Ace, one of the leading mines of the initial boom, lays off most of its workers, Jason watches the camp go into a decline. After a hard winter, during which a soup kitchen funded mainly by the directors of the Black Ace has helped feed the unemployed miners, there are signs of economic recovery, though not in the Black Ace itself. . . . On days when the sun came out and the snow began to melt, or changed shapes in the wind, blowing from the shanty peaks in little veils, the slope would come alive like a rabbit warren or a gopher colony. Women tied up in shawls and old coats, and children, usually in jackets too big for them, would appear on most of the roofs with scoops and brooms to get the weight off before the roofs collapsed. After an hour or two there would be an intricate design of dark roofs on the snow slope, all steaming a little gently down canyon if it was a still day. The coasting and shouting would begin in the angular lanes.

There were roofs directly below Jason now too, and his own cabin was in a colony. On the good days, even in the middle of winter, there would be sounds of hammering and sawing. Both slopes were built up all the way to the Black Ace, and new rooming houses and clubs were lining the narrower canyon below the National House nearly to the graveyard on its long point into the valley. Big houses with porches, painted gables and fretwork appeared on the steeps behind them, built twice and three times as high in front as in back. The town was turning into a frail city because one claim had come good on the north side of the peak, and word had leaked out that the new Toyabe shaft on the third divide had got a core drill into rich rock. Toyabe Eastern stock had gone up into the head of the list even before there was any ore out to a mill, and the third divide had been quickly covered by a patchwork of claims.

Jason went over to look at it one day. Only a few holes were being worked, but both slopes of the ridge were covered with little monuments of shale and rock, like an extensive but sparsely-settled cemetery.

Towards spring, rumors in the clubs had it that some of the big companies were already quietly buying claims in blocks, without even waiting for anything to prove up. There was evidence of this too, off the books, for prospectors and single miners who had sometimes been in the line at the soup kitchen for the Black Ace miners began to appear in new clothes, smoking expensive cigars, drinking champagne and buying for the house, playing faro for hours, and sometimes boasting happily that they got all they wanted now from the entertainers at the Jack O'Diamonds and didn't have to beg for the two-bit wrecks at the Silver Dollar, or buy an hour or two in the colony of one-room cabins on the west slope up under the Black Ace works. The clubs did a big business all night. There were new stores, and their owners built good houses. The barroom and dining room of the National House were full of well-dressed men who stared at everybody with cheerful belligerence and talked loudly and confidently. There were even two new churches going up. It was a secondary boom nearly as big as the first, and this expansion made Gold Rock feel strong. The *Reveille* began to speak of the community in terms of generations, as if it and they stared at the floor and sat very still. None of them said anything. For a minute the hall was quiet. Travers, sitting in back of the president . . . made a little grimace as of gentle contempt, and shook his head.

Then a young man with his miner's cap only pushed to the back of his head stood up in another part of the hall. He looked very angry because he was afraid.

"I can tell you something," he said loudly.

Bates leaned over to Jason and said, "That's Frank Casey. His old man's a permanent drunk now. The boy's a fool if he talks."

Travers said something to the president, and the president nodded. He looked at the boy as if trying to keep a serious face. When the boy began to talk, he hammered with the gavel, and called for order in a deep voice.

"We'll have order," he said. "You haven't been recognized."

"You know who I am," the boy said. "Travers knows, too."

A miner in the middle of the house called, "Let the kid talk."

The president pounded with the gavel again.

"You'll all observe the rules of order," he told them, "or I'll adjourn the meeting. I won't stand any rioting."

The men were quiet. They were all looking at the boy standing there. The boy had hooked both thumbs into his belt and taken a belligerent pose to stop his hands from trembling. He was a black-haired boy, with only the beginnings of a beard. He was tall, but stoop-shouldered and thin, with a prominent Adam's apple. The Adam's apple worked because he was swallowing.

"Now," said the president, as if relieved by the resumption of order after a storm, "what's your name?"

"Frank Casey," the boy said. His voice broke, because he was adolescent, and because of his shame. There was laughter.

"How old are you, Frank?" the president asked, winking at the audience. . . .

"I'm seventeen, if it matters."

"Mind your manners, sonny," the president said mildly. There was laughter again.

"What difference does it make how old I am?" the boy yelled suddenly. "I know some things I could tell. . . know the Black Ace ain't worked out. I know—"

The gavel descended sharply and repeatedly. Men moved uneasily.

"Do you work for the Black Ace, Casey?" the president asked loudly.

"I did."

"I didn't ask you that. I asked do you work for the Black Ace now."

"No," Casey said. "Does that matter, either? He was going to say something more, but the gavel stopped him again.

were the center of something as durable as rich farm lands.

Still, most of the men from the Black Ace were out of work. Something strange had happened to Black Ace stock. . . . In two weeks it had gone back up to ten dollars a share. But when nothing came out of the mine it slowly went down again. The soup kitchen was discontinued, because the Black Ace didn't add to its five thousand, and most of the private donors became convinced by the confident and bragging air of the whole town that the new boom made plenty of work if the Ace miners weren't too lazy to take it. Jason thought so, too. Even workers from the other mines thought so.

Another mass meeting was called at the Union Hall in March. Jason went because he was in the Golden Horn that evening, and Jim Bates, who had written a lot of the prosperity articles in the *Reveille*, insisted that he go.

Only a few of the Black Ace miners came. Harold Travers, who was popular because he had been a miner himself, and because he still often told jokes about investors and managers who had never seen the inside of a mine, spoke very sensibly. The Black Ace had produced nothing, he said. The directors had met several times and discussed stopping even the exploratory work. He showed that this work was being continued only because the company, out of responsibility to both its workers and shareholders, felt it should exhaust every possibility, at whatever expense, before admitting that it was done. He admitted they still had hopes. But even this small exploratory work was costing money, and nothing was coming in. Charity, he said, was very fine, but you couldn't drink forever from a pail filled once. He hinted that in a town booming like this, no man had to be out of work. He said that his heart, like any man's, was full of pity for women and children who suffered, and that he was open to any reasonable suggestion from the Union officers, but ended with a joke about the mule who starved between two haystacks, only he . . . put a haystack in the middle also, which the mule had already devoured.

The Union officers supported him vaguely, and made firm references only to the fact that miners owed work for their money. Most of the miners weren't much interested in any of this. Most of them had their own work, and it looked good for a long time. They knew there was expansion. Many of them had claims on the third ridge, and so much hope for the spring and summer that secretly they began to feel like owners, not miners, anyway. Finally the presiding officer, a bald man with a massive black beard, asked if any of the Black Ace men had anything to tell them that they didn't already know. He made it sound impossible.

The Black Ace men were together in one back corner. They were badly dressed, some of them really in rags, and looked tired. Everybody looked at them,

"Are you working anywhere now?"

"Yes," the boy said, flushing.

"Where?"

"Toyabe Eastern," the boy said.

"Any complaints about your job there?"

"No."

"Have you worked for the Ace since it was cut to this exploration shift?"

The boy didn't say anything.

"Have you?"

"No," the boy said, finally.

"But I can tell you—," he began angrily. The gavel banged again. Before the president spoke, Travers leaned forward and said something again. His grin showed that he understood it was all a joke. The president nodded, grinning too.

"Was there any pay ore coming out of the Ace when you last worked there?"

"No," Casey said, finally.

The president looked at him and shook his head in wonder. "Sonny," he said gently, "I'd take it easy if I were you. . . . You're a little hot-headed, but you're not lazy. And you've got a good-paying job. Just sit down, and think it over."

"Because I'm all right—," Casey began.

"Sit down, I said."

After a moment young Casey sat down. Some of the miners were talking among themselves. Travers got up and came to the front.

"With your permission, Mr. President?" The bearded man nodded, and waved a hand at the front of the platform.

"Men, I'm sorry," Travers said reasonably, "that young Casey should let rumor put him in this uncomfortable spot. I guess we all know how hard it is for any mine to close down without stories getting started." He waited as if he had asked a question. A good many of the miners nodded. Most of them wanted to go on to the clubs, or go home. They were afraid Travers would start an oration. They were a little restless. They looked around at the blue, silly, gold-fringed Union banners on the walls, and the crossed pick and shovel with a miner's cap between them in back of the platform. Travers stood there, looking at his boot toe, as if thinking. Finally he looked up.

"I'll tell you," he said. "I can't offer any more company money to help these men. We've gone as far as the shareholders will stand it already. But I don't want to have hard feeling, if I can help it, even over a rumor. Maybe some of these men have had trouble finding work. When it warms up some, we'll know where the real hard luck is. There'll be a lot of new properties opening up. In the meantime, I've been a miner myself. I still am, for that matter. And I've known some tough times. I'll make a donation out of my own pocket to start the soup kitchen again. I'll give twenty-five hundred." He stood looking at them.

A voice with a cockney accent called, "Good man, Travers." They all began to cheer.

"Travers should be a senator," Bates said to Jason. "He's wasting a magnificent talent. He would be, if he had only a salary."

Travers modestly bowed his head and held up his hand, like a minister about to invoke a blessing. He was impressive, standing there against the cheering, a broad man with a bull neck, big features and heavy, black brows, overlapping jowls, and a thick, wide hand held up that still looked like a miner's. Gradually the hall became quiet again.

"We'll have to excuse young Casey here," he said. "You expect a good kid to be a little wild. Though I think he should be told for his own good that in the long run nobody likes a natural troublemaker."

"The Union doesn't care for them, either," the president said. "It gives us a bad name with people if something important does come up."

Travers waited out this interruption politely, but as if it didn't matter. . . .

"Still, it's better for everybody if we spike rumor when it does begin. Are there any men here from the exploration shift at the Ace?"

For a moment nobody showed himself, and Travers looked around over the audience.

"There must be somebody," he said, grinning. "They wouldn't all be down at the Bonanza this early."

Everybody laughed. The Bonanza was a new club running on a new system. It had a much bigger dance floor than any of the others, and a floor show with twenty women. The show didn't amount to much, but the women would dance with anybody the rest of the time. They were all good-looking women, and of all types and sizes, from small, dark, quick ones to big, turkey-breasted blondes. Everybody knew these women didn't buy their stylish and dangerous San Francisco dresses and the little hats with their big plumes . . . on what they were paid for dancing in the chorus.

During the laughter a man in the back corner of the hall on the side away from the Black Ace miners stood up. He was very broad, but short. His broad face had thick, stubby features, and his hair and walrus moustache were white. He was embarrassed, and stirred restlessly on his feet, and moved his stiff hands on the back of the chair in front of him.

Travers, grinning at the laughter about his joke, held up his hand for quiet again.

When it was quiet, he said, "I guess Broger was too old."

It took even longer for this laughter to die off. The old miner . . . looked at his feet and pulled one side of his moustache.

When it was quiet again, Travers said, "Broger,

will you tell the men how long you've worked on this exploration shift?"

"All time," the old man said, looking up, and then down again. "I don' miss any day."

"Tell them how much you're making in that shift, will you, Broger?"

"Four dollar half, same like always," Broger said.

"Have we taken anything out of there but porphyry, Broger?"

"I see it all dig," the old man said. "We don't take out anything."

"Thanks, Broger," Travers said. The old miner sat down. The man beside him asked a joking question. He smiled bashfully, and shook his head.

After an immediate collection was taken up for the soup kitchen, the meeting was over. Jason saw young Casey go out. He was by himself, and didn't look around. The Black Ace workers went off in a little group, too.

[The Casey boy soon loses his job at the Eastern Toyabe. A month later, Jason learns young Casey has been found dead on a hill outside of town, apparently by his own gun. Some say suicide, some a hunting accident. Jason also learns, through an eccentric but kindly old man who helps him work his own small, unpaying claim, that the Casey's baby daughter is very sick. With the father a hopeless drunk, the boy unable to get work anywhere, and the other miners avoiding the family, there has been no medicine, nor even sufficient fuel or food to help combat the baby's sickness. When Jason comes to help, the child is already dead. The despairing mother thanks him, and innocently remarks that "Everybody is good now."]

Mrs. Casey was right about Gold Rock being good now. It was horribly shocked to hear of Frank being brought in dead, and partly chewed by coyotes, in the late afternoon, and little Eileen winking out before morning. The weak and dirty shack became full of flowers, many from people who had never seen any of the Caseys. Mr. Casey, sitting in the dark back corner of the Silver Dollar, was bought drinks by one after another of the miners, who . . . wept and blew their noses when he, sitting bolt upright, but with the tears beginning to run upon his stern, conservative and unshaven old face, complained of the years bad luck had followed him. The neighbors took care of the other children while Mrs. Casey got hold of herself. Other gifts of money were made. More food than could be used, even for a wake, piled up in the kitchen. The Miners' Union, in spite of the fact that Frank had quit it when he lost his job at the Toyabe, maintained that Mr. Casey was still an active member, and undertook the funeral expenses.

There was suddenly much clearer and indignant talk everywhere to the plight of other Black Ace miners and their families. Disinfected by righteousness, women from better houses went into shantytown, and afterwards expressed horror at what they had seen there. The children were bones and half-naked, they said. Food, blankets, clothing, firewood were supplied to these houses, and a bigger fund than either of the previous was made up in two days from unsolicited donations. Mine owners and foremen promised the Black Ace men . . . work when the spring boom really opened on the third divide and north of the peak.

At every club in town except the Silver Dollar and the Miner's Roost, which was the same kind without back rooms, collections were taken up. . . . Most of the money was in silver dollars, but there were gold pieces, too, three of them twenty-five dollar gold pieces. . . . The fund became so large that a widow's pension was established for Mrs. Casey through the bank. . . .

There was angry talk, even among the Irish and Italian workers of other mines, when the funeral made it publicly evident that Father Coran had not been caught in the burst of outgiving, and would bury Frank Casey on a knoll in the brush by himself, and not in either the Catholic cemetary of the important, or the Catholic cemetery of the unimportant, and would not permit the symbol of the cross to be erected over him, or any marker but a wooden board with his name.

Little Eileen's funeral, however, which was held on the second day, after a mass attended as if the Mighty had died, was tremendous. The only hearse of the Irish undertakers was painted white, and set with white plumes and drawn by white horses. Within, the child lay in a white casket buried under flowers. A procession of coaches and wagons and walkers in their Sunday best followed it down the road in the beginning dust in the clear sunlight, and thronged the cemetery from fence to fence. When she was left alone, Eileen had a headstone of white marble, with a white lamb lying on top of it. Even a few Chinamen and Paiute Indians stood outside the fence, silently, in short lines, and observed the ceremony without expression. . . .

[Three days later] most of Gold Rock was triumphant, because in the night after the burial somebody had put a granite tombstone on Frank Casey's grave, and in the next night some miners, with a chisel, had roughly cut a cross on the stone.

In May suddenly the streets were full of teams again, the boom began real work on the third ridge, the Black Ace men lost their look of ingratitude, and everybody in Gold Rock was minding his own business again.

[The following April, after the stock has dropped to ten cents a share, the Black Ace goes into bonanza.]

Old Button

by Robert Laxalt

There was a faraway moan in the wind, so muted and faint that it seemed almost to come from another world. Night had followed swiftly on the heels of the storm, and the corners of the bunkhouse were already thick with darkness, obscuring all but the worn, shining pommel of a saddle, a silver crusted bit on a bridle, and the dull gleam of a carbine on the wall. They listened to the moan in the wind and the rustling of the wood in the stove, and wished that Buzz would come quickly.

Frisco Jack turned his fixed gaze away from the red chinks in the stove and stared at the figure on the cot. His eyes narrowed as he saw grayness in the old face and the gnarled hands. There was a rustle of canvas from the cot and they knew he was awake. Frisco Jack rose swiftly and leaned over him, and even Henry, the Indian buckaroo, shifted in his chair and inclined his head toward the cot.

"Do it feel better now?" asked Frisco Jack.

When there was no answer, Frisco Jack groaned, "I'm sorry, Old Button. It were all my doing, me and my big mouth."

The voice from the cot was half gasp, half whisper. "It weren't your doing. It weren't your doing at all. It were that saddle. If it hadn't slipped, I wouldn't of been thrown at all."

Frisco Jack glanced at Henry, hoping he would say nothing. But there was no need to worry. In the red light from the stove, the old Indian's face was as silent and impassive as rock.

Old Button turned his head to look at Henry. "Who's there? Who's that there?" He squinted his eyes and peered into the darkness. "What the hell you doing here, black old Winnemucca?"

Henry said nothing, but there was a warm light of a smile in his black eyes at the familiar banter. He sat back in his chair and continued to stare silently at Old Button.

A gust of cold air cut like a knife through the warmth of the bunkhouse when Buzz opened the door. He did not even bother to shake the snow from his hat and coat, but strode swiftly to the cot. He held Old Button's wrist in his hands for a long moment, then placed his palm flat against the tiny cage of the old man's chest.

"Is it any better, old man?" he asked. "Suzy wants to know can you take some broth?"

Old Button shook his head. "I ain't hungry, Buzz. But you thank her anyway. I'll be all right."

Frisco Jack had been watching Buzz intently, noticing the grim line of his mouth. "When's the doc coming, Buzz?" he asked.

"He can't come tonight," Buzz answered flatly. "The wind's drifted the road shut tighter than a tick. They can't clear it until morning at least."

Frisco Jack leaped to his feet. "Damn his coward hide! A little snow maybe can stop him, but it won't stop me. Give me the pickup, Buzz. I'll take Old Button through."

Buzz shook his head. "Doc says we shan't move him. And besides, it ain't a little snow. It's a big one getting bigger every minute. If it don't break come daylight, we'll be in big trouble ourselves. All that stock in the North Fork and valley both has got to be moved to high ground before they wallow down in the drifts."

Old Button's voice whispered from the cot. "Now, Jack, you take it easy. I'll be fine here until morning." He was silent for a moment, and then he added, "Ain't nothing going to happen to me tonight. I ain't made to die in bed. You know that."

Frisco Jack closed his eyes helplessly at the uncertainty in the old man's voice. "I know that, Old Button," he said. "I ain't worried about you dying in bed. When your time comes, you'll go in the saddle, just like your daddy and his daddy before him, I know that."

Buzz glanced curiously at Frisco Jack before he interrupted. "We better get up to the ranch house and get some food in us. Suzy's keeping it warm." When Frisco Jack made as if to protest, Buzz motioned him still. Then he turned and leaned over the cot. "Will you be okay for a little while, old man?"

Old Button nodded and they rose to go. Henry was the last to pass the cot. He stopped for an instant and looked down at the old face and the little hands, even grayer now, showing through the brown of sun and wind.

Old Button's face twisted in the familiar scowl, but the words died unspoken. He stared at the Indian mutely, and as he stared, his mouth trembled.

"I'm scared, Henry," he whispered. "I ain't never gonna move from this bed again."

The Indian shook his head. "Old buckaroo never die when big work to be done. You go to sleep now. We got long day tomorrow."

They were waiting on the board stoop when Henry passed through the door, and Buzz asked him in a low voice, "He's done for, ain't he, Henry?"

When the Indian nodded slowly, Frisco Jack wheeled as if to re-enter the bunkhouse. "Then why the damned hell we leaving him?" he demanded in a tortured voice. "If he's got to die in bed, then by God, the least I can do is stay with him."

Buzz reached out and blocked the door. "It ain't decent to watch a man die, Jack. Leave him go alone."

Henry grunted in assent. "You not worry, Jack. Old Button find way alone."

433

Frisco Jack paused, puzzled and yet strangely comforted by Henry's words. He looked intently at the old Indian for a long moment, and then he led the others into the swirling darkness. As they crossed the yard, Buzz noted aloud with satisfaction that the heavy clouds had finally parted high overhead. The storm was breaking, and only the wind remained to play at whipping the snow about in mock fury.

Inside the bunkhouse, Old Button listened intently until the low rumble of voices faded away, then he lay back and stared into the darkness overhead. But when he realized that his eyes were closing, he rose with a start, fear gripping his heart with an icy hand.

Adjusting the pillow under his head, he peered about into the thick gloom. By the red, flickering light of the stove, he could see the hair chaps hanging from the peg on the wall.

"If I'd a worn those today," he muttered, "bet I wouldn't of been thrown so bad."

Then he had been thrown, after all. The saddle hadn't slipped. He had really been thrown, all right. Might as well face up to it, he thought. And it wasn't Frisco Jack's big mouth that was to blame for it all. It was his own.

They had all been sitting on the corral fence that afternoon, casting occasional glances at the clouds settling low and leaden from horizon to horizon, and waiting for Frisco Jack to step into the saddle.

Ordinarily, they wouldn't even have watched, but this was no ordinary horse. This was a powerful stallion caught from the wild bunch, black as midnight, with meanness shining clear through him. Frisco Jack had broken him to stand and saddle, but they all knew he would take no rider.

Even before Frisco Jack hit the saddle, the stallion took off, uncoiling like a piece of black lightning. And Frisco Jack hung on with both hands as the stallion fishtailed and snapped in two like a whip, churning up the corral dust and even ramming broadside once into the corral.

They yipped and shouted like wild men as Frisco Jack stuck it out for one pass around the corral. Then, one jarring twist jerked him off balance, another started him going, and the last heaved him into a corner.

The stallion didn't go after him, but bucked his way into another corner and stood there, his black sides heaving, his outlaw eyes rimmed with white, and his nostrils flaring like bellows. Frisco Jack picked himself up and limped to where the others sat, not even bothering to shake off the dust that covered him or feel the bloody bruise on his cheekbone. It was then that Old Button had said the wrong thing.

"Now, I ain't saying there just ain't no more buckaroos," he said aloud to no one in particular. "But I seen the day when my old Ma could ride that thing with a money piece between her boot and the stirrup."

But this time, Frisco Jack was in no mood for banter. He was skinned and shaken and mad. Instead of laughing, he pulled a silver dollar out of his pocket and flipped it angrily at Old Button.

"There's your money piece, old runny mouth," he spat out. "Let's see if you're as good a man as your Ma."

Even after Frisco Jack said it, he hadn't backed down, but stood there looking defiantly at Old Button. There was nothing else to do but pick up the dollar and start in the direction of the stallion.

It was then Buzz intervened. "Listen," he said, laughing in open amusement. "You ain't any chicken anymore. You haven't been on a bucker in ten years. That's too much horse for an old man like you."

Frisco Jack had chimed in then, grasping Old Button's sleeve and not even bothering to conceal his derision. "Who the hell you trying to kid?" he scoffed. "That ain't no old man's pony, you know."

But Old Button had shaken off Frisco Jack's hand, his face flaring with humiliation and anger, and moved for the stallion. They knew there was no stopping him then, so they backed up to the fence and waited for it to happen, hoping he would be thrown quickly.

The stallion stood shock still as Old Button hitched up his Levi's, rocked on his worn heels for an instant, and then placed the silver dollar on the stirrup. But Old Button wanted to make sure the stallion stayed still until he was firm in the saddle. Just before he swung his leg over, he reached up with his left hand and twisted the stallion's ear.

That old buckaroo trick got him into the saddle, all right. But that was all. On the first jump, Old Button felt something tear inside and he screamed aloud. The stallion cracked double once more, and the old man's light little body hurtled into the air and landed in the dirt like an old sack.

And so now it was done. All the little needles of hurt that old age had brought him through good natured insults, all the little pangs that he had suffered and tried so unsuccessfully to forget, had been climaxed by the shame of this day. And he would die not like a buckaroo, not like his daddy and his daddy before him, in the saddle. But like any old man, in a bed.

He covered his eyes with his arms, and for a long while, the hard folds of the canvas shook gently, and then became still.

It had been a terrible effort. He could not remember ever having cried before. And now that it was done, he felt an overwhelming drowsiness creep over his body.

Outside, the wind was moaning again, lonely and very near. It cried about the edge of the bunkhouse and whimpered at the crack under the door. The wood in the stove whispered as it settled for the last time. Old Button heard these things and watched with a distant helplessness as the drowsiness enveloped his body and grayed out the stove, the saddle in the corner, and the hair chaps on the wall.

The bunkhouse was cold when he awoke, and the single window was framed with an uncertain light. He sat bolt upright in bed and stared about him. The canvasses on the other cots had already been pulled high, and the bunkhouse was empty. He swung his legs quickly over the side of his cot, furious that the others had not awakened him earlier.

Then he remembered, and almost gasped in pain before he realized there was no pain. Gingerly, he pressed his fingers against his abdomen. There was no pain. The terrible bleeding he had felt inside the night before was gone, completely and surely gone. He could have shouted in amazement and joy.

But there was no time for that. Outside, the wind had not diminished, but had grown wilder. It was screaming like a madman now, roaring down upon the bunkhouse and hurling great sheets of snow across the window.

He dressed hurriedly, jerking on his high boots and hoping desperately that the others had not already left after the stock. Deep inside his clothes sack, he found a warm winter shirt and heavy, fur-backed gloves. Reaching under his mattress, he pulled out the long sheepskin coat, creased and musty from many months of confinement. And from the wall, he jerked down the hair chaps.

When he opened the bunkhouse door and stepped into the yard, the flying snow leaped wet and cold into his face. He turned his head towards the storm, and moved quickly through the drifts. In all his life, he could not remember a storm so fierce. It blotted out all the world except the tiny sphere in which he walked. Its wailing filled his ears and the snow stung his face, but he welcomed it with a savage hunger.

When he clumped into the ranch house and shrugged off the sheepskin coat, he could hardly suppress a grin at the chorus of astonished yelps that greeted him.

Suzy was the first to reach him. "You shouldn't be out of bed, Button," she exlaimed. "Not until the doctor's checked you."

He waved her aside and thumped his chest and stomach with quick blows. "Why, you think that little fall would lay me up more'n one night? You don't know much about old buckaroos. Ask black Winnemucca there. He'll tell you about old buckaroos."

The Indian said nothing, but he smiled slowly when Button sat down beside him at the table.

"You sure you're okay, Button?" asked Buzz intently.

"Hell yes, he's okay," Frisco Jack answered for him. "Look at him! Tough and hard as he ever was. You can't keep that one down when there's big work to be done."

Button grinned and began to eat his breakfast quickly, so that the others would not have to wait. He attacked the sausages and the eggs and the hotcakes ravenously, gulping down the steaming coffee between mouthfuls. He could not remember when breakfast had tasted so good.

When he was done, they rose together and clumped to the door, their heels thumping hollow against the wooden floor of the kitchen. It was a good sound, boots against the floor, thought Button.

Buzz faced them as they slid into their heavy coats. "We're shorthanded, but we can't take any chances on splitting up in this storm," he said. "The most of the stock is in the North Fork. We'll ride there first and hope to blazes we can get them to high ground today. But there ain't a chance in the world of saving them steers in the valley."

"I'll ride to the valley, Buzz," said Button simply. "I know that ground like the back of my hand. I can get them beefs to high ground, and you know I can."

Buzz stared hard into Button's eyes. "I know you can, Button. If there's any man can do it, it's you."

They pulled on their wide-brimmed hats and stepped into the screaming wind and flying snow. It was inconceivable, but the storm had actually become worse. The drifts in the yard were already up to their waists.

In the dim, early-morning light of the barn, they picked out the strongest horses they could find. But many minutes had passed before anyone realized what horse Button had chosen for himself. It was the black stallion.

"My God, that horse ain't broke!" exclaimed Buzz.

In answer, Button swung himself lightly into the saddle. The stallion took his weight without a tremor. He stood there, his black head raised high and his powerful barrel faintly lifting with each breath.

"Why, I guess you showed that horse yesterday," crowed Frisco Jack. "I guess that little ride broke you a horse, all right. I gotta hand it to you, Button. You're the best buckaroo ever I see."

Henry opened the barn door and they moved slowly into the drifted yard, the horses tossing their heads excitedly at the stinging flakes. At the outer gate, they grouped together for an instant in a wordless goodbye, and then they parted and went their different ways. When Button turned once in the saddle, Buzz and Frisco Jack and Henry were fading into a stormy mist. He felt a deep, sudden flow of kinship for them. Then he turned and set his jaw for the terrible job ahead.

At the last corral, Button laid his direction for the distant valley. North and south and east and west were lost in the white haze that whirled about him. It did little good to look into the face of the storm. He could see nothing, and the flakes cut like tiny daggers into the bare skin of his face. Raising his bandana until it covered his nose, he hunched forward in the saddle and prepared to travel by instinct alone.

The black stallion seemed unaffected by the storm. His powerful legs plowed tirelessly hour after hour through the high sea of drifts. Button saw the firm white jets of steam that issued from his nostrils and felt the power between his legs, and was secure.

When they came to the creek, almost hidden now by towering banks of snow, the stallion stopped. Button lifted his boots high and flicked the reins, and the stallion stepped surely into the rushing water. Button could only marvel that a horse could be so strong. They reached the far bank and resumed their plodding pace through a world of white.

For a moment, Button could not believe his eyes. The veil of the storm was split for the briefest of instants, and there before him were the steers, bunched together in the smothering whiteness. He had never expected to find them so easily, and for an instant, he was astonished that his sense of direction could be so true. Then, vaguely, he realized that his hand had been limp to the reins for a long time before. The stallion had found the direction.

He urged the stallion forward until his forequarters jarred against the rump of a steer. The startled animal gave one quick leap, struggled to go further, quit his plunging and turned to stare at them through snow-rimmed eyes.

Then, Button realized that the stock could never be driven to high ground. There was only one out to the dilemma, ride ahead to the foothills and bank on the almost impossible hope that the cavvy would be there. Turning the stallion, he skirted the herd and plowed toward the mountain.

Again, the stallion took his head and moved certainly forward, and when the wind suddenly began to subside, Button knew they were moving into the lee side of the foothills. When he saw the big band of horses huddled together, he yipped aloud in exultation. It was almost too much to comprehend. Again, he had found that for which he searched.

Quickly and methodically, he moved into the band and cut out some twenty horses. Uncoiling his rope, he tied the leaders together, then moved back and whipped them down into the valley. They went reluctantly, pitching and kicking. But they went, and that was the important thing.

In the hours that followed, he drove them back and forth between the valley and the foothills, pounding an ever clearer path through the drifts. But by the time he had finished prodding and thumping the steers into the beaten path, darkness was already beginning to fall.

And finally, the stallion's strength was going. He slipped and floundered often now, and the once proud head was low. His great chest heaved with shuddering breaths, and his legs were caving. Button knew that in the stallion had lain his only hope of finding his way back to the ranch. But this did not seem important somehow. A magnificent horse was dying, and Button felt a sadness that this should be.

Night had fallen black, and the slivers that pierced his face were invisible slivers. Yet, Button did not really notice. There was an overwhelming drowsiness creeping over his body, and he knew a happiness he had not known since the days of his youth. Gently, he reined the stallion into the storm and the blackness of the valley.

Index

— A —

Agriculture, 33-35, 152, 322-323, 333-334, 338-339, 345-346, 384
Albright, Archie, author, 33
Alkali Hot Springs, Nye Co., 276
Alladin, Las Vegas, 372-373
Alligator, 195
Amaral, Anthony, author, 46, 112
American Canyon, Pershing Co., 160
Anaconda Copper, 70, 75
Anti-Saloon League, 21-22
Archaeology, 42
Artemisia, 13
Ash Meadows, Nye Co., 281-283
Atomic Energy Commission, 400-401
Auction, livestock, 142-143
Aurora, Mineral Co., 16, 251-253
Austin, George B., miner, 177
Austin, Gregory G., author, 176
Austin, Lander Co., 181-184, 190-191, 193-195
Automobile, early, 69, 334, 345-346, 408
Averett, Walter, author, 307, 326-327

— B —

"Babe in the Woods," 182
Baccarat, game of, 353
Bally Manufacturing Corp., 355
Balzar, Governor Fred, 356
Bank Saloon, Tonopah, 350
Banks, 256, 335, 394-396, 407
Bannock, Lander Co., 189
Barbara Worth Site, 174
Barieau, Walter, gambler, 278-279
Baring, Walter, Congressman, 25-26
Barrett, Bill, businessman, 121
Bartlett, Bruce, author, 199
Bartlett, Judge, 117-119
Bartlett, Lt. Edward, 166
Bartley, Dave, engineer, 293
Bartley, Fred & Nevin, innkeepers, 346
Basic Magnesium Industries, 406
Basic Refractories, 282
Basic Townsite, Clark Co., see Henderson
Basketball, high school, 115
Basques, 34, 64-65, 168
Bat Shooting, 90
"Battle Born," 13
Battle Mountain, Lander Co., 28, 186, 193, 195, 291
Beatty, Nye Co., 389
Beer, 238
Beer Day, 138-139
Belcher Silver Mining Co., 85
Bell, Charlie, publicist, 25
Bell, Harry, colonizer, 71
Bell, Johnny, of Humboldt Co., 170
Bell, Laura, author, 392-393
Bell, Norman, author, 169
Bell, W. J., miner, 169
Belmont, Nye Co., 269-270, 386, 388-389

Bender, Ed, warehouseman, 410-411
Bernard, Lew, sheriff, 208-209
Beville, John, author, 342
Big Creek, Lander Co., 182
Bighorn Sheep, 12-13
Big Meadows, Pershing Co., 151
Bilbray, Jimmy Jr., politician, 25
Billiards, 149
Binion, Benny, casino owner, 362-364
Binion, Jack, casino owner, 362-364
Birds, in Nevada, 12, 116-117
Black Canyon, 339, 341, 348-349
Blackjack, game of, 352
Black Rock Desert, Humboldt Co., 174, 178
Blacks, 380-381
Bliss, Myrtle Damrow, author, 308
Block 16, Las Vegas, 327-328, 332
Blue Diamond, Clark Co., 316
Blue Eagle Ranch, Nye Co., 382
Blue Stone Mine, Lyon Co., 75
Boating, 66, 343-344, 348-349
Bodie, Calif., 69, 78
Bonelli's Ferry, Clark Co., 319
Bonneville, B.L.E., explorer, 27
Bonnie Claire, Nye Co., 280-281
Bonnie Claire Bullfrog Mining Co., 280
Books, collecting of, 424-425
Bootlegging, 74, 281-282, 299, 337
Bottles, collecting of, 421
Boulder City, Clark Co., 339-340, 343
Boulder Dam, 329, 339-341, 343, 348-349, 380
Bowler, Sam, author, 361
Bowles, Samuel, journalist, 15
Bowman, Don, author, 384
Boyle, Governor Emmet, 345
Brauer, Ann, author, 345-346
Brewer, George, Elko Co., 208
Briggs, Carl, author, 30, 59
Bringhurst, William, colonist, 318
Brothers, Earl, theatre owner, 343
Brown, Bob, author, 25
Brown, Joe W., casino owner, 363
Brown, Nellie (book), 210
"Brownstone Mansions," 236
Buchan, John, author, 170
Buckingham, Fritz C., rancher, 168
Buckskin, Humboldt Co., 169-170
Buckskin National Mining Co., 170
Bufkin, Donald, author, 318-319
Bullfrog-Goldfield RR, 280-281
Bullfrog Mining District, 271-272, 283
Bunce, Ellen, author, 81
Bunker, Edward, settler, 322
Bunker, Mary, midwife, 290
Bunkerville, Clark Co., 322-323
Bureau of Land Management, 28, 35, 215
Burro, J., 98
Burros, 272, 330-331, 337
Butler, Jim, of Tonopah, 28, 258
Butterfield, Henry, Indian Agent, 288
Butte Station, White Pine Co., 285
Bybee, M. Burrell Sr., author, 384

— C —

Caesars Palace, Las Vegas, 371-373
Cahlan, John F., author, 107, 360, 361
Caliente, Lincoln Co., 302-305, 309
Call, Anson W., settler, 318
Callville, Clark Co., 301, 318-319, 321
Camels, 261
Cameron, Mrs. Jake, midwife, 291
Camp Winfield Scott, Humboldt Co., 168
Candelaria, Mineral Co., 253, 255-258
Cannon, Howard, U.S. Senator, 25, 26
Capital Punishment, 217
Capitol Building, 45
Caples, Shirley, innkeeper, 346
Carbonari, Italian, 390-391
Carlin, Elko Co., 208
Carson City Appeal, 40
Carson City County, 36-51
Carson City Eagle, 41-43
Carson & Colorado RR, 254-258, 262, 407, 413
Carson County (1850's), 54
Carson, Kit, explorer, 317
Carson River, 43
Carson & Tahoe Co., 59
Carson Valley, Douglas Co., 53, 55, 56, 61
Case, Lee, miner, 156-157
Castaways, Las Vegas, 372
Castleton, Lincoln Co., 310
Cathcart, Joe C., author, 301-302
Catholics, 70
Caughlan, Larry, 213
Cedar Basin, Clark Co., 326
Central Pacific RR, 124, 151, 166, 170, 186, 395, 412
Chapin, Samuel A., politician, 10
Chapman, C.H., sheriff, 162-163
Charcoal Burners, 197-198, 390-391
Chase, Ogden C., promoter, 210
Chemin-de-fer, game of, 353
Cherry Creek, White Pine Co., 293
Childers, Roberta, author, 246
Chinese and Chinese influence, 59, 92, 181, 185, 201, 254, 255-256, 258, 273, 309, 335, 391, 404
Christensen, Vicki, author, 99
Chuck-a-Luck, game of, 352
Churches, 80, 292, see also Catholics, Mormons, etc.
Churchill County, 133-147
Citizens Committee of Battle Mountain, 195
Civil War, 89
Clampers, 31, see E Clampus Vitus
Clapp, Hannah K., educator, 45
Clark County, 314-349
Clark, Mrs., midwife, 290
Clark, Robert Morse, editor, 429-432
Clark, Senator J. Ross, 327-328, 332, 345, 395
Clark, Walter Van Tilburg, author, 429-432
Clark, William Andrew, banker, 395, 408
Clemens, Orion, of Nevada Territory, 41

Climax mine, 397
Cloudburst, 158
Clover Valley, Lincoln Co., 290
Club Bingo, Las Vegas, 370
Coalition Mining Co., 158
Cobb, Alan, author, 168
Cobb, Fremont, of St. Thomas, 326-327
Cobb, Ty, author, 94
Cobre, Elko Co., 293
Cohn, Morris, promoter, 71
Coleman, Ronald, building inspector, 193
Colorado River, 238, 301, 315, 318-319,
    321-322, 329, 339, 341, 343-344,
    348-349, 408-409
Columbus, Esmeralda Co., 258, 388
Commercial Hotel, Elko, 369-370
Comstock Lode, 28, 55, 59-60, 80, 85,
    125, 198
Consolidated Copper Corp., 293
Contact, Elko Co., 218-219
Copper Canyon district, Lander Co., 188,
    189
Copper City, Clark Co., 326-327
"Copperheads," 89
Cornish miners, 123
Cortez, Lander Co., 192
Cortez Canyon, 185
Cortez silver mine, 184
Cotton, 34
Cottonwood Cove, Clark Co., 348
Cottonwood Spring, Clark Co., 316
County Seat controversies, 69, 147, 154,
    193, 293, 318
Courtland, Al, dealer, 357
Covington, E. Gorton, author, 47, 90
Cox, Virgin, prospector, 144-146
Cox, Walter, author, 69, 74
Crandall, James, author, 80
Crane, James M., legislator, 54-55
Crane Company, 411
Craps, game of, 351-352
Creighton, Isabelle, author, 72
Crescent, Lincoln Co., 302
Crocker, Len E., author, 66
Crouch, Jordan J., author, 395-396
Crowell, Clara, sheriff, 190
Crown Point Trestle, Storey Co., 94-95
Crumley, Newton Jr., casino owner, 369-370
Crystal Mine, 397
Crystal Springs, Lincoln Co., 301
Cucha Payuches Indians, 315
Cuddeback, Leon, pilot, 418
Culbert, Elsa & Jerry, authors, 291-292
Curry, Abraham, of Carson City, 41

— D —

Dakin, Mary, midwife, 291
Daley, Jim, author, 358
Damrow, Constable Milton, 308
Dangberg, Grace, author, 53
Darling, Phyllis, author, 357
Dart, Elias, "fast mail" carrier, 287-288
Datin, Richard C., author, 261-262
Davidson, Jack, businessman, 211
Davis, Sam, journalist, 40, 47
Davis, Sammy Jr., entertainer, 373-374, 378,
    381
Dayton, Lyon Co., 69, 80, 124
Dead Horse Wells, Mineral Co., 388-389

Death Valley, 273, 280-281
Death Valley Scotty, see Scott, Walter E.
Deep Creek, White Pine Co., 285, 290
De La Mar, Captain Joseph Rafael, 287, 302
Delamar, Lincoln Co., 302-305, 307, 391
Delmue Ranch, Lincoln Co., 311
Dempsey, Jack, boxer, 298
Denton, Ralph, attorney, 25
Depression, 94, 188, 339-340, 356, 396, 407
De Quille, Dan, journalist, 60
Derby, Washoe Co., 104
Deseret, Mormon state of, 318
Desert Inn, Las Vegas, 366, 370, 372
Desert Showboat Hotel, Las Vegas, 419
Detter, "Doctor" Thomas, 210
Dietz, Arthur H., author, 309-311
Dini, Grace, author, 271-272
"Dinkey, The," 202
Divorce, 15, 113-114, 117-119
"Doby Doc," casino owner, 363
Doughty, Nanelia S., author, 255-256
Douglas, Binnie, author, 347
Douglas, William A., author, 64
Douglas Canyon, White Pine Co., 299
Douglas County, 52-67
Dracket, Joan, businesswoman, 119
Dreyer, Darrell, journalist, 26
Dry farming, 35, 333-334, 338-339
Duck Creek, White Pine Co., 288
Dude Ranches, 114, 117-119
Dunes, Las Vegs, 372-373
Dusang, Mrs., midwife, 291
Dutch Nick's, Carson City Co., 43-44

— E —

Eagle Ranch, 41
Eagles, 41, 213
Eagle Valley, Carson City, 41, 54
Eagle Valley, Lincoln Co., 305, 306
Earl, Philip I., author, 197
Early, Charles A. "Hap," game farm, 116
Earp, Wyatt, Virgil, and Morgan, 237-238
Earthquakes, 142
Eberhardt Mine, White Pine Co., 386
E Clampus Vitus, 30-32
Edgar, Bob, author, 216
Education, 69, 72, 96, 104, 203, 218
Edwards, Ben, 256-258
Edwards, Elbert, author, 321-222
Edwards, Jerome E., author, 278-279
Edwards, Thomas, miner, 43
Egan, Howard, author, 285-287
Eight Mile Station, White Pine Co., 288
El Dorado Canyon, Clark Co., 318, 334
El Dorado Club, Las Vegas, 357
Elko City, Elko Co., 214-215, 216-217,
    369-370, 418
Elko County, 22, 205-219
Elko Hot Hole, 214-215
Elks lodges, 265, 277
Ellis, Anne, 249
Ellis, Grace G., author, 142
Ellis, Red, hotel owner, 370
Ellison, Marion, author, 56
El Rancho Vegas, hotel, 357, 358, 360-361,
    370-372, 419
Ely, White Pine Co., 28, 289-290, 293-294,
    298-299, 382
Emery, Murl, boatman, 348-349

Pages 1-224 are in Volume 1
Pages 225-436 are in Volume 2

Emigrants, 33, 41, 133-135, 151, 201
Emigrant Trail, Humboldt River, 133-134
Empire City, Carson City Co., 43-44
Energy Research & Development
    Administration, 397-403
Environmental Protection Agency, 28,
    262-263
Equal Rights, 210
Equal Rights Amendment, 21
Escobar, Francis, of Austin, 194
Esmeralda County, 234-249
Eureka, Eureka Co., 197, 391
Eureka Consolidated Co., 197
Eureka County, 197-203
Eureka-Nevada Railway, 200
Eureka & Palisade RR, 199-200, 202
Evans, Gene, author, 130
Evans, Marguerite, author, 218

— F —

Fair, James G., 88
Fairview, Churchill Co., 138
Fallon, Churchill Co., 139-141, 142, 144-146
Farmers & Merchants Bank, Reno, 395
Faro, game of, 351
Faucett, Miles, of Carlin, 208
Fay, Lincoln Co., 308
Fayle, Leonard R., author, 330-331
Fey, Charles, slot machine inventor, 354-355
Fey, Marshall, author, 30, 354-355
Fiction, prostitution, 78
Fires, 69, 93, 97, 154, 174, 186, 200, 214,
    237-238, 248, 292
First National Bank of Nevada, 395, 407
First State Bank, 335, 395
Fish, 385, 387
Fish Creek, Eureka Co., 197-198
Fish Lake Valley, 258
Flag, state, 13
Flamingo Hotel, Las Vegas, 360-361, 370,
    373-374
Floods, 120-122, 152, 158, 246, 322-323
Flower Lake Valley, White Pine Co.,
    see Goshute Valley
Flumes, 59
Flying ME Ranch, 119
Fong, Wing, businessman, 404
Forbes, William J., journalist, 149
Ford, Gravelly, Eureka Co., 201
Fort McDermit, Humboldt Co., 165
Fort Ruby, White Pine Co., 288
Forts, 165, 168, 288, see also above named
    Forts; see also Camps
Fort Scott, Humboldt Co., 168
Forty Mile Desert, Churchill Co., 134
Fox, Theron, author, 269-270, 386
Francis, Sheriff D. G., 251-252
Freeport law, 410-411
Fremont, John C., 12, 126, 151, 210
Fremont Expedition, 214
Fremont Hotel, Las Vegas, 363, 372, 373
Frenchman Flat, 400
French's Ford, Humboldt Co., 170
Frontier Hotel, Las Vegas, 372; see also Last
    Frontier and New Frontier
Fur Trapping, 27

439

— G —

Gabbs, Nye Co., 282-283, 386, 406
Gallagher, U.S. Commissioner J. H., 299
Gambling, 274, 350-366, 419
Game farm, 116-117
Gaming chips, 423
Gans-Nelson prize fight, 245
Garces, Francisco, explorer, 317
Gardner, Paul K., author, 162
Garner, Aliza, author, 96
Garrecht, J. J., Hot Springs, 214-215
Gay, Sheriff Sam, 328, 348
Genoa, Douglas Co., 33, 53, 54, 113
George, Charles W., author, 423
Gerlach, Washoe Co., 174
Germino, Bill, author, 82
Getchel, Frank, the "Burro King," 337
Ghost Dance, 79
Gibbon, Thomas E., 332
Gibson, Captain R. A., author, 283, 324-326, 336
Glenbrook, Douglas Co., 59
Glenbrook mill, Douglas Co., 58
Glendale, Washoe Co., 291
Godecke, Freida, author, 61
Gold Butte mining district, Clark Co., 337
Golden Nugget, Las Vegas, 357, 370
Golden Slipper, Las Vegas, 370
Goldfield, Esmeralda Co., 28, 235-249, 276, 350, 389, 394-395, 407
Goldfield Hotel, 248, 276
Gold Hill, Storey Co., 94, 96
Gold Hill Hotel, 87
Gold Mountain mines, 280
Good, Joseph, cattleman, 330
Goodin, Bill, of Lovelock, 127
Goodsprings, Clark Co., 330-331
Goodwin, Victor, author, 124
Gordon, Louis, mine operator, 144
Goshute Indians, 287-289
Goshute Valley, White Pine Co., 287
Goshute War, 288
Grand Canyon, Arizona, 348
Grand Gulch, Clark Co., 337
Grant, General, 15
Grant, Nan Millard, author, 289
Grapevine Canyon, 280-281
Grass Valley, Lander Co., 185, 195
Gravelly Ford, 134
Gray, Bob, of the V.&T. RR, 99
Gray, Edwin, engineer, 293
Great Basin, 33-34
Great Seal, state, 10
Greek, Jimmy the, oddsmaker, 363
Greeley, Horace, author, 133
Greene, James M., author, 343
Greenfield, Lyon Co., 69
Gridley, Reuel, of Austin, 183
Griffith, D. W., movie producer, 358
Griffith, Edmond W., developer, 408-409
Griffith, Robert B., developer, 408-409
Grock, Charles A., of Elko, 24
Groom mine, Lincoln Co., 302
Grue, Charlie, of Hilltop, 192
Grutt, Leo and Gene, 259

— H —

Hacienda Hotel, Las Vegas, 373
Haenszel, Arda M., author, 334-335

Haenszel, Dr. Allen L., physician, 334-335
Hamilton, White Pine Co., 291-292, 293, 386
Hammond, Sheriff, 194
Hangings, 208-209, 251-252, 269-270
Hanks, Pinkerton Detective William, 307
Happy (horse), 112
Hardy, Harvey, author, 205, 327-328
Harrington, John, author, 333-334
Harris, Sheriff Joseph, 217
Harris, Walter J., banker, 395-396
Harrison's Guest House, Las Vegas, 380-381
Harte, Bret, 73
Haupt, Janice, author, 328-329
Haviland, Carl, of Winnemucca, 127
Hawthorne, Mineral Co., 264-265
Hayatas Indians, 315
Healy, Ann Lacher, author, 48
Hearst, George, mine investor, 185
Heit, Stella, author, 294
Hemenway Wash, Clark Co., 348
Henderson, Charles B., Senator, 22, 24, 406
Henderson, Clark Co., 406
Henroid, "Grandma," midwife, 290
Herrick, Dr. H. S., of Hamilton, 291-292
Highgrading, 303-305
Hiko, Lincoln Co., 301
Hilltop, Lander Co., 186-187, 192-193
Hilton Hotel, Las Vegas, 374, 378
"Hobo Jungle," 62
Hobos, 61
Hofer, T. R., promoter, 71
"Hog Pen" mine, Lincoln Co., 302
Holiday Hotel, Reno, 370
Holliday, "Doc," 237
Holliday, Fred, author, 237-238
Homesteads, 33
Hooker, Henry, rancher, 46
Hoover Dam, see Boulder Dam
Horn, Agnes (Hannie), of Delamar, 303
Horn Silver mine, 397
Horseshoe Club, Las Vegas, 357, 362-364
Hot Springs, 214
Houses, desert, 236
Howard, F. D., author, 236
Hughes, Howard, industrialist, 372-373, 404-405
Hull, Tom, hotel operator, 358
Humboldt County, 165-179, 356
Humboldt Hot Springs Spa, 214
Humboldt Lake, 134
"Humboldt mines," 149
Humboldt Register, 149-150
Humboldt River, 133-134, 201, 215, 356
Humboldt Sink, 134-135
Humphrey, Marguerite, author, 123
Humphreys, Noreen I. K., author, 41
Hunt, Frank, miner, 211-212
Hunting, 169
Hyde, Orson, settler, 54
Hydroplanes, 66

— I —

Ibapah, White Pine Co., see Deep Creek
Ice skating, 188
Independence Day Celebrations, 152, 272, 275-276, 292, 308, 311
Indian Messiah, 79
Indians, 10, 33, 53, 76, 78-79, 96, 165, 190, 285-290, 301, 305, 308, 315, 320, 334, 336, 345, 382, 391, 396-397; see also Paiutes, Shoshone, etc.

Indians, hostilities, 27, 175, 185, 288, 320, 334
Indians, legends, 129
Indians, rabbit drives, 65
Indian Springs Ranch, Clark Co., 345-346
Industry, 59, 64, 395-417
International Hotel, Austin, 86
International Hotel, Las Vegas, 374
Interstate 80, 126, 128, 188, 201
Irvin, Stan, legislator, 12
"Island," The, Clark Co., 320
Italian War, 197-198
I.W.W., 249

— J —

"Jackass mail," 287
Jackson, David, author, 397,403
Jackson, Nancy J., author, 117, 129
Jacobson, Ira N., author, 28
James, Will, artist, 51, 112
Jean, Clark Co., 330-331
Jennings Manufacturing Co., 355
Jensen, Phil, author, 423
Jews, 71, 385
Johnson, Albert Mussey, financier, 280-281
Johnson, Captain George A., explorer, 318
Johnson, Frank H. author, 351-353
Johnson, Nigger, nurse, 305
Johnson, William, author, 65
Johnson, W. R., 251-252
Johnston, Hank, author, 273, 280-281
Johnston, Velma, and mustangs, 50
Jones, Florence Lee, author, 343-344, 408-409
Jones, John P., Senator, 88
Jones, Joyce, author, 337
Jordan, Paul, author, 214
Journalism, 69, 149-150
Journalists, 40, 149, 175
Julia C. Bulette Chapter, E.C.V., 30-33
Jumbo, Humboldt Co., 176
Jumbo Gold Mine, 176
Jungo Hotel, 176
Juniper, 10

— K —

Kaye, Norman, author, 383
Kelley, Joseph, casino executive, 419
Kellogg, Cyrus W., of Stillwater, 136-137
Kendrick, Grace, author, 421
Keno, game of, 353
Kinkead, John, Governor, 197
Kinnear, John Charles, miner, 295
Kinnemich, Goshute Indian, 288-289
Kinney, Mary, midwife, 291
Kirman, Governor Richard, 395
Knapp, Sewell Alvin, 253-254
Knapp, Sewell Crosby, 253-254
Knapp's Landing, Mineral Co., 253-254
Knudson, K. O., author, 104
Knudtsen, Molly, author, 184
Kyle Canyon, Clark Co., 408-409
Kyle ranch, Las Vegas, 335

— L —

Labor, 249
Lady Luck Hotel, Las Vegas, 373; see also Hacienda Hotel
Lagoon, Dr. A. P., 294

Lake Bigler Toll Road, 59
Lake Lahontan, 129
Lake Mead, 66, 337, 339, 349, 409
Lake Tahoe, 59, 66, 95
Lambertucci, Victor, rancher, 277
Lamoille, Elko Co., 208
Lander County, 181-195
Lander County Taxpayer Association, 195
Landmark Hotel, Las Vegas, 372, 404-405
Lanner, Ronald M., author, 390
La Panta mining district, 254
La Rivers, M. B., author, 192
Larkswood Ranch, 40
Larson, Pansilee, author, 156
Last Frontier, Las Vegas, 358, 360-361, 365-366, 370, 371, 380, 419
Las Vegas, Clark Co., 302, 318, 321, 237-329, 332-335, 338-340, 342, 347, 356-367, 369-374, 376, 378, 380-381, 395, 397, 404-405, 408-409, 414-415, 419
Las Vegas Bombing & Gunnery Range, see Nevada Test Site
Las Vegas Club, 357, 419
Las Vegas High School Rhythmettes, 115
Las Vegas Land & Water Co., 332, 408
Las Vegas Springs, Clark Co., 320
Las Vegas-Tonopah-Reno Stage Lines, 414-415
Las Vegas & Tonopah RR, 280-281, 412, 414
Las Vegas Transfer & Storage Co., 414
Las Vegas Valley, 315-317, 409
Latimer, George & Belle, innkeepers, 345-346
Law, 162-163, 194, 197-198, 205-207, 208, 235-236, 251-252, 278-279, 281-282, 307, 326, 328, 332, 356-357, 410-411
Laws, R. G., merchant, 253
Lawson, Maude, author, 92
Laxalt, Paul, U.S. Senator, 25, 64
Laxalt, Robert, author, 64, 433-436
Leavitt, Aunt Lena, midwife, 291
Leavitt, Dudley, settler, 322
Leavitt, Phyllis M., author, 339-340
Lee's Ferry, Clark Co., 344
Legends, Indian, 129
Lemaire family, Battle Mountain, 186-189
Leonard, Paul A., author, 369-370
Levinson, Ed, casino owner, 363
Lewis, Ted, entertainer, 369
Liberty Bell, slot machine, 354-355
Lida, Esmeralda Co., 258
Lillard, Richard G., author, 16, 17
Lincoln, President Abraham, 18, 89, 105
Lincoln County, 300-313, 321-322
Lincoln Highway, 298
Lincoln Highway Association, 128
Livestock industry, 64
Logan, Sheriff Tom, 278-279
Logan City, Lincoln Co., 302
Lorenzi Park, Las Vegas, 338-339
Lost City, Clark Co., 320
Lovelock, George, rancher, 151
Lovelock, Pershing Co., 151-154, 162, 163
Lovelock Cave, 155
Lucky Boy mine, 264
Ludwig, Lyon Co., 78
Lund, White Pine Co., 290, 299
Lyon County, 69
Lytle, Freel, teamster, 303-305
Lytle, Mary Virginia, midwife, 291
Lytle, Wayne, author, 303-306

— M —

McCarran, Margaret, P., author, 37
McCarran, Patrick, Senator, 16, 37-39, 64, 200, 278-279, 360, 406
McCartney, Jim, author, 135
McCloskey, Jack R., author, 18
McCormack, Annie Laurie, midwife, 291
McDonald, D. C., prospector, 293
McDonald, Douglas, author, 116, 414-415
MacFarland, Ira & Alice, innkeepers, 346
McGill, White Pine Co, 294-298
McGill ranch, White Pine Co., 288
McGinn, Vincent, author, 274-275
McGriff, Edwin G., farmer, 333-334
McInnis, Helen, author, 253-254, 281-282
Mackay, John W., miner, 40
McKissick Opera House, Reno, 106
Maggio, Frank, author, 315-317
Mahoney, Bill, Mohave County Sheriff, 348
Mail, 203, 287-288
Maish, Clint Thomas, author, 422
Manhattan, Nye Co., 28, 267-268, 278-279
Manifest Destiny, 27
Marietta, Mineral Co., 258
Martin, Anne, feminist, 19-21, 24
Martin, Dean, entertainer, 373-374
Mason, Lyon Co., 69, 72-73, 75, 76, 78
Mason, N. H., rancher, 33
Masonic Lodge, 183, 335
Mason Valley, Lyon Co., 33, 69-70, 72, 253
Mason Valley Mining Co., 75
Mazuma, Pershing Co., 158-159
Meadows, Lorena, author, 256
Meadow Valley, Clark Co., 321
Medicine, 214-215, 290-292, 294, 334-335
Mercer, Jennie, author, 248
Mercury, Nye Co., 401
Mesquite, Clark Co., 322-323
Meyers, Dennis, author, 19, 24
MGM Grand, Las Vegas, 373-374
Midwives, 290-291
Mikulich, Sebastian, bus line developer, 414-415
Miller, Heinie, miner, 247
Miller, John S., author, 89
Miller, Mary K., author, 391-392
Mills Novelty Co., 354-355
Mina, Mineral Co., 262-263, 388
Minden, Douglas Co., 62
Mineral County, 251-265
Miners, 149-150, 247, 249, 262-263; see also Cornish miners
Mines and mining camps, 28-29, 60, 75, 80, 88, 96, 125, 149, 176-177, 184, 188-189, 198, 211-212, 251-252, 271-272, 296, 312-313; see also specific locations
Mingle, Mamie Frances, 264
Mining, 28-29, 73, 75, 176-177, 211-212, 262-263, 302-303, 397; see also specific locations
Mining companies, 75, 85, 158, 170, 197, 211-212, 251, 255, 276, 280, 293, 330; see also specific corporate names
Mining Litigation, 251
Minoletti, Julis, midwife, 290
Mint Hotel, Las Vegas, 372
Moapa Valley, Clark Co., 35
Mob, The, 360-361
Modena, Lincoln Co., 308
Molly McGuires, 269-270

Pages 1-224 are in Volume 1
Pages 225-436 are in Volume 2

Monk, Hank, stagedriver, 59
Monroe, "Cowboy" Nell, 307
Monte, game of, 351
Montgomery Hotel, Beatty, 389
Moody, Eric N., author, 101
Moore, Estelle, author, 71, 385
Mormons, 54-55, 290, 318-323
Mosse, Sonja, author, 410-411
Moulin Rouge, Las Vegas, 372, 381
Mountain Bluebird, 12
Mountain City Mining Co., 212
Mountain City nining district, 211-212
Mt. Diablo Mining co., 255
Mount Tenabo, 184-185
Movies, 174, 343, 404
Muddy River, 318-322
Muddy Valley, Clark Co., 321-322
Murbarger, Nell, author, 178
Museums, 99, 161
Mustang, 50-51
Myles, Myrtle T., author, 14, 190

— N —

"Nagah," 12-13
National, Humboldt Co., 169
National Reclamation Act, 34, 49
Natural resources, 28
Neddenriep, Anna E., 56
Nellis, 1st Lt. William Harrell, 347
Nellis Air Force Base, 347-409
Nelson, Clark Co., 334
Nelson Landing, Clark Co., 349
Nenzel, Joe, miner, 156-157
Neugent, Gus, prospector, 205
Nevada Air National Guard, 116
Nevada Bankers Association, 395-396
Nevada Central RR, 189
Nevada Consolidated Copper Corp., 298; see also Consolidated Copper Corp.
Nevada Copper Belt RR, 75-78
Nevada Douglas Copper Co., 75-78
Nevada Equal Franchise Society, 19
Nevada Historical Society, 161
Nevada Livestock Commission, 142
Nevada Northern RR, 293, 294, 413
Nevada Power and Transportation Co., 107
Nevada State, emblems, symbols, 10-14
Nevada State, Prison, 47, 217
Nevada Steam Transportation Co., 261-262
Nevada Test Site, 397-403
Nevada Transfer & Warehouse Co., 411
Nevada U.S. 40 Association, 128
Nevills, Norman D., river guide, 343-344
New Frontier, Las Vegas, 371; see also Last Frontier
Newlands, Francis, Senator, 22, 107, 407
Newlands, W. G., Senator, 34
Newspapers, 19, 20, 69
Nickel, Sam, rancher, 253
Nixon, U.S. Senator George S., 395-407
Noble Experiment, 21
Northern Belle lode, 255
Northern Hotel, Ely, 293
Northern Saloon, Goldfield, 237, 246
Northern Saloon, Rawhide, 260
Northern Saloon, Tonopah, 237
North Gabbs, Nye Co., 282
Norton, Olive Stanton, author, 293
Notes, Tom, miner, 235-236

Nye, Senator James W., 318
Nye County, 266-283, 382

— O —

Oak Spring mining district, 397
Oasis, The, Las Vegas, 338
Occidental Colony Company, 71
Oddie, Tasker L., Senator-Governor, 127, 237, 329
Old Frontier Hotel, Las Vegas, 342
(Old) Spanish Trail, 316
Olinghouse, Washoe Co., 123
Opera, 106
Oreana, Pershing Co., 152, 156
Ormsby, William, of Carson City, 41
Ormsby County, 36-51
Orr, Betty, author, 287-288
Osceola, White Pine Co., 235, 291
Overland Mail & Stage Line, 124
Overton, Clark Co., 291, 321, 337
Owen, B. J., author, 264
Oxborrow, Mary Leicht, midwife, 290

— P —

Pace, Frank, storekeeper, 307
Pacific Coast Borax Co., 258
Pacific & Colorado Navigation Co., 318
Pacific Freeport Warehouse Co., 411
Packard, Pershing Co., 160
Paher, Stanley W., author, 193, 424-425
Pahranagat Valley, Lincoln Co., 301-302
Pahrump Valley, Nye Co., 34, 316
Pah-Ute County, 317-319
Paiutes, 129, 165, 316, 320, 334, 336, 391, 397
Palisade, Eureka Co., 202
Palisade Canyon, 201
Panaca, Lincoln Co., 290, 321, 322
Paradise City, Humboldt Co., 168
Paradise Valley, Clark Co., 333
Paradise Valley, Humboldt Co., 170
Park, John S., banker, 335
Patterson, Edna, author, 213
Pearl, Josie, of Black Rock, 178
Perkins, Alberta, author, 320
Pershing County, 149-163
Pickhandle Gulch, Mineral Co., 255-258
Pigeon Springs, Esmeralda Co., 258
Pine Creek, Eureka Co., 200
Pine-nuts, 308, 390-392
Pine Valley, Eureka Co., 202
Pinyon pines, 390-392
Pioche, Lincoln Co., 302, 306-311
Piper's Opera House, Virginia City, 90, 96
Pistone, Dante, author, 45
Pittman, Key, Senator, 22, 64
Pizen Switch, Lyon County, 69, 74
Placerville Stage Route, 125
Pletzke, Dennis, author, 407
Poker, game of, 352; World Series of, 363
Police, 111
Political Innovations, 16
Politics, 15-27, 40, 149, 152, 161, 210, 318-319, 356-357, 360
Politics, woman suffrage, 19-23
Pony Express, 287
Postage stamps, 423
Potatoes, 35
Potosi, Clark Co., 318
Potts, Elizabeth, hanging, 208-209
Powell, Major, explorer, 344

Pray, Augustus W., sawmill owner, 59
Primeaux, Roy, businessman, 201
Primeaux, Tony, author, 183, 201
Primeaux Station, Eureka Co., 201-202
Prince, Lincoln Co., 309-311
Prince Consolidated Mining Co., 310
Prince Consolidated M. & S. Co. RR, 310-311
Prizefighting, 15, 245
Progressivism, 22
Prohibition, 22-23, 74, 101, 216, 281-282, 299, 332
Prospecting, 81, 192, 262-263, 282-283
Prospectors, 144-146, 262-263, 392-393
Prostitution, 16, 30-32, 78, 101-103, 259-260, 274-275, 298, 327-328; see also Red Light Districts
Pupfish, 387
Pyramid Lake, Washoe Co., 66, 117, 118, 129

— Q —

Queho, Paiute renegade, 334
Questa, E. J., banker, 370

— R —

Rader, Art, author, 412-413
Raffetto, Bertha, lyricist, 14
Railroads, 34, 94-95, 254, 280-281, 293-294, 302, 309-311, 330, 345-346, 395, 407-408, 412-413; see also Bullfrog Goldfield, Central Pacific, Eureka-Nevada, Eureka & Palisade, Las Vegas & Tonopah, Nevada Central, Nevada Copper Belt, Nevada Northern, Prince Consolidated, San Pedro Los Angeles & Salt Lake, Southern Pacific, Tonopah & Tidewater, Virginia & Truckee, Western Pacific
Rainmaker, 129
Ranch Inn, Elko, 370
Rawhide, Mineral Co., 138, 259-260, 389
Raymond, William, mine developer, 301
Read, Effie O., author, 298, 299, 307-308
Read, Ressie Walls, author, 295
Real del Monte Mining Co., 251
Reconstruction Finance Corporation, 24
Red Light Districts, 30-32, 101-103, 259-260, 274-275, 278-279, 327-328, 332, 347; see also Prostitution
Reese, Colonel John, settler, 33, 53
Reese, Kenley, author, 322-323
"Reese River," Lander Co., 182, 184
Reid, Dr. H. E., 108
Reid, Jean, author, 262-263
Reiley, Mrs. Larry, author, 249
Reipetown, White Pine Co., 298
Reno, Washoe Co., 22, 101-111, 113-115, 120-122, 395-396
Reno Electric Railway and Land Co., 107
Reno Police, 111
Reno Traction Co., 109
Reno Women's Christian Temperance Union, 102
Requa, Mark, mine, developer, 293
Rhyolite, Nye Co., 28, 271-272, 273
Richardson, T. T., author, 181
Richmond County, 197
Rickard, Tex, 237, 260, 293
Rio Tinto, Elko Co., 211-212
Rio Tinto Copper Co., 211
Rivera, Rafael, scout, 315-317

Riviera Hotel, Las Vegas, 371-374, 378
Robison, Ruby, author, 136
Roberts, E. E., politician, 101-102
Robertson, Joseph H., author, 13
Rochester, Pershing Co., 156-157, 160
"Rock Creek" Mike, 175
Rood, Standish, mining reporter, 301
Roosevelt, Teddy, in Nevada, 48
Roseyear, Marion Dobrowsky, author, 257-277
Ross, Ellen Frances, midwife, 291
Roulette, game of, 351
Royal Nevada, Las Vegas, 371-372
Ruby Valley Wildlife Refuge, 213
Ruddock, Gregory, author, 106
Ruggles, Lynn, author, 211
Rusco, Elmer, author, 92, 210
Russell, Colonel Bob, 342
Rustlers, 384
Ruth, White Pine Co., 293-294
Rye Patch Station, Nye Co., 267

— S —

Sadler, Reinhold, Governor, 71
Sagebrush, 13
Sahara, Las Vegas, 370-372
Saiger, Mort, casino host, 365-366
St. Joseph, Clark Co., 319-322
St. Mary's Hospital, Reno, 122
St. Thomas, Clark Co., 319-322, 326-327, 337
Sands, Las Vegs, 370-373, 378
San Pedro, Los Angeles, & Salt Lake RR, 302, 330, 332, 408, 412
Sapp, M. J. & Cass, fishermen, 385
Sawyer, Byrd Wall, author, 290-291
Scarselli, Eva, author, 57
Schell Creek Mtns., White Pine Co., 288
Schools, 97, 157, 277, 282, 296, 310, 312-313
Schurz, Mineral Co., 385
Schwartz, Daniel, colonist, 71
Scott, Walter E. "Death Valley Scotty," 273, 274, 280-281, 298
Scottsdale, Humboldt Co., 168
Scotty's Castle, 281
Searchlight, Clark Co., 324, 334-335, 336
Segerblom, Gene Wines, author, 161
"Semblins" (Wm. Forbes), 149
Senators, 16
Service Stations, 201
Sexton, John, Judge, 194, 202
Shamberger, Hugh, author, 247
Sharon, William, of Comstock Lode, 88
Shaver, Georgia, author, 296
Sheep, 64
Sheriffs, County, 162, 190, 194, 208, 217, 237, 248, 251, 328
Shipler, Guy, author, 15
Shockley, William H., mining engineer, 255-256
Shoshones, 33, 286, 288
Showboat Hotel, Las Vegas, see Desert Showboat
Siegel, Benjamin "Bugsy," 358, 360-361
Sierra Pacific Power Co., 411
Sierra Seminary, 45
Sierra shanties, 127, 172, 201-202
Silver (Bald Eagle), 213
Silver Cafe, Las Vegas, 404
Silver Canyon, Lincoln Co., 302
Silver City, Lyon Co., 82, 93

Silver City Guard, 82-83
Silver Club, Las Vegas, 419
Silver Party, 40
Silver Peak, Esmeralda Co., 258
Silver Slipper, Las Vegas, 370
Singing Sands Mtn., 137
Single-Leaf Pinyon, 10-12
Six Companies, Inc., 349
Slagowski, Charlene, author, 202
Slocum, Capt. "Click," 82
Slot machines, 352, 354-355
Slumbering Hills, Humboldt Co., 176
Smith, Ann Warren, author, 19
Smith, Captain, U.S. Cavalry, 288
Smith, Ed, of Winnemucca, 127, 172
Smith, F. M. "Borax," 256, 258
Smith, Harold T., author, 21
Smith Valley, Lyon Co., 71
Smith Valley Colony, Lyon Co., 71
Smithville, Nye Co., see North Gabbs
Smokey Valley, 384
Snake Creek Range, White Pine Co., 299
Snake Valley, 235
Snowshoe Thompson Chapter E.C.V., 31
Sodaville, Mineral Co., 255-256, 262
Song, Nevada State, 14
Southern Pacific RR, 175, 189, 199-200,
    218, 412-413
South Gabbs, Nyc Co., 282
Spanish exploration, 315-317
Spanish Springs Station, Nye Co., 267-268
Sparks, John, Governor, 49
Sparks, Washoe Co., 34, 108, 109
Sparks Nugget, 378
Spooner's Summit, Douglas Co., 59, 60
Sports, 90, 115, 188
Springmeyer, George, rancher, 23, 63
Springmeyer, H. H., rancher, 63
Spring Valley, White Pine Co., 288, 291
Sproule, Charles, editor, 208-209
Spude, Robert L., author, 85
Squires, Charles "Pop," author, 328-329,
    332
Stage roads, 124
Staggs, Grover C., 176
Star City, Pershing Co., 160
Stardust, Las Vegas, 371
Stead, Bill, and boats, 66
Stead, Lt. Crosten, 116
Stead Air Force Base, Reno, 116
Steninger, E. M., editor, 175
Steninger, Mel, author, 208
Steptoe Valley, White Pine Co., 287, 288, 293
Stevens, Frank, lawyer, 205
Stevenson, Pat, author, 144
Stewart, Bob, author, 251
Stewart, Patricia, author, 165
Stewart, Senator William M., 318
Stillwater, Churchill Co., 136, 396
Stingaree Gulch, 259-260
Stockade, in Reno, 103
Stock certificates, 422
Stockman's Hotel, Elko, 370
Stoddard, Robert L., radio broadcaster,
    130-131
Stoddard, Sylvia Crowell, author, 40
Stokes, J. G. Phelps, mine financier, 190
Stokes Castle, Austin, 190-191
Storey County, 85-99
Strange, Vivian, contractor, 211
Strate, Larry, author, 335

Strip, Las Vegas, 357, 358, 360, 362, 365-366,
    370-374, 378, 381, 419
Stubbs, Don, author, 356-357
Stump Spring, Clark Co., 316
Sullivan, Carl, prospector, 388-389
Summerfield, Winslow, author, 113
Sutcliffe, Washoe Co., 117
Swackhamer Family, Battle Mtn., 186-189
Swallow, Matilda, midwife, 291
Sweet, Ben, author, 406

— T —

Taber, Stanley, of Elko Co., 209
Taylor, Clyde, prospector, 176
Taylor, White Pine Co., 287-288, 299
Taylor Grazing act, 34
Teamsters, 44, 69, 267-268, 283, 303-305
Techatticup mine, Clark Co., 334-335
Tecopa, Paiute Chief, 336
Teel's Marsh, 258
Telegraph, 181
Temperance societies, 21, 332
Tempiute, Lincoln Co., 302, 312-313
Telephone, 93
Territorial Legislature, 41
Territorial Prison, 41
Terry, Eliza Jane, midwife, 290
Thompson, Lyon Co., 75, 77
Thompson, "Snowshoe," 57
Thorp's Wells, see Bonnie Claire
Three Card Monte, see Monte
Thunderbird Hotel, Las Vegas, 370, 372`
Tikapoo, Indian, 305
Tingley, Icyl C., author, 158
Tipton, Ruth, author, 174, 282-283
Tobin, Phil M., legislator, 356-357
Toll Roads, 42, 124
Tommyknockers, 123
Tonopah, Nye Co., 28, 235-236, 237-238,
    256, 258, 262, 267-268, 272, 274-279, 350,
    384, 395, 407, 414
Tonopah Club, 274, 407
Tonopah Mining Co., 237
Tonopah & Tidewater RR, 280-281, 412
Towell, David, Congressman, 25
Towner, Charles, rancher, 345
Townsite auction, 254, 408
Trade tokens, collecting of, 425
Transportation, 126, 261-262, 267-268,
    280-281, 283, 289, 303-305, 330-331,
    334, 345-346, 410-411, 412-413, 414-415,
    417-418
Tritle, Frederick A., of Comstock Lode, 85
Trolley Car System, 107-109
Tropicana Hotel, Las Vegas, 372-374
Truckee, Captain, 165
Truckee-Carson Irrigation Project, 139, 141
Truckee River, 120-122, 136
Turkey Drive, 46
Tuscarora, Elko Co., 201
Twain, Mark, humorist, 10, 15, 41, 44,
    426-427
Twenty-one, see Blackjack

— U —

Ubehebe Copper Mines & Smelting Co., 280
Union Pacific RR, 333, 412-413
Unionville, Pershing Co., 149-150
United Airlines, 418
United Nevada Industries, 22

Pages 1-224 are in Volume 1
Pages 225-436 are in Volume 2

U.S. 50 highway, 126-128
U.S. 40, 126-128, 187, 193
U.S. Gypsum, industrial railway, 413
U.S. Mint, at Carson City, 42, 47
U.S. Naval Ammunition Depot, 264
University of Nevada, 104-105, 115, 139,
    404

Valley Livestock Sales Yard, 142-143
Van Bokkeleyn, Jacob, Provost Marshal,
    251-252
Van Duzer, Clarence D., District Attorney,
    407
Varney Air Lines, 418
Victor Mining Co., 276
Victory Highway, 201
Vigilantes, 251-252, 269-270
Virginia City, Storey Co., 28, 33, 40,
    85-99, 261, 395
Virginia City Bankers Association, 395
Virginia & Truckee RR, 37-38, 43-44, 48,
    62, 71, 94, 99, 118
Virgin River, 315, 318-319, 321-323
Virgin Valley, Clark Co., 290, 291, 318-319,
    322-323
Vesey's Hotel, Gold Hill, 87
Via, Lewis L., author, 190

— W —

Wabuska, Lyon Co., 76, 78, 253, 254
Wagner, Jack R., author, 75
Wahmonie, Nye Co., 397, 414
Walker, Ardis Manly, author, 27
Walker, Corrine, author, 302-303
Walker Lake, 253-254, 385
Ward, Artemus, author, 182
Ward, Jack, shooting of, 326-327
Ward, White Pine Co., 287, 290
Warehousing, 410-411
Warm Spring's Hotel, 41-42
Warm Springs Ranch, Clark Co., 334
Washoe County, 101-131
Wasson, U.S. Marshall Warren, 251-252
Wasson's Camp, Lyon Co., 253
Water, 258
Watkins, "Sport," 307-308
Weaver, James L., author, 91
Weed Heights, Lyon Co., 75
Weepah, Esmeralda Co., 414
Weight, Harold O., author, 259-260,
    388-389
Wellington, Lyon Co., 71
Wells Cargo Co., 417
Wells Fargo & Co., 124, 394-395
Wenban, Simeon, mine operator, 184-185
Werner, Laura Gallagher, author, 288-289
Western Pacific RR, 177, 412-413
Westlake, Jim, author, 111
West Las Vegas, Clark Co., 380, 409
West Point, Clark Co., 321
Wheeler, Sessions S., author, 235-236
Wheel of Fortune, game of, 353
"Whispering Ben," Paiute, 345-346
"Whispering Pat," bootlegger, 299
White, Bob, of Elko Co., 216-217
White Mountain Water Co., 255

Pages 1-224 are in Volume 1
Pages 225-436 are in Volume 2

White Pine County, 284-299
White River Valley, White Pine Co., 299
Whitney Mesa, Clark Co., 315
Whittemore, C. O., attorney, 332
Wide-Open Gambling Bill, 356
Wier, Jeanne Elizabeth, historian, 19,
    426-427
Wilkinson, Ruth Bradley, author, 312-313
Willard, Bill, author, 370-374
Williams, G. Budd, rancher, 138
Williams, Ike, miner, 262-263
Williams, Tommy, muleskinner, 283
Wills, Chill, casino host, 364
Wilson, Ken, author, 247
Wilson, Mildred M., author, 380-381
Wilson, Walter C., author, 267-268
Windows, Margaret, midwife, 290
Wines, Hazel Bell, legislator, 161
Wines, Judge Taylor, 195
Wingfield, George, financier, 20, 144,
    395, 407
Winnemucca, Humboldt Co., 150, 170-173,
    179, 407
Winnemucca, Sarah, 165-166
Wittenberg Warehouse & Transfer, Tonopah,
    267
Wixom, Emma "Nevada," 183
Woman Sufferage, 190
Women's Movement, 190
Women's Rights, 45, 165
Wood, Emy, of Washoe Co., 119
Woodburn, William, attorney, 23
Wovoka, Indian Messiah, 79
Wovoka Dancers, 79
Wright, Harold Bell, 174
Wright, William V., author, 425
Wymore Ranch, Lyon Co., 71

— Y —

Yellow Jacket mine, Comstock Lode, 88
Yellow Pine Mining Co., 330
Yerington, H.M., financier, 69-70
Yerington, Lyon Co., 28, 69, 74, 75-78
Yoakum, Jim, author, 387
Young, Brigham, colonizer, 321-322
Young, Cliff, author, 26, 50-51
Young, James, author, 33
Yount, Samuel E., of Goodsprings, 330
Yucca Flat, 400, 403

— Z —

Zabriskie & Shockley's bank, 256
Zanjani, Sally S., author, 63
Zoology, 12, 112, 195

Books available from
Nevada Publications
4135 Badger Circle, Reno, Nevada 89509 • 702-747-0800

PUBLISHERS AND DISTRIBUTORS OF MORE THAN 180 SOUTHWESTERN DESERT BOOKS.

Nevada Ghost Towns & Mining Camps
by Stanley W. Paher

HERE IS NEVADA'S ALL-TIME BEST SELLING HISTORY BOOK, with more than 52,000 copies printed. Large 8-1/2 x 11 format, 500 pages, 710 illustrations, maps and index. The largest ghost town book of all time. In all, 668 ghost towns are described with travel directions. Contains more pictures and describes more localities than any other Nevada book. Nearly every page brings new information and unpublished photos of the towns, the mines, the people, and early Nevada life. This book won the national "Award of Merit" for history. Cloth with color dust jacket, index, glossary.

The perfect companion to the above book...
NEVADA GHOST TOWNS & MINING CAMPS *Illustrated Atlas* VOL. ONE – Northern Nevada, Reno - Austin - Ely, and points north. VOL. TWO – Southern Nevada, Death Valley - Mojave Desert. Each 104 pages, 7 x 10. Combined hardcover edition, 208 pages.

DESTINATION: LAKE TAHOE THE STORY BEHIND THE SCENERY by Stanley W. Paher. The stunning color cover of a stern wheeler on Emerald Bay provides a felicitous introduction to this new book about Lake Tahoe, North America's largest alpine lake. More than 60 color photographs show the scenery, the sternwheelers, the historic sites, the hikers, and the water and winter sports enthusiasts. The photographs of long, calm stretches of surface blue waters give the reader a sense that Lake Tahoe is a world apart. And it is!

GEM TRAILS OF NEVADA by James Mitchell. 120 pages, illus. Nearly 60 sites for gemstone collecting are described and located on maps giving locations to the 1/10 mile. About 30 Nevada minerals are described.

THE COMPLETE NEVADA TRAVELER, by David W. Toll. 192 pages, illus. The author divides Nevada into five regions describing each of them— history, services for travelers, annual events, and assorted trivia. Current information for Cowboy Country (northern Nevada), Reno-Tahoe Territory, Pony Express Territory (central Nevada), Pioneer Territory (mid-southern Nevada), and Las Vegas Territory. Interesting photographs interspersed amid a well-written and lively text. This book will surely prove helpful to any Nevada visitor.

PLACER GOLD DEPOSITS OF NEVADA, by Maureen Johnson. USGS Bull. 1356. 118 pp., index. Valuable catalog of locations, geology, production; 115 placer sites, all located on two-color map.

BOOKS ON EMIGRANTS

FEARFUL CROSSING, by Harold Curran. 212 pages, large 8-1/2 x 11 format, illus., paperback. The author describes the development of the trail and the lives and fortunes of those crossing Nevada. Extensive quotes from emigrant journals and other authorities give intimate insights into daily emigrant living: trouble with Indians, feeding animals, fighting, deaths, food preparation, etc. Author Harold Curran of Reno has explored the trail giving personal insight into problems of travel over difficult terrain. In addition to giving a history of the main Humboldt trail, this book also describes the Applegate cutoff. Paperback.

FORTY-NINERS: THE CHRONICLE OF THE CALIFORNIA TRAIL, by Archer Butler Hulbert. 340 pages, illus. The author furnishes a thorough rambling account of a July 14 to August 10 emigrant trek across northern Nevada. Accurate footnotes are a guide to places visited along the route. Inferences determined by field work supplement this modern arrangement of emigrant diary material, with facts culled from diaries of gold rushers, 1849-1853. There is much description of emigrant life interspersed with colorful anecdotes. Paperback.

THE CALIFORNIA STAR 212 oversized pages. In this faithful reproduction of the San Francisco weekly paper in 1847 are numerous descriptive references to the Donner Party and other northern California pre-state happenings, such as port activity in San Francisco, ranch life, development of transportation, etc. Prime source material. Hardback.

GHOST TRAILS OF CALIFORNIA, by Thomas Hunt. 228 pages, large 8-1/2 x 11 format, illus. Author covers all early emigrant routes: the main Humboldt River route through northern Nevada; the Hastings cutoff in eastern Nevada; the Applegate-Lassen route, a short cut which left the Humboldt route in north-central Nevada; the Carson Pass route with its 40-mile desert crossing from the Humboldt Sink to the Carson River; the popular Stevens-Donner route along the Truckee River; the Beckwourth Pass route through Feather River Canyon; Nobles' Route which branched off the Applegate-Lassen route, and the Sonora Pass route which followed the Walker River into California. More than 160 color pictures carry captions excerpted from emigrant journals. A large, beautiful color map and a portfolio of maps trace the routes of every major emigrant trail.

Treasure Guides
Theron Fox, ed. 24 pages, 6 x 9, illus.
For use with modern road maps.

ARIZONA TREASURE HUNTERS GHOST TOWN GUIDE. Maps 1867 and 1881 show 1200 place names— mining camps, mountains, rivers and creeks, railroads, abandoned roads, forts, canyons and passes.

EASTERN CALIFORNIA TREASURE HUNTERS GHOST TOWN GUIDE. Maps 1880 and 1881 show 700 place names–mining camps, abandoned roads, water holes, etc.

NEVADA TREASURE HUNTERS GHOST TOWN GUIDE. Maps 1867 and 1881 show 800 place names — mining camps, abandoned roads, springs, mountains, rivers, lakes, water holes, and even a camel trail.

OREGON TRAIL, VOYAGE OF DISCOVERY, by Dan Murphy. 64 pages, 9 x 12. Maps. During the 1840-1850s the emigrant trail from Missouri to Oregon was annually traveled by thousands of argonauts seeking new homes. The author dramatically describes the 2,000 mile journey along grassy prairies, past river crossings and over rugged mountains. Emigrants endured storms, hardships, Indians, and tragedy. Extracts from several emigrant diaries describe every segment of the trail. Stunning photographs of river crossings, plants and animals found en route, topography, wagon ruts that have survived 150 years of weather and human intrusion, high mountains, buffalo, and flower-studded valleys. Also available, **The Mormon Trail,** from Nebraska to Utah. Featuring the same lavish color format, and **The California Trail,** these presentations of an important part of America's heritage are thoughtfully designed with lively text interspersed by color photographs. For the emigrant trail buff this is an essential tool. Maps.

CLASSIC HISTORIES

HISTORY OF NEVADA, 1540-1888, by H. H. Bancroft. 332 pages, 6 x 9. This is a reprint of the 1888 history of the early explorers through Nevada through the beginning of statehood in 1864 up to the date of publication. Large chapters discuss the Comstock Lode and other mining regions, state government, Indian wars, transportation, agriculture, etc. Cloth.

HISTORY OF UTAH, 1840-1886, by H. H. Bancroft. 808 pages, illus., maps. Utah became a territory in 1850, three years after the Mormons came to settle Salt Lake Valley. Here is a detailed history of the early growth and development of Utah, as well as a balanced treatment of Mormon developments. Cloth.

HISTORY OF NEVADA, 1913, by Sam P. Davis. 2 vols., 1344 pages, 60 illus. Originally issued in 1913, this landmark history is a compilation of special treatises on Nevada geography, Indians, territorial life, law and crime, mining history, politics, journalism, education, religion, transportation, business and finance, agriculture, divorce, the military, reclamation, and biographies of prominent early 20th century Nevadans. The new index has 6,000 subject entries. Cloth slipcase.

DEATH VALLEY'S SCOTTY'S CASTLE, by S.W. Paher. 48 pages, large 9 x 12 format, heavily illustrated in color. Built with funds supplied by a Chicago insurance executive benefactor, the Castle ultimately took its name from a local prospector who publicized it and jealously guarded its development — Walter "Death Valley" Scott. Besides a history of Scott, there are about fifty intricate color pictures of the Castle itself.

DEATH VALLEY GHOST TOWNS, VOL. I, by S. W. Paher. 32 pages, 9 x 12, map, 50 old-time photographs. Though Death Valley is known for its colorful eras of borax mining, there were gold and silver rushes also. The first one included Panamint and Calico, while the early 20th century boom produced Rhyolite, Greenwater, and others. About 35 mining camps are included. Color cover.

VIRGINIA CITY — COMSTOCK LODE

MARK TWAIN IN VIRGINIA CITY, by Mark Twain. 192 pages. Twain portrays the life and the people of Virginia City, including the mining litigation, breaking in of a horse, fighting a tarantula, a funeral and the Washoe zephyrs. He camped out at Lake Tahoe, mined for silver, labored in a silver mill and worked as a reporter for Virginia City's *Territorial Enterprise.* Drawings and cartoons.

MARK TWAIN, YOUNG REPORTER IN VIRGINIA CITY, by Katharine Hillyer. 92 pages, illus. The author provides an informal collection of Twain episodes at the *Territorial Enterprise,* in the 1860s.

CAMELS IN NEVADA, by Douglas McDonald. 32 pages, illus. In Nevada, camel pack trains hauled salt, wood and even freight, also aiding early surveyors. Modern camel races in Virginia City are recounted. Color cover.

SKETCHES OF VIRGINIA CITY, N.T., by J. Ross Browne. 48 pages, illus. In 1860 agent J. Ross Browne visited the newly discovered Comstock and commented extensively on the miners and their madness over minerals, the Chinese, the Indians, stagecoach drivers, proprietors, barroom brawlers, etc. Charming, humorous cartoons of these appear in the book, originally entitled *A Peep at Washoe.*

VIRGINIA CITY'S INTERNATIONAL HOTEL, by Richard C. Datin. 49 pages, illus. Subtitled *Elegance on C Street.* This book recreates the history, the people, and the splendor of Virginia City. The International Hotel typified it all, kings, financiers, president U. S. Grant, and queens of the footlights.

COMSTOCK MINING & MINERS, by Eliot Lord. 478 pages, illus., maps. This comprehensive and well-written narrative history of the Comstock Lode traces the birth of the silver mining industry in turbulent Virginia City right up to the original date of publication, 1883. There is much on day-to-day life, mining and milling techniques, and Comstock Lode personalities. A landmark Nevada book.

JULIA BULETTE AND THE RED LIGHT LADIES OF NEVADA, by Douglas McDonald. 32 pages, illus., map. A devoted Nevada researcher has put together the best written historical sketch to date of Virginia City's famed prostitute, who was murdered in 1867. An overview of Nevada prostitution occupies the last part of the book, augmented by interesting photographs. Color cover.

THE BIG BONANZA, by Dan DeQuille (William Wright). 488 pages, illus., with intro. by Oscar Lewis. Indexed. Subtitled "An authentic account of the discovery, history, and working of the Comstock Lode," *The Big Bonanza* covers every phase of the epic rise of Virginia City, especially the special technology required to work the deep silver mines. Color cover.

VIRGINIA CITY, SILVER REGION OF THE COMSTOCK LODE, by Douglas McDonald. 128 pages, Large 9 x 12 format, 75 illus., index. The discovery and development of the West's largest silver lode is recounted in extensive text and both line drawings and photographs. There are essays on familiar Comstock figures such as the Big Four, Adolph Sutro and the discoverers, and also information on stock manipulations, the unions, and various institutions. Camels, the V & T R.R., Mark Twain, Law and Order, square-set mine timbering, and the tommy-knockers are all featured. Old and new maps help tell the story of this great mining town. Cloth, Paperback.

DEATH VALLEY GHOST TOWNS, VOL. II, by S. W. Paher. 32 pages, 9 x 12, illus. Mining camps of the Death Valley National Monument — Skidoo, Panamint City, and Old Stovepipe Wells — are joined by those immediately to the west, including Cerro Gordo, Darwin and Cartago. There are essays on "The Prospector," the Tonopah & Tidewater Railroad and desert driving hints. Color cover.

TONOPAH-GOLDFIELD

GOLD IN THEM HILLS, by C. B. Glasscock. 330 pages, illus., map. Intro. by David Myrick. Author saw the reversals of fortune, had a part in the frenzies, experienced the hardships. Chapters 2-4 tell the development of early Tonopah; chapters 5-17 discuss Goldfield's freighting, high-grading, big mines, society and the fast-talking promoters. Greenwater and Rawhide also are included. This informally written book will surely be enjoyed by all who love old Nevada. Color cover.

TONOPAH, NEVADA SILVER CAMP, by S.W. Paher. 16 pages, 9 x 12, map. The silver discovery at Tonopah in 1900 triggered the fast-paced 20th century Nevada mining era. Here is a summary of the mining boom days in text and historic pictures.

GOLDFIELD by Hugh Shamberger. 240 pages, illus. The early history, the mines, the struggle for water, the building of railroads and the Gans-Nelson fight of 1906 are described. Author details corporate mining and highgrading.

GOLDFIELD: BOOM TOWN OF NEVADA, by S.W. Paher. 17 pages, 9 x 12. Nevada's greatest gold stampede, Goldfield, prospered from 1903 until 1918. Here is a summary of those boom days with photographs showing the crowds, the businesses, and the ore. Maps show nearby points of interest.

MY ADVENTURES WITH YOUR MONEY, by George Graham Rice. 334 pages, 110 illus. Here are the memoirs of get-rich-quick financing of central Nevada and Death Valley mines, with interesting anecdotal material. Author capitalized the stocks of Goldfield, Greenwater and Rawhide mines, listed them on the national exchanges, and reaped the profits until convicted of mail fraud in 1911.

DEATH VALLEY GHOST TOWNS, by S. W. Paher. 48 pages, 9 x 12, map. The heart of the above two books combine to form this heavily illustrated hardbound volume. Color dust jacket.

NEVADA TOWNS AND TALES, S. W. Paher, ed. 2 vols., 224 pages ea. 8-1/2 x 11. Formerly the Nevada Bicentennial book as base, these volumes include much new art and pictures to replace the advertisements of the earlier work. Chapters focus on economic, social and geographic factors. Other major sections discuss state emblems, gambling, politics, mining, business, and casino entertainment. There is much material on ghost towns, prospecting, legends, early day women, ranching, native animals, industries, banking and commerce, railroads, atomic testing, transportation, etc. Indexed. Color cover.

CALLVILLE, HEAD OF NAVIGATION, ARIZONA TERRITORY, S. W. Paher, ed. 40 pages, 9 x 12, illus., maps. The story of steamboat activity on the Colorado River, and area mines and Indians. The last part of the book contains Colorado River Indian lore, with 20 color plates.

GUIDE TO HIGHWAY 395, Los Angeles to Reno, by Ginny Clark. 207 pages, illus. Guide to parks, history, ghost towns, geology, fishing, hiking trails, especially between Bishop and Reno.

WESTERN ARIZONA GHOST TOWNS, by Stanley W. Paher. 64 pages, 9 x 12, illus., color cover. Within a day's drive of Las Vegas and Kingman are more than two dozen ghost towns, each described in a lively text with historic photographs. Among them are Oatman, Eldorado Canyon, Searchlight and Chloride. Other mining camps in the vicinity Yuma and Parker are: Gila City, Laguna, LaPaz, Ehrenburg, and more. Also information about the steamboats. A stunning 1862 full-color map of the Colorado River is reproduced on the back cover.

NEVADA STATEWIDE

TOURING NEVADA: A HISTORIC AND SCENIC GUIDE, by Mary Ellen and Al Glass. 253 pages, illus. Nevada travel descriptions for visitor and resident alike. Maps and index are definite aids. Color cover.

ONE HUNDRED YEARS AGO IN NEVADA by Jock Taylor. 372 pages. One page stories from 1864 depict mining, transportation, prospecting, etc.

GEOLOGY OF THE GREAT BASIN, by Bill Fiero. 250 pages, illus. A fine treatment complete with maps, charts, and analysis of Nevada geology.

THE SAGEBRUSH OCEAN, Stephen Trimble. 248 pages. Handsome coffee table book on the Great Basin. Important new Nevada book. Paper.

HIKING AND CLIMBING IN THE GREAT BASIN NATIONAL PARK, by Michael Kelsey. 192 pages, illus., maps. Besides the usual guide book information, this one includes Lehman Caves, geology, plant life, and mining. In all, 47 hikes or climbs. Color cover

NEVADA POST OFFICES, AN ILLUSTRATED HISTORY, by James Gamett and S. W. Paher. 160 pages, 7 x 10, illus. About 760 Nevada towns had post offices and here is a detailed list of them. There are chapters on the Pony Express, Wells-Fargo, and how to collect postal materials. Numerous postal related illustrations greatly enhance the usefulness of this research tool. Printed on high quality paper. Full color dust jacket.

GHOSTS OF THE GLORY TRAIL, by Nell Murbarger. 316 pages, illus., indexed. Subtitled "Intimate glimpses into the past and present of 275 western ghost towns," *Ghosts of the Glory Trail* is a fast-moving chronicle depicting the early-day mining stampedes. All Nevada counties are represented either in the 39 chapters on specific towns (such as Aurora, Rhyolite, Candelaria, Hamilton, Unionville, Belmont, Tybo, El Dorado Canyon, Tuscarora, Delamar, etc.) or in the ghost town directory with 275 listings, some in California and Utah. Color cover.

GUIDE TO HIGHWAY 395, Los Angeles to Reno, by Ginny Clark. 207 pages, illus. Guide to parks, history, ghost towns, geology, fishing, hiking trails, especially between Bishop and Reno.

BODIE

BODIE...BOOM TOWN. GOLD TOWN! The Last of California's Old-Time Mining Camps, by Douglas McDonald. 48 pages, illus., color cover. 7 x 10. Though Bodie was discovered in 1859, no significant mining was begun until after rich strikes in 1877 brought about a furious mining rush two years later. The height of the boom occurred in 1880, though the mines were still active until 1920. Illustrations show the mines and miners, street scenes, buildings, the mill, bullion, and the crowds which made up Bodie.

BODIE BONANZA, by Warren Loose. 246 pages, illus. A Bodie native chronicles the social picture of the camp during its heyday (1878-1880), lacing the text with news stories of the fortunes, failures, the rowdiness, businesses, the "red lights," and entertainments. A closing chapter surveys later happenings at what is now Bodie State Park.

MINING CAMP DAYS, by Emil W. Billeb. 229 pages, illus. The author provides insights into Nevada and eastern California mining camps after 1905. Dozens of unpublished photographs were taken by this observer-participant, augmenting a good text.

NEVADA, AN ANNOTATED BIBLIOGRAPHY, by Stanley W. Paher. 585 pp., 7 x 10, illus. A western Americana researcher's guide and description of more than 2,544 books relating to the history and development of Nevada, all annotated with valuable information. The 74-page index has 3,500 subjects; listed are 33 other bibliographies referring the researcher to countless Nevada materials. Printed on high-quality paper, sturdily bound.

LAS VEGAS, AS IT BEGAN, AS IT GREW, by Stanley W. Paher. Large 9 x 12 format, 181 pages, 210 duotone illus., maps, index. In the 19th century Las Vegas was first a Spanish Trail waterhole, then a religious mission and also a ranch. The town was founded in 1905 as a railroad town but developed into a gambling center during distinct boom periods. The reader is led every step along these transitions in both the text and a careful selection of previously unpublished photos. Cloth,

THE STORY OF THE HOOVER DAM, 144 pages, 9 x 12, illus. The book's 23 sections offer a progressive history of the undertaking from its genesis in Congress in the '20s to its dedication in 1935. In between was costly preliminary work and important political developments. The text, augmented by about 200 photos, tells about the engineers, the surveyors and the army of risk-taking laborers who enacted the perilous work..

NEVADA LOST MINES AND BURIED TREASURES, by Douglas McDonald. 128 pages, 6 x 9, illus. Legends of lost mines in Nevada date from the Gold Rush of 1849 when westbound emigrants discovered silver in the desolate Black Rock Desert. The author recounts 74 of these stories which also include tales of buried coins, bullion bars, stolen bank money, etc. Two-color maps show general treasure localities. Color cover.

CHLORIDE MINES AND MURALS, by artist Roy E. Purcell. Life in this Arizona mining camp is recalled by a lifelong resident. Unpublished photos show the Chloride of old. The Chloride murals are also interpreted.

NEVADA MINING BOOKS

320 DESERT WATERING PLACES IN SOUTHEASTERN CALIFORNIA AND SOUTHWESTERN NEVADA, by W. C. Mendenhall. 104 pages, illus., index. Color map 14 x 20. This 1909 Water Supply Paper covers numerous places between Death Valley and the Salton Sea. There are 323 springs, all described and keyed to the colored map.

MINES OF THE GOLDFIELD, BULLFROG AND OTHER SOUTHERN NEVADA DISTRICTS by F. L. Ransome. 144 pages, maps, index. Color map 22 x 28 laid in. This 1907 bulletin also covers Searchlight, Eldorado, Crescent and Gold Mountain. Two contemporary illustrated articles, capture the flavor and excitement of the mining era.

MINES OF CLARK COUNTY, 80 pages, illus., map. This 1937 report covers southern Nevada districts: Eldorado Canyon, Gold Butte, Goodsprings, St. Thomas, Searchlight, Sunset.

MINES OF HUMBOLDT AND PERSHING COUNTIES, 128 pages, illus., map. This 1938 report covers north-central Nevada districts: Golconda, National, Rabbithole, Rochester, Seven Troughs, Unionville, etc.

MINES OF LANDER AND EUREKA COUNTIES, 136 pages, illus., map. This 1939 report covers eastern Nevada districts: Battle Mountain, Kingston, Lewis, McCoy, Cortez, Eureka, Mineral Hill, Palisade, Union, etc.

MINES OF CHURCHILL AND MINERAL COUNTIES, 128 pages, illus., map. This 1940 report covers many west-central Nevada districts: Fairview, La Plata, Wonder, Aurora, Broken Hills, Candelaria, Rawhide, etc.

MINES OF THE SILVER PEAK RANGE, KAWICH RANGE AND OTHER SOUTHWESTERN NEVADA DISTRICTS, by S. H. Ball. 218 pages, maps, index. Color map 22 x 28. This 1907 bulletin also covers Amargosa Mountains, Death Valley, and the Panamint Range.

MINES OF CHERRY CREEK AND OTHER EASTERN NEVADA DISTRICTS, J. M. Hill. 214 pages, maps, index. This 1916 bulletin includes Gold Butte, Ruby and Toano Ranges, Tecoma, Ward, Aurum and Taylor.

MINES OF BATTLE MOUNTAIN, REESE RIVER, AUSTIN AND OTHER NEVADA DISTRICTS, J. M. Hill. 200 pages, maps, index. This 1915 bulletin covers California's Lassen and Modoc Counties, Douglas County, Peavine, and Pine Grove.

MINES OF TUSCARORA, CORTEZ AND OTHER NORTHERN NEVADA DISTRICTS, by W. H. Emmons. 220 pages, maps, index. This 1910 bulletin covers Midas, Edgemont, Tenabo, Lander, and Lewis districts. Includes F. L. Ransome's 1909 bulletin on Humboldt County featuring Seven Troughs, Pahute and Sonoma Ranges.

AN ESSENTIAL REFERENCE **MINING DISTRICTS AND MINERAL RESOURCES OF NEVADA,** by Francis C. Lincoln. 295 pages, maps, index. This compilation summarizes 307 mining di-tricts, with historical summaries and bibliographies keyed to dozens of other mining publications and articles in various journals through 1923. Nevada's mineral locations also noted by types.

Nevada Publications

PUBLISHERS AND DISTRIBUTORS OF
MORE THAN 180 SOUTHWESTERN DESERT BOOKS.

Write for our complete catalog

4135 Badger Circle, Reno, Nevada 89509

702-747-0800